Financial Statement Analysis in Europe

J.M. Samuels, R.E. Brayshaw and J.M. Craner
Department of Accounting and Finance,
Birmingham Business School,
University of Birmingham

CHAPMAN & HALL
University and Professional Division

London · Glasgow · Weinheim · New York · Tokyo · Melbourne · Madras

Published by Chapman & Hall, 2–6 Boundary Row, London SE1 8HN, UK

Chapman & Hall, 2–6 Boundary Row, London SE1 8HN, UK

Blackie Academic & Professional, Wester Cleddens Road, Bishopbriggs, Glasgow G64 2NZ, UK

Chapman & Hall GmbH, Pappelallee 3, 69469 Weinheim, Germany

Chapman & Hall USA, One Penn Plaza, 41st Floor, New York NY 10119, USA

Chapman & Hall Japan, ITP-Japan, Kyowa Building, 3F, 2–2–1 Hirakawacho, Chiyoda-ku, Tokyo 102, Japan

Chapman & Hall Australia, Thomas Nelson Australia, 102 Dodds Street, South Melbourne, Victoria 3205, Australia

Chapman & Hall India, R. Seshadri, 32 Second Main Road, CIT East, Madras 600 035, India

First edition 1995

©1995 Chapman & Hall

Typeset in Friz Quadrata by Fox Design, Bramley, Surrey
Printed in England by Clays Ltd, St Ives plc

ISBN 0 412 54450 4

A catalogue record for this book is available from the British Library

Library of Congress Catalog Card Number: 94-71828

Contents

PART THREE FINANCIAL STATEMENT ANALYSIS: EUROPEAN CASE STUDIES

Preface

The need for a book on this topic first became apparent to the authors when involved in teaching post graduate courses on financial statement analysis. Increasingly such courses form part of either an MBA or a postgraduate accounting programme which attracts students from many different countries. The increasing internationalisation of financial activities means that emphasizing the accounting practices of just one country leads to the neglect of the rich variety of practices to be found in the many countries represented in the class. It is always possible to analyse the accounts of companies from different countries, but most textbooks dealing with financial statement analysis (as opposed to international accounting) are based on the principles and practices of just one country.

The second factor which led to the book being written was a research project being undertaken by the three authors, which was attempting to reconcile the financial statements of companies from six countries. The research was being funded by the Chartered Association of Certified Accountants. The intention was to bring together a team of academics with at least one from each of the six countries. The representatives from each country would analyse the information contained in the annual report and accounts of a company to recalculate the profit of each of the five foreign companies to conform with the practices and principles of their home country. This turned out to be a massive and daunting task and in the end led the authors to be a little bit more sympathetic to the EU's policy of mutual recognition than they had been previously.

The third part of the book gives some indication of the flavour of the research. The list of academics who cooperated in the research or who assisted in different ways to the material in this book is shown.

The analysis of the accounts of real companies using the practices and principles of a number of countries is an instructive and pedagogically fruitful exercise. The authors suggest that this case study approach may usefully be adopted on Accounting courses with an international emphasis.

In addition to our European colleagues listed separately we are also pleased to acknowledge the assistance of Karen Hanson, Cynthia

Franklin, Margaret Watson, Peter Feige and Wolfgang Uhlrich in preparing the manuscript of this book.

Any errors in the book or situations in which we have been economical with the truth are the responsibility of the three principal authors.

J.M. Samuels
R.E. Brayshaw
J. M. Craner

Department of Accounting and Finance
The Birmingham Business School
University of Birmingham, UK

The book has been written in association with

Professor Serge Evraert
(Université Bordeaux 1)

Professor Jean G. Degos
(Université Bordeaux 1)

Drs Ruud Vergoosen
(Vrije Universiteit Amsterdam)

Drs Jeanette Droog
(Vrije Universiteit Amsterdam)

Professor Leandro Calvo
(Universidad Autonoma de Madrid)

Dr Begona Giner
(Universidad de Valencia)

Dr Giovanni Liberatore
(Universita degli Studi di Firenze)

Professor Gunther Gebhardt
(Johann Wolfgang Goethe-Universität, Frankfurt am Main)

PART ONE

The Analysis of Financial Reports in Europe

1

Techniques of Financial Statement Analysis

Objectives

- To explain the rationale for the approach to financial statement analysis adopted in this book.

- To describe the potential users of financial statement data and their differing perspectives.

- To explain and illustrate the calculation of key financial ratios relating to profitability, efficiency and risk.

- To discuss the usefulness and drawbacks of using financial statement analysis in company appraisal.

Introduction

This book is the product of cooperation between academic accountants working in universities in a number of European Union (EU) countries. The EU is an important world economic unit within which harmonization of political, institutional, legal and economic factors are aspirations which are being slowly (very slowly in some cases) achieved. The level of trading between member states is increasing and so is the volume of financial transactions. There is a need for financial information about companies in different EU countries and a first source of this information will often be the published financial statements. Although there have been moves towards harmonization of financial reporting through the adoption of the Fourth and Seventh Directives by member countries the number of options still available (see Chapter 4) mean that direct comparability is still difficult. Many books and articles on comparative accounting reporting use the USA as a benchmark. This is unsurprising as many of the publications originate from the USA and there is much data available particularly relating to non-US companies filing adjusted statements for USA stock market quotation purposes. It is not the intention of this book to advance a prescriptive method for adjusting financial statements produced in all European Union countries. Instead we focus on a limited number of significant member states to illustrate the problems which arise both in intra- and inter-country analysis and comparisons. To do otherwise would require a massive text in the state of constant revision; financial reporting is a dynamic process with new legislation and recommendations emerging on an almost day-to-day basis while the European Union also continues to evolve with new members seeking to attain full or associate membership.

In this book we are concerned with the comparative analysis of companies based in a number of different member countries of the European Union. The companies involved are usually of a significant size and the principal financial statements prepared are:

- income statement/profit and loss account;
- balance sheet;
- statement of cash flows or funds flow statement.

The analysis of company financial statements is undertaken with the purpose of extracting significant information relating to a company's activities, profitability, efficiency and degree of risk. This is achieved by using ratios relating to key financial variables and further analysis of the statements and the notes relating thereto.

The information contained in company financial statements is historic. Accounts are prepared for a company's financial year and only become available some months after the end of that year. The information given in the income statement, or profit and loss account as it is called in some countries, shows the operating results for the financial year just ended, the balance sheet shows the financial position of the company at the end of the financial year while the cash flow statement summarizes the source and application of cash funds for the financial year. Although we have focused on three financial statements the annual reports produced by large publicly quoted companies in Europe are often substantial documents containing supplementary and supporting information to the financial statements which are validated by external independent auditors. A major contention of this book is that in order to make valid comparisons between companies – and this could apply just as much to intra-country comparisons as to inter-country comparisons – it is necessary to adjust for different reporting practices in different companies and countries. In this context the notes and other information supplied with the financial statements assume great significance. It is contended that to make comparisons of financial ratios and other information based on the raw figures shown in company financial statements may be misleading and that it is necessary to take into consideration the information on accounting policies and other matters contained in the full annual financial report.

Chapters 2, 3 and 4 discuss the usefulness of financial statements and the problems in making comparisons between financial statements given the alternative acceptable treatments available for reporting key financial information. The rest of this chapter will be concerned with identifying the various users of financial statements, factors affecting the information contained in financial statements and a description and discussion on the techniques of financial statement analysis.

Users of Financial Statement Information

The type of information required from the analysis of financial statements may well vary depending upon the user for whom the information is required. Users could be classified in a number of ways depending upon their relationship with the company and/or the type of information they require. One possible classification would be: 'outside' users who would include shareholders, lenders, suppliers and customers; 'intermediary' users, for example security analysts and the financial press; and 'inside' users who would be mainly managers and employees or their representatives.

Another suggested division is between 'contractual claimers', who are mainly interested in information relating to the default risk of the company, and 'residual claimers' with claims on residual profits and net worth. The first group would include creditors, suppliers and staff while the most important members of the second group would be shareholders and the tax authorities. We will now identify the main purposes for analysing financial statements and the different factors which might be stressed in each case.

Current and prospective shareholders (including security analysts)

The most quoted purpose for analysing financial statements in the English language literature is to enable current and prospective shareholders to make decisions on buying, holding or selling equity shares in the company. This analysis presupposes that it may be possible to identify mispriced securities and this matter is discussed in detail in Chapter 3. As shareholders obtain their return from dividend income and changes in market price of shares they will be interested in analysing the past operating profitability of the company including its efficiency of asset management in order to enable predictions to be made of future profitability and dividend paying capability. The required return of any investment is linked to the perceived risk of that investment and, therefore, the accounts will be analysed for indicators of risk affecting equity investment in the company. From an accounting statement perspective risk analysis will be focused on asset management, particularly working capital and cash management, and the impact on risk of borrowed funds.

Lenders

Bankers and other providers of funds to the company will usually see their return in the form of interest payments. Conditions will also be laid down as to how the principal loan advanced is to be repaid. This may be either over the term of the loan or in total at maturity. The loans themselves may be for differing time periods. In some countries finance is provided in the form of short-term bank loans (in the UK as bank overdrafts) with other loans extending up to periods of 20 or more years as would be the case with corporate bonds. Analysts will be concerned that the company can both pay the interest payments as they fall due and repay the principal in accordance with the agreed terms. The analyst will, therefore, focus both on the short-term prospects of the company, examining the ability of the company to generate sufficient cash to cover interest payments and any periodic repayment of capital, and also the long-run profitability of the company through to maturity of the loans. Loan conditions may incorporate covenants whereby lenders require the company to maintain minimum agreed ratios of earnings to interest charges and stay within maximum levels of debt-to-equity ratios. In both cases the lenders will wish to monitor the company's performance by reference to successive financial statements and, in addition, check the accounting methods used by the company. Conversely, the company could be tempted to adopt accounting policies which enhance ratios – this is another matter discussed in length in Chapter 3.

Executive managers/directors

Company directors and senior managers may be users of the information contained in their company's published financial statements for a number of reasons. One possibility is that their performance-related pay may be linked to numbers contained in the accounting statements. Additional remuneration may be triggered by levels of sales, operating income or return on asset figures. Bearing in mind that accounting policies will be determined by top management, an agency problem arises in that management could be tempted to adopt policies which maximize the numbers on which their pay is based to the detriment of the company generally. Managers may also use financial statement information as an input to their financing, investment or dividend decisions. The impact of proposed new borrowings on the debt-to-equity ratio or interest coverage ratio may be a significant factor. In addition the managers may well be concerned at the impact of a new project on short- and medium-term profitability ratios.

Customers

A customer that relies on a company to provide an important product may well wish to check on the financial health of the company. There could be significant costs if the supplier was unable to supply the product as and when needed and this is increasingly the case with the adoption of just-in-time management methods. The supplier's financial statements will, therefore, be analysed for profitability, financial stability and long-term viability. Profitability analysis will also be useful in negotiating new contracts.

Suppliers

Where credit is extended to a company the supplier company will wish to confirm the ability of the creditor company to pay as and when required. Clearly the ability of the creditor company to generate cash is important and attention will be given to the profitability, liquidity and level of borrowing of the customer. The amount of time spent on analysis will be related to the significance of the customer in terms of size and length of credit. Much of this type of information may be obtained

Techniques of Financial Statement Analysis

from a professional credit analyst or from a database. However, there can be occasions when mechanically prepared information based on raw data may be inadequate for the analyst's needs.

Employees

Employees and their representatives will be concerned with the long-term viability of the company and its level of profitability. In the first case they will be trying to assess future employment prospects while in the second case levels of profitability may be used in future pay negotiations.

Government and other agencies

The most obvious use of financial statements by governments is for tax calculation and collection. This may be both income tax and value added tax. In some countries the accounting profit is taken to be the taxable profit (e.g. Germany) while in other countries the accounting profit is adjusted to arrive at a taxable profit (e.g. United Kingdom). In the Netherlands separate financial statements are often drawn up for tax purposes. Differences in determining taxable profit may clearly affect accounting policies adopted by companies under different tax regimes. Companies engaged in government contracts may also find their accounts under scrutiny to ensure that excess profits are not being earned on government contracts. In addition the accounts of regulated utility companies providing, for example, gas or electricity supplies will be used to monitor the rate of return being earned and contribute to the determination of charges.

Other interest groups

Other groups concerned with the way in which large companies conduct their financial affairs will vary over time and from country to country. Groups currently concerned with the policies of large corporations will include environmental lobbies, representatives of minority groups and host countries of multinational companies. Companies are aware of the interest of these groups and their commercial and political significance and make efforts to provide information, sometimes in the form of special statements.

We have discussed above the various potential users of financial information produced by the company. In one or two cases we have mentioned conflicts of interest which may arise between company management and other users of financial statements. Although financial statements are audited by independent auditors in accordance with company laws and accounting standards, responsibility for preparation of the financial statements lies with the directors of the company. Where the interests of directors may be affected by the results and financial position shown by the financial statements they may be tempted to show the most optimistic position possible. Inter-country comparisons may be affected by the existence of different methods of financing, the relative importance of financial markets and legal rules, particularly those relating to the calculation of taxable profits. Although the adoption of the Fourth and Seventh Directives of the EU may seem to indicate that companies should treat similar business transactions in the same way in their financial statements the existence of optional treatments relating to significant items means that companies in different countries – and indeed different companies within the same country – may be treating identical transactions in quite different ways. This points to the need to undertake analysis which goes beyond the mere computation of ratios based on figures in the financial statements but also considers the varying policies adopted by companies relating to key items in the income statement and balance sheet. The need for these adjustments and their scope is developed in later chapters. We turn now to discuss the principles of financial statement analysis.

Analysing Financial Statements

The analysis of financial statements incorporates the study of significant relationships within the financial statements at a particular time and with trends in these relationships over time. There are a number of ways in which ratios can be categorized and defined. The important thing for the analyst is to be consistent in the definition of ratios when making comparisons between companies or over time. It should be stressed that both the proposed categories and the definition of ratios are not necessarily the only definitions used by analysts. In some cases a number of different measures are presented. Bearing in mind that the main purposes of undertaking financial statement analysis is to obtain insights into profitability, efficiency and risk, one possible way of categorizing ratios is as follows:

- profitability ratios;
- ratios relating to the efficiency of asset management;
- risk, short-term cash management and borrowing ratios;
- stock market data (ratios using accounting information and current share price).

We will now consider each of these headings in turn using the published accounts of ICI plc contained in Appendix 1 at the end of the book to illustrate ratios etc.

Profitability

This will be a key area for analysts' attention. A problem in analysing a business's ability to make profits is that profits may arise from a variety of sources. High profits may be derived from a mixture of skills within the business and ideally analysts would like to identify those skills which contribute most to a particular company's level of profits. For example, a company which imports raw materials and manufactures a finished product will have its profits affected by a variety of factors which would include the buying department's ability to negotiate keen prices for raw materials, the finance department's skill in managing exchange rate exposure, the skill of the workforce in producing fault-free products, the ability of production engineers to manage the production process, and the ability of top management to identify new products and provide overall management for the business which enables it to flourish. Unfortunately it is not possible to derive this information from the published accounts of companies as much of it will be aggregated into single profit figures. Indeed, it could well be the case that even inside companies this detail of information may not be made available.

Profitability ratios

Profitability could be examined by relating profit either to sales or to capital employed in earning that profit. Profit may also be related to assets employed. In fact figures for assets and capital employed will be the same although different assets and capital employed figures may be used depending on whether total assets, net trading assets, shareholders' assets or some other variation is used. In each case the appropriate profit figure must be related to the equivalent capital employed figure.

In fact high profitability could be the result of a high mark-up on goods sold and/or an efficient usage of assets indicated by a rapid asset turnover.

Key profitability ratios

- Return on sales $= \dfrac{\text{Operating profit}}{\text{Sales}}$

- Return on net assets or capital employed $= \dfrac{\text{Operating profit}}{\text{Capital employed}}$
(Capital employed is defined here as Fixed assets plus Net current assets)

- Asset turnover $= \dfrac{\text{Sales}}{\text{Capital employed}}$

- Return on capital employed (ROCE) $= \dfrac{\text{Operating profit}}{\text{Sales}} \times \dfrac{\text{Sales}}{\text{Capital employed}}$

ROCE could be increased either by a higher profit to sales ratio or a faster asset turnover as sales to capital employed (CE) increases. Different businesses, although they may be earning similar levels of ROCE, may have entirely different returns on sales and asset turnover ratios. A discount store may have low profit margins and rapid turnover of assets while an industrial manufacturing company might have a higher profit margin but a slower turnover of assets.

The purpose of examining historic profitability is to get some idea of how well the company has been using the assets in the past so that projections can be made about future levels of profits. In using this information operating conditions prevailing in the past must be considered. Has the company done well in general buoyant economic conditions? Is the company producing better or worse results than its competitors given the circumstances? Is the current or anticipated economic climate better or worse than that prevailing in the year(s) reviewed?

The operating profit used is often taken as earnings before interest and taxation (EBIT). This gives the profit earned irrespective of the way in which the business is financed and enables comparisons to be made between companies financed in different ways.

The matching assets or capital employed figure is fixed assets plus working capital where working capital comprises current assets minus current liabilities (creditors due within one year). Using the ICI 1991 Group accounts we can take EBIT to be the trading profit of £1033 million. Capital employed as defined above would give us the figure of total assets less current liabilities of £7605 million. However, this figure includes investments in associated companies, quoted investments and cash where the related income has not been included in EBIT; in addition short-term creditors include borrowings and non-trading items of taxation and dividends. An appropriate capital employed figure could be:

ICI plc

	£m	£m	£m
Fixed assets			
Tangible assets			5128
<u>Less</u>: Assets in course of construction			<u>874</u> (Note 11)
Current assets (Note 15)			4254
Stocks		2025	
Debtors	2636		
<u>Less</u>: Associated companies	<u>34</u>	<u>2602</u>	
		4627	
<u>Less</u>: Other creditors (Note 18)	2894		
Adjust for associated			
companies and taxation	(374)		
Dividends	<u>(242)</u>	<u>2278</u>	<u>2349</u>
			<u>6603</u>

This is a simple illustration of the need to relate profit to the appropriate capital employed. The difference between the simply defined capital employed and adjusted capital employed is substantial both in absolute terms, £1002 million, and in percentage terms, a reduction of 13%. In this example the year-end capital employed figure has been used. It could be argued that the average capital employed (usually of start and end of year) is more appropriate. Similar arguments can be advanced relating to other ratios. If the business is growing rapidly then the use of average figures may be necessary but in mature businesses year-end figures will usually suffice. Bear in mind that whichever method is adopted it must be followed consistently from year to year and in making comparisons between companies.

ICI like most large companies operates in a number of identifiable business sectors and different geographic regions. Analysts will be able to make better predictions about the future if they have more information on the performance of the company both in its different business sectors and geographic regions. In Note 7 this segment information is given. This note provides us with the basic information we need to calculate profitability. Interestingly the net operating assets figure given is £6531 million which, although not the same as the adjusted figure we calculated, is reasonably close. We will use the figures shown in Note 7 but in some cases the analyst will have to rely on his or her own adjustments if the appropriate information is not given directly in the notes.

ICI plc

Return on sales $= \dfrac{1033}{13\,195} = 0.078\ (7.8\%)$

Return on capital employed $= \dfrac{1033}{6531} = 0.158\ (15.8\%)$

Asset turnover $= \dfrac{13\,195}{6531} = 2.02$

ROCE $=$ Return on sales $\times$ Asset turnover

$= 0.078 \times 2.02$

$= 0.158$

Similar figures can be computed for the different business segments and Table 1.1 shows this information for 1991.

TABLE 1.1
ICI plc profitability ratios by business segment: 1991

SEGMENT	RETURN ON SALES	ASSET TURNOVER	ROCE	PERCENTAGE BY SALES
Bioscience	23%	1.8	42%	22%
Speciality chemicals	3%	1.9	6%	41%
Industrial chemicals	4%	2.4	9%	27%
Regional business	2%	2.3	5%	10%

We are beginning here to get useful information about the business activities of the company and a similar table could be prepared for the different geographic regions. A single year's figures only have been calculated and a time series of several years' figures would normally be examined to identify discernible trends in the levels of profitability and mix of business activities. Cross-sectional analysis can also be undertaken by comparing this company's performance with other companies carrying on similar activities. A problem with this type of analysis is finding companies with the same range and balance of activities.

Rate of return on shareholders' funds

The previous profitability ratios examined, return on sales and return on assets or capital employed, examined the overall profitability of the company irrespective of the financing of the company. Analysts, as was noted earlier, will often be assessing the company from the perspective of equity investors. It is appropriate therefore to look at the profit available to shareholders in relation to their investment in the company. The profit will be after charging interest and may also be after charging taxation. We are focusing here on the so-called 'bottom line' figure.

The profit for ICI will be £542m which is after interest, tax and minority interests while the shareholders' funds will be the capital and reserves figure of £4792 million.

$$\text{Return on shareholders' funds} \quad = \quad \frac{542}{4792} \quad = \quad 0.113 \, (11.3\%)$$

When examining time series trends or making cross-sectional comparisons any significant changes in accounting policy will need to be considered. Large differences in capital employed may result both from different approaches to group accounts, merger or acquisition accounting, and, where acquisition accounting is used, differing treatments of goodwill arising on consolidation. As goodwill may be charged against reserves as ICI does there can be substantial differences compared with companies who capitalize goodwill. When the capitalized amount is amortized then lower profit and higher assets/capital employed will result.

Efficiency/ Turnover Ratios

These ratios are used to try and assess how efficiently management is using and managing company assets. We have already discussed the overall asset usage in terms of the sales to capital employed ratio. Further information may be gained by examining the constituent parts of the capital employed figure as follows:

1. $\dfrac{\text{Sales}}{\text{Fixed assets}}$

2. $\dfrac{\text{Sales}}{\text{Net current assets}}$

In (1) we calculate the sales per £ invested in fixed assets while (2) gives us the sales per £ of working capital. Companies sustaining high turnover ratios would normally be regarded as more efficient and making greater use of their resources.

Within the working capital figure a number of other ratios can also be calculated.

3. $\dfrac{\text{Sales}}{\text{Trade debtors}}$

In this computation sales should relate only to credit sales and in the case of ICI it seems likely that all sales can be assumed to be on credit. With other companies a higher proportion of sales maybe for cash and unless a breakdown is given between cash and credit sales the ratio obtained using the total sales figure may be fairly meaningless.

The ratio is often used to calculate the average collection period of debtors in the form:

4. $$\frac{\text{Trade debtors}}{\text{Sales}} \times 365 = \text{Collection period in days}$$

If we use the information in the ICI accounts to compute collection period we get:

$$\frac{1877}{12\ 488} \times 365 = 55 \text{ days}$$

This period can be monitored over time and compared with industry norms and competitors to assess the credit management of a business.

A similar calculation will give the average time taken by a company to pay its creditors. This creditors' payments period is given by:

5. $$\frac{\text{Trade creditors}}{\text{Purchases}} \times 365$$

In this case we need to know the amount owing to suppliers of goods and the actual goods purchased in the year. Although Note 3 to the ICI Accounts gives a 'Cost of Sales' figure this will include wages and other manufacturing costs. However, the company includes in its information a sources and disposal of value added (a value added statement). This shows a figure of materials and services used amounting to £8285 million. The accounts payable figure will be taken as trade creditors of £1004 million and accruals of £478 million totalling £1482 million and shown in Note 18 to the accounts.

ICI plc

	£m
Materials and services used	8 285
Add: Closing stock	2 025
	10 310
Less: Opening stock	2 214
Estimated purchases	8 096

$$\text{ICI payments period} = \frac{1482}{8096} \times 365$$

$$= 67 \text{ days}$$

This may be an over-estimate as the accruals figure may include a provision for wages payments. (Wages have specifically been excluded from the figure of materials and services used.)

This figure will again be monitored over time and comparisons made with industry norms and other similar companies. A high and/or rising payments period could be thought to be a sign of weakness and a danger signal. However, it could equally signal a company of strength! The figure calculated for ICI seems to show that the company takes longer to pay its bills than it does to collect in money from debtors. This is not surprising as it reflects the relative strength of companies operating in an environment of recession and high real interest rates. In such an environment companies with commercial strength, usually the larger companies, are able to take longer periods of credit from their suppliers (often smaller companies) while at the same time pressing for earlier payment from their customers (again often smaller companies). In such circumstances it tends to be the smaller companies that are squeezed at both ends. In interpreting the length of, and changes in, the collection period the analyst must consider both the size of the company and its relative bargaining strength in the industry concerned.

A further series of turnover ratios can be calculated for stocks/inventories. The stock turnover ratio is:

$$\frac{\text{Cost of goods sold}}{\text{Stock}}$$

Using the cost of sales figure of £7429 million shown in Note 3 and the stock figure of £2025 million gives:

$$\text{Stock turnover ratio} = \frac{7429}{2025}$$

$$= 3.7 \text{ times}$$

This ratio shows the number of times stock is being turned over in sales each year. Clearly the more rapidly a business can throughput its stock the higher profits are likely to be. However, caution needs to be exercised in drawing conclusions on stock turnover. The balance sheet shows the stock figure for one day in the year only. If stock varies throughout the year, perhaps because the business is seasonal, then stock turnover may not mean very much. The ratio can also be affected by methods used in stock valuation and this could affect international comparisons where LIFO might be used which would typically give a lower inventory figure than the FIFO valuation method used in the UK. Alternative treatments of overheads in stock valuation could also result in differences.

The turnover ratio equation could also be revised to give the number of days sales the company has in stock. This would be calculated as follows:

$$\frac{\text{Stock}}{\text{Cost of goods sold}} \times 365$$

In the case of ICI this would be:

$$\frac{2025}{7429} \times 365 = 100 \text{ days}$$

This is a comparatively high level of stock for manufacturing companies which on average carry stocks in the region of 90 days' sales. However, we need to compare ICI's figures with similar companies rather than manufacturing companies in general as chemical companies manufacture some products which require long and complex processes. It would also be useful if we could obtain information relating to different categories of inventory – raw materials, work in process and finished goods. The information on this is given in Note 14 on Stocks and if each component part of stock is expressed in numbers of days we get:

Raw materials	30
Stocks in process	13
Finished goods and goods for resale	57
	100

A further refinement would be to relate levels of stock by segment of business to tie in with the segmental profitability analysis but unfortunately this degree of information is not available even in the informative notes provided to the ICI accounts.

An additional ratio can be calculated by expressing stock as a proportion/percentage of total assets:

$$\frac{\text{Stock}}{\text{Total assets}}$$

Again this ratio could be affected by the balance sheet date and the degree of stability in the stock figure throughout the year. Another factor making inter-firm comparisons difficult is the differing treatment of similar assets in terms of inclusion (e.g. intangibles), valuation and depreciation policy.

Financial Risk Analysis

In an earlier section we reviewed ratios relating to profitability; as investors will weigh return from investments against relative risk we need to see what clues ratio analysis can give us of the risk relating to different companies. Although the finance literature distinguishes between systematic or market risk and non-systematic or firm-specific risk, it is the latter with which we are particularly concerned when we analyse accounting statements.

Companies go bust when they are unable to pay their debts, be they trade suppliers or loan creditors. Ratio analysis tends to focus on short-term cash management and long-term debt liabilities. As well as calculating ratios based on the balance sheet and income statement, cash flow information will be useful in assessing the ability of a company to meet its obligations as and when they fall due.

Liquidity ratios

These ratios assess short-term liquidity and examine the ability of the company to meet its short-term commitments. They are concerned with the management of short-term assets and liabilities. In fact we have already discussed three relevant ratios relating to debtors, creditors and stock and we will now review three other ratios used in liquidity analysis.

Current ratio

This is the ratio of current assets to current liabilities (creditors due within one year). For ICI at the end of 1991 this was:

$$\frac{5466}{3410} = 1.6$$

Traditionally the satisfactory norm accepted for the current ratio was regarded as 2.0 indicating a healthy position. However, with the high interest rates of the 1970s and 1980s firms have tried to slow down payments to suppliers allowing the latter to finance a greater part of their working capital requirement. The point was made earlier that it was often the larger companies with their greater commercial influence that did this at the expense of smaller companies. A current ratio of 1.6 for a manufacturing company like ICI would be regarded as very acceptable as it is quite common for such companies now to have current ratios of 1.5 down to 1.

Current ratios and quick ratios (see below) will also vary with the type of business activity. Supermarket companies, for example, often have current liabilities well in excess of current assets and therefore very low current ratios. This is because they have little owing to them, selling almost exclusively for cash, and have low stocks relative to sales because of the type of product sold. At the same time they will be buying on credit and like other large businesses taking as much time to pay as possible. Indeed higher than average current ratios in any kind of business may reflect poorer business conditions. In a recession period less business may be undertaken, current liabilities paid and investment curtailed leading to a build up in cash, whereas in a boom period investment may be resumed and current liabilities increase as business increases. A high current ratio can sometimes indicate a company that has been successful but has now run out of ideas.

Quick ratio

This is a variant of the current ratio and matches current assets less stocks to current liabilities. For ICI at the end of 1991 this was:

$$\frac{3441}{3410} = 1$$

The traditionally satisfactory level for this ratio was 1 as in the case of ICI calculated above. However, as current ratios have fallen towards 1 so the quick ratio has inevitably trended down below this level. The reason for excluding stock is that it enables us to focus on those assets which are already cash or near cash thus giving a better indication of the company's ability to pay its short-term liabilities. As mentioned in connection with the current ratio, levels of quick ratios will vary both over the trading cycle for a particular company and between companies depending upon the different types of business activity undertaken.

Operating cash flow to current liabilities ratio

A problem in using current assets as an indicator of a company's ability to pay its liabilities is that it is a static measure of short-term assets taken at one day in the year; it gives no indication of the cash being generated by the company in its trading activities which will be the key to meeting its continuing obligations. Using the information provided by the cash flow statement for ICI this ratio is:

$$\frac{\text{Cash flow from operations}}{\text{Current liabilities}} = \frac{1458}{3410}$$

$$= 0.43$$

Although the preparation of cash flow statements is a fairly recent innovation in the UK an empirical study undertaken in the USA found that a ratio of 0.40 or more was common for a healthy firm.[1]

Long-term debt ratios

These ratios are used to assess the company's ability to meet both interest and principal payments on loans as they fall due. If payments cannot be made as agreed then the company becomes insolvent and may have to be reorganized or go into receivership or liquidation. In the difficult years of the late 1980s and early 1990s many companies have faced up to restructuring or gone into liquidation because their debt obligations became too burdensome to service.

A key factor in meeting debts and debt interest will be the company's ability to generate profits over time. If the company is making good profits it should either be generating sufficient cash flows to enable it to meet debt obligations or to enable cash to be raised from other sources. The measures of profitability previously discussed will figure in the appraisal of the company together with leverage (gearing) ratios, interest coverage ratio and cash flow ratios.

Leverage (gearing) ratios

These ratios are used to measure the amount of long-term debt used by a company. There are a number of ratios used with the most common being:

- Long-term debt ratio $=\dfrac{\text{Long-term debt}}{\text{Long-term debt + Shareholders' equity}}$

- Debt to equity ratio $=\dfrac{\text{Long-term debt}}{\text{Shareholders' equity}}$

- Long-term debt to assets ratio $=\dfrac{\text{Long-term debt}}{\text{Total assets}}$

It would be expected that all these three measures would give similar signals if tracked over time and the analyst may select only one to track over time or compare with other companies.

The debt ratios for ICI for 1991 are:

- Long-term debt ratio $=\dfrac{1788}{1788+4792}=$ 0.27 (27%)

- Debt to equity ratio $=\dfrac{1788}{4792}=$ 0.37 (37%)

- Long-term debt to assets ratio $=\dfrac{1788}{11\,015}=$ 0.16 (16%)

All these ratios indicate comparatively low levels of debt in the capital structure but all could be criticized for concentrating on long-term debt and ignoring other liabilities. A more comprehensive measure of indebtedness is the ratio of total debt to total assets and for ICI this is:

- Debt ratio $=\dfrac{3410+1947}{11\,015}=$ 0.49 (49%)

This ratio now includes all external sources of finance in the numerator. This is important in the UK and other countries where companies may obtain significant finance from bank loans and overdrafts which, although they may legally be repayable on demand, are regarded as a permanent or semi-permanent part of the company's financing.

The ratio calculated for ICI of 49% would be regarded as satisfactory. In the UK 50% (or 1 : 2) is seen as an acceptable ratio of total debt to total assets. This implies that it is reasonable to finance half the assets of the company by debt. Other variants of debt which could be included in the numerator are 'long- and short-term borrowings', i.e. excluding other creditors. However leverage ratios may be calculated they should be computed consistently both over time and when making comparisons between companies.

Unfortunately the use of leverage ratios is clouded by accounting policies relating to both liabilities and assets. The use of 'off-balance sheet' financing has proliferated in recent years and although some practices (e.g. finance leasing) now require capitalization for reporting purposes other practices may go unreported. Indeed, although obligations under finance leases have to be reported on the face of company balance sheets, operating leases do not, although they are noted, and analysts should refer to any information given in the notes on these and other matters. A further problem relates to the company's policy with regard to asset recognition and valuation. Intangibles are a particularly difficult category of asset. Some analysts suggest that only tangible assets should be included in the total assets figure. This would mean excluding assets such as goodwill, patents, etc. The argument is that tangible assets provide greater security as asset backing and intangibles should therefore be ignored. In many cases companies will already have charged purchased goodwill arising on acquisition against reserves (this is the policy adopted by ICI) and these companies' leverage ratios will be higher than companies capitalizing and amortizing goodwill. This point has not been lost on the finance directors of the companies writing off goodwill immediately, some of whom seek to overcome the problem by valuing 'brand names' and including them as intangible assets. Because these brands are regarded by the companies as having enduring values they typically improve the asset and leverage positions of the companies without affecting reported profits as any changes in value are dealt with through reserves rather than the profit and loss account.

Yet another problem in measuring leverage ratios lies in defining debt and equity. An issue of debentures or unsecured loan stock is clearly debt, while ordinary shares and associated reserves can be classified as equity, but in recent years capital issues have become more complex leading to problems of classification. Examples include puttable convertibles of the type issued by Burton Group plc and a number of other companies.

These bonds carry the right to a fixed payment and can be converted into ordinary shares on specified terms on or between specified dates; however, in addition, holders have the right to have the bonds repaid by the companies at pre-specified redemption values should conversion not take place. Should these bonds be classified as debt or equity? When first issued companies tended to regard these issues as equity. It was assumed that holders would wish to convert to equity. However, as the fortunes of the companies changed and their share values plunged it became apparent that conversion would not take place and that repayment would be required not just of the original amount subscribed but of the enhanced redemption value. This revision drastically affected the balance sheet perception of many companies.

We can see that there are many problems in measuring realistic and relevant leverage ratios. In fact this emphasizes the point that financial statement analysis is more than just 'number crunching'. Ratios can be useful but need to be computed after completely reviewing and understanding the published financial statements, the notes relating to them and any other information given. Even though regulations relating to financial reporting are constantly being updated astute company advisers are also active in devising ever more sophisticated forms of financial instrument.

Because of the problems associated with balance sheet measures more stress may be placed on ratios related to profit or cash flows.

Interest cover ratio

A commonly used ratio is interest cover which is calculated by dividing earnings before interest and tax by the annual interest payment and shows the number of times interest is covered by current earnings. The ratio for ICI is:

$$\text{Interest cover} \quad = \quad \frac{1033 + 30 + 83}{303}$$

$$= \quad 3.8 \text{ times}$$

In calculating this ratio the trading profit has been increased by the share of associated companies' earnings and interest received; the denominator is the gross interest payable in the year. If interest cover falls below 2 then the company would start to be considered risky; ICI's cover is adequate but currently lower than in previous years because of the depressed profits during the recession. In the company's own summarized financial information loan interest is shown as £195 million which represents the interest on long-term loans, interest on short-term borrowings is netted off against interest receivable. If the cover figure is calculated on this basis the effect is a reduction of £108 million in both numerator and denominator giving a cover figure of 5.3, a substantial improvement on the figure calculated above.

The interest cover ratio can be criticized in that it uses earnings rather than cash flows in measuring ability to pay interest. If the interest cover ratio is comparatively low then the figure of operating cash flow can be used in the numerator.

Cash flow ratio

A similar cash flow ratio to that calculated for short-term liabilities can be calculated using total rather than current liabilities as the denominator. For ICI this would be:

$$\text{Operating cash flow to total liabilities ratio} \quad = \quad \frac{\text{Cash flow from operations}}{\text{Total liabilities}}$$

$$= \quad \frac{1458}{3410 + 1947}$$

$$= \quad 0.27$$

Healthy US companies commonly have ratios of 20% or more;[2] if this is transferable to the UK then ICI's solvency is sound.

Because of the problems discussed, particularly in connection with asset recognition and valuation, there seems scope for developing more measures based on cash flow information. This is particularly pertinent given the almost universal change from funds flow to cash flow statements in published financial statements. In the UK and some other countries cash flow statements are now an accounting standard requirement.

As part of the Group financial record ICI includes a summarized cash flow statement covering the previous five years; other companies are increasingly producing this type of information. The statements can be used in a number of ways including monitoring to what extent investment is being financed by retained earnings and how much new financing is being used in the business. Other information contained in the five-year Record can be used to try and analyse new financing between debt and equity thus giving an indicator of growth in debt financing.

Ratios and insolvency (bankruptcy) prediction

The early 1990s have seen many formerly highly rated companies encounter financial difficulties.[3] These have ranged from temporary liquidity problems, through the need to restructure to ultimate insolvency. The ability to successfully predict future financial difficulties would be extremely valuable as it would enable both investors and creditors to take action at an earlier stage. Although financial ratios taken individually can indicate strengths and weaknesses there may nevertheless be satisfactory explanations where ratios appear out of line. The crucial question to answer is whether any particular combination of ratios can give insights into a company's financial strength.

A number of researchers have attempted to discriminate between the financial characteristics of successful companies and those facing failure. The objective has been to develop a model which uses financial ratios to predict which companies have the greatest likelihood of becoming insolvent in the near future. Altman in the USA is perhaps the best known of these researchers; using a statistical technique known as multiple discriminant analysis he developed a model using the combination of ratios which gave the best prediction of bankruptcy.[4] From 22 potentially useful ratios he narrowed the list down to the five which were regarded as being the most useful grouping in predicting bankruptcy. Using these ratios he calculated 'Z-scores' with lower scores indicating increasing risk of bankruptcy.

Altman calculated the Z-score as follows:

$$Z\text{-Score} = 1.2 \left(\frac{\text{Net working capital}}{\text{Total assets}} \right) + 1.4 \left(\frac{\text{Retained earnings}}{\text{Total assets}} \right)$$

$$+ 3.3 \left(\frac{\text{Earnings before interest and tax}}{\text{Total assets}} \right)$$

$$+ 0.6 \left(\frac{\text{Market value of equity}}{\text{Book value of liabilities}} \right)$$

$$+ 1.0 \left(\frac{\text{Sales}}{\text{Total assets}} \right)$$

Using this model the Z-score for ICI would be:

$$\text{Z-score} = 1.2 \left(\frac{2056}{11\,015} \right) + 1.4 \left(\frac{3131}{11\,015} \right) + 3.3 \left(\frac{1033}{11\,015} \right)$$

$$+ 0.6 \left(\frac{8603}{3410 + 1947} \right) + 1.0 \left(\frac{12\,488}{11\,015} \right)$$

$$= 3.03$$

When using this model Altman concluded:

Z-score < 1.81   =   High probability of bankruptcy

Z-score > 3.0   =   Low probability of bankruptcy

Z-score <3> 1.81   =   Indeterminate

Each of the ratios used represents a different measure of profitability or risk. The ratios use figures illustrated earlier in the chapter with two exceptions. The numerator of the second term 'Retained earnings' is the figure for accumulated retained earnings. This ratio seeks to capture long-run profitability and maturity of the company. The other figure is used in the fourth term which is a measure of leverage; the numerator used is the market value of equity (calculated in this case by multiplying the number of shares in issue at the balance sheet date by the market price per share at that date). By using market value the ratio incorporates the market view of the company's value, risk and future profitability. It could also be argued that use of a market value figure overcomes some of the problems identified with asset valuations; however, it should be noted that all the other figures used are based on the annual accounts and that the book value of total assets is used as the denominator in four out of the five terms.

Altman and others have extended this research to include other variables, specialized industries and international aspects. In the UK Taffler has been the most prominent researcher. His 1982 paper reported that after testing 50 ratios the five most significant from a discrimination point of view were:[5]

1   $\dfrac{\text{Earnings before interest and tax}}{\text{Total assets}}$

2   $\dfrac{\text{Total liabilities}}{\text{Net capital employed}}$

3   $\dfrac{\text{Quick assets}}{\text{Total assets}}$

4   $\dfrac{\text{Working capital}}{\text{Net worth}}$

5   $\dfrac{\text{Cost of sales}}{\text{Stock}}$

In both Altman's and Taffler's models the current profitability ratio (EBIT to total assets) was most important in discriminating between insolvent and solvent companies. This makes the point that if a company is successful in generating profits (and one assumes positive cash flows) it can overcome short-term liquidity problems. Also if a company makes profits but is otherwise being poorly managed it is likely to prove an attractive takeover target.

Although the different bankruptcy models have varied substantially they have, on average, accurately predicted 70% to 90% of insolvencies up to two years prior to insolvency. Altman's model was able to predict with 95% accuracy one year prior to insolvency and with 72% accuracy two years prior to insolvency. The accuracy diminished substantially as the lead time to insolvency extended beyond two years.

This approach to insolvency/bankruptcy prediction has been criticized on a number of counts. First of all there is no underlying theory relating to the process by which companies become bankrupt; the variables used in the different models result from a computational exercise undertaken on a sample of companies. The discriminant models are developed by matching a company known to be bankrupt with a similar healthy company matched for size and business activity. As most large firms operate in several industries matching can be difficult, also matching by size and industry means that these factors cannot be included in the variables although they may be significant in themselves. Because firms already known to be bankrupt are used, the models are based on relationships which match that sample for that period of time. It is not clear that past experience will always be transferable to future situations given the dynamic environment in which businesses operate.

The Bank of England also examined the scope of the technique and were not very encouraging. They concluded that 'careful analysis of accounts over a long period together with scrutiny of other published information is likely to provide the best, indeed the only basis for any adequate assessment by an outsider of the financial position of a company.'[6] The Bank is putting the onus back on the individual analyst and this reinforces the view that careful, thorough and individual analysis on a company-by-company basis is the necessary approach to company analysis.

However, despite these criticisms the discriminant approach is still used and a number of companies supply information on a commercial basis. Their attraction lies in their use of a small number of financial ratios aggregated into a single Z-score figure. Given the problems discussed above the scores should be used as indicators rather than firm evidence and further examination should be made of potential problem companies.

Stock Market Ratios

These ratios use accounting information combined with market values to compute ratios deemed important to investors and others interested in the performance of the company's issued capital.

Price to earnings ratio (P/E)

This is calculated by dividing the current market price by the last reported earnings per share figure. The resulting figure gives the number of years' earnings represented by the current price. In late August 1992 the price of ICI ordinary shares was 1112p. The reported earnings per share (earnings available to ordinary shareholders divided by number of shares in issue) for the year ended 31 December 1991 was 76.4p. The current P/E was:

$$P/E \ = \ \frac{1112}{76.4} \ = \ 14.6$$

The simplistic interpretation of P/E ratios is that high P/Es reflect higher anticipated growth with, perhaps, a lower risk; low P/Es would be anticipating lower growth and higher risk. The P/E ratio is, however, a mixture of current price reflecting expectations about the future and the historic profit for the most recent accounting period. If profits are temporarily depressed the P/E may be artificially high because, although profits are lower, the share price may not have fallen very much if the profit reduction is only considered temporary. Conversely, if profits were temporarily inflated then the P/E may appear relatively low. In addition, the average P/E ratios may differ between countries. If earnings figures are calculated in a very conservative way, as is thought to be the case in Germany for example, the average P/Es will tend to be higher than in other countries with a different attitude towards profit measurement as in the UK or the Netherlands. This means that P/Es must be interpreted with caution.

Dividend yield

This ratio expresses the most recent annual gross dividend as a percentage of the current market value. The actual net dividend for ICI in 1991 was 55p; when grossed up to allow for basic rate tax this becomes 73.3p. The current dividend yield in August 1992 was:

$$\text{Dividend yield} \ = \ \frac{73.3}{1112} \ = \ 0.066 \, (6.6\%)$$

Investors in ordinary shares normally expect to receive part of their return in the form of dividends and part in the form of capital appreciation. The dividend yield shows the current rate of return being received in the form of dividends.

This is another ratio which uses current market value and a historical figure, in this case dividend paid. In 1992 a number of companies had very high dividend yields as conventionally calculated and prima facie may have appeared attractive securities for inclusion in a high yield portfolio. However, the high yields were brought about by the sharp reduction in share price in anticipation of a substantial reduction, and in some cases complete withdrawal, of future dividend payments.

Dividend cover

This ratio uses only accounting data and is analogous to the interest cover ratio previously discussed. In this case profits available to pay a dividend are divided by the total dividend payment for the year. The 1991 figure for ICI is:

$$\text{Dividend cover} \quad = \quad \frac{542}{391} \quad = \quad 1.4$$

This ratio gives an indication of the safeness of the dividend payment. At 1.4 ICI's cover is relatively modest; it has maintained the same dividend for the past three years despite profits dropping very substantially. The early 1990s have seen many companies with declining dividend cover as they have struggled to maintain dividends in the face of falling profits. A normal expectation would be for dividend yield and dividend cover to be negatively correlated.

Asset value per share

This is another measure used by security analysts which is also wholly accounts based. It is calculated by dividing net assets attributable to ordinary shareholders by the number of shares in issue. For ICI at 31 December 1991 the asset per share figure was:

$$\text{Asset value per share} \quad = \quad \frac{4792}{711} \quad = \quad £6.74$$

The asset value is often compared with the market value (currently £11.12) to see to what extent the current price is supported or backed by assets. Where the asset value exceeds the market value it is sometimes seen as indicating a likely takeover target. However, this figure, like any other ratio, should not be used in isolation but in the context of a comprehensive evaluation of the company.

Debenture/loan stock measures

Investors in quoted fixed interest securities, as well as focusing on the interest cover figure, will also calculate return ratios. The first is similar to the dividend yield and is the interest yield; this is calculated as follows:

$$\frac{\text{Gross annual interest payment per unit}}{\text{Current market value per unit}}$$

This is sometimes referred to as the 'flat yield' as it only considers the annual interest payment and does not consider any change in value to maturity. A more complete measure of the return on fixed interest securities is the yield to maturity, or redemption yield. This is a discounted present value calculation and is the average annual interest rate arising from an investment undertaken at the current market price after allowing for the amount and timing of all future cash flows of interest and redemption payments.

Conclusions

Financial ratio analysis has been used for many years to assess profitability and risk from the viewpoint of lenders, investors and other transactors with the company both current and prospective. Norms were developed as yardsticks against which other companies could be measured both for their potential and soundness. It was always recognized that ratios were, at the least, industry based and that comparisons needed to be made between companies in similar lines of business activity with ratios calculated on a consistent basis. It is now apparent that, given the increasing use of creative accounting techniques to put the best view possible on a company's results and financial position,it is not enough to calculate financial ratios from the figures stated on the face of the financial statements. The notes to the accounts contain additional and often vital information which the analyst must study carefully, and where appropriate amendments must be made to the figures in the accounts. If this is true when we make intra-country comparisons then it is doubly so when we make comparisons between companies resident in different countries.

Another matter that must be approached with care is the significance of ratios when calculated. A number of references have been made to 'norms'; these are generally taken to mean acceptable levels of ratios in mid-cycle conditions. Ratios will vary depending on trading conditions, and the economic conditions existing during the period(s) covered by the accounts being analysed is an important consideration. It must also be questioned whether levels of ratios are expected to be similar in different countries. Would we expect a debt-to-equity ratio of 1 : 1, even if calculated on a similar basis after allowing for different accounting policies, to mean the same for companies operating in different countries? This seems unlikely as institutional factors affecting debt capacity vary between countries.

We may have seemed to raise more questions than we have answered! However, from the outset we must realize that for financial statement analysis to mean anything we need to sharpen our accounting knowledge and analytic skills. In the chapters that follow this theme is developed.

References

1. Casey, C. and Bartzcak, N. (1984) 'Cash flow – it's not the bottom line', *Harvard Business Review*, July–August, 61–66.
2. Stickney, C.P. (1990) *Financial Statement Analysis, A Strategic Perspective*, Harcourt Brace Jovanovich, 243.
3. Different terms are applied in different countries to the financial distress of companies. In the UK individuals go 'bankrupt' while companies become insolvent and go into liquidation. In the USA the term bankruptcy is applied to companies.
4. Altman, E. (1968) 'Financial ratios discriminant analysis and the prediction of corporate bankruptcy', *Journal of Finance*, September 589–609.

5. Taffler, R.J. (1982) 'Forecasting company failure in the UK using discriminant analysis and financial ratio data', *Journal of the Royal Statistical Society*, Series A (General), **145** (3), 342–358.

6. 'Techniques for Assessing Corporate Financial Strength', *Bank of England Quarterly Bulletin*, June 1982, pp 221–223.

Further Reading

Foster, G.	(1986) *Financial Statement Analysis*, 2nd edn, Prentice Hall.
Holmes, G. and Sugden, A.	(1992) *Interpreting Company Reports and Accounts*, 4th edn revised, Woodhead-Faulkner, Cambridge.
Rees, W.	(1990) *Financial Analysis*, Prentice Hall.
Stickney, C.P.	(1990) *Financial Statement Analysis, A Strategic Perspective*, Harcourt Brace Jovanovich.
White, G.I., Sondhi, A.C. and Fried, D.	(1994) *The Analysis and Use of Financial Statements*, John Wiley & Sons.

Problems

1. You have been asked to use accounting information contained in a database to compare the profitability, efficiency and risk-profile of a number of companies. Identify the accounting ratios you would use in this analysis and comment on any problems there might be in drawing conclusions from the analysis undertaken.

2. A number of different groups may consult a company's financial report for information. Name four groups who would be interested in the performance of a company and the type of information each would consider important.

3. Comment briefly on each of the following:
   a measurement of assets figure to be used in return on assets calculation;
   b measurement of equity to be used in debt-to-equity calculation;
   c drawing conclusions from a time series of ratios.

4. Discuss the use of bankruptcy prediction models in identifying companies likely to become insolvent in the near future.

5. Obtain a copy of the financial report and accounts of a large industrial company. (The London *Financial Times* offers a service whereby readers can obtain a copy of certain companies financial reports; these are mainly UK companies but some overseas companies' reports are also available. Alternatively you could contact a company of your choice in a country of your choice requesting a copy of the latest financial report.)

   Using the accounts obtained compute key profitability, efficiency and liquidity ratios and compare them with the ICI ratios. Comment on the results obtained.

6. Using the accounts obtained for Problem 5 above compare the accounting policies for depreciation, goodwill and pension costs with those used by ICI, commenting briefly on your results.

2

The Management of Earnings Disclosure

Objectives

- To consider why the numbers used in ratio analysis are not always reliable.

- To explain what the management of earnings disclosure means.

- To introduce the various techniques for carrying out the management of earnings disclosure.

- To discuss why such methods might be used by those controlling a company.

- To consider the reasons why accounting standards cannot prevent such practices.

Introduction

In the previous chapter we considered the most common method of analysing financial accounts. As explained financial ratio analysis is widely used both by outside investors when making investment decisions, and by managers within a company when analysing performance. Ratios must, however, be used with caution. It is unwise simply to divide one number by another and think that the numerical outcome tells you something. Unless the person calculating the ratio understands what lies behind the numerator and the denominator the ratio is meaningless.

Almost every number in a company's balance sheet and its profit and loss account is accompanied by a note. The first step in financial analysis is to read the footnotes and accompanying statement of accounting policies in order to try to understand the basis on which the numbers in the accounts have been calculated. How can an analysis of accounts mean anything unless we read the explanation of how an accounting number is arrived at? This is what the footnote attempts to do, or should attempt to do. Footnotes might appear to many users of accounts to be boring but they are important to obtaining more than just a superficial understanding of accounts.

It should not be assumed that every company makes the same assumptions about the future and uses the same methods to arrive at a valuation or to measure income and expenditure. This is the danger in analysing accounts based on data provided by one of the many computerized information agencies. They provide the ratio, but not always the footnotes. Often they claim the ratios are standardized to make comparisons meaningful. They might make some adjustments, but they cannot make all that are necessary. As Part Three of this book will illustrate, a thorough adjustment of accounts to make them truly comparable is very complex, time-consuming and in fact involves quite a lot of guesswork.

A further and more serious problem is that unfortunately sometimes the accounting numbers do not always mean what they appear to mean. The user has to, what is called, 'read between the lines' to see what is the company's true financial position. Financial ratios are only as reliable as the accounting numbers on which they are based.

Everyone has contact with some form of accounting data, and most people are confused and misled by them. This explains the power and importance of accountants in our society: their ability to represent and interpret financial information gives them considerable influence over decisions.[1]

Many users of accounts may only have a superficial understanding of the techniques of accounting. Therefore it is easy for them to be misled by a well-presented set of accounts, with a large number of footnotes apparently disclosing the information the financial analysts believe is important.

Preparers of accounts have been known to engage in what can be called 'window dressing', 'income smoothing', 'creative accounting' or 'accounting magic'. All of these practices can produce accounts that an auditor can sign as true and fair. It should be emphasized that all these 'techniques' are legal, they are not fraudulent. They are designed to present the company's performance in the best possible light. They should keep the financial analyst on his or her toes – they mean financial ratio analysis is not as simple as dividing one number by another and expecting the result to be the answer to a question on profitability, liquidity or gearing.

In the 1980s the expression 'creative accounting' came into common usage, even being used by those who know very little about the techniques and theories of accounting. The idea behind the expression, namely that it is possible for accountants, and those who are in a position to influence accountants, to 'create' the impression that they want to give, is not a new one. Over the previous 20 years in the USA and UK there had been a number of occasions in which a 'credibility gap' had developed between those who use accounts and those that prepare them, the users having on occasion reason to doubt the financial position of a company as reported.

In fact for decades the concept of 'income smoothing' had been known and on occasions used in the preparation of accounts, the idea being that it gives a better impression to show a steady performance, with profits growing at a reasonable rate, rather than to show a dramatic increase in performance in one year, followed by a less than dramatic performance the next year. There is clearly nothing new about what has become known as the 'management of earnings disclosure'. Why should we expect managers to always want to disclose the 'true' position? It is not surprising that given the opportunity they would wish to produce results which show them in the best possible light – which indicates that they are doing a good job. They may receive performance related financial rewards, but even if they do not they will want to appear to be 'good' managers. This is for their own job security and personal satisfaction.

However, by definition only in the region of one half of companies can show above average performance – all managers would want their companies to appear to be in the top half. How far can managers go, how far do they go, to create a favourable impression regarding their company's performance?

There is, of course, no such thing as a (true) correct profit or loss figure to reflect a year's activities. There is a range of possible profit or loss figures that can be produced depending upon the assumptions that are made. At one end of the range is what some would regard as the 'exaggerated' profit figure, and at the other end is what others would regard as the excessively cautious profit figure. The fact that there is a possible range of profit figures (even with perfect accounting standards), and not a unique figure, should not come as a surprise to anybody who knows something about accounting. The profit and loss account reports the performance over a period of time, but the business does not usually come to an end at the close of that period: contracts may be only half completed; goods may have been produced but not sold; equipment that has been purchased is still usable; and not all customers have paid for goods and services received. Accounting reporting does not just involve measuring what has happened in the past; of necessity, it involves making assumptions about certain aspects of what will happen in the future.

In this chapter we will begin by considering the role of accounting theory in accounting standard setting. We will then examine the problem areas which allow preparers of accounts the opportunity to 'manage' the level of earnings they disclose. These problem areas are the ones users of accounts need to be aware of, and to scrutinize in the financial reports of companies.

Before making concluding comments, we will examine why managers might wish to adopt creative accounting techniques, and examine the evidence on manipulation.

Accounting Policy

Accounting is concerned with the measurement and communication of useful financial information, and as such exists for its practical merit. If accounting reports turn out to be of little or no practical use, then the justification for an accountant and auditor disappears. If the users of accounting reports lose faith in such reports then they will not wish to contribute towards the cost of their preparation nor to the cost of the audit process. The benefits will not justify the cost.

The credibility of financial accounts is what justifies the accounting profession. If the public and/or the government feel that the accounting profession is no longer to be trusted, if it is felt that it is not acting responsibly, then changes will be introduced. The accounting profession therefore has to take steps to eliminate or reduce the opportunities for creative accounting. It has to ensure that the credibility gap disappears, or at least that it is only a small percentage of companies who are able to manage earnings disclosure to the extent that it misleads the user.

Perhaps surprisingly, in the UK and USA, the objective of financial statements is continually being discussed. In 1991 an exposure draft in the UK on the subject stated: 'The objectives of financial statements is to provide information about the financial position, performance and financial adaptability of an enterprise that is useful to a wide range of users in making economic decisions.' It does point out that financial statements do not provide all the information that users need to make economic decisions. It also mentions that financial statements also show 'the results of the stewardship of management, that is, the accountability of management for the resources entrusted to it'.[2]

Financial statements serve different purposes within the social and economic systems of the European countries included in this study. Two major purposes are:

- the provision of information; and
- the regulation of distributions.

The emphasis laid upon these two purposes differs considerably between the countries with which we are concerned. The **provision of information** is the declared primary objective of financial statements in the countries forming or following the Anglo-Saxon accounting tradition (e.g. the United Kingdom, the Netherlands). The **regulation of distributions** is of less importance in these countries especially as compared to the countries following the continental European accounting tradition (e.g. France, Germany, Italy).

In Germany commercial financial statements play a central role in the regulation of distributions both to shareholders and especially to the fiscal authorities. Distributions to shareholders are restricted to the amount of profit displayed in the commercial financial statements. Moreover, management has the discretion – within certain restrictions – to retain up to 50% of the profit of the year without the consent of the shareholders. With regard to distributions to the fiscal authorities, commercial financial statements and tax financial statements are linked by the so-called authoritative principle. The valuation methods in commercial accounts generally follow the tax treatment. Because of the tax consequences accounting choices result in practices that are conservative by international comparison and have resulted in the creation of hidden reserves. Accounting creativity is aimed at minimizing taxable income rather than in boosting equity or profits shown in the commercial financial statements. The conflict with the informational objective is apparent.

When we consider financial statements as a means of providing information there has in recent years been in most countries a change in emphasis. Traditionally financial accounting has been more concerned with providing information that could be used for an ex post evaluation of past performance, rather than providing information concerned with the present or the future. This concern with reporting the results of the past, which is referred to as stewardship, has the advantage that the data is more reliable than when based on future expectations.

There have been, however, increasing pressures in all countries from investors and financial markets for the financial accounts to adopt a more forward-looking role. The response to this pressure has been greater in some countries than in others. This move away from the stewardship role makes accounts more relevant to many users, but it is at the expense of reliability. It must be remembered that accounting data by its nature is in many ways unreliable, and 'by moving the emphasis of accounts from the less relevant past to the more relevant future, we are likely to increase the element of uncertainty'.[3]

There are many uses of accounting data, and many different ways of supplying the information. A single approach to providing asset values and profit figures is unlikely to be optimal to all users. As explained some users of accounting statements are interested in stewardship, in ensuring that funds have been used properly in the past and that their investment in the company is secure. In Germany, traditionally, the emphasis has been to prepare a set of accounts that will be useful to creditor groups, these being banks and other companies to whom money is owed. As explained other users are interested in information that can be used for prediction purposes. It is doubtful that one set of measurement rules can provide information that will satisfy the differing needs of all the users of financial statements. Any choice of accounting method will depend on which class of user(s) the statement is aimed at.[4]

Certain of these groups, for example the loan creditor group and the government, will at times be more interested in the reliability they can attach to the figures in the reports than in using the figures in an attempt to ascertain the future earning power of the company. At times where tax, fraud or the legality of dividend payments are involved, the less subjective the figures are, the better.

If the objective of financial reports is to communicate economic measurement of, and information about, the resources and performance of the business, what rules should be applied to measure the resources currently being employed and the past performance? Is a consistent and comprehensive set of rules and procedures really needed to guide practice? Do we need to bother with theories of accounting?

Watts and Zimmerman argue that accounting theories serve a number of overlapping functions.[5] One is the need to describe existing practice, to be able to rationalize what we at present do. A second is the need to meet the demand of those who require financial information for prediction purposes. A third is what is referred to as the 'justification demand'. This is the need to have a theory to support the measurement practices that a particular interest group wants adopted because such practices will benefit them at the expense of another group. A fourth is to meet the demand of governments and regulatory bodies who are concerned with the role that financial statements play in wealth transfers and in discussions on the efficiency of enterprises and the public interest.

The accounting profession has attempted to reduce the range of choice available to the preparers of accounts by introducing accounting standards. Unfortunately standard setters do not have an agreed accounting theory to guide the standards. This is not because of a lack of literature on accounting theory, it is because of a lack of agreement. Many writers refer to accounting standard setting as a political process, rather than as a resort to theory.[6]

Watts and Zimmerman express the view that much of the work on accounting theory is a waste of time. They refer to much 'normative' work as attempts to 'supply excuses which satisfy the demand created by the political process'. They believe that 'financial accounting theory has had little substantive direct impact on accounting practice or policy formulation'. They see accounting theory as an economic good. The demand for theories arises partly because accounting procedures are a means of achieving wealth transfers. Because one interest group may wish to achieve a wealth distribution different from that of another, it needs a theory, an accounting theory, to help justify the wealth transfer. Therefore, 'a variety of accounting theories is demanded on any one issue'.

The accounting standards that we have, and those that will be produced in the future, are pragmatic. They are each the result of the interplay of three forces: political pressure, existing accounting practice and accounting theory. The process of arriving at a standard means that it is a compromise. A board prepares the standards after consultation with many people and a number of relevant interest groups. With so much consultation, and so many organizations and pressure groups having an influence on the final standard, there is bound to be a fair amount of give and take. It must not even be thought that the practice that eventually becomes the accepted standard has received unanimous approval at all stages of its development. It could well have passed any particular stage only by a vote, say with an outcome of ten in favour and eight against.

This point is being emphasized not in any way to discredit a statement of standard practice, but to show why the approved practice is not 'right' and all other possibilities 'wrong'. It is the practice accepted by the balance of a particular group of people and interest groups as being the best at a particular time. A different group of people involved in the various stages of the development of the standard, or the same people consulting at a different time, could well have produced a different standard. A further point is that an alternative possible practice, one that was not recommended by the Standards Board, but which received minority support, might be almost as acceptable as the one that is recommended. It is not a matter of deciding upon the right practice, but of deciding upon the practice that is the most acceptable one out of a number of possibilities, all of which have something to be said for them. The accounting standard-setting procedure is a bargaining process.

There has been much work undertaken to produce a conceptual framework for accounting but no agreement has been reached. This is not really surprising as there are major divisions of opinion amongst those involved with making decisions on such matters. In the UK there are those who argue that the balance sheet is the most important statement and it should reflect the current value of assets and liabilities, and there are those who disagree, seeing the profit and loss account as more important. The latter believe that producing a profit which can be used to determine the level of distribution is most important. There are also disagreements between those who support an economic approach to accounts and those who support the legalistic approach.[7]

Creative Accounting

In the early 1940s, the Institute of Chartered Accountants in England and Wales (ICAEW) produced guidance statements for members on the best practice to follow in preparing accounts. These were recommendations on accounting principles, an attempt to narrow the range of possible reporting practices. The recommendations did not escape criticism. As early as 1953, Baxter was concerned (but not surprised) at the lack of theoretical foundation for these recommendations: 'Is it wise for any group of men to say what is true or right in matters of theory?' Baxter argued that it was not possible to support any particular practice on the grounds of theory alone.[8] Despite the fact that recommendations were being produced, accounting reporting practices did not escape further criticism. In the 1960s Stamp, among others, argued that there was a need for the recommendations, the guidance statements, to be more firmly based on the objectives of accounting.[9]

In addition to this academic criticism, there was criticism from the users of the financial statements. First a 'credibility gap' developed and later an 'expectations' gap. The users of financial statements often did not know how to interpret the accounts that were being produced. In preparing their accounts, some companies were choosing from the range of accepted practices those that made the profit position of the company appear in the best possible light. The companies that used this imaginative form of accounting were often run by people whom the Americans would refer to as 'financial gunslingers', following practices described in the UK as 'creative accounting'. Other companies were preparing accounts based on the traditional accounting principles of 'conservatism' and 'prudency'. Hence the credibility gap: a reader of a set of accounts could not always tell whether it had been prepared on the basis of a conservative set of principles or on the basis of the highest possible profit. In the UK an accounting standards committee was established in 1970.

Different countries have adopted different approaches to the establishment of generally accepted accounting principles. In France, for example, from 1947 there existed a 'Plan Comptable General' which introduced uniform charts of accounts. The Commission that produced the Plan (National Accounting Council – CNC) continues to give technical guidance on points of interpretation. The Stock Exchange regulating body (Commission des Opérations de Bourse – COB) has also been influential in introducing improved accounting reports and greatest disclosure.

The Netherlands, on the other hand, have relatively liberal statutory accounting and financial reporting requirements but very high professional practice standards. Prior to 1970, Dutch legal requirements for accounting, auditing and financial reporting were very few in number, very general in nature and by and large insignificant economically. After an Act in 1970 on the Annual Accounts of Enterprises the basis was laid down for subsequent statutory accounting developments. Consequently the influence of company law has steadily increased since the early 1970s.

The Act remains permissive and general. Consequently, the Act is further interpreted by the Enterprise Chamber of the Court of Justice and the Council for Annual Reporting. Nevertheless, the only binding and legally enforceable accounting rules are those specified in the accounting and financial reporting provisions of the Act

The Act provides that interested parties may complain to an Enterprise Chamber if they feel that the financial statements submitted do not comply with the law. 'Interested parties' is defined broadly and includes shareholders, employees, work councils and trade unions. The public prosecutor may also bring proceedings. The Enterprise Chamber is composed of three judges and two experts; there is no jury involved.

The Enterprise Chamber may order rectification of the financial statement and/or may influence future financial statements. Although the rulings of the Enterprise Chamber are applicable only to the defendant company, the Enterprise Chamber may indicate grounds for its decisions which may influence the reporting practices of other companies. Failure to comply with the Court's rulings may be punished by fines or imprisonment of management.

Guidance as to what are generally acceptable accounting principles is provided by the guidelines published by the Council for Annual Reporting. The Council is composed of representatives of the preparers, the users and the auditors of annual accounts. The users are represented by trade unions and the Dutch Association of Investment Analysts. Thus not all categories are represented in the Council; for example, there are no direct representations of shareholders or of the Amsterdam Stock Exchange.

Companies are not obliged to follow the guidelines (although most of them do so), nor need they or their auditors state that the guidelines have been applied; audit reports are not qualified for departure from the guidelines.

Even though the Council's work is highly influential, it does not have statutory power.

Any credibility gap is important, because one of the factors that influence investors, bankers and others in their decision-making is how they interpret the financial statements presented to them. The investors' decisions are important, for not only do they affect the demand for a company's shares, but at times of mergers and takeovers they can affect the survival of a company in its existing form. In the UK the reputations of some businessmen were built up on the basis of their use of creative accounting. Even conservative executives sometimes had to abandon their more prudent assumptions when preparing accounts, or run the risk of seeing their companies taken over because they were not producing the performance of what were thought to be the more dynamic companies. There was clearly a need for accountants to tidy up reporting practices.

The accounting profession in the UK has in the 1990s changed its accounting standard-setting procedures to try to reduce the opportunities for the management of earnings disclosure. Accounting standard-setting is one attempt to improve the reporting system. It is, however, not the end of the story, and within five to ten years it is reasonable to assume that we will be trying other methods to improve communication between businesses, shareholders, potential investors, employees, the government and all other users of accounts.

In the 1970s the business world, the financial community and the accounting profession had high expectations from accounting standards. By the mid-1980s, considerable disillusionment had set in. In the UK, the level of non-compliance was increasing. Regrettably, the Accounting Standards Committee was not even monitoring the level of non-compliance. The position changed in the 1990s. A Financial Reporting Review Panel was established, to examine the annual report and accounts of companies to ensure that the practices followed complied with accounting standards and statutory requirements. The panel has the power to take action which can lead to a company being required to prepare revised accounts.

The panel has been successful in that a number of companies have as a result of criticism made changes and adjustments to their published accounts. The panel's most spectacular success has been with Trafalgar House where criticism of the reclassification of certain properties from current assets to fixed assets and of the treatment of a number of other items led to revised accounts. The criticism also led to other changes which resulted in the removal of the chairman and the managing director of the company.

There was one other area of major concern with accounting standards. The accounting standard-setting bodies either could not agree on the appropriate treatment or else took too long to come to a recommendation. Accounting at a time of changing prices is an example of the first problem; off-balance-sheet financing is an example of delay.

In the USA there was concern that, on many of the major issues that were emerging in the fields of finance and accounting, there were no standards or recommendations with regard to the appropriate accounting treatment. It was taking a considerable time for the FASB to produce a standard, and during this period the preparers of accounts could do as they liked, to the confusion of the users. The FASB, in an attempt to overcome this problem, set up an 'Emerging Issues Task Force'. In the UK there was also a considerable lag between the time when an accounting issue emerged and the time when, if at all, a standard or statement was produced. A similar task force has been set up in the UK entitled the 'Urgent Issues Task Force'.

It is intended that the information disclosed, and the financial statements produced, will give a 'true and fair' view of the state of affairs of the company. Perhaps, however, our expectation of the outcome is too high. Existing knowledge is such that standards cannot be produced that will lead to accounting numbers that command universal support. Many of the problems are not amenable to logical analysis.

Methods of Managing Earnings Disclosure

Davidson, Stickney and Well, in discussing what they refer to as 'accounting magic' define the managing of earnings disclosure as: 'A process of taking deliberate steps within the constraints of generally accepted accounting principles to bring about a desired level of earnings.'[10]

Holmes and Sugden writing in 1990 refer to the fact that analysts expect some companies to 'try to show continuous growth year after year and to pull out all the stops to avoid reporting a downturn'.[11] They list certain accounting practices that 'some' companies have used to enhance their profits; the list includes the following issues:

- depreciation of buildings and intangible assets;
- capitalization of costs, for example interest, start-up costs, research and development;
- writing off costs direct to reserves;
- the treatment of acquisitions and disposals;
- extraordinary and exceptional items;
- income recognition.

Smith lists twelve possible accounting techniques that can be used as a means of manufacturing profit.[12] These techniques are:

1. write down of pre-acquisition costs or potential future costs;
2. profits on disposal of a business;
3. deferred purchase consideration;
4. extraordinary and exceptional items of income and expenditure;
5. off-balance sheet finance;
6. contingent liabilities;
7. capitalization of costs;
8. brand accounting;
9. changes in depreciation policy;
10. convertible securities;
11. pension fund accounting;
12. treatment of foreign currency items.

In fact all alert users of accounts know which are the items that allow for earnings manipulation. It is not always easy, however, to ascertain from the information disclosed exactly how a particular item has been treated. Part Two of this book deals with those items in detail, giving examples from different countries. At this point we will only deal briefly with the problems.

Evidence of Manipulation

Lev in his survey article on the usefulness of earnings research, concludes that 'prima facie evidence on manipulation of financial information is widespread'.[13] He quotes from Scholes et al. who found evidence of income smoothing.[14] Even banks have been found to manage their earnings disclosure. Allen and Saunders found 'almost 85% of banks in the sample window dressing their balance sheet upwards'.[15]

McNichols and Wilson found evidence that firms manage their earnings 'by choosing income-decreasing accruals when income is extreme'.[16] The reason a firm might wish to reveal lower income is to avoid criticism from regulatory agencies. The researchers believe, however, that, whereas managers are able to alter some accruals, the discretionary component of total accruals is only a small portion.

A question that has worried investors and analysts for some time is what percentage of companies engage in the management of earnings disclosure. There are high profile cases that hit the headlines, such as Asil Nadir and Polly Peck, and Robert Maxwell and his group of companies. But the impression that those who are engaged in finance like to give is that these are just isolated cases, and that 99% of companies do not engage in deliberate manipulation in order to mislead.

It came as something of a shock therefore when, in the UK in 1992, Smith wrote his book entitled *Accounting for Growth*.[17] The contents of the book were greeted by many with surprise, also the fact that the author was an insider. The contents should not, however, have been a surprise to anyone engaged in the actual analysis of company accounts.

The results he reported were based on an analysis of the actual reporting practices of the major one hundred UK companies. Smith's research received widespread publicity as at the time of undertaking the research he was a banking analyst for UBS Phillips & Drew, one of the major UK brokers. He examined 12 areas in which dubious accounting methods were possible, and found that one company adopted as many as nine of these manipulative techniques. Two companies used eight, four used seven, 15 used six. To be fair there were a number of companies that only adopted practices for managing disclosure in one of the 12 areas, and there were a few companies that had no dubious practices.

An interesting case study is that prepared by Brink that examines changes over a long period of time and illustrates the problems involved. Brink analyses the actual changes in Philips' accounting policies from 1912 to the present time.[18] He also attempted to attach motives for the changes and the choices made by the board of the company. As Brink pointed out, his conclusions are subjective as 'no research was conducted into what went on behind closed doors in the managers' boardroom.'

Philips is a particularly interesting company to examine as not only is it one of the largest European companies, it also has a respected reputation in the field of financial reporting. Brink points out that the company has with 'increasing frequency changed the principles used in determining its results'. With respect to recent changes Brink believes the reasons given in the financial reports to explain the changes have not always been convincing. 'The figures leave the strong suspicion that an improvement in the company result was a motive. Every important change in accounting occurred in a period of decreasing results, and each change led to a higher result.'

There were some occasions, however, where the company appeared to change its own policies in response to changes in accounting standards. For the company to have maintained its own policies and just to respond to the changes being forced upon it by external authorities would have led to a deterioration in the reported results of the company. Brink believes that 'in such situations, a company like Philips has a legitimate right, or even a duty, to change its policies on this point'. This is what the management of earnings disclosure is all about. The analyst has to decide whether the change in a company's accounting policies is a response to a 'genuine' need to change or an attempt to window dress.

It should be pointed out that what can appear to be manipulation can in fact be a genuine reflection of changed circumstances. For example, reducing the depreciation charge by lengthening the useful life of an asset could just be recognizing new knowledge. It would have been difficult for an airline company to appreciate the useful life of a Boeing 747 when it was first introduced.

Problems can arise, not because of any attempt to manipulate the reported figures, but just because of the fact that accounts have to be prepared every 12 months. At the end of an accounting period, many transactions will be incomplete, and in order to estimate profits many assumptions have to be made. It is possible for those who want to, to take advantage of this, and to bring forward in time the reporting of profit, by speeding up the recognition of income or delaying the recognition of expenses. Four examples of areas in which assumptions need to be made are:

1. life of assets – affects annual depreciation charge;
2. credit sales – means cash has not been received, so there is a need to estimate the probability of a customer paying: the directors of a company decide when they wish to recognize a debt as bad;
3. estimate of cost of producing finished goods and work in progress – this affects the value of inventory: the directors decide when to write off certain items of finished goods as obsolete;
4. long-term contracts – there is a need to estimate the percentage of work completed and so the amount of profit earned as at a certain date.

The way in which the company handles all the above items and many more affects the reported profit figure and the asset valuations. To assist the reader of the accounts in understanding what lies behind the figures some explanations are given in the annual accounts. There is a statement of accounting principles and numerous footnotes. But even in the 'best' set of accounts with the highest level of disclosure there is much the reader of the accounts will not be able to completely understand about the treatment of the four items mentioned above. This is naturally the position considering the complexity of modern business. The result is that the user is reliant on the auditor's statement that the accounts are 'true and fair'.

However, there is more than one 'true and fair' profit figure for any company. Hence the opportunity to manage earnings disclosure arises in even the most 'reliable' company.

The user of accounts must beware. The user cannot hide behind the accountant who prepared the accounts or the auditor who signed them. Accounting is not an exact subject. As one UK businessman said 'if I want to I can mislead, whatever happens to accounting standards'.

If the market is efficient, it should not be fooled by creative accounting techniques. Watts and Zimmerman conclude that boosting earnings through accounting changes to increase the corporation stock prices will in most cases be a futile exercise.[19] The words 'in most cases' should be noted.

Most studies detect little or no reaction in the share prices of a company to new accounting disclosures or to changes in accounting practices. Changes in inventory valuation methods, foreign currency translation methods, reporting the earnings of related companies and moves from the merger to the acquisition accounting approach have been studied. No consistent evidence has been found that the resulting change in earnings per share fools the market.

However, the directors of companies do still continue to manipulate earnings per share figure. They know of the existence of the EMH theory but they still act as if they believe that the 'adjustment' or 'window dressing' of the financial accounts is worthwhile. Perhaps the fact that it has only been found that manipulation does not mislead the market in most cases encourages them. It has not been found that it does not work in all cases. The directors hope that their company accounts might be one of the few that the market does not 'read' properly in the short term.

As explained in the next chapter there are doubts as to how efficient are the major stock markets.

Why Earnings Management Occurs

The reasons why the earnings figures that are disclosed might be managed include the following.

- Directors' remuneration schemes can create an incentive to manage earnings figures. Directors' bonus schemes are on occasions linked in some way to earnings per share. Directors often have only short-term contracts, sometimes one year or less. Why not speed up the recognition of profit so as to benefit from it as early as possible? The director may not be in office when profits on long-term ventures would normally pass through the accounts.
- Asymmetry in information – managers have 'private' information that they can use when determining compensation or profit-sharing rules among interested parties in the company.
- Directors or one shareholder group may want to impress a 'prospective' shareholder group with the firm's past performance (inviting/encouraging takeover bid/buy-out).
- Following a takeover bid, management wishes to impress its existing shareholders with its past performance.
- Firms will smooth income to create an impression of a low variability in income: to impress lenders, therefore attracting low interest rates.
- Earning fixation – In the UK (and in the USA) the users of accounts and consequently the preparers of accounts have become obsessed with the earnings figures – with what is sometimes called the 'bottom line'. Whereas at one time in the

UK, and still in some other countries (Germany), accounts had a stewardship role, now the emphasis has shifted to earnings performance. It is the earnings per share and the associated price earnings ratio that dominate analysis of a company's performance and consequently investment prospects.

Tinic refers to the 'functional fixation hypothesis' which in the stock market context means that 'decision makers who are unfamiliar with different methods of producing accounting outputs rely on bottom line accounting numbers without paying attention to the procedures used in generating them'.[20] If this hypothesis were proven it would mean that the efficient market hypothesis was incorrect, and that share prices do not reflect all available information. Tinic was not able to resolve the issue as to which hypothesis best explained stock market prices. The hypothesis does, however, illustrate the danger in users of accounts relying on the 'bottom line'.

The hypothesis would indicate that techniques of accounting that boost earnings per share, whatever the effect on the balance sheet, are desirable. Following an acquisition an immediate write-off of goodwill to reserves helps boost earnings in the current year and future years. Classifying an item as a 'brand value' rather than goodwill also helps earnings. Brand values do not necessarily have to be written down.

These techniques boost profits at the expense of the balance sheet. If the overall accounts were analysed these policies to boost short-term earnings would not be so important. It is partly the result of what has been called an 'earnings fixation' we see the management of earnings disclosure.

- Perhaps the underlying reason why we see the management of disclosure in the UK (and the USA) is because of the system of corporate governance. It should be emphasized that the system of corporate governance varies from one country to another. (Corporate governance is an expression referring to the relationship between those who provide the money for the company and those that manage the company.)

In the present business culture in the UK, the two key factors in the director/shareholder relationship are:

- senior management is accountable to shareholders; and
- senior managers are judged essentially by the value they create for shareholders.

A recent discussion paper issued by the Bank of England raised the question of whether there is the possibility that the UK system, 'so excellent when viewed in isolation, may put (the UK) at a disadvantage in international competition compared with those who have superior linkages and lines of accountability ... and a greater sense of patience?'[21]

The debate centres on whether the divorce of ownership and control that exists in the UK puts us at a disadvantage to our European and

Japanese competitors. A similar concern exists in the USA. The UK and US systems are similar; they contrast with the closer relationship between providers of finance and managers to be found with our major competitors.

The objective of maximizing shareholder wealth is not sufficiently precise, and we are unclear whether we mean long-term wealth or short-term wealth. We are, we know, unclear how to measure company performance; perhaps the stock market is less 'efficient' than we have believed with the result that available funds have not been allocated to where they can be most effectively used.

An exchange of views has been taking place in the pages of the *Harvard Business Review*. Jensen, one of the leading writers on mergers and acquisitions, wrote an article entitled 'The eclipse of the public corporation'.[22] He expressed the view that in certain industries for a variety of reasons our present relationship between owners and managers is out of date, is changing and needs further change. He would support an alternative system.

His views are representative of those who want fundamental change. He makes the point that many investors are dissatisfied, and that managers have been putting their own interests first over the last ten to twenty years.

Golden parachute type contracts and other perks have shown that managers are not taking the interest of the investor seriously enough. The clear separation of ownership and control has worked against efficiency and growth. Jensen believes that managers are looking after their own interests.

Another problem with the UK system of corporate governance is the pressure on institutional investment managers to show good relative returns each quarter in the funds they manage. If they find their performance in the lower ranking too often they will be removed.

But as is pointed out by Rybczynski the problem is not just the way in which institutional investment managers' performance is judged, but also the fact that the managers of companies can find themselves in a position where the maximization of performance during their periods of control is not consistent with the maximization of a company's long-term performance.[23] Rybczynski raises the problem of information asymmetries in the UK, in particular the poor flow of information from the company to its shareholders. This is why it is necessary to read between the lines of the accounts. The system of corporate government in the UK encourages the management of earnings disclosure.

Rapport, disagreeing with Jensen, argues against fundamental change. He believes the existing system will be improved when the USA (and UK) move to a 'governance system that provides effective monitoring of and checks on managerial authority'.[24] The present system of financial reporting in the UK and USA, it seems agreed, is not an effective monitoring system.

The system of corporate governance varies from country to country. In Germany companies have a two-tier board structure. The supervisory board consists of representatives of many interest groups, with far more outside directors involved than is found in a UK company. In Chapter 5 of the book, the levels of disclosure on governance in the financial reports from the different countries is considered.

Most countries have some criticisms of their own system. In Germany the minority shareholders feel their interests are not represented. It is the large banks, through their direct shareholdings, the loans advanced, the advice they offer as stock brokers and the votes they can control through the proxy system that have a degree of power over companies that worries many people.

Accounting Response

Despite the difficulties, the profession in the UK and in other countries is continually attempting to improve financial reporting and address the criticisms. The Accounting Standards Board (ASB) is proposing that an 'operating and financial review' (OFR) be included as part of the annual report of large companies.[25] The 'review' would discuss the factors affecting future financial performance, but would not include a profit forecast. It would comprise three main elements: a commentary on the operating results, a review of financial needs and resources, and a commentary on shareholders' return and value.

The first part would examine the main influences on the operating results, discussing such issues as products, customers, inflation and exchange rate movements. The analysis of financial needs would hopefully confirm that the business could meet its short-term needs and give broad details of future investment and financing plans. The commentary on returns would discuss dividends, but perhaps more significantly would identify assets not fully reflected in the balance sheet, for example investment in brands, advertising and training.

Undoubtedly statements such as an OFR would help reduce the credibility gap. It would help shareholders to understand the position of the company much more than the present chairman's statement. Such statements are usually far too general.

A problem with the proposal is that the production of such an OFR would be voluntary. Even if a company decided to produce such a 'review' it could contain a large number of words but reveal very little. An additional drawback is that the 'review' would not be subject to audit. One could therefore have a credibility gap relating to the 'review' itself.

The Accounting Standards Board in the UK and the International Accounting Standards Committee (IASC) are trying to reduce the opportunities for creative accounting. The ASB's new definition of assets is the 'rights or other access to future tangible economic benefits controlled by an entity as a result of past transactions and events'. With such a definition companies would be forced to account for more assets in the balance sheet than at present. An asset under this definition is not a particular item of property, but the rights deriving from ownership, or use. With this definition even operating leases would be included on the face of the balance sheet.

A similar 'radical' change in definition is proposed for liabilities. A liability is defined as the 'obligation to transfer economic benefits as a result of past transactions or events'. It is also proposed that companies should account on the face of the balance sheet for 'contracts for future performance where both parties have rights and obligations under the contract'. Traditionally, if disclosed at all, such information has been shown in footnotes.

The above are proposals. There are difficulties that would result if accepted, for example how to value the new types of asset and liability, but if adopted they would certainly reduce the opportunity for creative accounting.

The IASC in its proposals has followed the ASB in ending the distinction between extraordinary and exceptional items, and requiring all such items to be included before arriving at earnings per share. This would end one opportunity for boosting earnings per share figures. The proposals from the international body also call for more disclosure on the financial effects of discontinued operations and changes in accounting estimates.

Conclusions

Clearly from what has been written above the user of financial statements should beware. Very few companies resort to creative accounting to the extent that it would seriously mislead a user, whether a banker or investor. But some companies do, and it is precisely the companies that do resort to such techniques that are the ones with which an investor or banker can lose large amounts of money.

Remember 'for every foolish borrower there is a foolish lender'. It is perhaps surprising that bankers do not spend more time analysing in detail the accounts of companies that they lend to. It is because of this that in the 1980s a number of leading industrialists were able to mislead the banks.

The bankers' replies to the criticism that their analysis at that time was superficial are as follows.

- They do not have time to undertake a detailed analysis – if they do not lend another banker will do so, and the banks are competing for market share. They could not in the late 1980s take a long time over making a decision.
- The loan officer making the decision hopes not to occupy the same position in the bank if and when the loan turns out to be bad. He or she will have been promoted. They will be more likely to have been promoted if they go along with the 'herd' in their lending decisions. If they start questioning the creditworthiness of companies and individuals that the financial community in general regard as outstanding they will face criticism. It will be some time before they will be proved to be right or wrong.
- Why look at the actual accounts, when all the analysis (ratios etc.) has been done for you by a computerized data agency? Unfortunately, such agencies are not particularly reliable when it comes to dissecting the accounts of those companies who engage in creative accounting.

The system of corporate governance that exists in the UK and USA encourages a certain amount of management of earnings disclosure – the user has to read between the lines to ascertain how much such management has taken place.

There are significant differences between countries within the EU in the form of ownership and control of companies. The UK system is directed towards the promotion of free markets, and close links between investors and managers are discouraged by laws and rules, a major concern being the prevention of insider dealing and the protection of minority interest shareholders. The result is that with an arm's length relationship between owners and managers the financial reports take on a greater significance. Also there is less opportunity for owners to monitor the decisions and policies of managers.

In France and Germany, traditionally far less emphasis has been placed on the operations of the stock markets. There are therefore less restrictions on the closeness of the relationship between owners and managers. More information is exchanged informally. The opportunities to manage disclosure are therefore less. The financial reports are therefore of less significance, with a more established informal communication system.[26]

Another important difference between countries within the Union arises because of the different structure of financing by companies. As is well known, UK companies have traditionally worked with lower levels of gearing than companies in other European countries. Debt and equity lead to different forms of corporate governance. Debt governance works mainly through rules, with covenants and other legal restraints restricting the actions of those who manage companies. Equity governance, on the other hand, allows much greater discretion. With a greater proportion of funds being provided through equity, those who run UK companies are more concerned than management in other European countries in creating a favourable impression in the stock market. With an over-active market in corporate control the short-term survival of the UK manager depends on it.

References

1. Whittington, G. (1992) *The Elements of Accounting: An Introduction*, Cambridge University Press.

2. Accounting Standards Board (1991) Exposure Draft: *The Objective of Financial Statements and the Qualitative Characteristics of Financial Information*, ASB.

3. Whittington, op. cit.

4. McMonnies, P. (Ed) (1988) *Making Corporate Reports Valuable,* Institute of Chartered Accountants of Scotland.

5. Watts, R.L. and Zimmerman, J.L. (1978) 'Towards a positive theory of the determination of accounting standards', *Accounting Review,* January.

6. Horngren, C.T. (1973) 'The marketing of accounting standards', *Journal of Accounting,* October.

7. Ernst & Young (1993) *The Future of UK Financial Reporting,* Thought Leadership Series, September.

8. Baxter, W.T. (1953) 'Recommendations on accounting theory', *The Accountant,* October; reprinted in Baxter, W.T. and Davidson, S. (eds) (1962), *Studies in Accounting Theory,* Sweet & Maxwell, London.

9. Stamp, E. (1969) 'The public accountant and the public interest', *Journal of Finance,* Spring.

10. Davidson, S., Stickney, C. and Weil, R. (1987) *Accounting: The Language of Business,* 7th edn, Horton, Arizona.

11. Holmes, G. and Sugden, A. (1990) *Interpreting Company Reports and Accounts,* 4th edn, Woodhead Faulkner, Cambridge.

12. Smith, T. (1992) *Accounting for Growth,* Century Business, London.

13. Lev, B. (1989) 'On the usefulness of earnings and earnings research: lessons and directions from two decades of empirical research', *Journal of Accounting Research.*

14. Scholes, M.S., Wilson, P. and Wolfson, M.A. (1990) 'Tax planning, regulatory capital planning and financial reporting strategy for commercial banks', *Review of Financial Studies,* **3**(4), 625–650.

15. Allen, L. and Saunders, A. (1988) 'Incentives to engage in bank window dressing: manager vs stockholder conflicts'. Working paper, Hofstra University.

16. McNichols, M. and Wilson, P. (1988) 'Evidence of earnings management from the provision for bad debts', *Journal of Accounting Research,* **26**, Supplement, 1–31.

17. Smith, op. cit.

18. Brink, H.L. (1992) 'A history of Philips accounting policies on the basis of its annual reports', *European Accounting Review,* **1**, 255–275.

19. Watts, L. and Zimmerman, J. (1990) 'Positive accounting theory: a ten year perspective', *Accounting Review,* **65**, 131–156.

20. Tinic, S.H. (1990) 'A perspective on the markets fixation on accounting numbers', *The Accounting Review,* **65** (4), 781–796.

21. Charkham, J. (1989) *Corporate Governance and the Market for Companies: Aspects of the Shareholders Role,* Bank of England Discussion Paper, London.

22. Jensen, M.C. (1989) 'The eclipse of the public corporation', *Harvard Business Review,* September-October.

23. Rybczynski, T. (1989) 'Corporate restructuring', *National Westminster Bank Review,* August.

24. Rapport, A. (1990) 'The staying power of the public corporation', *Harvard Business Review,* January-February.

25. Accounting Standards Board (1993) *Operating and Financial Review,* ASB.

26. Van Hulle, K. (1992) 'Harmonisation of accounting standards: a view', *European Accounting Review,* **1** (1), 161–172.

Further Reading

Schipper, K. (1989) 'Commentary on earnings management', *Accounting Horizons,* 91–102.

Smith, T. (1992) *Accounting for Growth,* Century Business, London.

Griffiths, I. (1986) *Creative Accounting,* Firethorn Press.

Problems

1. Identify the various user groups interested in information about multinational companies. Discuss whether their needs are likely to be satisfied by the annual report and accounts of companies.

2. What is the goal of mutual recognition? What are its advantages? What are its disadvantages?

3. What are the reasons why the senior executives of a company might wish to manage the disclosure of earnings information?

4. What are the reasons why the relationship between the movement over time of a company share price and the movement in its earnings are not statistically related?

5. How might the divorce of the ownership of the business and the control of the business influence accountability and financial disclosure?

6. Discuss whether or not you believe it to be important for a company to provide accounting information to a wide audience including employees, consumers and the government.

7. Look at the accounts of ICI and suggest areas where the managers would have an opportunity to smooth annual earnings figures should they choose to do so.

8. From a set of financial accounts obtain the earnings per share figures for each of the last ten years (these should be available from the comparative statistics shown in the accounts). Plot the change in earnings per share over time to see if a random pattern does emerge. Comment on the significance of the results you obtain.

9. Why has it proved to be so difficult for accounting standard setters to produce a conceptual framework for accounting?

3

Accounting Reports and Stock Market Prices

Objectives

- To examine the evidence on whether the information contained in financial statements really matters.

- To examine how the information contained in financial statements is 'used' by the stock market.

- To ascertain the relationship between earnings announcements and share price movement.

- To discuss the findings on the movement in earnings figures over time.

- To describe the efficient market hypothesis and to examine the evidence on whether stock markets are efficient.

- To consider whether analysts do correctly interpret the information contained in annual reports.

Introduction

In the first two chapters we have been concerned with how to analyse financial accounts. We now consider whether or not the information contained in such financial statements really matters. This might seem a surprising question to consider. With banks employing large numbers of credit officers who decide whether loans should be advanced, and with other financial institutions employing large numbers of financial analysts to advise on which companies' equity shares are a good investment, it might seem obvious that financial statements matter.

Certainly credit and financial analysts do examine the information reported in financial accounts. Certainly larger companies spend a fortune producing 'glossy' annual reports containing the financial statements. But such statements are only one piece of information that analysts have access to when they are forming opinions on the financial health and prospects of a company. They have information on the state of the economy, the likely future of the industry, any news releases from the company concerned, any information obtained at meetings with executives of the company and they will have received interim profit figures. The analysts therefore will have formed expectations about the financial performance of a company before they see the actual annual financial statement and before the company announces its annual earnings.

The share price of a company will be moving throughout the year as new information becomes available. Draper has estimated that in the UK, on average, 55% of share price movement can be explained by market-wide effects, a further 15% by industry factors and only 30% by firm-specific news. This relates to movement throughout the year. The annual financial reports are only one element of firm-specific news.[1] The results of a large amount of academic research, (mainly undertaken in the USA) indicating that in general there is not usually a strong movement in share price following the announcement of a company's earnings figures is therefore not really so surprising – the price has been moving throughout the year in anticipation of the results.

We will in this chapter examine exactly what is the significance of a company's financial statement. Does the market correctly interpret the information given in the accounts? Do analysts read between the lines of the accounts? Can the capital market be fooled by creative accounting? How efficient are stock markets?

In the second section we will consider the stock market's reaction to the release of earnings information, and in the third section we examine the usefulness of financial statement information in forecasting future earnings. The following section investigates the literature on stock market efficiency.

We will conclude that the usefulness of accounting statements is as follows.

- It allows analysts to confirm or deny their earnings predictions. If their predictions are confirmed there will be no share price movement. If their predictions are shown to be incorrect there will be share price movement. Accounting information is only one source of information. It could be that much of the information contained in the accounts has already been anticipated by the time of the earnings announcement.
- The annual accounts (and interim statements) can be helpful in forecasting the results of future periods.
- The accounts have a stewardship role. They enable shareholders and creditors to monitor the performance of the board of directors. Some information (not enough) is given on the financial rewards received by the directors. Some information is given which enables the risk of investing in the company to be ascertained.
- Banks and other lenders can obtain accounting information that is not disclosed in the published accounts.

Market Reaction to Earnings Information

A number of studies have examined the use made by investment analysts of annual financial reports.[2] Studies based on the situation in the UK and the Netherlands show that the annual reports and communications with management are the two most important sources of information for analysts. These are followed in the order of perceived importance by interim reports, any offer prospectuses and press releases, with advisory services of least importance.

It must be remembered that information is coming to analysts continuously over time and they react to such information on a continuous basis. The share price is therefore continually changing to reflect this information. On the other hand, annual reports are only produced once a year. In theory the price of a share in the market place reflects the true value of a share, the true value being based on what information is available at any time.

Within a free market system what impact does the disclosure of the financial results of a company have on investors? A number of studies have shown that at the individual company level the share price does react to the announcement of earnings, but in general the movement at the time of the announcement is not as great as might be expected. The reason for this is that the market has anticipated much of the year-on-year news content of the annual financial reports. Earnings announcements and the subsequent publication of the annual report allow the revision of expectations to be made. Investors and bankers form expectations of all future variables that they consider to be significant in the valuation of bonds and shares but there is uncertainty attached to these valuations. The announcement of earnings figures resolves one source of this uncertainty.

In an early pioneering study, Ball and Brown found that for US companies most of the information contained in the final report had already been anticipated before its release; the anticipation was very accurate, and the drift upwards or downwards in share price had begun 12 months before the report was released.[3] With regard to the value of the information contained in the final report, no more than 10–15% has not been anticipated by the month of the report. The value of the information conveyed by the report at the time of its release constitutes on average only 20% of the value of all information coming to the market in that month. About 70% of all information appears to be offsetting, which means that it is of no lasting use for decision-making, although it may cause investors to act in the short run. Therefore only 30% of all information coming to the market at the time of the final report has a continuing value.

Investors build up expectations about earnings, and when actual results are announced some proportion of any movement will already have been anticipated. Therefore this expected part of any movement should already have been reflected in the share price. If the market is efficient, only the unexpected part should not already have been reflected in the share price as only the unexpected part of the total information would be new. The efficient market should then ensure that the security's price reacts quickly and in the appropriate direction.

The early work of Ball and Brown was based on quite simple analysis. Since then there have been hundreds of other studies into the relationship between a company earnings and its stock market returns.

The more recent studies have refined the analysis but have not enhanced our understanding of the extent to which earnings figures are utilized by investors. The evidence over the past 20 years shows a consistent picture with earnings and earnings related information explaining between 2% and 5% of the time series variability of share price returns over short periods of time, and up to 7% for longer periods of time.

This apparently minor role of accounting earnings numbers in security valuation might seem worrying particularly as the justification for the expensive accounting reporting system is to provide useful information for decision-making. What is the explanation for it? Lev offers three explanations, of which the third is of the most significance for our purposes.[4] The first explanation is that earnings figures might be very useful to investors but that the statistical techniques used by academic researchers are not good enough to detect this fact. A second possible explanation is that investors are irrational and that stock markets are less efficient than is sometimes assumed.

The third explanation is that because published earnings are based on many assumptions and strategic management choices as to which accounting policies to adopt, the actual figures published are not the ones used by analysts. In other words it is the information content of the actual reported profit figure that is low and not useful in predicting future profits. If analysts carry out their own adjustments to the published figures, it could be that these adjusted figures show a very good relationship with security returns.

It is in fact strange that nearly all researchers take the published earnings figures at face value and use these in their statistical analysis. We know that adjustments are required in order to be able to compare the published earnings of one company with those of another. This is necessary, even without allowing for 'creative' techniques, just to make the assumptions comparable. Much of the research on the usefulness of earnings figures has been wasted effort because it ignores the quality of the published earnings figures and the adjustments needed to make figures comparable. Recent research in the USA into the market reaction to earnings announcements emphasizes the significance to the results of the 'quality' of the earnings figures. If the figures are distorted, different investors will interpret them in different ways, leading to a confused market reaction.

The point has been made that not all people who analyse accounts or who undertake research in the earnings/share price area actually look at the published accounts. Often they make use of the on-stream data supplied by many agencies. As Brennan points out, 'the careful consideration given by practising accountants to the manner in which earnings are reported, and to which items are included in earnings, stands in marked contrast to the casual attitude of most researchers towards the definition of the variable under investigation'.[5]

Much of the research into the information content of accounting reports is undertaken by non-accountants, who have access to the large computerized databases. It is easy to regress one set of numbers (readily available) on another set (equally readily available). It is not easy to go through a set of accounts considering every footnote and trying to assess its implications. It is time consuming and requires more than a basic knowledge of accounting. It requires the researcher to read between the lines. Perhaps therefore we should not be too worried that a large amount of academic finance research finds it difficult to discover a relationship between unadjusted published earning figures and share price movements.

Accountants know it is not possible to compare the earnings figures of one company with another without making adjustments. As Holmes and Sugden point out there are at least five reasons in the UK not to trust company financial accounting figures at their face value.[6] One is that 'present accounting rules can and do make nonsense of some figures'. They give the example of the preferred method in the UK of dealing with purchased goodwill. The second reason is that the present rules give companies far too much flexibility. This has been referred to in Chapter 2, and is clearly a reason why unadjusted figures should not be used in statistical analysis.

The third reason is the enormous influence that quite small changes in accounting policies can make on reported profits. The bottom line, the profit figure, is the result of adding and deducting very large numbers. A one per cent difference in inventory valuation can make a huge difference to profits. Can companies really value inventories that accurately? The fourth reason is the clever new financing arrangements that are continuously being devised that are not always correctly represented in the accounts. The fifth reason is that auditors are too close to the directors, and not close enough to the shareholders. The first four reasons point to the need to analyse and make adjustments for comparative purposes. The quality of the reported earnings figures is the key factor, not the unadjusted reported figures.

Accounting reports do matter therefore, but they need careful analysis. They should not be accepted at face value. Those who develop creative accounting techniques are very skilled in the craft of accounting; those who hope to be able to unravel the accounts need to be equally skilled.

One object of the process of harmonization of accounting standards in the EU has been to assist in bringing about an effective and efficient European capital market. It is argued that if analysts in one country are unable to correctly interpret the financial accounts of a company in another country, this will not lead to efficient portfolio investment decisions. Misunderstandings and indeed uncertainty will limit the gains that could be achieved from a single market in finance. Choi and Levich in a recent empirical study conclude that 'a major implication of our findings is that accounting differences are important and affect capital market decisions of a significant number of market participants we surveyed regardless of nationality, size, experience, scope of international activity and organizational structure.'[7]

Forecasting and Financial Statement Information

It has been shown that forecasts produced by financial analysts outperform forecasts based on just historical data, whether accounting numbers or otherwise. This is not really surprising – analysts have meetings with directors of companies, and obtain qualitative information relevant to determining a company's and industry's future earnings prospects. There is a consensus between practitioners and academics that a firm's future earnings are a major determinant of its current share value. It is therefore useful to see whether there are models which will help in the forecasting of future corporate earnings.

In this book we are concerned with analysis based on financial accounts. Therefore the first question we need to consider it how useful is the analysis of the movement of accounting data over time. For example, can data relating to earnings in past periods be used usefully to forecast future earnings? It might be thought that by studying the movement in the numbers in the financial accounts over time it is possible to predict future earnings. Indeed the frequent publication by companies in the accounts of five- or ten-year comparative statistics suggests that the companies are indicating to users that such time series data is helpful.

Unfortunately, like the daily changes in share price, changes in corporate earnings also appear to behave as if generated by a random process. Successive earnings changes are largely independent over time.

Little and Raynor in an early UK study on this topic plotted the movement of changes in a company's earnings and found that:

- in the short run it is virtually impossible to find any consistent earnings growth;
- in the long run it is hard to discover any repetition of earlier growth behaviour.[8]

The name 'higgledy-piggledy growth' was used to describe the observed patterns of company earnings growth. One implication of these findings is that so called 'good management' of a company cannot be expected to continue to exert its effect by producing an above-average growth of earnings for the company for period after period. 'Good management' may produce above-average earnings for a time, but in the study it was shown that such performance was not sustained consistently over a decade, the comparatively short period studied.

There are theoretical reasons why one might not find consistency in the short run. One cannot, for instance, expect management to be able to readjust their plans in the short run in response to changes in the overall level of economic activity. Many short-run changes are beyond the control of management, so one would expect the return on capital to fluctuate over time, depending on such factors as capacity utilization. In the long run, however, economic theory would suggest that a management team that is considered to be of above-average quality would lead to an above-average return on capital employed.

The random walk in earnings theory does not deny that good management exists and perhaps lasts within a company over a long period of time. But good (or, for that matter, bad) management is not reflected in earnings figures which remain each year above (or below) the average annual growth in earnings figures. There are a number of reasons why this apparently paradoxical situation prevails. One explanation is that monopoly power and good management may counteract each other. The good management may be striving in the highly competitive sectors of the economy. In the monopolistic sectors, where the higher profits are easier to obtain, less efficient management may prevail. Consequently in examining above- and below-average performance, one is not really identifying the quality of the management. Profit performance depends on opportunities. Another explanation is that perhaps management does not try to maximize growth in earnings.

It may be thought that monopolistic advantages and accounting practices should produce a tendency for a good earnings record to persist. But the studies of short-term profit behaviour suggest that any such tendency has been completely swamped by the impact of shock either within the company, industry or economy. These have occurred with considerable frequency, and management has not always been able to act quickly enough to keep up its performance. Such non-recurring events are likely to be of less importance over the long term, but despite this, the comparisons of growth rates for a particular company over successive five-year periods have revealed little conformity.

Ball and Watts examined the movement of earnings figures in US companies.[9] Their test was slightly different. They found that if one examines changes in earnings figures for a company from one year to the next, the run of signs for the changes follows a random walk pattern.

There have been many later studies but the results have not changed the conclusion that the movement over time in company earnings follows a random walk pattern.

Perhaps, however, we are expecting too much for a company to consistently show an above average growth in earnings. If earnings increase by 10% in one year (which is, say, above average) for the earnings only to grow at 2% over the next year (i.e. below average) is not such a bad performance. We could observe other measures of success, for example above-average levels of profitability rather than above-average growth in profits. Beaver has shown that percentage rates of return on assets do not necessarily follow a random walk.[10]

However, Beaver found that there is a tendency for the accounting percentage rate of return to revert to the mean. That is above average-rates for a company over time move down to the average rate, they do not persist, but this reversion 'takes place over several years'.

Other researchers have also examined the rate of return on capital employed and obtained similar results. It can be concluded that the evidence indicates no consistent behaviour pattern in companies in general. This means that on the basis of unadjusted published earnings figures it is difficult to forecast.

Better results can be obtained when forecasts are based on quarterly accounting data. Unfortunately such data is only published by US companies. Better results can also be obtained when the forecasting model is disaggregated with an analysis of the geographical and industrial segmented data relating to a company, and on information on the economic situation of the countries in which the company operates and on the future of the industries in which it is engaged.

The usefulness of the information content of accounting earnings figures whether for forecasting or other purposes varies considerably from one firm to another. As Smith's study showed, some firms adopt more creative accounting techniques than others.[11] Therefore the analyst should employ firm-specific models in formulating an appropriate response to earnings announcements.

Stock Market Efficiency

We have said that the market awaits the earnings announcement and the publication of accounts of a company in order to confirm or refute its expectations. Does the market correctly interpret the published results? Is the market efficient?

Three types of efficiency can be identified: allocational, pricing and operational. Allocational efficiency means that the market channels funds to those firms and organizations with the best real investment opportunities. Allocational efficiency requires both pricing and operational efficiency. The absence of either can lead to the misallocation of resources.

Operational efficiency means that buyers and sellers of securities can purchase transaction services at prices that are as low as possible given the costs associated with having these services provided. Pricing (fair game) efficiency implies that the actual market price of a share on a day approximates to its intrinsic value on that day. Prices at any point in time are said, if the market is efficient, to 'fully reflect' all available information that is relevant to the determination of values. By definition, then, any new relevant information is quickly and accurately impounded into share prices.

When the efficiency of the stock exchange is discussed in the literature of finance, it usually just means efficiency with respect to pricing. Virtually all testing of the efficient market hypothesis (EMH) has been based on testing for pricing efficiency. Unfortunately the data are not readily available for testing for allocational or operational efficiency.

The process by which the value of a share is arrived at is not often discussed. In an efficient market there should be a number of potential buyers of a share and a number of potential sellers. They could all have slightly differing views about the 'true value of a share'. Some investors will be more informed than others. Some will interpret the information differently to others. Some would base intrinsic value on the future earnings ability of the company, some on the past. The price that is settled upon is some sort of weighted consensus of these different views.

If there was homogeneity in beliefs, it would be as if all decision-makers acted as one. When we recognize heterogeneity of beliefs then how efficient the market is in the pricing of shares becomes less certain. We have the problem of how we aggregate the views and beliefs of the different traders in the market.

If the stock market is efficient, share prices would be expected to 'fully reflect' the available information. To test whether it is, we must specify how the process of price formation for a company's shares is expected to operate. It is generally assumed that the share price would adjust to give shareholders the required level of returns, allowing for risk, suggested by the informa-tion being considered. This is known as a 'fair game' model.

This means, in its simplest form, that as information which suggests higher profits for a company becomes available, the price of that company's shares is expected to rise up to a point where the expected yield is comparable with that of other shares in a similar risk class. If information which suggests increased risks for a company becomes available, unless there are also expected higher returns, the share price will adjust to give a yield comparable with that of other shares in this same higher risk class.

The EMH can be tested at three levels. What is known as the weak form test attempts to ascertain whether knowledge and analysis of past price data can be used to advantage. If it can, it means that the fair game model has to be rejected. The semi-strong test examines whether knowledge of all publicly available information can be used to beat the market. The strong test considers whether any knowledge, publicly available or not, can be used to beat the market.

The financial accounts of a company provides information to the market. How does the market react to such information? Does the market pick up the correct signals from the annual accounts? The semi-strong form test of the EMH is concerned with whether the current price of a share reflects public knowledge about the company, and whether the speed of price adjustment to the public announcement of information is fast enough to eliminate the possibility of abnormal gains. Thus the question of whether it is worth some effort to acquire and analyse this publicly available information with the hope of gaining superior investment results, if answered in the negative, would support the EMH. There is a large amount of evidence suggesting that in certain major stock markets the share price adjustment is quick and in the appropriate directions, thus confirming the EMH at least as far as the semi-strong test is concerned.

For a stock market to be efficient, at any time the share price of a company should reflect the value of that company on the basis of its expected future earnings. With an efficient market, the share price at any time will reflect its true value, that is its intrinsic value.

There is a large body of evidence that suggests that the capital markets of New York and London are efficient. There is less evidence regarding the 'efficiency' of the markets of Paris and Frankfurt. There is little evidence supporting the efficiency of the other capital markets in the European Union. We will begin by examining the literature relating to the UK and USA and then return to the markets of other countries. We will conclude this section by referring to some of the doubts that now exist with regard to the efficiency of stock markets.

In 1978 Jensen told us that 'the efficient market hypothesis is the best established fact in all of the social sciences.' In 1988 he went further, telling us that 'no proposition, in any of the sciences, is better documented' than the efficient market hypothesis. It is true that there is much research evidence indicating that stock market prices (in the USA) appropriately incorporate all currently available public information. Nevertheless these are sweeping statements, particularly as Jensen does admit in the 1988 study that the evidence is 'not literally 100 percent in support' of the hypothesis.[12]

It must be remembered that there are important differences between the stock markets in Europe and the US stock markets. In the UK the financial institutions own a much higher percentage of the shares of UK companies than is the case with financial institutions in the USA. As Peacock and Bannock point out, this means that in the UK there are not always a large number of buyers or sellers of a company's shares, which as every first-year economics student knows is a necessary condition for perfect competition.[13] We should be careful before assuming that findings based on the situation in the USA apply to the UK.

Researchers have been kept busy on both sides of the Atlantic for over thirty years studying how share prices react to new information. It has almost become heresy for financial economists to suggest that the stock market is less than efficient. But for a share price to reflect publicly available information (which is what has been found) does not mean that the share price reflects the fundamental value of the share (sometimes referred to as the true or intrinsic value of the share).

One basic problem is that we do not know what is the 'fundamental value' of a share. We have to rely on valuation models that of necessity need to be based on certain assumptions. Even having estimated a true value we then have to decide how far away from this true value does the actual price of a share have to be, before we say the market is underestimating or overestimating and is therefore inefficient. A third problem is what percentage of quoted companies need to have their shares under- or over-priced before we say the market is inefficient.

Black caused a stir when, in his presidential address to the American Finance Association, he stated: 'I think almost all markets [he was referring to US stock markets] are efficient almost all of the time.' Almost all he explains means at least 90% of the time.[14] In fact if 10% of the prices do not reflect true value this gives a lot of opportunity for 'bargain purchases' of undervalued shares.

Black's views of what the relationship between a true (intrinsic) value and the actual share price should be in an efficient market leaves a lot of room for those engaged in investing in equities to exploit price gaps. Black refers to the market being efficient if it results in the actual price of a company's shares being within a factor of 2 of its true value. This factor of course represents his view of a reasonable price and Black admits it is arbitrary, but he states 'intuitively, though, it seems reasonable to me, in the light of sources of uncertainty about value.' The above comments suggest that either the market is not so efficient at interpreting the information given in company financial statements or that the statements do not give sufficient information for the intrinsic value to be determined.

One problem that often arises is a misunderstanding of the meaning of the word 'efficiency' in the context of the efficient market hypothesis. The expression is being used in the context of the hypothesis in a much narrower sense than the dictionary definition. There are different levels of efficiency. What is referred to as the efficient market hypothesis merely states that share prices quickly adjust to reflect publicly available information. It does not mean that everyone interprets the information in the same way.

As Stiglitz points out the existence of asymmetric information means that 'managers can take actions which affect the returns to those who provide capital'.[15] In the 1980s the 'management of earnings disclosure' became an art and unfortunately became not uncommon both in the USA and the UK. The manipulation of reported earnings means that one group of market participants have information and an understanding not available to other participants. On the question of understanding, doubts arose particularly in the late 1980s as to whether financial analysts, who had the necessary information, were able to understand its true importance.

Modigliani, a Nobel economic prize winner, has expressed concern with the efficiency of the stock market. He believes that irrational investors are present in the market.[16] He wrote in 1988, that he had 'become a bit disenchanted with the indiscriminate use of superrationality as the foundation for models of financial behaviour'. Modigliani examines the effects of inflation on market valuation. He believes the market fails to 'understand how to value equities in the presence of significant inflation, which results in systematic, predictable error'. Modigliani and Cohn offer an explanation for some of the unexpected movements in share price, namely the existence of irrationality on the part of a subset of investors.[17] Campbell and Kyle show how the presence of such a subset of irrational investors can result in under- or over-valuation of shares persisting over time.[18]

De Bondt and Thaler suggest that some parts of the stock market overreact to the disclosure of current earnings.[19] Bhattachara, reviewing the literature on the valuation of equities in the stock market, concludes 'the accumulation of evidence presents, in my view, a murky picture vis-à-vis the prevalence of rational (information efficiency) valuation in the stock market'.[20] Roll and other researchers have found that significant movements in individual share price and stock market indices cannot on many occasions be related to public news, and vice versa.[21] The announcement of fundamental news does not on occasion move prices. It is not just news that leads to movements in share prices, the action of uninformed investors also moves prices.

The fact that the major stock markets of the world were efficient was for a long time accepted as an act of faith. To suggest otherwise was to imply that one did not really understand the concept and did not know how to follow the vast empirical evidence on the topic. Recently, however, the evidence is being re-examined. The current position is that those who believe in efficient markets argue that there is strong consistent evidence that markets such as London and New York are efficient, but they admit that there are some anomalies.

Fama and French have shown that it is possible to predict the prices of the shares of small firms.[22] Most of the research on testing the EMH has been conducted with data relating to larger firms. It has been shown that the standard statistical tests of the hypothesis cannot detect some possible inefficiencies in the market. As has been known for some time, when the strong form test of the EMH is applied there is evidence that inside dealers can achieve abnormal returns. The weak form test has shown that there are time and seasonal anomalies.

The anomalies referred to, it is claimed by supporters of the efficient markets, are not of major importance. The ones that have been found only affect a minor part of stock market activity. There does not seem to be anything systematic about them which would give grounds for concern that the stock market is not on the whole a fair game.

It is accepted that discrepancies do exist between actual share prices at any one time and what are thought to be 'true' (intrinsic) values. Bernard and Thomas have shown that the market only allows small discrepancies to arise, which they estimate to be on average up to a

2% difference for larger firms and up to a 6% difference for smaller firms.[23]

The studies mentioned above have all been published in the USA and are primarily based on the situation in that country where there has been a vast amount of research testing the efficient market hypothesis. Whittington, in his overview of financial accounting theory, asserts that 'the empirical approach has become almost a cult among ambitious young academics, especially in the USA ...' and refers to 'the age of the computer' which facilitates this type of research.[24]

There is a certain amount of evidence relating to the efficiency of the London stock exchange, but much less evidence on the efficiency of the other stock exchanges in Europe. In fact the concept of the efficient market hypothesis is of more interest and of more significance in some countries than in others. This is because in some countries stock exchanges are of more importance in the financial system than in others. This is discussed in Chapter 5 on corporate governance. Most of the literature on the efficient stock market is from Anglo-Saxon countries. In Germany, where the banks have a major role in the provision of finance and advice on buying and selling securities in the stock market, there has been less pressure to investigate the efficiency of the stock market.

Coenenberg devotes twenty-five pages of his leading German textbook on financial accounting to the efficient market hypothesis.[25] In his introductory remarks on the topic he puts the EMH into perspective. He points out that the 'capital market oriented approach' is merely one way of discussing accounting theory and, moreover, that this approach has its origins in the particular accounting and finance context of the USA. Coenenberg's view that empirical financial accounting theory is basically concerned with the usefulness of external financial reporting for society is an idea that Watts and Zimmerman would most probably reject as a normative value judgement.

Coenenberg in his book describes in some detail the methodology of the 1968 Ball and Brown study. However, he does not deal with the more sophisticated studies which have been carried out in the USA and the UK since 1968. The reason why Coenenberg concentrates on the Ball and Brown study is that the German EMH tests have been modelled very much along the lines of this 'classic' paper. Another explanation for the few German EMH studies is that a major obstacle to be overcome by researchers until comparatively recently was the lack of an adequate database.

The results of the German EMH tests that have been undertaken are consistent with the findings of the studies which were carried out in the USA and the UK. Stock prices not only react to the publication of annual reports, but the German investors also seem to anticipate to some degree the information which is published in the accounts. As far as the anticipation of information is concerned Coenenberg singles out companies which, due to their size, are obliged by the Commercial Code to disclose more data than their smaller counterparts. The stock price reaction after the publication of the annual reports of these big companies is relatively minor, thus reflecting that there are less surprises made public via the accounts of large companies than small.

Finally, according to Coenenberg the German EMH test seems to indicate that German investors do not simply take reported figures at face value. However, he points out how difficult it is in Germany to interpret the aims of accounting policies correctly, especially with the so-called authoritative principle and the resultant trade-off faced by management between a minimization of the company's tax burden and the optimistic profits impression which it may want to convey in its report. Furthermore, he argues in this context that, depending on the amount of published information, it is not always possible to identify the impact of accounting policies clearly.

Choi and Levich 'take it as given that US capital markets are highly efficient'.[26] They refer to 'the conventional notion that European capital markets are more likely to be inefficient in a weak form sense'. It will be remembered that weak form efficiency implies that knowledge of past changes in share price will not be useful in predicting future changes in share price. If stock markets are not weak form efficient then it is possible to predict future price changes on the basis of past price changes.

Choi and Levich point out that contrary to what may be thought the evidence is that many European stock markets are weak form efficient. Hawawini examined the literature on weak form efficiency of the markets in 14 European countries.[27] He concludes in most of these countries 'when returns are measured over intervals longer than a week, the Random Walk Model cannot be rejected'. This says nothing of course about movement within a week. There is much less literature on the semi-strong efficiency of European markets. Hawawini's review of the literature for France and the UK indicates that these countries are semi-strong efficient but that Germany is not. The studies indicate that for France and the UK the share prices that are set by the market do not leave opportunities for abnormal returns for investors who have publicly available information. The findings are that market prices quickly reflect accounting information and those operating in the market are not mislead by changes in accounting rules.

Although most of the evidence produced over the last twenty years indicates that the major stock markets of the world are efficient in a weak form and semi-strong form sense, doubts are now being raised. It is becoming fashionable to criticize the idea that stock markets are efficient. The problem is that the theory has perhaps been oversold in the past. There are two directions which this criticism is taking. One direction is fundamental to the idea that we can test whether or not a market is efficient.[28]

New mathematical analysis of stock market prices shows there is often unexpected predictability. This is explained by the fact that those who trade in the market do not all think the same way. They reason differently about the information they receive, they have different time horizons and different attitudes towards risk. It has been suggested that the more advanced computer models now being developed allow opportunities to outperform the market at least for a while. Such opportunities result from the way in which information is interpreted and used by the participants in the market. The information is efficiently and fairly distributed – it is how it is used that creates opportunities.

As Schneider, in his German critique of the efficient market hypothesis, points out, the hypothesis does not say anything about how market participants incorporate news into investment decisions.[29] Lev proposed that research should be undertaken which aims at 'understanding the use of financial information by investors, that is, a thorough investigation of the financial statement analysis process'.[30] This book is about financial statement analysis. We know how to analyse financial statements, but we do not know what use individual analysts will make of the information.

The second class of criticisms is based on the acceptance that stock markets are more or less efficient, but that there are loopholes that exist that can be exploited. Certain anomalies have been found in share price behaviour. These are discussed below.

Short-term overreaction

The more powerful statistical techniques now being employed in statistical analysis are revealing a number of anomalies. One of the most important of these, from the point of view of long-term decision-making, is that the market tends to 'overreact' in the short run.

Experimental and survey evidence indicates that there is a tendency to over-weight recent information and under-weight basic data. From a stock market point of view this means investors overreact to earnings figures, and as a result stock prices can and do depart at least in the short run from their underlying fundamental values. The returns from a company investment in long-term projects such as those in R&D and advanced manufacturing systems are not reflected in the earnings figures for the early years of a project's life. Therefore, although such investments increase the fundamental value of a company, they are not immediately reflected in the market price of the company's shares.

De Bondt and Thaler and other researchers have found evidence that in the USA investors overreact to short-term earnings movements.[31] Investors focus on the immediate past and do not look beyond the immediate future. There is a close correspondence between share price returns and changes in the short-term earnings outlook. Investors, on average, have an excessively short-term orientation. There is no reason to believe that these results, based on the situation in the USA, do not apply to the UK; we have a similar financial system. As explained, the implications are not good for companies that undertake investments that will not show early earnings figures. They indicate that it is important to show 'good' current earnings figures

These findings are not, of course, what one would expect from an efficient market. But there is now increasing evidence that share prices do take swings away from fundamental values. The evidence is that these 'erroneous' movements away from fundamental values are eventually corrected: there is a mean reversion in share prices.

Poterba and Summers[32] also show that there are transitory components in share prices; that is, there can be a move in the short run away from fundamental values. They found this with UK data as well as US data. These transitory components are large in relation to what one would expect with stock market efficiency. This overreaction of the market to good and bad short-term earnings figures leads to volatility in investors' returns. As Shiller[33] concludes the volatility in the market returns for investors is greater than what one would expect if market prices reflected fundamental values.

The implication of the short-term overreaction for those preparing accounts is to encourage them to emphasize short-term performance – to show a 'good' earnings per share figure. Long-term investments are reflected in the share price in the long run; they increase the fundamental value of the company, but the present value of such investments is not necessarily reflected in the price in the short run. This encourages 'the management of earnings disclosure'. It is why financial reports have to be read with care.

There are certain other stock market anomalies. They are less concerned with the impact of financial reports, than other factors, and so will only be briefly mentioned.

Time and seasonal anomalies

Studies (particularly in the USA) have shown that there is a tendency for mean share price returns to vary as follows.

- **Hours of the day**. Prices rise during the last 15 minutes of the trading day. They fall on the first 45 minutes of trading on Mondays. One possible explanation of the latter result is the weekend effect.
- **Day of the week effect**. It has been found that there are below average returns on Mondays.
- **Month of the year effect**, with high returns in January in the USA, and in April in the UK. One popular explanation of this outcome is the end of the tax year. In March in the UK, shareholders with losses sell shares and depress prices. In April they buy the shares back again.

Size anomalies

This is important from the point of view of analysing financial statements. Research has shown that in the long run the returns from investing in smaller companies give a slightly higher return than the average market performance across companies of all sizes. If the market is efficient this should only happen if the market risks from investing in smaller companies are above the average market risk. An investor knowing of this irregularity could devise trading rules to produce consistent above average returns.

Research in the USA found that smaller companies outperformed other companies over time on average by 4% per annum on a compound basis. Research was later conducted on data from many other countries and similar results were obtained. Dimson and March[34] published results for the UK based on the performance of as many as 1200 companies with market capitalizations or £100 million or less. They found that, on average, the small firms outperformed the larger firms by 6% per annum.

How can this size effect be explained? Among the explanations that have been offered are the following.

- **Lack of information**. The market has less information about small companies than about large companies. Analysts spend less time studying the financial position of small companies. It is less likely therefore that the market price of smaller companies represents the fundamental value of the share, of that company, than for a large company. This means that there is an opportunity for the aware investor to make above average returns through investing in smaller companies.

  For the market to be efficient in the valuation of a company it is necessary to have analysts studying the performance of a company. This is a problem in smaller capital markets, where there may not be enough analysts. It is a problem in the larger markets, because it is not possible for analysts to be knowledgeable about all companies quoted.

- **Risk**. Do smaller companies have higher non-diversifiable risks (betas) than large companies? If this is the case then investors would want above average return to compensate for the risk. It has in fact been shown that smaller companies do have above average betas, but it has also been shown that this difference in betas is not sufficient to give a complete explanation of the size effect.

Conclusions

Clearly annual reports including the financial statements do matter – if only in that they can confirm or refute the expectations of those who forecast company performance. Accounting standards, both on issues of measurement and on levels of disclosure, make it easier to analyse financial statements, but there is still much uncertainty – there always will be. The user must beware – the most revealing set of accounts and the most thorough audit cannot be expected to disclose all short-term attempts at managing the level of earnings disclosure.

The problem does not become easier. As businesses become more complex, accounting becomes more complex. New methods of financing are continuously being devised. Indeed in the City of London large sums of money were on offer at the end of the 1980s to those who could devise new forms of special-purpose financial transactions, the object being to avoid users of published accounts discovering the true commercial reality of a particular financial arrangement. The accounting standard statements and regulations will always be behind the new methods – but hopefully not too far behind, which is the reason for the creation in the UK and USA of 'Urgent Issues Task Forces'.

There is and probably always will be a credibility gap. It takes time to detect those who are breaking the law, whether it is physical crime or white-collar crime. There always will be a gap as long as it is possible for Asil Nadir (Chairman of Polly Peck) to answer a question as to whether or not he is a 'crook', by stating: 'How can I be when everything I do is disclosed in my company's accounts, the accounts are prepared according to accounting standards and certified as true and fair by the auditors?'

This is why accounts can be dangerous – a superficial knowledge of accounting is dangerous. The user has to be able to read between the lines. The scandals that occur do not mean accounts are not valuable, but it would be better if we did not have so many problems in interpreting financial reports. The accounting standard setting bodies around the world are attempting to make the understanding of accounting statements easier, and to reduce the scope for choice on the part of preparers.

If there were an agreed theory of accounting and agreed objectives, it would be possible to choose between alternative accounting principles and practices on a rational basis. There is no agreed theory, and there are disagreements on objectives.

Among the obstacles the FASB saw to the acceptance of a universal theory of accounting were:

- the problem of relating theory to practice;
- the allocation problem;
- the difficulty with normative standards;
- difficulties in interpreting security price behaviour research;
- the problem of cost-benefit considerations in accounting; and
- limitations of data.

One approach to the problem of choosing between alternative reporting practices is to measure the impact of accounting reports and changes in accounting practices on stock market prices, and this has been the subject of much research. The rationale for the approach is that shareholders and potential investors are important users of accounting reports and it is worthwhile observing how they use the information provided, and using the reactions of this group to decide on which accounting practice is best. This is, of course, only a partial analysis.

The approach can be criticized in that it ignores the externalities. Shareholders make decisions on the basis of financial information; their decisions affect many people, and if we are concerned with setting a standard that needs to maximize general welfare rather than shareholders' welfare, then we need to be concerned with the wider impact of the accounting reports.

References

1. Draper, P.R. (1985) 'Industry influence on share price variability', *Journal of Business Finance and Accounting,* Summer, 169–186.

2. Arnold, J. and Moizer, P. (1984) 'A survey of the methods used by UK investment analysis to appraise investments in ordinary shares', *Accounting and Business Research,* Summer; Vergoosen, R.G.A. (1993) 'The use and perceived importance of annual reports by investment analysts in the Netherlands', *European Accounting Review,* **2**(2), 219–243.

3. Ball, R. and Brown, P. (1968) 'An empirical evaluation of accounting income numbers', *Journal of Accounting Research,* Autumn, 159–178.

4. A good survey article is that of Lev, B. (1989) 'On the usefulness of earnings and earnings research: lessons and directions from two decades of empirical research', *Journal of Accounting Research.*

5. Brennan, M.J. (1991) 'A perspective on accounting and stock prices', *Accounting Review,* January, 67–79.

6. Holmes, G. and Sugden, A. (1990) *Interpreting Company Reports and Accounts,* 4th edn, Woodhead Faulkner, Cambridge.

7. Choi, F.D.S. and Levich, R.M. (1991) 'Behavioural effects of international accounting diversity', *Accounting Horizons,* June.

8. Little, I.M.D. and Rayner, A.C. (1966) *Higgledy Piggledy Growth Again,* Basil Blackwell.

9. Ball, R. and Watts, R. (1977) 'Additional evidence on the time series properties of reported earnings per share', *Journal of Finance,* **32**(5), 1802–1808.

10. Beaver, W.H. (1968) 'The information content of annual earnings announcements', Empirical Research in Accounting, Selected Studies. Supplement to Vol. 6, *Journal of Accounting Research,* 67–92.

11. Smith, T. (1992) *Accounting for Growth,* Century Business, London.

12. Jensen, M.C. (1978) 'Some anomalies evidence regarding market efficiency', *Journal of Financial Economics,* **6**, June/September, 95–102; Jensen, M.C. (1988) 'Takeovers: their causes and consequences', *Journal of Economic Perspectives,* **2**(1).

13. Peacock, A. and Bannock, G. (1991) *Corporate Takeovers and the Public Interest,* Aberdeen University Press.

14. Black, F. (1986) 'Noise', *Journal of Finance,* **41**, 529–534.

15. Stiglitz, J.E. (1988) 'Why financial structure matters', *Journal of Economic Perspectives,* **2**(4), 121–126.

16. Modigliani, F. (1988) 'MM – past, present, future', *Journal of Economic Perspectives,* **2**(4), 149–158.

17. Modigliani, F. and Cohn, R.A. (1979) 'Inflation, rational expectation, and the market', *Financial Analysts Journal,* **35**(2), 24–44.

18. Campbell, J.Y. and Kyle, A.S. (1988) *Smart Money, Noise Trading and Stock Prices Behaviour,* Princeton University, Mimeo.

19. De Bondt, W.F. and Thaler, A.H. (1987) 'Further evidence on investment overreaction and stock market seasonality', *The Journal of Finance,* July.

20. Bhattachara, S. (1988) 'Corporate finance and the legacy of Miller and Modigliani', *Journal of Economic Perspectives,* **2**(4), 135–147.

21. Roll, R. (1988) 'R-Squared', *Journal of Finance,* **43**, 541–566.

22. Fama, E.F. and French, K.R. (1988) 'Permanent and temporary components of stock prices', *Journal of Political Economy,* **96** 246–273.

23. Bernard, V.L. and Thomas, J. (1990) 'Evidence that stock prices do not fully reflect the implications of current earnings', *Journal of Accounting and Economics,* **13**, 305–340.

24. Whittington, G. (1986) 'Financial accounting theory: an overview', *The British Accounting Review,* **18**(2), 4–41.

25. Coenenberg, A.C. (1988) *Jahresabschluß und Jahresabschlußalyse*, 10th edn, Verlag Moderne Industrie, Landsberg am Lech.

26. Choi, F.D.S. and Levich, R.M. (1990) *The Capital Market Effects and International Accounting Diversity*, New York University, Irwin.

27. Hawawini, G. (1984) *European Equity Markets: Price Behaviour and Efficiency*, New York University Monograph Series in Finance and Economics.

28. *The Economist*, Supplement: 'Frontiers of Finance', 9–15 October 1993.

29. Schneider, D. (1990) *Investition, Finanzierund und Besteuerung*, 6th edn, Gabler Verlag, Wiesbaden.

30. Lev, op. cit.

31. De Bondt and Thaler, op. cit.

32. Poterba, J. and Summers, L.H. (1988) 'Mean reversion in stock prices: evidence and implications', *Journal of Financial Economics*, **22**, 27–59.

33. Shiller, R.J. (1981) 'Do stock prices move too much to be justified by subsequent changes in dividends?' *American Economic Review*, **71**, 421–436.

34. Dimson, E. and March, P. (1986) 'Event study methodologies and the size effect', *Journal of Financial Economics*, **17**(1), 113–142.

Further Reading

Bromwich, M. (1992) — *Financial Reporting, Information and Capital Markets*, Pitman, London.

Demski, J. and Feltham, G. (1994) — 'Market response to financial reports', *Journal of Accounting and Economics*, **17**.

Dimson, E. (ed.) (1988) — *Stock Market Anomalies*, Cambridge University Press, Cambridge.

Economist, The, Supplement: 'Frontiers of Finance' 9–15 October 1993.

Fama, E.F. (1991) — 'Efficient capital markets II', *Journal of Finance*, **46**, 1575–1617.

Firth, S.M. (1983) — *Stock Market Efficiency*, Philip Allan, Oxford.

Zarrowin, P. (1990) — 'Size, seasonality and stock market overreaction', *Journal of Financial and Quantitative Analysis*, **25**, 113–125.

Problems

1. Why is the efficient market hypothesis not considered to be such an important issue in Germany as in the UK?

2. Examine the function of the EMH in your own country. Is there any evidence of semi-strong efficiency? What are the implications of this for the release of accounting information?

3. Discuss how the importance of a stock market to the financing of a firm will affect its reporting practices. Compare the situation of one country of your choosing to that of another country.

4. Making use of a database plot the movement in the share price of one company over time. Can you identify national industry or company events that led to changes in the price?

5. In the UK there have been over the last five or six years one financial scandal after another – Polly Peck, Maxwell Communications, Queens Moat. If the stock market is so efficient how can such cases arise?

6. Obtain details of the share price of a company for each day over a one month period. Plot the change in the share price from day to day. Is the movement random? What statistical test could be undertaken to examine whether or not it is random?

4

European Accounting Diversity

Objectives

- To establish the evidence for, and to examine the causes of, diversity in accounting practice between countries in Europe, and in particular between certain European Union (EU) member states. (The description European Community (EC) will be used for pronouncements made before adoption of the description EU.)

- To examine the problems of measuring accounting diversity.

- To describe and discuss the attempts by the EU and the International Accounting Standards Committee (IASC) to reduce or otherwise deal with diversity.

- To explain the rationale for adjustment as a device for dealing with diversity.

Evidence of Accounting Diversity

There is considerable evidence of the existence of major differences in reporting practices in the EU countries. A dramatic source of such evidence may be found in a case study undertaken by Touche Ross,[1] one of the 'big six' professional accounting firms. In this study a hypothetical company, based upon data drawn from real companies, was created and partners in practices in seven of the member states of the Community were asked to prepare financial statements based upon their own domestic rules or practices. The results (Table 4.1) show that profit could vary from ECU 131 million in Spain to ECU 192 million in the United Kingdom under the most likely set of policies in each country, that is a difference in reported profits of 46%. Further, the study examined the possible variations in profits permissible within countries. This extended the potential range of variation from ECU 27 million in Germany to ECU 194 million in the United Kingdom, that is a potential (if unlikely) difference of 618% for the same set of operating activities. If combined with the range of methods of accounting for assets and liabilities this gave a possible variation of rates of return on net assets of 18% in Belgium to 27% in the UK. This illustrates the degree of variation in practice which exists both within individual countries, as discussed in Chapter 2, and between countries.

TABLE 4.1

A case study of accounting diversity (millions of ECUs)

Comparison of profit achieved

	B	D	E	F	I	NL	UK
Operating profit (average 264)	274	261	250	264	243	264	289
Net profit (average 151)	135	133	131	149	174	140	192

Variations of profit within countries

Maximum achievable	193	140	192	160	193	156	194
Most likely	135	133	131	149	174	140	192
Minimum achievable	90	27	121	121	167	70	171

Comparison of return on net assets

Net profit	136	133	131	149	174	140	192
Net assets	720	640	722	710	761	764	712
Return (%) (average 21.2%)	18.6	20.5	18.2	21.0	23.2	19.0	27.0

Source: Touche Ross & Co. (1989)

More prosaic evidence of the variation of practices may be found in a growing number of textbooks dealing with comparative international accounting and of manuals or guides to the differences in accounting practice (for example, Alexander and Archer,[2] Coopers & Lybrand[3]). A further source of evidence of variations in practice within and between countries can be found in the surveys carried out by the Fédération des Experts Comptables Européens (FEE) in 1989, 1991 and 1992.[4]

These variations may be categorized as either:

- **measurement issues** – these are concerned, *inter alia*, with valuation, recognition, allocation, estimation and presentation; or
- **disclosure issues** – these are concerned with the amount of detailed description and transparency of data disclosures.

The differences in accounting practice can therefore be seen to exist and to be significant. We will examine some of the empirical research into the magnitude of these differences later in this chapter.

What are the Causes of Accounting Diversity?

There exists an extensive literature on the possible causes of accounting differences and on attempts to classify countries by examining the relationships of differences and causes.[5,6] As the purpose of this book is to deal with the issues from a financial analysis perspective rather than from that of accounting theory the discussion will be somewhat summarized. However, a bibliography will provide the interested reader with a source for more detailed reading.

Accounting is a purposive social activity and should meet the needs of users in specific social environments. Although an alternative 'critical' perspective would suggest that accounting fails to meet this role and acts as a means of reinforcing the power of some member or group in society. Whichever of these scenarios we accept, it is clear that the environment in which accounting operates will influence its development and that different environments give rise to different accounting. The following factors, therefore, might be posited as the primary environmental (not in the green sense!) influences.

Source of finance

The different sources of business finance will be an obvious and dominant cause of accounting difference. In the UK the importance of equity finance has resulted in the acceptance of the shareholder as the primary user of financial statements. In other European countries this is not the case – in Germany, for example, the banks play a key role in financing commerce and industry. In other countries the role of government in providing finance is important and in others the role of direct personal investment outside of a regulated capital market may be influential.

Corporate governance

The nature of business ownership and the size and complexity of firms will give rise to different requirements of accounting information. Although this is closely interrelated with the sources of finance we believe that it is worth separating as it gives rise to a wider range of issues. The role of managers/directors in determining accounting policy has been alluded to in Chapter 2. The significance here of the governance of enterprises and the power which this may or may not give to individual managers is in the influence it gives these individuals over the development of accounting practice in general, and the choice of policy in specific cases. The role of the manager/director is itself governed by the degree of 'freedom' of action which they are granted. In the UK this freedom is extremely widely interpreted whereas in other European countries there often exist supervisory or oversight boards who will curb the powers of the individual managers.

Nature of the legal system

History has left us with two distinct legal traditions in Western Europe. Firstly, the common law system in which case law and judicial precedent builds a body of rules which supplements and interprets a basic level of statute law. This system gives rise to a flexible system which involves a certain element of judgement and interpretation. The other system is a codified or Roman system of law (*dirigisme*) where the code of law covers all specific eventualities in a detailed and prescriptive manner. The influence of the legal system is on the way in which accounting rules are formulated, expressed and interpreted. Thus, the UK has a common law approach which accepts that the concept of 'true and fair' may give rise to a range of acceptable alternatives. Germany and France, however, have codified systems which give rise to detailed charts of accounts with specific and often unique rules for each accounting problem (the black letter approach).

The influence of taxation

One specific consequence of the different legal systems may be the role of taxation law in determining specific accounting practice. In some countries tax legislation may require the application of certain accounting principles, this is the case in Germany. An alternative approach is to have two sets of figures, one for tax purposes and one for reporting purposes, as, for example, in the UK and the Netherlands where the publicly reported accounting profit is adjusted to comply with the different rules for computing taxable profits. There exists a range of levels of influence of taxation within the European states.

The influence of the profession/interference of the state

The system of accounting regulation and the determination of account-ing practice may be dominated either by an independent accounting profession or by the state. Again, these two distinct alternatives can be seen to be operating at various levels within Europe. In the UK, histori-cally, the profession has been large, powerful and has predominantly regulated accounting. In Germany and France, although the profession may influence the development of accounting, it is the state that has regulated accounting policy.

The relationship between the profession and the state is a complex one and even the notions of 'profession' and 'state' are subject to various interpretations. The requirements of the European Community Eighth Directive have given rise to institutional change at some level in most member states and thus the role of the auditor/accountant is a dynamic one. Another important interface is that between the account-ing profession and the legal profession and this has developed in different cultural and economic environments. The implications of this for the regulation of accounting and auditing rules and practice are obvious. However, the changing environment is a rich source for criti-cal and sociological studies and anyone who wishes to understand the profession/state/'other' professions nexus should examine these studies (for example Miller and Power[7] and Dezalay and Sugarman[8]).

We would argue that the above are the dominant influences on accounting differences within Europe and in examining the specific differences throughout this text we will refer back to these fundamental causes. The literature suggests other causal factors such as the level of economic development, education, social climate and mores. However, we would suggest that within the restricted context of Western Europe these are secondary influences.

A number of attempts to classify accounting systems have been undertaken, for example DaCosta, Bourgeois and Lawson,[9] Nair and Frank,[10] Nobes[11] and Gray.[12] These usually take a global perspective and attempt to place individual countries within the classification sys-tems. For our purposes we believe that a more useful approach is to establish two possible models with which and between which we can identify the countries we are concerned with.

Nobes and Parker[13] suggested that the two main types of financial reporting are the 'micro/professional' and the 'macro/uniform' systems. In order to represent the nature of the countries which are used for our analysis we have used these two systems as models between which there are variations. Thus, in Table 4.2 the 'micro/professional' system is model A and the 'macro/uniform' system is model D, between which are two other states reflecting lesser or greater correspondence with these two models, that is B and C.

TABLE 4.2
Array of factors and accounting environment models

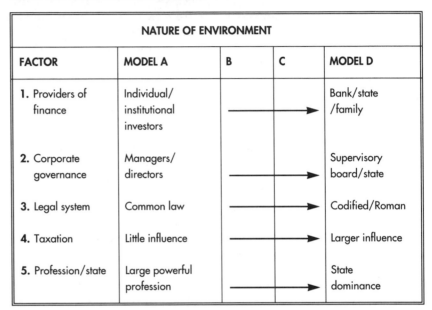

NATURE OF ENVIRONMENT				
FACTOR	MODEL A	B	C	MODEL D
1. Providers of finance	Individual/ institutional investors			Bank/state /family
2. Corporate governance	Managers/ directors			Supervisory board/state
3. Legal system	Common law			Codified/Roman
4. Taxation	Little influence			Larger influence
5. Profession/state	Large powerful profession			State dominance

We have applied these accounting environment models to the principal EU member states referred to in the later parts of this book. Table 4.3 gives an indication of the most appropriate model for each factor which constitutes the accounting environment. This is a very subjective analysis and is based upon our hypothetical models.

TABLE 4.3
Application of accounting environment models

	FACTORS				
COUNTRIES	1	2	3	4	5
United Kingdom	A	A	A	A	A
Netherlands	B	C	C	A	A
Italy	C	C	D	B	D
Spain	C	C	D	C	D
France	C	D	D	C	D
Germany	D	D	D	D	D

Thus the UK shows complete correspondence with Model A, with the Netherlands showing a reasonable level of similarity. Germany shows correspondence with Model D, with Italy, Spain and France showing a more or less close correspondence with models C and D. This array of factors and models is a simplification of a complex real world but is a reasonable representation and helps us to an understanding of the different environments of accounting.

The dangers of this type of classification analysis have been pointed out in recent years, that is they are intrinsically subjective and do not reflect the heterogeneity of accounting systems or the application of them, and are static reflections of a dynamic world. However, as a primary indicator of accounting differences they serve a useful starting point. If we wish to focus on the real differences we must look much closer.

The question of how these environments affect the detailed accounting rules will be seen in Part 2 of this book. However we might usefully generalize at this stage and suggest that the main areas which will be influenced and thus different are:

- conservatism vs. true and fair;
- historic cost vs. valuations;
- levels of disclosure;
- income smoothing;
- provisions and reserves;
- groups, consolidation and related issues;
- depreciation, deferred taxation and other allocations.

The Measurement of Accounting Diversity

In measuring accounting differences there are four initial problems, namely (a) the source of the comparative data to be used; (b) the standard (if any) to be used to measure the differences; (c) the type of issues to be analysed; and (d) the bias which may exist in the perspective of the measurer.

Source of the comparative data

The principal issue is whether to examine 'de jure' regulations or to use 'de facto' practice, that is are we to compare the rules of accounting between countries or sets of actual financial statements, or some combination of these?

The advantage of a de jure approach is that it eliminates the effect of accounting choices which individual enterprises might exercise. It can also take into account the full range of acceptable practices within a country and between countries. Further, it enables comparisons to be made of national rules with those of international bodies such as the IASC and the EU. However, it is known that within countries accounting practice may vary considerably and still comply with the rules or 'generally accepted accounting principles' (GAAP) of that country. This degree of non-compliance may vary between countries. In the real situation there is a degree of diversity and consequently the analysis should be based upon actual practice. Tay and Parker[14] analyse the recent research studies of this issue. They conclude that:

First, if harmonization activities are the result of concern about the comparability of accounts produced by companies from different countries, then a measurement study should focus on actual reporting practices rather than regulations, that is on 'de facto' rather than 'de jure' harmonization.

Second, actual reporting practices may be assessed most accurately from annual accounts or detailed survey of such accounts. (p.90)

A further complication may arise in determining the data to be used in a de facto comparison. Some studies use real data from one or more sets of published reports, for example Davidson and Kolhmeier,[15] and in a more recent study Emenyuno and Gray.[16] Other studies use hypothetical data sets to study differences, for example, Simmonds and Azieries[17] and Walton.[18]

Nature of the comparison

The nature of the comparison is, of course, determined by the objective of the research. It may be either between rules or practice between one or more countries, or between the rules or practices of a country and a set of international rules or practice (see Fig. 4.1).

FIGURE 4.1
Nature of the comparison of accounting practices.

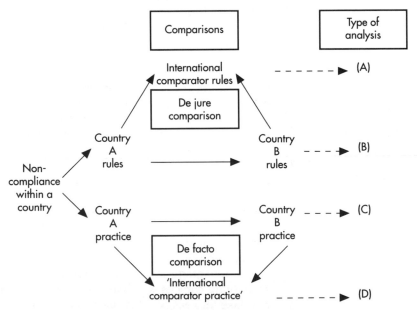

Studies of the degree of harmonization or standardization often use a set of international rules as the comparator, from which to measure diversity both between countries and/or the changes over time. The problem which these studies encounter is that it will be necessarily a de jure analysis (see Figure 4.1, Type (A)), as it is difficult, if not impossible, to establish a set of de facto practice (see Figure 4.1, Type (D)). Efforts to use an assumed form of practice have been undertaken, such as measuring diversity from US GAAP; however, these suffer from the weakness of comparing actual practice with an hypothetical practice.

An alternative measurement basis will be used in this book where the objective is to establish diversity without reference to an international comparator. This may be either de facto or de jure analysis (see Figure 4.1, Types (B) and (C)). The comparative merits of these have been examined above.

Issues to be analysed

We can make a basic distinction between 'measurement issues' and 'disclosure issues' as follows:

- measurement issues concern the way in which transactions and events are reflected in the financial report and comprise the choice between alternative methods of recognition, valuation, income determination, consideration, estimation and presentation;
- disclosure issues concern the extent and detail of data provided in the financial report. (p.213)

An issue which was raised by Van der Tas[19] was whether measurement and disclosure could be measured on the same basis. He argues that whereas measurement issues are concerned with the restriction of choice between a number of alternative policies, disclosure on the other hand is more open ended:

In disclosure issues standards may differ substantially but will seldom conflict because few standards will prohibit companies from disclosing particular information in the financial report. (p. 213)

This argument was examined in a response by Tay and Parker[20] who suggested that harmonization is 'in a sense value neutral'. They argue that the question they are examining is not the suitability of accounting practice but the degree of closeness that the harmonization process has brought about. The potential importance of information not required to be disclosed in a harmonized set of rules is a separate issue.

In conclusion, we suggest that this debate is an important one for the purposes of establishing the degree of diversity of accounting. We will examine both elements, that is measurement and disclosure, in our analysis.

Measurer bias/neutrality

Given that accounting diversity is a complex phenomenon and that the interpretation of the different accounting treatments may be subjective even within a country we suggest that the attitudes and understanding of the measurers may be a relevant factor. The difficulty for any researcher in this area is the ethnocentric perspective of accounting practice that is inevitable. Some researchers have attempted to reduce this influence by using the view of academic or practising accountants from other countries.[21,22]

It would appear to us that the degree of intimacy necessary to fully understand the practices of any country require the measurer to have a comprehensive and continuing exposure to that accounting environment and culture.

A further problem occurs in the language in which the reports are expressed. The linguistic problem is that of fully appreciating the nuances of the financial terminology used. As McLeay[23] points out 'even for professional analysts the language barrier is a significant problem in international financial analysis'.

Should Differences in Accounting be Eliminated?

The elimination of the differences which have been referred to in this chapter will clearly be a difficult, costly, and time-consuming task. The questions then are what benefits might accrue from such elimination, and what obstacles must be overcome?

Benefits to users

The principal beneficiaries would be those who use financial statements for decision-making and who make decisions on an international basis. Thus, investors and creditors will be better able to understand financial statements of companies in foreign countries if they are similar to those of domestic companies. The same will apply to employees, government and taxation authorities, and in particular financial analysts.

Benefits to producers

Multinational companies and firms of accountants will benefit in having fewer sets of accounting rules and practices to operate. Thus, staff time will be saved and staff become more transferable and technologies will be simplified.

Obstacles

The principal theoretical obstacle to elimination of differences is that they exist **because** of the different environments in which they developed. Thus, it may well be counter-productive to make accounting a single global set of procedures as the world which will use the accounting is not itself homogeneous in its needs. This may well give rise to a form of accounting nationalism by which countries will resist the abandonment of their own unique accounting form for an imposed external internationalism.

A practical obstacle is the sheer complexity of accounting practice throughout the world – elimination of differences in the face of this complexity is an heroic task. Further, if it is to be done then we need to consider who would do it. It requires a supra-national body which is universally accepted to have authority to determine and possibly regulate accounting.

The net result of these benefits and obstacles has been that the complete elimination of differences is now not seen as a realistic goal by those involved. However, progress has been made towards eliminating differences in two ways.

- **Harmonization** is the process of making financial statements equivalent or comparable between countries by either adopting the same practice or by disclosing differences between different practices.
- **Standardization** is the process of producing international accounting standards which will then be used by countries to develop or adjust their own standard practices.

Although the difference between these two approaches may seem artificial the means by which they are accomplished is significantly different.

The harmonization of accounting practice in the EC/EU

In 1957 the Treaty of Rome established the objects of the Community as to establish the free movement of persons, goods and services, and capital. The Common Industrial Policy (1970) calls for the creation of a unified business environment including the harmonization of company law and taxation and the creation of a common capital market. There are no specific provisions in the EC treaty to harmonize accounting standards and the accounting provisions form part of the programme of company law harmonization. Article 34(3) states that this programme seeks to allow freedom to establish companies in member states, protect the interests of members and third parties, free the movement of capital by providing common protection and to remove the barriers to cross frontier co-operation in the Community. Investors and creditors will, it is hoped, be given equivalent safeguards throughout the Community and thus be able to make investment decisions with more confidence in the legal and economic framework of the host country.

However, as Van Hulle[24] points out the directives are primarily there to protect current members (shareholders) and third parties and he suggests that '(potential) investor protection is not the primary objective of this harmonization .... In this respect, the approach that the Community follows must be distinguished from the capital market approach which is the basis for accounting standard setting in other parts of the world.' This distinction is important as, in principle, the differences due to the requirements of potential investors and providers of finance identified above may still remain after harmonization has been achieved. The primary objective is not to standardize accounting to either a UK, continental or a hybrid approach to financial reporting but in protection of third parties. However, in practice it is less clear as to how the objectives of 'investment decision usefulness' and shareholder/creditor protection relate and where and how the requirements of harmonization differentiate them. This potential conflict of objective was discussed in Chapter 2 of this book.

Van Hulle[25] suggests that the other main characteristics of harmonization, in addition to the company law approach outlined above, are as follows.

- Equivalence and comparability are the aims of harmonization – this is not the same as the development of a uniform system of accounting.
- Accounting regulations and practices will be part of the law and will not be set by the accounting profession.
- Harmonization is a multilingual and multicultural process.

Given the diversity of the accounting environment we have referred to above harmonization is likely to be fraught with difficulty and if the objective is simply creditor protection then it may not be worth the effort when other means of achieving this might be employed. However, it might be suggested that harmonization is still worthwhile, if in addition to the primary objective of the protection of members and creditors, other benefits may be derived from the harmonization process, for example:

- in some countries company law has tended to concentrate on the interests of shareholders and investors. EC legislation takes a more diverse view giving more weight to the interests of a wider set of interested groups, for example employees and consumers;
- the 'capital market approach' will be achieved as the financial analyst will be able to more easily understand and interpret financial information from different countries;
- the preparation and presentation of financial information by multinationals may be much simplified if the different accounting procedures are brought closer together;
- other groups such as auditors, revenue authorities and governmental bodies may also benefit from the process.

Thus, the harmonization process has a rather narrow legislative objective but in practice the process should be considered in its wider context.

The due process of EC harmonization

This section will examine the due process or legislative framework of harmonization.

The instrument used in harmonizing EC company law and accounting is the Directive. A Directive is not primary legislation but once agreed is binding on all member states who must incorporate it into national law within a specified period. This gives the requirements of the Directives two characteristics:

- they will be binding on all EC companies once incorporated into national law; and
- national provisions should be interpreted in the light of the Directives.

It is essential that the rules enshrined in the Directives are interpreted in the same way throughout the Community. This gives the law which arises through Directives a unique quality.

The procedure by which Directives are adopted is lengthy and in some instances byzantine. The procedure often involves compromise between the interests of different member states and this gives rise to the inclusion in Directives of options.

Options take two forms: (a) options given directly to companies, and (b) options given to member states. The Commission favours the first of these forms as they can constrain the effect of the option, but member states may resist this attempt to legislate at a European level. A further distinction of options is between those concerned with valuation and those with definitional items. The latter are the more substantive issues and their existence produces a reduction in the real level of harmonization. However, options have proved to be a lubricant to the political nature of harmonization and some member states have used them in order to give companies a degree of flexibility.

Member states are given several years to implement Directives. If they fail to meet the deadline the Commission will remind them of their responsibilities and may ultimately take them before the European Court of Justice.

The Directives relevant to corporate law as at 1993 are outlined in Table 4.4.

TABLE 4.4
Directives relevant to corporate accounting (adapted from Nobes and Parker[13])

DIRECTIVES ON COMPANY LAW	DRAFT DATES		DATE ADOPTED	TOPIC
First	1964		1968	Ultra vires rules
Second	1970	1972	1976	Separation of public companies, minimum capital distributions
Third	1970 1975	1973	1978	Mergers
Fourth	1971	1974	1978	Formats and rules of accounting
Fifth	1972	1983		Structure, managements and audit of companies
Sixth	1978		1982	De-mergers
Seventh	1976	1978	1983	Consolidated accounting
Eighth	1978		1984	Qualifications and work of auditors
Ninth				Links between public company groups
Tenth	1985			International mergers of public companies
Eleventh	1986			Disclosure about branches
Twelfth	1988			Single member company
Thirteenth	1989			Takeovers
Vredeling	1980	1983		Employee information and consultation

The timing of the implementation of the relevant legislation in member states has not been uniform, as shown in Table 4.5.

TABLE 4.5
Year of legislation

	B	D	E	F	I	NL	UK	P	GR
Fourth	1985	85	89	83	91	83	81	89	87
Seventh	1990	85	89	85	91	88	89	91	87

This implementation delay is compounded when one considers the additional delay between the passing of a national law and the practical effect on company financial statements. For example, in Italy the first financial statements to comply with the Fourth Directive were for the year ended 31 December 1991 and with the Seventh for the year ended 31 December 1994 even though the Directive was adopted by the EC Council of Ministers in 1983.

We might summarize the problems of the due process of harmonization as follows:

- The political nature of the EU leads to compromise on issues which it might be argued require positive solutions to accounting problems. On the other hand the diverse nature of the EU (as it has existed until now) may make compromise the best solution. In order to reduce the impact of options the Seventh Directive 'provides for a revision of the most important options at a later stage in order to achieve great transparency and harmonization. This will not be an easy task' (Van Hulle[26]). The use of options is at the root of this issue and re-search into the nature and use of options may be valuable.
- The length of time which is involved in the EU adopting a Directive can in some instances reduce its effectiveness in reacting to the dynamic environment in which accounting operates. The Seventh Directive, for example, was in preparation for nine years before adoption by the EC, and the Fourth failed to include accounting issues which were of current concern, for example accounting for leases, special purpose transactions and pensions.
- The delay between adoption by the EU and the practical application in different member states compounds the problems of the relevance of the rules to the current accounting environment.

To illustrate these problems we will briefly review the Fourth and Seventh Directives.

The Fourth Directive

The first draft of the Fourth Directive was published in 1971 before the UK or Eire became members and was primarily influenced by German law. However, the 1974 draft after the entry of the UK and Eire, was considerably altered and clearly shows the effect of the accounting practices of these two countries. The most important articles of the Directive include the following.

- The predominance of the true and fair view concept. This was introduced in the 1974 draft and clearly shows Anglo-Saxon influence (the model A approach).
- The requirement for standardized formats of financial statements within a number of permitted options. This shows the Franco-German (model D) influence of uniformity (somewhat watered-down by the options).
- The options to permit or require some form of inflation accounting. Here the Anglo-Dutch influence is obvious (model A/B).

The compromises between different national interests and the consequent introduction of options are obvious from the above. Even so, the Directive achieved a considerable level of potential harmonization and led to changes in the accounting practices in individual member states. The most fundamental of these changes has been the introduction of the 'true and fair view' concept to continental Europe. The countries which have had to introduce this concept have found considerable difficulty in interpreting, understanding and applying the concept to their domestic circumstances.

In practice, it would seem that they have interpreted the rule in the context of their own legal culture, and the effect of the changes inherent in a 'true and fair' approach have been limited by these interpretations. This is discussed in more detail in Part Two of this book. Secondly, the standard format requirements had some effect on the UK, Eire and the Netherlands, but again, in practice, if one even casually examines financial statements from different member states the options available give rise to a divergence of presentation.

Finally, the options made available with respect to the revaluation of assets and the introduction of inflation adjusted accounts has had little impact. There is still a variety of valuation practices being followed ranging from German adherence to historical costs, through UK laissez-faire to Dutch replacement cost accounts.

The Seventh Directive

The Seventh Directive was adopted by the EC in 1983 after a lengthy and tortuous path through due process. The most important issues to be dealt with were (a) the determination of the members of a group, (b) the requirement for and methods of group accounting to be used, (c) merger accounting and (d) accounting for goodwill.

The first of these issues, in Article 1, became contentious with a conflict between a 'de jure' approach and a 'de facto' approach and gave rise to the first of many options to be allowed in this Directive. In fact Nobes[27] points out that:

There are 51 obvious options, as outlined in a survey of EC Implementations conducted earlier this year by the Fédération des Experts Comptable Européens. If they are all assumed to be yes/no options, that is approximately 2×10^{15} or 2 zillion.

This rather tongue-in-cheek analysis is exaggerated but shows the potential for member states to differ in accounting practice. In implementing the Directive none of the major options were adopted uniformly, that is there is no issue on which complete standardization has been achieved. However, the differences in practice between countries which existed before the Seventh Directive were so great that any harmonization is significant. Further, this Directive had a hidden agenda which was to 'improve' group accounting within the Community. A simpler way of harmonizing practice in group accounting would have been to adopt what was existing practice in a number of member states, namely to have no requirement for group accounts at all!

We can, therefore, see some progress towards harmonization taking place. The question of course is how far have we progressed and how much further is possible or desirable. A subjective view of the success of the process may be found in the proceedings of a European Commission conference in which views of officials from member states ranged from fulsome praise to strong criticism. The summary by Mr Fitchew, the European Director General for Financial Institutions and Company Law, concluded that:

> *There was warm welcome for the degree of harmonization already achieved but the situation is not perfect in the sense that gaps and deficiencies exist. In particular it was not possible to say that there is a good comparability between accounts from member states as would be desirable for efficient functioning of the internal market and financial markets in particular.[28]*

Considerable academic research has taken place on measuring the success of international accounting standards but much less on EC harmonization. Tay and Parker[29] and Van der Tas[30] have suggested models of measuring the success of harmonization; however, both models suffer from the inherent complexity of the problems in terms of accounting theory, legislative practice, politics and the transition from these to accounting practice.

The Van der Tas analysis was a comprehensive examination of accounting for deferred taxation practices over a ten-year period in 154 European listed companies. The conclusions are that as regards individual accounts:

- the degree of harmony of the primary accounts, excluding reconciliation data in the notes to the accounts, is low and shows no significant movements during the examined period;
- the degree of harmony, taking reconciliation data in the notes into account, increases sharply over the examined period.

Similar conclusions are reached for the consolidated accounts.

We would argue that what Van der Tas has found for deferred taxation might not be true for other accounting issues and that the analyst needs to be aware of the quality of adjustments being made. Part Three of this book will return in detail to this problem.

This perceived lack of success in harmonization has led the EC to re-examine the process and what it is trying to achieve. The EC Commission in January 1990 organized a conference to discuss the future of harmonization. The principal decisions made at this conference were as follows.

- There was an agreement that the options in the Directives should reflect real differences between member states and should not be reduced.
- Harmonization through Directives was a lengthy and highly politicized process and Recommendations might be more effective vehicles for progress.
- An Accounting Advisory Forum would be created which would advise the Commission on issues not already dealt with and provide guidance on the position to be taken in the international accounting harmonization debate. (This body has not been successful and in a 'turf-battle' for influence has been outmanoeuvred by FEE.)

These decisions reflect a significant change in the harmonization process. Perhaps more significant still is the underlying philosophy that has moved from one of reducing accounting choice, and thus diversity, to one of mutual recognition.

Karel Van Hulle[31] of the EC Commission summarizes this philosophy:

We do mutually recognize the accounts of companies from different member states because we believe that – although the rules are not exactly the same – there is broadly speaking equivalence between the accounts of a French and a Dutch company or between the accounts of a German and an English company. In this respect it should be stressed that reconciliation is not a good answer to overcome differences in accounting treatment.

As we attempt to demonstrate in this book we find little broad equivalence and we do find a need for analysts to produce reconciliations (provided they have an understanding of the uncertainties involved). We believe mutual recognition is as yet an unworkable solution to the practical problem of accounting diversity.

International Accounting Standards

In 1973 an International Accounting Standards Committee (IASC) was formed by the professional bodies of nine countries. This body has grown, and by 1990 it had representatives from over 70 countries. The Committee produces what are referred to as International Accounting Standards. The aim of the IASC is 'to formulate and publish in the public interest accounting standards to be observed in the presentation of financial statements and to promote their worldwide acceptance and observance'.

The member bodies of IASC agree to support the standards and to use their best endeavours to ensure that published financial statements comply with the standards, to ensure auditors enforce this, and to persuade governments, stock exchanges and other bodies to back the standards.[32] The application of these standards depends on the willingness of the professional bodies in the different countries to promote them and on the importance of the particular professional bodies in their own countries. The IASC has had an influence on the development of standards within many countries and in particular in developing countries. In the UK the accounting bodies support the works of the IASC, although they do not subordinate their authority for standard-setting to this international body.

A number of criticisms were levelled at the IASC at the OECD Paris conference in 1986. The principal criticism was of the range of options available under international standards (see above for similar criticisms of the EC). The response of the IASC was to issue E32, *Comparability of Financial Statements*, which seeks to reduce the number of alternatives, or failing this to identify preferred alternatives. A survey of multinational enterprises to assess their attitudes to E32 found that the respondents expected a 'modest, useful improvement in international financial reporting' and that companies in Europe (except Germany!) generally expected greater benefits than those in non-European countries surveyed. The IASC has cooperated with IOSCO (International Organization of Securities Commissions) in order to arrive at a proposed agreement that if companies engaged in multinational securities offerings complied with IASs they would be accepted by all stock exchanges in the countries involved.

However, at the present time IASC standards are not enforceable and it may be that a political conflict with the EC may be a barrier. Van Hulle[33] states: 'For the Community the execution of this project will not remain without difficulties. It will require changes in both Community and national law.'

For our purposes, therefore, the IASC is a source of possible reduction of accounting differences but within a European perspective plays a significantly lesser role than the EU. Other standardizing bodies or those playing a similar role such as the OECD and the UN are not dealt with here as their influence has, as yet, been small.

Adjustment for International Accounting Diversity

It is clear that the attempts to reduce accounting diversity have not been successful. Further, although the research in measuring accounting diversity has produced an interesting background to understanding the extent and possible causes of the problem, the fact remains that analysts will still have to deal with the consequences of diversity. This section will examine the evidence of analysts making adjustments for diversity.

Gray[34] uses the European Federation of Financial Analysts Societies' method of standardizing accounting information to arrive at figures for ratio analysis and for forecasts of earnings. His conclusions on these adjustments is that:

> ... the analyst's adjustments to company accounts can only remove the impact of some of the more obvious differences in accounting

treatment and are thus likely to provide a somewhat modest assessment of the full position.

Despite these limitations, the European method does provide a common yardstick for comparative purposes, which is perceived to be of significance to security analysts in the process of making investment decisions. (p.66)

Another approach has been to examine the range of results of ratios expected from accounting data in different countries. Aron[35] examined the different PE ratios produced by American and Japanese accounting and attempted to explain the probable causes of these differences. Choi et al.[36] adopted a similar approach aimed at current ratios. However, other researchers, for example Hagigi and Sponza,[37] have pointed out the dangers of producing algorithms which attempt to adjust for diversity without looking at the underlying accounting detail.

Choi et al.[38] examined a number of the international data services which supply company statistics and suggests that these services will increasingly attempt to 'restate foreign accounting data to a common frame of reference'. He concludes that at least for the present a preferred course of action might be for firms to produce unadjusted numbers accompanied by sufficient data to provide readers with the opportunity to restate.

Direct evidence of adjustment by users was provided by Choi and Levich[39] who conducted interviews with the major participants in the capital market, namely institutional investors, corporate issuers, underwriters and regulators. Their findings show that approximately one-half of these participants believe that their decisions are affected by accounting diversity. They also found that of this half a significant proportion attempted to deal with the diversity by adjustment. For example, in the institutional investor group, of the nine investors who responded that accounting measurement differences were a problem seven 'coped by restating foreign accounts to an accounting framework more familiar to the user'. Further evidence of the use of adjustment was found with the other market participants in the study. However, Choi and Levich also note that those who do make adjustments still believe that their decisions are affected by diversity, and that restatement was not sufficient to remove the problem. In their conclusion they suggest that:

... either (a) existing restatement algorithms are still at a very crude stage of development, (b) existing algorithms are not being applied effectively or (c) no algorithm is capable of producing a proper and meaningful restatement. If restatement fails to be an effective coping mechanism because of (a) or (b) then more effort in restatement may result in a payoff. If the true answer is (c) then investors may be right in developing their skills to read and interpret foreign financial statements in their original form. (p.11)

We would argue that the detailed restatement of accounting information is the most realistic approach to producing useful information and that the existing or improved 'algorithms' of adjustment can produce an effective means of coping with accounting diversity in some, but not all, cases.

The limiting factor in determining the usefulness of adjustment is the reliability of the individual adjustments which are made to the information and this is determined by the analyst's knowledge of the policies/ measurement bases operated and the disclosures available to make meaningful adjustment.

The scenario suggested by Choi of data services presenting information which would enable adjustment to be made appears to us to have the problem in that it may disguise the reliability of the information used in adjustment and thus the quality of the resultant numbers.

To summarize, we believe that adjustment can play an important role in dealing with accounting diversity, and that this 'effort may result in a payoff', if users can assess the quality of the adjusted numbers by an understanding of the relative reliability of the adjustments.

In our view investors and other users of accounting information for financial analysis would benefit from a clear understanding of how they might approach such assessment.

Conclusions

The purpose of this chapter has been to set out the nature and causes of differences in accounting practice in Europe in an attempt to give a perspective to the detailed analysis which follows. Further, we have reviewed the harmonization process and its aim to make European financial statements more comparable. We conclude that, although there has been some success in achieving this goal, financial analysts still face a difficult task and that in analysing pan-European financial statements they need to consider the detailed measurement and disclosure differences. The quality of their analysis depends upon the quality of the detailed adjustments.

References

1. Simmonds, A. and Azieries, O. (1989) *Accounting for Europe-Success 2000 A.D.,* Touche Ross.

2. Alexander, D. and Archer, S. (1992) *The European Accounting Guide,* Academic Press.

3. Coopers & Lybrand (1991) *International Accounting Summaries,* Wiley & Sons, New York.

4. Fédération des Experts Comptables Européens (1991) *FEE European Survey of Published Accounts,* Routledge.

5. Miller, P. and Power, M. (1992) 'Accounting law and economic calculation', in Bromwich, M. and Hopwood, A. (eds), *Accounting and the Law,* Prentice Hall.

6. Dezalay, Y. and Sugarman, D. (eds) (1994) *Professional Competition and the Social Construction of Markets,* Routledge.

7. Miller and Power, op. cit.

8. Dezalay and Sugarman, op.cit.

9. DaCosta, R.C., Bourgeois, J.C. and Lawson, W.M. (1978) 'A classification of international financial accounting practices', *International Journal of Accounting,* Spring.

10. Nair, R.D. and Frank, W.G. (1981) 'The harmonization of international accounting standards 1973–79', *International Journal of Accounting,* Fall.

11. Nobes, C. (1983) 'A judgemental international classification of financial reporting practices', *Journal of Business Finance and Accounting,* Spring.

12. Gray, S.J. (1988) 'Towards a theory of cultural influence on the development of accounting systems internationally', *Abacus,* March.

13. Nobes, C.W. and Parker, R.H. (eds) (1991) *Comparative International Accounting,* Prentice Hall.

14. Tay, J.S.W. and Parker, R.H. (1990) 'Measuring international harmonization and standardization', *Abacus,* **26**(1), 84.

15. Davidson, S. and Kohlmeier, J.M. (1966) 'A measure of the impact of some foreign accounting principles', *Journal of Accounting Research,* Autumn.

16. Emenyuno, E.N. and Gray, S.J. (1992) 'EC accounting harmonization: an empirical study of measurement practices in France, Germany and the UK', *Accounting and Business Research,* **23** (89).

17. Simmonds and Azieries, op. cit.

18. Walton, P. (1992) 'Harmonization of accounting in France and Britain: some evidence', *Abacus,* **28** (2).

19. Van der Tas, L.G. (1992) 'Evidence of EC financial reporting practice harmonization: the case of deferred taxation', *European Accounting Review,* 213.

20. Tay, J.S.W. and Parker, R.H. (1992) 'Measuring international harmonization and standardization: a reply', *Abacus,* **28** (2).

21. Simmonds and Azierles, op. cit.

22. Walton, op. cit.

23. McLeay, S. (1991) 'International financial statement analysis', in Nobes, C.W. and Parker, R.H. (eds) *Comparative International Accounting,* Prentice Hall.

24. Van Hulle, K. (1989) 'The EC experience of harmonization (Part 2)', *Accountancy,* October, 76.

25. Van Hulle, K. (1992) 'Harmonization of accounting standards: a view', *European Accounting Review,* **1**(1), 161–172.

26. Van Hulle (1989), op. cit.

27. Nobes, C.W. (1990) 'EC group accounting: two zillion ways to do it', *Accountancy,* December.

28. European Commission (1990) *The Future of the Harmonization of Accounting Standards within the European Community,* EC Documentation Office.

29. Tay and Parker (1992), op. cit.

30. Van der Tas, op.cit.

31. Van Hulle (1989), op. cit.

32. Nobes and Parker (1991), op. cit.

33. Van Hulle (1989), op. cit.

34. Gray, S.J. (1988) 'The impact of international accounting differences from a security analysis perspective: some European evidence', *Journal of Accounting Research,* Spring.

35. Aron, P. (1991) 'Japanese P/E ratios in an environment of increasing uncertainty', in Choi, F.D.S. (ed) *Handbook of International Accounting,* Wiley, Sons.

36. Choi, F.D.S., Sang Kee Min, Sang Oh Nam, Hisaaki Hino, Junichi Ujiie and Stonehill, A.J. (1983) 'Multinational finance: the use and misuse of international ratio analysis', *Journal of International Business Studies,* Spring/Summer.

37. Hagigi, M. and Sponza, A. (1990) 'Financial statement analysis of Italian companies: accounting practices, environmental factors and international corporate performance comparisons', *International Journal of Accounting,* **25** (4).

38. Choi et al., op. cit.

39. Choi, F.D.S. and Levich, R.M. (1991) 'Behavioural effects of international accounting diversity', *Accounting Horizons,* 11.

Further Reading

Alexander, D. and Archer, S.   (1992) *The European Accounting Guide,* Academic Press.

Choi, F.D.S. and Mueller, G.G.   (1984) *International Accounting,* Prentice Hall International.

Fédération des Experts Comptables Européens   (1991) *FEE European Survey of Published Accounts,* Routledge.

Nobes, C.W. and Parker, R.H. (eds)   (1991) *Comparative International Accounting,* Prentice Hall.

Problems

1. Analyse two European countries of your own choice, using the accounting environment factors and models from this chapter.

2. Financial accounting policy-making can be seen as a political process both from a domestic and an international perspective. What evidence is available for this politicization?

3. Using two specific accounting issues, examine the degree of diversity amongst EU countries in terms of both measurement and disclosure.

4. Do you believe that harmonization of accounting in the EU is a worthwhile objective? To what extent do you think past efforts have been successful.

5. Using the current pronouncements of the IASC, list those items not specifically covered by EU Directives and discuss the relative merits of IASC standardization compared with EU harmonization.

PART TWO

**Financial Reporting Issues:
European Analysis and Examples**

5

Corporate Governance

Objectives

- To explain what corporate governance is all about.

- To discuss the different systems of corporate governance that exist within the European Union.

- To examine the information provided in the annual report and accounts of companies on matters relating to corporate governance.

Introduction

Although achieving harmonization of measurement practice is unlikely for the foreseeable future, this does not mean that a level of harmonization in disclosure could not be achieved. There should be less difficulties to overcome in reaching agreement on the minimum level of information to be shown in financial reports than in agreeing on what is the truest and fairest way to measure profits. All that is required is a willingness to disclose the same level of information, there are no theoretical issues to be resolved.

At a time when the European Union is attempting to introduce common policies on such issues as employment practices and social security through its Social Chapter, it should be quite a small step to get companies to disclose information on such matters as numbers employed, pension arrangements, market segmentation and directors' remuneration. Unfortunately even harmonizing on disclosure is likely to be met with resistance. This is because still basically financial reports and accounts are seen as having a different role, as being of greater significance in some countries than in others.

As long as Europe has different systems of corporate governance from one country to another, then not only will harmonization in measurement not be possible but nor will harmonization in disclosure.

Corporate governance is a dull sounding title; the word governance evokes thoughts of colonial administrators, prisons and powerful teachers. It is, however, a very important subject, being concerned with the balance of power between the owners, directors and bankers of a company. It has become a major issue in the UK culminating with the publication in 1992 of the *Report of the Committee on the Financial Aspects of Corporate Governance* (The Cadbury Report).[1]

In 1989, in a Bank of England discussion paper the question was posed on whether or not there was the possibility that 'our market system ... may put us at a disadvantage in international competition by those who have superior linkages and lines of accountability ... and a greater sense of patience.'[2]

In the opinion of the Cadbury Report: 'The basic system of corporate governance in Britain is sound. The principles are well known.' The report did, however, recommend a number of changes to the existing system. The changes proposed are only minor, attempting to tighten up the existing system, rather than alter the system. The committee did not consider whether the British system put UK companies at a disadvantage.

It is not always appreciated how the system of corporate governance varies from one country to another and the impact of such differences on financial reporting. We will briefly illustrate different models of corporate governance and the implication of the different models on financial disclosure. We are arguing that fundamental differences exist within the EU and that there are few signs that the systems are moving closer together. The user of accounts cannot expect the matters disclosed by companies according to the practices of one system will be the matters disclosed by companies following the practices of another system.

If the EU had continued with a policy of encouraging harmonization through Directives this may have led to similar levels of disclosure, but mutual recognition takes away any urgency to conform. It is now either up to the marketplace, to individual country legislation or to those desiring more self-regulation to persuade companies to disclose similar information.

Following discussions on corporate governance, we will examine the extent of harmonization of disclosure on issues of corporate governance in financial accounts.

The amount of information disclosed in a financial report depends on the importance attached by users of accounts to the content of the report. In the UK (and the USA) the centre of corporate control of a company is the stock market. The centre of control is 'external' to the company. The financial report is therefore of considerable importance conveying to those who control the company the information they believe they need. Of course the agents of the shareholders, namely the directors, can influence what is disclosed.

In contrast in Germany (and in Japan) the centre of control is 'internal' to the company. In Germany it is the supervisory board. The directors typically represent interest groups important to the company. The composition of the supervisory boards of the 100 largest companies in Germany is shown in Table 5.1 Information needs to be made available to these supervisory boards by the board of management.

The fact that certain information that is disclosed in UK company accounts is not disclosed in German company accounts does not matter from the point of view of the effectiveness of corporate control.

Corporate Governance

In both systems those who need information have it available. In the German system it is available within the company.

In the twentieth century in the UK (and USA) the ownership of the company has become divorced from the control of the company. The managers/directors are referred to as the agents of the shareholders in whose interests they are assumed to be acting. A great deal of the theory of the firm is based upon this assumption. The annual financial report is part of the system of reporting to the owners on the way in which their company is being run and shareholders have an opportunity of expressing their opinions at general meetings. Ultimately, if the owners are not happy, they will wish to sell their shares in the marketplace.

TABLE 5.1
Composition of the supervisory boards of the 100 largest German enterprises, 1988 (number of seats)

Private banks	104
Other banks	32
Insurance companies	25
Trade union representatives	187
Other employee representatives	542
Representatives from industry and other business enterprises	385
Other shareholder representatives (lawyers, notaries, representatives of shareholder associations, etc.)	152
Politicians, civil servants	69
	1,496

Source: Federal Association of German Banks.

In the UK takeovers and mergers have become the main form of exercising control. Directors know that following a takeover of their company it is they that are most likely to lose. Research has shown that 90% of directors of companies that have been taken over lose their jobs within two years of the takeover. It is this fear of takeover that, it is argued, is the best way of keeping managers on their toes.

This then is the external 'market' control system. Financial account-ing practices in the UK are geared to satisfy this system. The system has its critics, the chief criticism being that it leads to short-term decision-making. This problem arises because managers, being insecure allow short-term factors to dominate their thinking. Investors do not hold a high proportion of their wealth in any one security; they prefer to hold a diversified portfolio. This means the investors also have short-term horizons, preferring to be able to trade in securities as opportunities arise rather than have a long-term stake in a company. Takeovers and mergers are not the best ways of reorganizing an industry – they are expensive. It is not always the 'good' company that takes over the 'bad' company – the market for corporate control is not always efficient. In the UK the economic effects of 30 years of mergers and takeovers has been neutral. More recently there has been criticism that the level of remuneration of directors (the agents of shareholders) is only loosely linked to the performance of the company. It also is claimed this external control system has led to creative accounting practices.

In Germany the existing system also faces criticism. There are monopoly arguments against the power of the banks. Daimler-Benz producing accounts to conform to US GAAP, has led to a debate over accounting policies and practices in Germany. There are German companies who criticize Daimler-Benz for being willing to change from the traditional conservative approach. The chief financial officer of the company, in defending the company against criticism, made the following point.

> During the last few decades the English language has become the world language without a resolution of the UN or any other institution. It just happened. Well, something very similar is happening in international accounting; the Anglo-Saxon principles are gaining more and more ground and thus getting nearer and nearer to becoming the world's accounting language.
> (Quoted in *The Independent*, 24 April 1993.)

In this chapter, we are not concerned with the rights and wrongs of these criticisms in the two countries, just with the fact that they have been made. If those with an internal system are to move to the external 'market' system, they would need persuading that the above criticisms of markets and short-termism are not justified. They could ask why they should move to higher levels of disclosure, including disclosure on governance, when the results of providing additional information to the market do not seem worthwhile in terms of economic performance.

The model where the centre of corporate control is within the company leads to cross shareholding and interlocking directorships. Supporters of the system argue that this leads to more secure managers and more stable shareholdings which leads in turn to a longer-term approach to decision-making. Criticisms of the internal system include the fact that too much power is in the hands of the large banks and industrial groups. There is minority shareholder dissatisfaction with the inadequate disclosure and their lack of power. They complain about low levels of dividend payments, and being in a position to do nothing about it.

The German banks dominate the equity market, and they as company bankers are in a good position to obtain insider information. Until recently only a few banks had internal rules to prevent traders exploiting insider information.

There is insider trading on the stock market. In fact in Germany until recently insider trading was not against the law, but against voluntary market codes. Now there are laws making it a criminal offence. In 1993 a member of the Supervisory Board of Daimler Benz had to resign following an inside information scandal.

Takeovers of inefficient firms can be very difficult. There are restrictions on shareholder voting power. It has been suggested that the boards of many German companies are indifferent to a large percentage of the owners. If the directors on the board of management can satisfy the representatives of the main interest groups represented on the supervisory board they can feel secure.

Whether or not the move towards global markets, with companies and investors becoming increasingly international in their outlook means that there will be a convergence of views on corporate control remains to be seen. As has been mentioned those familiar with the 'internal' based system can point to the weaknesses of the external market system. For those with an external control system to move towards an internal system would lead to worries about lack of democracy, and increased power (and possible wealth) for some interest groups.

Problem areas

For a financial analyst or a shareholder to understand what is happening within a company from the point of view of corporate control it is necessary to have knowledge of at least the matters listed below.

- Who are the principal shareholders?
- Who are the directors of the company?
- How many shares are owned by the directors and do they have options to purchase further shares?
- What is the level of financial remuneration of directors?
- What is the management structure? What is the membership and role of board subcommittees?
- What is the company's mission statement?

To illustrate the differences that exist in Europe with regard to disclosure, we will show the range of practices adopted to deal with such issues.

Who Owns the Equity Shares

Germany

In Germany and in some other continental countries there is a difficulty in identifying who owns a company, because all or many of the shares issued by the company are bearer shares rather than registered shares.

The Deutsche Bundesbank has estimated that in 1990 the structure of share ownership in Germany was as follows:

Private households	17%
Enterprise	42%
Banks	10%
Insurance companies	12%
Public sector	5%
Foreigners	14%

These figures highlight one of the distinguishing features of corporate governance in Germany, namely the large interlocking share ownership, with one company holding shares in another company. This relationship extends to interlocking directorship.[3]

In recent years there has in fact been a tendency for the large German banks to reduce their industrial participation through share ownership. However, they still exert a considerable influence on companies as a result of their representatives having seats on supervisory boards and the use they can make of the proxy votes they can exercise on behalf of shares deposited with them by banking clients. Shares approximating to 40% of the total market value of all domestic companies are deposited in German banks.

German companies usually provide very little precise information on who owns their shares. Bayer, in a section on the 'investor' in their 1991 accounts, point out they are listed on 15 stock exchanges outside Germany. They state:

> The main objective of listing on stock exchanges outside Germany is to attract new investors, especially in view of the oversupply of blue-chip chemical stocks on the German market.
>
> To enhance our image, we have intensified our investor relations activities in international financial centres through direct presentations and personal contact with institutional investors. In 1991 we gave numerous presentations in Germany and abroad to update financial analysts and fund managers on the company's performance. The wide diversity of stockholders makes Bayer one of the few truly publicly owned companies in Germany, as reflected in the high share turnover. Some 213 million Bayer shares with a total value of DM 58.1 billion were traded on the German stock market in 1991, making Bayer stock one of the five most actively traded securities in Germany. Bayer's is also one of the most liquid German stocks on the London Stock Exchange.

In their 1993 accounts Bayer give details on who owns the shares (Extract 5.1). Siemens point to the problem of identifying shareowners, and indicate the solution to the problem that they have adopted (Extract 5.2).

VEBA point out that their shares are broadly held, and again disclose the division between foreign and domestic ownership (Extract 5.3).

The German companies provide information which is of some interest, but still do not disclose key information for a true understanding of the power structure within the company. They do not usually state who are their major shareholders.

There are of course exceptions, Daimler-Benz being one. They have less problem than most in identifying their shareholders (Extract 5.4). This extract from the company's accounts illustrates and reinforces the points made in the introduction to this chapter on corporate governance in Germany. It emphasizes the stable and reliable shareholder structure, and the fact that the company need not worry about any takeover attempts. Who the Daimler-Benz shareholders were can be seen from Extract 5.5. In 1993 the company obtained a quotation in New York, and will consequently widen their shareholder base.

Extract 5.1 – Bayer AG 1993 accounts, Bayer and the Investor.

A survey of the number and structure of our stockholders was carried out as of November 1, 1993. Bayer is a widely held corporation, and its stock is well distributed internationally. Foreign investors hold 47 percent of the shares. We consider the increase in foreign ownership during the past ten years to be the outcome of our efforts to interest the international investment community in Bayer stock. This applies particularly to U.S. investors, who now own some 12 percent of the company. Heading the list of non-German stockholders are the British, with 15 percent of the capital stock. Swiss investors are in fourth place. There are also significant holdings of Bayer shares in the other countries where Bayer has stock exchange listings.

Since the last survey was carried out in 1988, the total number of stockholders has declined by 80,000 to 295,000. At the same time the percentage of the stock held by institutional investors has grown, showing that individuals are increasingly investing in the stock market through mutual funds. 282,600 individuals in Germany and abroad hold 29 percent of the capital stock directly. This figure includes 56,000 company employees who together own about 4 percent of Bayer. No single holdings in excess of 5 percent were registered in the survey.

Foreign Stockholding by Country
% of Capital Stock

	1993	1988
United Kingdom	14.8	15.1
U.S.A.	11.5	4.8
Belgium	4.4	4.0
Switzerland, Liechtenstein	3.9	12.7
United Arab Emirates	1.6	0.8
Netherlands	1.2	1.9
Sweden	1.2	0.3
Japan	1.2	1.1
Luxembourg	1.1	0.8
France	1.0	2.1
124 (115) other countries	4.7	4.2
	46.6	**47.8**

Stock Ownership by Stockholder Group

	Number of Stockholders				% of Stock Held	
	1993	in %	1988	in %	1993	1988
Private Individuals	282,600	95.8	355,700	94.9	28.9	37.3
Insurance companies, banks	2,100	0.7	3,500	0.9	42.9	38.0
Mutual funds	1,600	0.5	1,100	0.3	18.6	10.1
Industry, commerce	4,500	1.5	6,000	1.6	3.3	8.5
Others	4,200	1.5	8,700	2.3	6.3	6.1
	295,000	**100.0**	**375,000**	**100.0**	**100.0**	**100.0**

Shareholder structure

With the assistance of banks in Germany and abroad, we conducted a survey of our shareholder structure as at October 1, 1990, which identified around 95% of our capital stock.

The survey confirmed the trend toward a continuing institutionalization of our shareholder structure. The proportion of capital stock held by German and foreign insurance companies, pension funds, investment companies and banks increased from 24% to 35%. Since 1986, the proportion of foreign institutional investors has grown about 120% from DM207 million to DM454 million in 1990, reflecting in part the growing interest of these investor groups in the German stock market following the country's unification. In all, around 44% of the capital stock is held by foreign shareholders.

In addition, the survey revealed for the first time a decline in non-institutional investors. However, with a share of 45% (1986: 52%), private shareholders still hold the largest portion of capital stock, representing the biggest single group of investors. Their number grew from 506,000 in 1986 to 533,000 in 1990, partly due to an increase in the number of our employees in Germany participating in the employee stock program.

Siemens AG now has a total of around 583,000 shareholders, an increase of 45,000 since the last survey in 1986 and twice as many as the 285,000 reported in the first survey conducted in 1970.

VEBA Shares Broadly Held

According to the most recent shareholder survey, carried out in February 1990, a good 540,000 people hold shares in VEBA. Some 52,000 of them are VEBA employees. Foreign investors hold 39.8% of the share capital (1986: 21.5%), while 53.6% (1986: 73.6%) is in the hands of domestic shareholders. 6.6% (1986: 4.9%) could not be accounted for in the survey (chart 19). The next shareholder survey is planned for 1993.

It is well known that there are extensive cross shareholdings in German companies. A Monopolies Commission Report disclosed that in 1984 there were 88 cross shareholdings arranged among Germany's top 100 companies. Traditionally a large German company has had one bank as a major shareholder. For example, Deutsche Bank have owned 28% of Daimler-Benz equity, but this fact is not usually disclosed in the company's annual financial reports. German banks as a group own more than 25% of at least 33 major industrial companies.

One reason why banks in Germany have acquired large blocks of equity shares in companies has been to help those companies during periods of financial difficulties. In fact the large private banks during the 1980s were pursuing a policy of reducing their holdings of equity in companies where they were holding more than 25% of the shares.

Of course as well as banks holding large blocks of shares in a company, there is often a holding of a large block by another company. Again the typical annual financial report of a company does not disclose which other company or companies is a major shareholder. Some indications can, however, be obtained from observing who are members of the supervisory board.

In 1984 the supervisory board of 79 of the largest 100 German companies had at least one member who was a member of the management board of another top 100 company. There is a relatively small circle of German top executives who sit on the boards of other companies, a system of interlocking boards often based on interlocking shareholdings.

France

A number of companies do disclose who their principal shareholders are, as in Extract 5.6 from the accounts of Elf Sanofi.

Deutsche Bank, which holds 28 % of our share capital, has been a large shareholder of Daimler-Benz since the late twenties. The Mercedes-Benz Aktiengesellschaft Holding (MAH), Frankfurt am Main, has held a 25.23 % stake since it was founded in 1975. Stern Autombil-Beteiligungsgesellschaft und Stella Automobil-Beteiligungsgesellschaft each hold a 25 % stake in MAH.

Stern and Stella enjoy an institutional following who consider their investments on a long-term basis. The remaining 50 % of the MAH shares are broadly distributed and belong to about 50,000 shareholders. This ensures that no single shareholder is able to dominate the MAH.

The third largest shareholder is the government of Kuwait, whose equity stake amounts to about 14 %. After the end of the Gulf war, it has again been speculated that Kuwait would have to sell substantial portions of its large-scale shareholdings for the purpose of financing the continuing burden of reconstruction. The Kuwait Investment Office, which is domiciled in London and which also is administering the Daimler-Benz package, has let us know that a sale of Daimler-Benz shares is not being contemplated.

The remaining 33 % of our share capital is widely held by about 300,000 investors both at home and abroad. If the scattered ownership of MAH is taken into account as well, about 45 % of our share capital is then, directly or indirectly, broadly distributed.

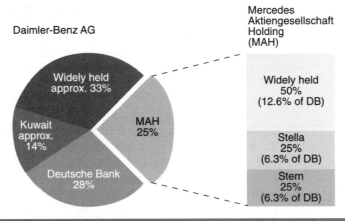

An examination of the accounts of SNEA reveals the following shareholdings:

State	54%	Unit trusts	6%
Foreigners	20%	French institutions	6%
Private shareholders	14%		

Clearly the corporate power in SNEA lies with the government, who also have control of ELF Sanofi's share ownership.

Corporate Governance

The principal stockholders of Elf Sanofi are:

- Société Nationale Elf Aquitaine (S.N.E.A.) . . . 45.94%

- SAFREP (a wholly-owned

  subsidiary of S.N.E.A.) 14.91%

No other stockholder has declared an interest in excess of
2.5%.

as at December 31, 1991

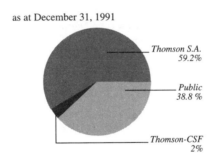

Thomson S.A.
59.2%

Public
38.8%

Thomson-CSF
2%

Ownership thresholds – The Company's by-laws provide that any shareholder or group of share-holders must inform the Company whenever they increase or decrease their holdings in the Company to 1% of the total number of shares or a multiple of that figure. The Company has been informed of no such changes in 1991.
In addition, to the knowledge of the Company, no shareholder other than Thomson S.A. holds more than 5% of voting rights.

Clearing house inquiry into the identity of owners of shares in bearer form and the number of Thomson-CSF shares held by each shareholder: Conducted by the Paris clearing house (SICOVAM) on December 31, 1991, this inquiry focused primarily on large portfolios. It identified the owners of 31 million shares (72% of the float), of whom 55% are foreign and 45% French shareholders. Mutual funds and French institutional investors have increased their holdings between December 1990 and December 1991.

■ *Stock options:* At end-1991, Thomson-CSF held 2,230,117 of its own shares on account of the two stock options plans detailed below:

Pechiney report that 74% of their common shares were held by the Republic of France and 26% by 45 banks and other financial institutions, including one bank and one insurance company, each with 10% of the common shares. It is the non-voting preferred shares of Pechiney (being one third the number of ordinary shares) which are held by the public and are quoted on the stock market. The situation in Pechiney is common to that in other companies which are wholly or partly state owned. Rhône-Poulenc was nationalized in 1982. It has a similar complicated capital structure.

Thomson-CSF show a large holding by Thomson SA, which is itself largely state owned. Thomson refer to an enquiry to establish the ownership of bearer shares, a similar exercise to that which is undertaken by some companies in Germany (see Extract 5.7).

Extract 5.8 – Royal Dutch/Shell Group of Companies 1992 accounts, Highlights.

STRUCTURE OF THE GROUP

The Royal Dutch/Shell Group of Companies has grown out of an alliance made in 1907 between Royal Dutch Petroleum Company and The "Shell" Transport and Trading Company, p.l.c., by which the two companies agreed to merge their interests on a 60:40 basis while keeping their separate identities. Today the title describes a group of companies engaged in the oil, natural gas, chemicals, coal and metals businesses throughout the greater part of the world.

Parent Companies

As Parent Companies, Royal Dutch Petroleum Company and The "Shell" Transport and Trading Company, p.l.c. do not themselves directly engage in operational activities. They are public companies, one domiciled in the Netherlands, the other in the United Kingdom.
The Parent Companies directly or indirectly own the shares in the Group Holding Companies but are not themselves part of the Group. They appoint Directors to the Boards of the Group Holding Companies, from which they receive income in the form of dividends.

Shareholdings

There are some 325,000 shareholders of Royal Dutch and some 300,000 of Shell Transport. Shares of one or both companies are listed and traded on stock exchanges in eight European countries and in the USA.

The estimated geographical distribution of shareholdings at the end of 1992 was:

	Royal Dutch	Shell Transport	Combined
	%	%	%
United Kingdom	1	97	39
USA	42	3	26
Netherlands	36	*	21
Switzerland	13	*	8
France	4	*	3
Germany	2	*	1
Belgium	1	*	1
Luxembourg	1	*	1
Others	*	*	*

* Less than 1%

Carrefour, a large publicly owned company in France, gives no detailed breakdown of share ownership. It does, however, report who its major shareholder is. In the 1991 accounts in the section on shareholder information, it reports: 'The de Noyange Group's interest in Carrefour increased from 18.45% at 1990 year end to 18.58% at 1991 year end.'

Extract 5.9 – W.H. Smith Group plc 1993 accounts, Shareholders.

At 29 May 1993 the analysis of the Company's ordinary shareholders was:

	'A' Ordinary Shares		'B' Ordinary Shares		Number of shareholdings	
	Number	%	Number	%	'A'	'B'
Private holders	26,648,008	10.89	58,067,862	41.71	17,099	1,306
Banks and nominees	157,336,076	64.29	60,962,260	43.79	2,671	109
Insurance companies	32,960,647	13.47	7,877,971	5.66	117	7
Investment trusts	13,709,576	5.60	5,362,160	3.85	349	15
Pension funds	9,040,338	3.69	5,772,500	4.15	37	7
Commercial and industrial companies	813,177	0.33	29,682	0.02	160	7
Miscellaneous	4,239,252	1.73	1,146,315	0.82	108	6
	244,747,074	100.00	139,218,750	100.00	20,541	1,457

Notes:

(i) Private holders includes trustee holdings for the W H Smith Group Profitshare Scheme of 4,003,345 'A' Ordinary Shares.

(ii) Miscellaneous includes charities, local authorities, hospitals and colleges.

Details of directors' shareholdings and share options are shown on page 61 and in note 21 to the financial statements on page 56.

Details of other shareholdings which at 6 August 1993 amounted to 3% or more of the total number of issued 'A' Ordinary Shares or 'B' Ordinary Shares and of which notification has been received by the Company are:

		Number of shares held			
	Class of share	Beneficially	As a trustee	Total	% of class
The Prudential Corporation group of companies	A	13,120,238	–	13,120,238	5.36
The Prudential Corporation group of companies	B	8,960,472	–	8,960,472	6.43
J J Cotterell	B	–	11,040,000(a)	11,040,000	7.92
Dowager Viscountess Hambleden	B	4,170,770	23,170,858(b)	27,341,628	19.63
Viscount Hambleden	B	–	27,423,448(c)	27,423,448	19.69
W H Smith Pension Trust	B	15,248,810	–	15,248,810	10.95
J H Wise	B	–	11,227,500(d)	11,227,500	8.06

Notes:

(a) 11,040,000 shares held jointly with J H Wise.

(b) 23,114,548 shares held jointly with Viscount Hambleden, The Hon. Philip Smith and P J C Troughton and 56,310 shares held jointly with Viscount Hambleden.

(c) 23,114,548 shares held jointly with the Dowager Viscountess Hambleden, The Hon. Philip Smith and P J C Troughton, 4,059,400 shares held jointly with P J C Troughton and 56,310 shares held jointly with the Dowager Viscountess Hambleden.

(d) 11,040,000 shares held jointly with J J Cotterell.

They also make reference to company by-laws which require shareholders to report any holding of 1% or more of shares. Thomson-CSF had a similar requirement. It is necessary for shareholders to inform the company of such a holding because with bearer shares, the company does not know if any other company or investor is building up a substantial shareholding. The company does not, however, disclose the existence of such holdings in its financial report.

The Netherlands

No information on shareholdings is given by the vast majority of Dutch companies. The Royal Dutch/Shell Group of companies do not provide details of who owns their shares, but do give an interesting and unusual estimated geographical breakdown of the distribution of ownership of the shares of the two companies (Extract 5.8).

UK

In contrast to the lack of information given by companies in most European countries, UK companies give quite detailed disclosure. This analysis is usually by size of holdings and sometimes by category of shareholders, with individual shareholdings of over 3% being listed. Details from the annual reports of W.H. Smith and Yorkshire Chemicals are shown in Extracts 5.9 and 5.10.

Extract 5.10 – Yorkshire Chemicals plc 1992 accounts, Directors' Report.

SUBSTANTIAL SHAREHOLDINGS

As at 19th February 1993 (the latest practicable date prior to the printing of this report) the directors had been notified of, or were aware of, the following shareholdings representing three per cent. or more of the issued share capital of the company.

	Ordinary Shares	Percentage of Ordinary Share Capital
Prudential Corporation plc (beneficial and non-beneficial)	2,344,650	6.18
Schroders plc (non-beneficial)	1,948,000	5.13
Barclays Bank PLC (non-beneficial)	1,810,814	4.77
City of Bradford Metropolitan Council	1,720,000	4.53
Cheshire County Council	1,635,248	4.31
TSB Group plc (non-beneficial)	1,462,200	3.85
M&G Group plc (non-beneficial)	1,310,000	3.45
Australian Mutual Provident Society	1,264,000	3.33
British Coal Pension Fund	1,240,862	3.27
Scottish Amicable Investment Managers Limited (non-beneficial)	1,138,336	3.00

Save as set out above, the directors have not been advised of any person who, directly or indirectly, is interested in three per cent. or more of the issued share capital of the Company and are not aware of any person or persons who, directly or indirectly, jointly or severally, exercise or could exercise control over the Company.

Italy

Little or no information is supplied by most Italian companies with regard to share ownership. It should be appreciated that Italian companies are tightly controlled. By the early 1990s only seven companies had offered more than 50% of their shares to the public, but five of these still have majority control exercised by a small group. In only two companies, therefore, were a majority of shares widely held.

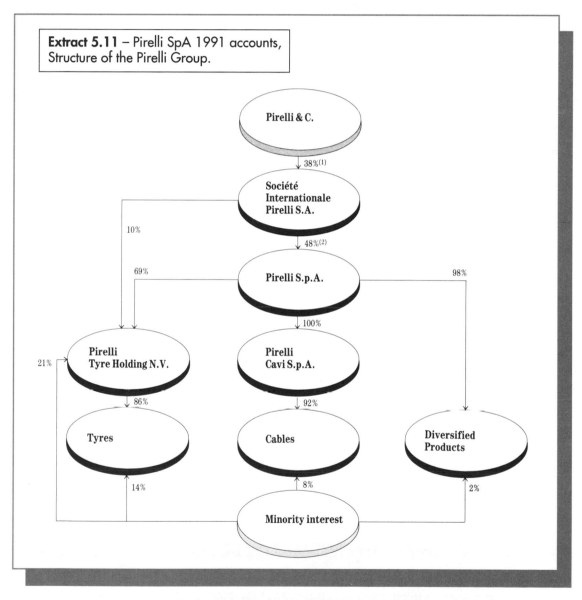

Extract 5.11 – Pirelli SpA 1991 accounts, Structure of the Pirelli Group.

In Extract 5.11, certain details regarding the structure of the membership of the Pirelli Group are shown. In terms of market capitalization Pirelli ranks about eighth largest company by size in Italy. It has ambitions to be seen as a major international firm with its shares traded in international financial markets. It therefore supplies much more information than is usual in Italy. Pirelli & Co. (the private family company) owns 38% of Société Internationale Pirelli SA which owns 49% of Pirelli SpA (the quoted company). However, this does not mean that outsiders own 51% of the listed company as there are various other controlled holdings.

The system of corporate governance varies from country to country. In Italy there is not the same level of pressure for the public disclosure of information as exists in the UK. There is not such a separation of ownership and control, and there are more informal information channels.

Spain

In Spain there is more disclosure than in most of the other countries being considered, but there is no consistency in the amount of information disclosed.

State ownership is revealed by FOCOEX (Extract 5.12). Banco Santander disclose their largest shareholdings, plus an intriguing geographical breakdown of shareholdings as distributed by region within Spain (Extract 5.13).

Board of Directors

Up to this point in the chapter we have been concerned with who owns a particular company. Corporate governance is concerned with the relationship between the owners of a company and those who control the company. We now turn to those who control the company, namely the directors.

Extract 5.14 – Akzo NV 1991 accounts, Management and Supervision.

Supervisory Council

G. Kraijenhoff, Chairman
F.H. Fentener van Vlissingen, Deputy Chairman
H. Kopper, Deputy Chairman
A. Batenburg
J.G.A. Gandois
H.H. van den Kroonenberg
H.A. van Stiphout
C. van Veen
H.G. Zempelin

Board of Management

A.A. Loudon, Chairman
C.J.A. van Lede
M.D. Westermann

Secretary

Th.J.A.W. Schregardus

In theory directors run the company in the interests of shareholders. Economic theory suggests the corporate objective should be to maximize shareholders' wealth, and in theory directors are agents of the company. Directors clearly, however, have their own interests to consider. In order to achieve 'goal congruence' between owner and controller some reward structure is considered desirable that ties together the interests of the two groups.

We will now examine what information is made available to the owners of the company as to who are the directors of the company and the information on the rewards they receive. When an analyst is examining a company it is important to observe qualitative factors as well as quantitative. The future success of a company depends on the quality of the decision-makers. Studies on failed companies point to the significance to success or failure of the people involved in decision-making. It is factors such as bad investment decisions, lack of financial control and dominant chief executives that lead to failure. The accounting numbers with which this book is concerned are the results of bad decisions and lack of financial expertise. They are a symptom of failure, not the cause. An analysis of a company needs therefore to be concerned with who are the directors, what is the relationship between them and what is the forum for making decisions. The analyst needs to be aware of how many of the directors are insiders and how many outsiders.

Extract 5.15 – Pirelli SpA 1991 accounts, Board of Directors.

Board of Directors

Chairman	Leopoldo Pirelli*
Executive Deputy Chairman	Marco Tronchetti Provera*
Deputy Chairmen	Alberto Pirelli* Filiberto Pittini*
Managing Directors	Piero Sierra* Marco Tronchetti Provera*
Directors	Henry C.M. Bodmer Carlo De Benedetti Alberto Falck Luigi Orlando Giampiero Pesenti Ambrogio Puri Cesare Romiti Alfred Sarasin* Vincenzo Sozzani*
Secretary of the Board	Adalberto Castagna

* Members of the Executive Committee

Companies in all the countries in the Community provide a list of the names of members of their board of directors. With the two-tier system names are given for both the supervisory board and the board of management.

Ernst von Siemens, Dr.-Ing. E. h.
Munich
Honorary Chairman
(deceased December 31, 1990)

Heribald Närger, Dr. jur.
Munich
Chairman

Rudolf Mooshammer
Munich
Deputy Chairman
Mechanic

Wolfgang Schieren, Dr. jur.
Munich
Deputy Chairman
President of the Board of Management,
Allianz Aktiengesellschaft, Munich
(until October 1, 1991)
Chairman of the Supervisory Board,
Allianz Aktiengesellschaft, Munich

Alfred Bock
Erlangen
Technician

Ulrich Cartellieri, Dr. jur.
Frankfurt on Main
Member of the Board of Management,
Deutsche Bank AG, Frankfurt on Main

Rolf Diel
Düsseldorf
Chairman of the Supervisory Board,
Dresdner Bank AG, Düsseldorf

Eberhard Fehrmann
(until March 31, 1991)
Bremen
Managing Director,
Chamber of Salaried Employees, Bremen

Alfons Graf
Amberg
Master Toolmaker

Herbert Grünewald, Prof. Dr. rer. nat.
Leverkusen
Chairman of the Supervisory Board,
Bayer AG, Leverkusen

Maximilian Hackl, Dr. jur.
Munich
Chairman of the Supervisory Board,
Bayerische Vereinsbank AG, Munich

Heinz Hawreliuk
Frankfurt on Main
Head of the Shop Stewards Department
on the Executive Committee, IG Metall

Ralf Heckmann
Munich
Telecommunications Installer

Detlef Kreyenberg
Munich
Dipl.-Ing.

Reimar Lüst, Prof. Dr. rer. nat.
Bonn
President of the Alexander von Humbolt
Foundation, Bonn-Bad Godesberg

Werner Neugebauer
Munich
Regional Manager for Munich, IG Metall

Franz Rehm
Munich
Precision Mechanic

Helmut Reithmeier
Munich
Electrical Technician

Alexander von Seidel
Düsseldorf

Nikolaus Senn, Dr. jur.
Zurich
Chairman of the Board of Administration,
Union Bank of Switzerland, Zurich

Dieter Spethmann, Prof. Dr. jur.
Düsseldorf
Chairman of the Management Board,
(until March 21, 1991)
Thyssen AG vorm. August Thyssen-Hütte,
Düsseldorf

Horst Wagner
(as of May 23, 1991)
Berlin
Regional Manager for Berlin-Brandenburg,
IG Metall

What varies from country to country is the amount of detail given relating to each director. In most countries just a list of names is given, and no information on the position of the person or their qualifications is provided in the accounts. A typical example of a simple listing is that in Extracts 5.14 and 5.15 for Akzo in the Netherlands and Pirelli in Italy.

At the other extreme are the listings shown by German companies, an example being the disclosure of Seimens (Extract 5.16). This enables

President and
Chief Executive Officer
Karlheinz Kaske, Dr.-Ing.
Special responsibilities:
Corporate Research and Development,
Corporate Relations, Berlin Executive
Offices, Semiconductors

Deputy Chairman
of the Managing Board
Heinrich von Pierer, Dr. jur.
(as of July 2, 1991)
Power Generation (KWU) (until July 2, 1991)
Special responsibilities: International Regions,
Power Generation (KWU),
Power Transmission and Distribution

Karl-Hermann Baumann, Dr. rer. oec.
Corporate Finance

Hans Baur, Dr.-Ing.
Special responsibilities: Public Communication
Networks, Private Communication Systems,
Defense Electronics

Hermann Franz
Corporate Planning and Development
Special responsibilities: Drives and
Standard Products, Automotive Systems,
Medical Engineering, Osram

Claus Kessler, Dr.-Ing.
Corporate Production and Logistics
Special responsibilities: Passive Components
and Electron Tubes, Electromechanical
Components, Audio and Video Systems
(as of April 1, 1991)

Gerhard Kühne, Dr. jur.
Corporate Human Resources
Special responsibilities: Centralized Services
(as of April 1, 1991: including Domestic
Regional Administration)

Horst Langer, Dr.-Ing.
Special responsibilities: Siemens Corporation
(until December 31, 1990: Chief Executive
Officer of Siemens Corporation),
Industrial and Building Systems, Automation,
Transportation Systems

Hans-Gerd Neglein
Regional Administration
Special responsibilities: Audio and Video
Systems (until March 31, 1991),
Consultant to corporate management
(until September 30, 1991)

Hans Günter Danielmeyer,
Prof. Dr. rer. nat.
Corporate Research and Development

Erwin N. Hardt, Dr. oec. publ.
Public Communication Networks

Hans Hirschmann
Power Generation (KWU)

Adolf Hüttl
Power Generation (KWU)
(as of July 2, 1991)

Volker Jung, Dr. Eng. h. c.
International Regions
(as of July 2, 1991)

Wolfgang Keller, Dr.-Ing.
Power Generation (KWU)

Eberhard Kill
Industrial and Building Systems

Jürgen Knorr
Semiconductors

Werner Maly
Medical Engineering

Anton Peisl, Dr. oec. publ.
Corporate Relations

Peter von Siemens
Centralized Services Munich

Carl-Heiner Thomas
Drives and Standard Products

the readers of the accounts to see the 'qualifications' of each person who is a member of the board. With most German companies it demonstrates the interlocking membership of such supervisory boards.

In the UK in the past little information was provided other than the name and, when relevant, the title of the person. There are of course exceptions to this – ICI, for example, give details of the major positions held by each director outside ICI. As with German companies, this can often reveal an element of interlocking directorship (Extract 5.17). The information disclosed on this matter has improved following the Cadbury Committee recommendations.

In the UK and Germany it is popular with many companies to show photographs of board members, either individually or collectively. The reason for this is unclear, unless the respectable appearance of the board members is designed to give shareholders confidence. One suspects in some parts of the world, for example the USA, this visual presentation is designed to show the ethnic mix of the board or the sexual balance. This, however, is unlikely to be the case in Europe.

Sir Patrick Meaney
Aged 66. A Non-Executive Director since 1981. He is Chairman of The Rank Organisation Plc, Chairman of A. Kershaw & Sons Plc, and a Deputy Chairman of Midland Bank plc. He is also a Director of MEPC plc and of Tarmac PLC.

Lord Chilver, FRS
Aged 65. A Non-Executive Director since 1990. He is Chairman of ECC Group plc, Chairman of Milton Keynes Development Corporation, and a Director of Porton International plc.

Sir Denys Henderson
Aged 59. A Director since 1980 and Chairman since 1987. He has particular responsibility for Group strategies and Group Public Affairs. He is also a non-executive Director of Barclays PLC and The RTZ Corporation PLC.

R C Hampel
Aged 59. A Director since 1985 and Chief Operating Officer since October 1991. He is responsible to the Chairman for the operations of the Group and for Acquisitions and Divestments. He is also a non-executive Director of British Aerospace PLC and the Commercial Union Assurance Company plc.

C Hampson
Aged 60. A Director since 1987, he currently has Group overview responsibility for the industrial chemicals business and is Non-Executive Chairman of ICI Chemicals & Polymers Ltd. He is Group Safety, Health and Environment Director. He is also a non-executive Director of Costain Group PLC.

T H Wyman
Aged 62. A Non-Executive Director since 1986. He is also a Director of American Telephone and Telegraph Company, General Motors Corporation, United Biscuits (Holdings) plc and S. G. Warburg Group plc.

F Whiteley
Aged 61. A Director since 1979 and Deputy Chairman since 1987. He is currently Group Personnel Director and has Group overview responsibility for Engineering.

Sir Antony Pilkington
Aged 56. Appointed a Non-Executive Director in March 1991. He is Chairman of Pilkington plc and a Director of National Westminster Bank plc.

J D F Barnes, CBE
Aged 56. A Director since 1986, he is currently Territorial Director for the Western Hemisphere and is Group Planning Director. He is also a non-executive Director of THORN EMI plc.

Sir Jeremy Morse, KCMG
Aged 63. A Non-Executive Director since 1981. He is Chairman of Lloyds Bank Plc.

Miss Ellen R Schneider-Lenné
Aged 49. Appointed a Non-Executive Director in March 1991. She is a member of the Board of Managing Directors of Deutsche Bank AG and a Director of Morgan Grenfell Group plc.

C M Short
Aged 57. A Director since 1990, he is currently Group Finance and Group Information Services Director.

A T G Rodgers
Aged 51. Appointed a Director in January 1991, he is currently Territorial Director for the Eastern Hemisphere and has overview responsibility for Group Advertising.

P Doyle, CBE
Aged 53. A Director since 1989, he is currently Group Research and Technology Director. He is also a member of the Medical Research Council and of the Prime Minister's Advisory Council on Science and Technology.

W G L L Kiep
Aged 66. A Non-Executive Director since 1982. He is Managing Partner of Gradmann & Höller, the German insurance group, Chairman of the Supervisory Board of Glunz AG, a Director of Marsh & McLennan Companies, Inc., New York, a Director of the Bank of Montreal and a member of the Supervisory Board of Volkswagen AG.

P A Volcker
Aged 64. A Non-Executive Director since 1988. He is Chairman of James D. Wolfensohn Inc. and Professor of International Economic Policy at Princeton University. He is also a Director of Nestlé S.A., The Prudential Insurance Company of America and of MBIA Inc.

The disclosure of any academic and/or professional qualifications of the board members varies from country to country. In the UK it is common to indicate if they have professional accounting qualifications, but not to give their scientific qualifications. This could be a significant point, illustrating that accounts are prepared to satisfy different user groups in different countries. Bayer, for example, disclose that on their supervisory board they have 9 out of 22 members with doctorates, three being professors. On their management board 10 out of 21 members have doctorates.

By contrast, the 1991 accounts of ICI show photographs of the 16 directors. Brief biographical notes on each director do not disclose whether or not they hold academic or professional qualifications. Presumably some do, but one wonders why it is not thought to be worthwhile to tell the reader of the accounts about this fact. It is disclosed, however, that seven of the twelve hold director appointments in major banks and another two of the twelve directorships in insurance companies.

Three-quarters of the ICI board are obviously qualified from a financial point of view. One would have thought that one of the leading scientific-based companies would have thought it worthwhile mentioning whether their board members held scientific qualifications. However, one member of the ICI board is a professor – a professor of international economic policy in the USA.

In case it is thought Siemens are an exception amongst German companies, this is not so. On Bayer's board of management of 11, they have two professors plus six doctorates. On the Hoechst board of management of 13, there are three professors plus six doctorates.

Extract 5.16 earlier showed the supervisory board and managing board of Siemens. It will be seen that on the supervisory board, as well as chairmen of banks, one finds master toolmakers and precision mechanics. A similar mix is found on the supervisory boards of other German companies. Table 5.1 on page 93 shows the composition of the supervisory boards of the largest 100 German enterprises – the rich variety of backgrounds of directors can be seen.

As mentioned in the introduction to this section, the information most British companies supply about their directors is surprising. It is geared to impress a financial community. The information disclosed by ICI is reproduced in Extract 5.17. This is representative – in fact ICI disclose more than most UK companies. There are of course exceptions – Yorkshire Chemicals give a fuller description of their directors, and it is revealed that apart from accountants, secretaries and economists, they have a chemist and a production engineer (Extract 5.18).

The British and German companies in fact reveal more than those in the other four countries being examined. In France, Italy, the Netherlands and Spain usually only the names of the directors are given without details of their background or of any other directorships they hold. Extract 5.19 shows the entire details given with regard to Pechiney; this is representative of the disclosure on this matter by French companies. It is similar to the listings to be found in Spanish and Italian companies.

The typical UK board contains a number of non-executive directors (NEDs). The Cadbury Committee 'believes that the calibre of the non-executive members of the board is of special importance in setting and maintaining standards of corporate governance'. They recommend that their calibre and numbers should be such that 'their views will carry significant weight in the board's decisions'. The committee recommends that there should be at least three non-executives, and that they should be able to bring independent judgement to bear in board decisions.

This emphasis on the role of NEDs followed a number of financial scandals in UK companies. It was felt that if NEDs took a more active role these scandals could be avoided. The user of accounts needs to be able to ascertain whether the NEDs on a board are sufficiently independent and of the right quality to be able to influence policy and control.

The German and Dutch system of supervisory boards is a different method of corporate control. An interesting observation on the merits of the two systems was made by the finance director of a company from what was at the time Czechoslovakia. The role of the non-executive in the UK had been explained at a seminar, and the local director commented:

You are telling us that the owners of British companies, the institutions, act through NEDs who they have not chosen. That these men are selected by the people they have to at the same time work with and monitor. That they are those whose salaries they fix. They have to be independent even though fully responsible, yet also give

---

Extract 5.18 – Yorkshire Chemicals plc 1992 accounts, Directors.

Riccardo Caresani (69). Joined the group in 1974 to establish marketing operations in Italy. Appointed non-executive director of Yorkshire in 1988 with special responsibilities for advising on the further development of the European Subsidiary network.

John F. Dawson (53). Colour chemist and Fellow of the Royal Society of Chemistry. Joined the company in 1961. Varied senior level experience of research and development, production and general management. Appointed group technical director in 1976.

John Walker (52). Joined the company in the production department in 1961. Became production executive of colours division in 1982. Appointed a divisional chief executive in 1985, group director in 1986, and operations director Europe in 1990.

Malcolm J. Wilson (44). Chartered Accountant. MA in Economics and Jurisprudence. Substantial experience within large multi-national groups. Joined Yorkshire as finance director on 1st November 1991.

Extract 5.19 – Pechiney Group 1990 accounts, Organisation of the Group.

Board of Directors

Jean Gandois, Chairman	Yves Quéré
Raymond Barbier	Claude Labbé
Christian Bècle	André Levy-Lang
Pierre de Boissieu	Claude Mandil
Pierre-Michel Chabaud	Philippe Remond*
Robert Dupont	Antoine Riboud
Fernand Engler	Felix Rohatyn
Jean-Pierre Falque-Pierrotin	Denis Samuel-Lajeunesse**
Michel Garnier	Louis Schweitzer

good advice and be good company men. And they are part time. This is voluntary, and all the papers are full of British company scandals where it seems the non-executives either did nothing or were not aware of what was happening.'

The Czechoslovakian director concluded: 'We Czechs are just ordinary people, so we shall have to take lessons from the likes of Volkswagen.'[4]

Disclosure of Amount of Shares and Options Held by Directors

In the UK the Companies Act requires information to be disclosed in the annual report on the interests of each director in the share capital and debentures of the company. This clearly applies not only to the holding of shares but also share options. UK companies therefore provide full information on this point. See, for example, the extracts from the accounts of Marks & Spencer (Extract 5.20).

It is unusual to find this amount of information in the accounts of companies from the other countries being considered, with the exception of Spain. Banco Santander provide a detailed breakdown of the shares held by directors (Extract 5.21). As mentioned earlier they also provide a breakdown of shareholdings by size and region and disclose who are their major shareholders. In the other countries the law does not require such disclosure and companies do not volunteer this information.

Although it is only in the UK and Spain that it is common to give details of actual shareholdings of directors, in the other four countries being studied reference is often made in the accounts to share option schemes for executives, key employees or employees. It seems to be increasingly common for companies to offer some or all of their employees and executives shares in the company. Sometimes such share offers are at a discount on market price, sometimes not. In some countries there are tax advantages in taking up the options, in some not.

In all countries insufficient information is given to enable the reader of the accounts to understand fully what is really happening. A number of companies across countries give sufficient information to whet the appetite but no more.

Share options when exercised will of course result in directors holding shares, but as explained above, in four of the countries we are not told of the actual holdings of directors collectively or individually. This is assuming of course that directors are classed as executives or key employees.

The extracts from the Marks & Spencer 1992 accounts illustrate the problem of identifying the value, realized and potential, of the option scheme to directors. Extract 5.20 shows the shares accrued by directors at the beginning and end of the financial year. It also shows the number of options held at the beginning of the year and the number granted in the year and exercised or lapsed in the year. In one of the notes in their accounts they provide a great amount of detail on the option schemes, with details of the option (exercise) prices. But it is not possible to link the two tables and so ascertain the profit made by an individual director on exercising options (Extract 5.22). The Marks & Spencer notes on this topic are typical of those found in the UK. There are, however, a

26 Directors' interests in shares and debentures

The beneficial interests of the directors and their families in the shares of the Company and its subsidiaries, together with their interests as trustees of both charitable and other trusts, are shown below. These include options granted under the Savings Related Share Option, Approved Senior Staff Share Option, and Delayed Profit Sharing Schemes. Non-executive directors are not eligible for the Approved Senior Staff Scheme. Further information regarding employee share options is given in note 12 on pages 41 and 42.

Interests in the Company

Ordinary shares — beneficial and family interests

	Shares		Options			
	At 1 April 1991 or date of appointment	At 31 March 1992	At 1 April 1991 or date of appointment	Granted in year	Exercised/ lapsed in year	At 31 March 1992
Sir Richard Greenbury	44,311	21,062	1,012,236	344,594	984,751	372,079
C V Silver	40,904	47,106	917,387	256,924	878,422	295,889
J K Oates	13,990	17,739	704,800	238,670	80,000	863,470
N L Colne	61,725	66,479	676,560	147,827	158,394	665,993
R W C Colvill	10,285	13,230	379,783	125,220	94,000	411,003
C Littmoden	14,989	19,214	224,800	92,668	70,473	264,995
J A Lusher	24,323	32,398	563,019	146,284	579,886	129,417
P G McCracken	7,658	8,922	248,460	143,888	180,992	211,356
S J Sacher	396,150	399,194	463,549	144,933	143,912	464,570
P L Salsbury	16,307	22,069	414,215	95,677	209,347	300,545
The Hon David Sieff	292,913	296,402	684,352	106,776	294,661	496,467
A K P Smith	183,299	186,113	881,353	111,745	298,884	694,214
P P D Smith	8,533	7,393	243,585	133,479	79,240	297,824
A Z Stone	8,628	11,232	283,657	119,942	103,745	299,854
D G Trangmar	34,134	38,045	437,286	155,940	489,245	103,981
Dr D V Atterton	4,204	4,204	—	—	—	—
Sir Martin Jacomb	—	6,665	—	—	—	—
D G Lanigan	2,631	3,103	6,181	3,275	—	9,456
D R Susman	57,386	58,863	—	—	—	—
The Rt Hon The Baroness Young	2,508	3,847	—	—	—	—

Ordinary shares — trustee interests

	At 31 March 1992		At 1 April 1991	
	Charitable Trusts Shares	Other Trusts Shares	Charitable Trusts Shares	Other Trusts Shares
S J Sacher	205,000	170,118	391,690	171,368
The Hon David Sieff	20,000	87,542	30,000	67,242
D R Susman	570,100	—	570,100	—

Preference shares and debentures

At 31 March 1992 N L Colne owned 500 4·9 per cent preference shares (last year 500 shares). Mr C Littmoden owned 10 4·9% preference shares and 10 7% (at date of appointment 10 4·9% preference shares and 10 7% preference shares). None of the other directors had an interest in any preference shares or in the debentures of the Company.

Interests in subsidiaries

None of the directors had any interests in any subsidiaries at the beginning or end of the year.

Between the end of the financial year and one month prior to the date of the Notice of Meeting, there have been no changes in the directors' interests in shares and debentures of, and in options granted by, the Company and its subsidiaries.

Extract 5.21 – Banco Santander 1991 accounts, Management Report.

DIRECTORS

	Direct Shareholding	Indirect Shareholding	Total
Emilio Botín-Sanz de Sautuola y García de los Ríos	340,354	173,036	513,390
Jaime Botín-Sanz de Sautuola y García de los Ríos	222,286	76,415	298,701
Rodrigo Echenique Gordillo	11,308	600	11,908
Ignacio Soler de la Riva	1,283	964,146	965,429
Juan José Martínez Vázquez	14,227	—	14,227
César Martínez Beascoechea	25,780	—	25,780
Ramón Quijano Secades	33,022	12,707	45,729
Joaquín Chapaprieta Ornstein	588	—	588
Angel Jado Becerro de Bengoa	332,157	—	332,157
Juan Secades y González-Camino	52,244	—	52,244
Dimas Blanco Valdivielso	6,280	—	6,280
Rafael Alonso Botín	9,694	—	9,694
José Luis Díaz Fernández	4,492	—	4,492
Mr. John J. Creedon	972	505,221 (1)	506,193
Matías Rodríguez Inciarte	4,198	—	4,198
Joaquín Folch-Rusiñol Corachán	402,160	454,116	856,276
Sir Michael Herries (Royal Bank of Scotland)	—	—	—
Rt. Hon. George Younger (Royal Bank of Scotland)	—	1,620,650 (2)	1,620,050
Ana P. Botín-Sanz de Sautuola y O'Shea	965	661	1,626
Emilio Botín-Sanz de Sautuola y O'Shea	300	—	300
Juan Rodríguez Inciarte	2,961	—	2,961
	1,465,271	**3,807,552**	**5,272,823**

(1) Owned by Metropolitan Life Insurance.
(2) Owned by The Royal Bank of Scotland.

small number of companies that disclose the complete picture – typical of these is Wolseley (Extract 5.23).

In criticizing the practice of most companies in the UK it needs to be recognized that UK companies are much more open in what they disclose on this matter than companies from other European countries.

Bayer, Siemens and VEBA make reference to employee share schemes. Siemens started their scheme in 1969. In 1991 they disclose that they purchased their own shares at a price of DM 586 in order to be able to offer them to employees at a preferential price (DM 322). The accounts disclose, however, that such action is being contested by shareholders, and they explain that they are having to devise a new scheme for future years (Extract 5.24). Bayer reveal that employees of the company now own between 4% and 5% of the total shares, as a result of their option scheme (Extract 5.25).

Reference is often made in company accounts to executive share option schemes. Elf explain that the first phase of their plan would benefit 291 beneficiaries, and the second phase would benefit 135. It is most unusual in any of the countries for the number of beneficiaries to be given.

The Elf executives should indeed 'benefit', for the exercise price for the options under the first phase is FF 130, and the second phase FF 187. During 1991 the company was purchasing its own shares in the stock market at an average price of FF 291.

Thomson-CSF provide quite an amount of information about two stock option schemes they have for 'officers' of the company. We are not told who the officers are, and cannot work out the extent to which an officer might benefit (Extract 5.26). This is typical of the level of disclosure on the matter in French company accounts.

In the Netherlands no details are usually given of the actual share-holding of directors, but reference is often made to stock options held by executives and other key employees. The 'Shell' Transport and Trading Company provides a footnote in their accounts explaining a certain amount about their scheme. The information is, however, very limited, and does not indicate who holds options, or the value or potential value of such options (Extract 5.27).

A similar note appears in the accounts of Akzo, referring again to key employees. They did disclose the exercise price of such options (Extract 5.28). The 1990 accounts of Daf show such a scheme exists for directors and senior officers. Unfortunately in 1993 Daf went into receivership, and so such options probably resulted in no benefits.

Directors' Remuneration

The financial rewards to directors come in a number of forms including:

- fees;
- basic remuneration (salary);
- performance related bonuses;
- pension contributions;
- executive share option schemes;
- cheap loans.

12 Share schemes

a Profit sharing:

The Trustees of the United Kingdom Employees' Profit Sharing Schemes have been allocated £16·2 million (last year £15·3 million) with which to subscribe for ordinary shares in the Company. The price of each share is 329·0p, being the average market price for the three dealing days immediately following the announcement of the results for the year ended 31 March 1992.

b United Kingdom Senior Staff Share Option Schemes:

Under the terms of the 1984 and 1987 schemes, following the announcement of the Company's results, the Board may offer options to purchase ordinary shares in the Company to executive directors and senior employees at the higher of the nominal value of the shares and the average market price for three consecutive dealing days preceding the date of the offer. The 1977 scheme has now expired and no further options may be granted under this scheme. Although options may be granted under both the 1984 and 1987 schemes, the maximum option value that can be exercised under each scheme is limited to four times earnings. Outstanding options offered under all senior schemes are as follows:

Options offered	Number of shares 1992	1991	Option price	Option dates
(1977 Scheme)				
May 1985	278,447	832,427	137·000p	May 1988 – May 1992
May 1986	248,199	778,878	211·000p	May 1989 – May 1993
May 1987	483,825	1,188,686	232·333p	May 1990 – May 1994
(1984 Scheme)				
October 1984	769,149	1,415,665	115·667p	Oct 1987 – Oct 1994
May 1985	223,584	408,810	137·000p	May 1988 – May 1995
May 1986	95,037	519,294	211·000p	May 1989 – May 1996
May 1987	495,906	1,216,306	232·333p	May 1990 – May 1997
October 1987	481,484	683,923	202·000p	Oct 1990 – Oct 1997
May 1988	1,305,400	3,266,313	176·000p	May 1991 – May 1998
October 1988	29,424	64,234	158·000p	Oct 1991 – Oct 1998
May 1989	2,747,147	2,971,722	175·000p	May 1992 – May 1999
October 1989	61,038	61,038	188·000p	Oct 1992 – Oct 1999
May 1990	2,982,917	3,184,801	206·000p	May 1993 – May 2000
May 1991	3,640,246	—	254·000p	May 1994 – May 2001
(1987 Scheme)				
October 1987	645,755	735,811	202·000p	Oct 1990 – Oct 1994
May 1988	3,064,513	6,412,682	176·000p	May 1991 – May 1995
May 1989	2,996,692	3,195,184	175·000p	May 1992 – May 1996
October 1989	61,038	61,038	188·000p	Oct 1992 – Oct 1996
May 1990	3,720,915	4,030,566	206·000p	May 1993 – May 1997
May 1991	2,942,151	—	254·000p	May 1994 – May 1998

No options were offered in October 1990 and October 1991.

21. Transactions with directors and their interests (continued)

The following directors hold options to subscribe for ordinary shares of 25 pence each granted under the employees' savings related share option scheme and the executive share option schemes.

	Subscription Price	Option period expires in	Savings Related Options at 31 July 1992	1 August 1991	Executive Options at 31 July 1992	1 August 1991
J. Lancaster	279.0p	1996	—	—	31,400	31,400
	229.0p	1998	—	—	24,000	24,000
	271.0p	1999	—	—	26,000	26,000
	303.0p	2000	—	—	26,000	26,000
	†406.5p	2002	—	—	26,000	—
D. A. Dibben	229.0p	1998	—	—	12,800	12,800
	271.0p	1999	—	—	14,000	14,000
	303.0p	2000	—	—	14,000	14,000
	†406.5p	2002	—	—	14,000	—
W. C. Ferris	229.0p	1998	—	—	8,000	8,000
	271.0p	1999	—	—	9,500	9,500
	228.0p	1995	4,736	4,736	—	—
	303.0p	2000	—	—	14,000	14,000
	†406.5p	2002	—	—	14,000	—
	††312.0p	1997	2,403	—	—	—
J. W. Footman	229.0p	1998	—	—	16,000	16,000
	271.0p	1999	—	—	18,000	18,000
	303.0p	2000	—	—	18,000	18,000
	†406.5p	2002	—	—	18,000	—
R. Ireland	279.0p	1996	—	—	19,600	19,600
	229.0p	1998	—	—	13,600	13,600
	271.0p	1999	—	—	15,000	15,000
	228.0p	1995	3,473	3,473	—	—
	303.0p	2000	—	—	15,000	15,000
	298.0p	1996	1,006	1,006	—	—
	†406.5p	2002	—	—	15,000	—
	††312.0p	1997	2,403	—	—	—
J. W. G. Young	229.0p	1998	—	—	12,800	12,800
	271.0p	1999	—	—	14,000	14,000
	303.0p	2000	—	—	14,000	14,000
	†406.5p	2002	—	—	14,000	—
	††312.0p	1999	7,211	—	—	—

†Granted 25 March 1992.
††Granted 23 April 1992.

During the year ended 31 July 1992 no director exercised options over the company's ordinary shares.

There were between 31 July 1992 and 20 October 1992 no changes in the interests of the directors in the shares of the company.

None of the directors of Wolseley plc has a beneficial interest in the shares of subsidiary undertakings or in the debenture stock of the company. Save as disclosed, and apart from contracts of employment, none of the directors had a material beneficial interest in any contract of significance to which the company or any of its subsidiary undertakings was a party during the financial year.

Employee stock

Beginning in 1969, Siemens AG was one of the first German corporations to offer its employees the opportunity to purchase stock at a preferential price. Around 176,000 employees, or 71% of those entitled, took advantage of the latest offer. The high acceptance rate underscores both the interest in our model of employee participation and the return earned on investments in Siemens. This accomplishes the goal of providing incentives for employee participation and at the same time contributes to a stronger equity base.

The company's employee stock purchase plan was again very popular in 1991, with 90 percent of those eligible taking advantage of the opportunity to purchase Bayer shares at a discount. Employees hold some 4-5 percent of the capital stock of Bayer AG.

The Fourth Directive (Article 43) requires the notes on the accounts to provide information on 'the amount of emoluments granted ... to the members of the administrative, managerial and supervisory bodies by reason of their responsibilities'. This is very loose wording. Are the responsibilities referred to those as members of the board. or as executives? Is it intended the emoluments of each director should be shown or just the total?

In most companies there is only a limited amount of information provided to shareholders on directors' remuneration. It might be argued that the amount that is provided is all that is needed, and if shareholders and the market wanted more, they are in a position to demand it. We will briefly examine the arguments for and against more disclosure.

For the agency relationship to work between owners and managers/ directors it is essential that the owners can monitor the rewards received by their agents. It is therefore important that shareholders are confident that directors are being paid in a way that ensures the unity of their respective interests. Shareholders need a detailed understanding of how directors benefit from performance related bonuses,

Extract 5.26 – Thomson–CSF 1991 accounts, Notes.

• **Treasury stock and deferred compensation**

Thomson-CSF implemented two stock-option plans in favour of officers of the Company, decided by the Board of Directors on December 30, 1987 and April 17, 1990. In December 1987, Thomson-CSF purchased from Thomson S.A. 1,500,000 of its own shares, and during the first quarter of 1990 1,000,000 of its own shares on the Paris Stock Exchange, for the purpose of allocating 1,500,000 and 1,000,000 stock options respectively to around 200 and 300 officers and other employees of the company. Exercise price per option amounts to FF 117. The following schedules summarize movements occured since January 1, 1990 :

12/30/1987 plan	Treasury stock: number of shares	Per share (FF)	Treasury stock (MFF)	Deferred compensation (1) (MFF)	Total
As of January 1, 1990	1,396,307	123	(172)	(58)	(230)
Options exercised	(7,700)	1		–	1
Allowance for deferred compensation	–		–	17	17
Unexercised expired options (2)	(36,700)	4		–	4
As of December 31, 1990	1,351,907	123	(167)	(41)	(208)
Options exercised	(81,080)	10		–	10
Allowance for deferred compensation	–		–	17	17
Unexercised expired options (2)	(19,440)	2		–	2
As of December 31, 1991	1,251,387	123	(155)	(24)	(179)

04/17/1990 plan	Treasury stock: number of shares	Per share (FF)	Treasury stock (MFF)	Deferred compensation (1) (MFF)	Total
As of January 1, 1991	1,000,000	136	(136)	–	(136)
Delivery	–		–	(12)	(12)
Options exercised	(13,070)	2		–	2
Allowance for deferred compensation	–		–	2	2
Unexercised expired options (2)	(8,200)	1		–	1
As of December 31, 1991	978,730	136	(133)	(10)	(143)

Extract 5.27 – The 'Shell' Transport and Trading Company plc 1992 accounts, Report of the Directors.

Share options

Certain Group companies have option plans, the operation of which during 1992 is summarized in Note 32 to the Group financial statements. The Shell Petroleum Company Limited and Shell Petroleum N.V. are two of the companies with such plans for executives, the shares involved being those of the Company and Royal Dutch. The outstanding options of the Directors at the end of the year are for not more than five years at prices not less than the fair market value of the shares at the time of the grant of options.

The Shell Petroleum Company Limited also operates a savings related share option scheme which has been approved by the Inland Revenue under the Finance Act 1980. Under this scheme options over shares in the Company are granted to employees of UK Group companies at prices not less than the fair market value of the shares on a date not more than 30 days before the date of grant of the option and are normally exercisable after completion of a five years' contractual savings period.

No issue of new shares is involved under any of the plans or schemes mentioned above.

The interests of the Directors under all the share option plans or schemes of Group companies (in terms of options exercised by or granted to them during the year or outstanding in their favour at December 31, 1992) are shown in Note 8 to the financial statements of the Company.

Extract 5.28 – Akzo NV 1991 accounts, Notes.

Stock options
Options to purchase shares of Akzo N.V. common stock have been granted to key employees under a stock option plan introduced in 1990. Until May 4, 1995, these options are exercisable at a price of Hfl 120.40 per share. The options granted in 1991 expire on April 29, 1996, and entitle the holders to acquire shares at a price of Hfl 115.10 per share. At December 31, 1991, there were options outstanding for 122,596 shares of Akzo N.V. common stock (1990: 80,150).

---

share option schemes and the extent to which each of these elements makes up the directors' full remuneration package.

Gower reasons that there is a need to disclose directors' remuneration because '...it is too obvious that the system lends itself to abuse, since directors will be encouraged to bleed the company by voting themselves excessive salaries and expense allowances.'[5] The UK

Companies Act 1985 attempts to minimize these dangers by providing for full disclosure of the total emoluments received by directors. Unfortunately, the Act has not turned out to be effective in this respect.

It can be argued that there is no need for shareholders to be concerned with the finer details of directors' remuneration. If a management team is not administering a company efficiently, this will eventually be reflected in the share price of the company. They then run the risk of becoming a target for a takeover by a more efficient management team. Thus, assuming a desire for continued tenure by the management team of a company, the market for corporate control will effectively discipline them and do the work for the shareholders.

Unfortunately, the evidence from the UK and USA on the success of mergers and takeovers in securing the most efficient use of resources is far from clear. In the wake of the events of the 1980s, it is difficult to assume firstly that an inefficient management team will always be noticed; secondly, that they will be uncovered in time to save the company, and thirdly, if they are uncovered, that those who succeed them will be necessarily any more efficient.

There are in fact considerable differences between countries with respect to the detail disclosed on directors' remuneration. In the UK there is a comparatively high level of disclosure on most aspects of directors' compensation. In Italy, no information is given. In Germany, the Netherlands, France and Spain usually only a total figure is presented. Over the last decade, and particularly since the late 1980s, increasing concern has been expressed about various aspects of directors' remuneration. Apart from critical comment on the level of remuneration of some directors, questions have been raised about the level of disclosure, the extent of board accountability to shareholders and the methods used to reward directors. It was as a result of such mounting criticism that the Cadbury Committee was set up.

The UK Companies Act 1985 requires certain information to be given in notes to the company's annual accounts. This includes the figure for emoluments which must distinguish between payments received in respect of services as a director and other emoluments. The former usually represents fees paid for attending board meetings and other duties which relate solely to duties as a director. Such fees apply particularly to non-executive directors. The amounts executive directors receive as salary, bonuses and other benefits appear as 'other emoluments'. Some companies separate the payments made as pension contributions from other emoluments.

Following recent adverse comments, an increasing number of companies are disclosing fuller information about directors' performance related pay. However, most do not provide enough information to enable shareholders to form an opinion on the merits of the scheme. Some companies differentiate between rewards based upon short-term performance and those based upon long-term performance. At the most extreme vague comments appear which state that bonuses are related 'to the financial results of the group' or 'growth in earnings per share'.

Extract 5.29 shows the detail provided by Glaxo, and Extract 5.30 the detail provided by the Bank of Scotland. This latter extract is particularly interesting in the detail provided on employee incentives.

In Germany at best only the total amount of remuneration received by the board of management and the supervisory board is disclosed. See, for example, Extract 5.31 for VEBA, which in fact provides more information than most German companies.

Most larger German companies provide information on the total payment of directors' remuneration, but no details are given on the remuneration of the highest paid directors, and no breakdown into payments within different size bands. This is the situation with most German companies – see, for example, Extract 5.32 from the accounts of Bayer.

In the Netherlands, France and Spain as with Germany most large companies provide information on the total amount paid to directors, but no details. See, for example, the extracts from the accounts of Saint Gobain (5.33) and Akzo (5.34).

The FEE survey of published accounts indicated that between 40% and 80% of companies in Germany, France and the Netherlands provided some information. A French company is required to submit an annual social balance sheet to its staff committee. This is not really a balance sheet but a series of disclosures. This 'bilan social' is available for any shareholder who requires a copy and does not form a part of the annual report. One of the matters on which the company has to report is employee remuneration and associated costs. This includes details of the ten highest salaries and details of any employee profit-sharing scheme.

Corporate Governance

'Shareholders have delegated many of their responsibilities as owners to the directors who act as their stewards. It is for the shareholders to call the directors to book if they appear to be failing in their stewardship … they can insist on a high standard of corporate governance' (Cadbury Report, para. 6.6). At one time the annual reports were seen as primarily fulfilling this stewardship role. More recently they have been prepared with the primary emphasis on influencing the valuation of the company.

The Cadbury Report in emphasizing accountability and stewardship seems to be trying to restore the balance. If companies complied with the report's 'the code of best practice' it would be easier to be able to decide if directors were failing in their stewardship role.

In the UK corporate governance has become a major issue, and following the Cadbury Report a number of companies have produced statements on this matter in their annual reports. Typical of such statements is that produced by ICI (Extract 5.35). As can be seen they disclose the membership and terms of reference of their Audit Committee, Remuneration Committee and Appeals Committee.

Not all UK companies support the Cadbury Report recommendations. In the 1992 accounts of Hanson the chairman writes 'much has been said recently about corporate governance, but most of the advice has been long on accountability and short on encouraging efficiency and enterprise'. Marley in their 1992 accounts are also critical. The chairman writes:

6. REMUNERATION OF DIRECTORS

Directors are remunerated for services to the Company and its subsidiary undertakings on terms competitive with international market rates that reflect the skill and experience they bring to the conduct of their responsibilities and reward individual performance and contribution to the performance of the Group. Executive Directors receive salary and benefits, payments linked to performance, pensions and options on the Company's shares. Non-Executive Directors receive fees for their services to the Board and its Committees.

	1993 £000	1992 £000
a) Remuneration of Directors of the Holding company for services to the Company and its subsidiary and associated undertakings:		
Fees	147	150
Performance related payments	1,676	718
Other emoluments	5,903	4,573
Contributions to pension schemes	1,541	1,628
Funding of past service pension deficit	4,700	–
Payments to former Directors	220	123
Pensions to former Directors	252	8

b) The emoluments of the Chairman, excluding pension scheme contributions, were £1,442,713 (1992 – £1,185,727), including a long term performance related payment of £410,400 (1992 – £192,200).

c) The emoluments, excluding pension scheme contributions and including performance related payments, of the Directors of the Company, including the Chairman and overseas Directors, were:

Exceeding £000	Not exceeding £000	1993 Number	1992 Number	Exceeding £000	Not exceeding £000	1993 Number	1992 Number
25	30	4	5	470	475	–	1
35	40	1	–	535	540	–	1
40	45	–	1	555	560	–	1
50	55	1	–	565	570	1	–
60	65	1	–	570	575	1	–
70	75	–	1	590	595	1	–
80	85	1	–	630	635	1	–
90	95	1	–	720	725	1	–
165	170	–	1	740	745	1	–
255	260	1	–	970	975	–	1
405	410	–	1	1,185	1,190	–	1
425	430	1	–	1,320	1,325	1	–
435	440	–	1	1,440	1,445	1	–
450	455	–	1				

d) Directors participate in a long term performance related incentive plan based on growth in earnings per share above a minimum level over rolling four year periods. Payments are adjusted by reference to the relative performance of a comparator group of pharmaceutical companies. Pending completion of his first four year period, a Director may be awarded annual bonuses based on individual and Company performance. Performance related payments and annual bonuses are shown as Directors' remuneration when paid. Amounts payable under the long term performance related incentive plan are provided in the accounts on an annual basis. The amount charged in the profit and loss account for the year ended 30th June 1993, reflecting this year principally a greater difference between the relative performance of the Company and the comparator group, was £4,912,600 (1992 – £751,490), of which £1,141,400 (1992 – £250,550) relates to the Chairman.

EXECUTIVE STOCK OPTION SCHEME

This performance related scheme was introduced in 1985 and from start has differed significantly from comparable schemes run by other companies.

Under Inland Revenue rules, an employee can be only hold options up to a maximum subscription value of four times his or her taxable earnings. Senior executives in many companies are granted options up to or close to this limit, only once or perhaps two or three times during their careers.

Bank policy, however, has been to increase the motivation by spreading the potential awards over a period of 10 years, so that as long as the individual performs well, he or she will receive approximately one tenth of his or her total permissible options regularly each year. Spreading the options in this way makes people think in terms of their performance. It also diminishes the danger of the options' value being reduced or eliminated by share price fluctuations which may have little or nothing to do with the Bank's results.

The other distinctive feature of the Bank's Scheme is that it includes staff at lower levels than most other schemes. Each year, about 25 percent of the total options available are rewarded to staff in grades below what would normally be considered 'senior executive level' in a large organisation. These awards, for exceptional performance, are particularly valuable in encouraging and realise a profit at such a time as the proprietors and can only realise a profit at such time as the proprietors have already enjoyed the 'added-value' of a rise in the share price.

SAVINGS-RELATED STOCK OPTION SCHEME

This scheme was set up at the same time as the Executive Stock Option Scheme and allows any member of staff to enter into a five or seven year savings contract, with the proceeds being taken either in cash or in Ordinary Stock. In this case, the subscription price reflects a 20 per cent discount on the market price, as allowed by the Inland Revenue.

Arising from the three Schemes, staff had the following beneficial interests in Ordinary Stock of the Bank as at 28th February 1993:–

	Number of Employees	Ordinary Stock units of 25p each
1. Profit Sharing Scheme:–		
Stock held in trust through Profit Sharing Scheme	6,702	13,688,448
Stock held by staff in own name (who also hold stock through Profit Sharing Scheme as above)	5,459	13,233,897
2. Executive Stock Options Outstanding:–		
Management Board and Divisional General Managers (or equivalent)	29	5,638,809
Assistant General Managers and Senior Managers (or equivalent)	108	4,511,847
Staff below Senior Manager level	328	3,139,497
Retired staff	21	948,696
	486	14,238,849
3. Savings Related Stock Options Outstanding:–	6,330	20,875,944

After excluding double counting for staff having an interest under more than one scheme and retired staff, a total of 9,240 staff (being 55 per cent of the total staff including part-time employees currently employed by the Group) therefore have an interest in 61,088,442 Ordinary Stock units of the Bank (being 5·1 per cent of the total capital stock of the Bank on a fully diluted basis).

Extract 5.31 – VEBA AG 1991 accounts, Notes.

Provided that the Annual General Meeting of VEBA AG on June 4, 1992, approves the proposed dividend, total payments to the members of the Supervisory Board will amount to DM 1,520,015.00 and total payments to the members of the Board of Management including remuneration for the performance of their duties at subsidiaries to DM 11,670,982.31.

Total payments to retired members of the VEBA Board of Management and their surviving dependants as well as in connection with the succession in title of former subsidiaries amount to DM 6,141,246.50, including remuneration for the performance of their duties at subsidiaries.

A provision of DM 49,882,596.00 has been made for the pension commitments of VEBA AG to retired members of the VEBA Board of Management and their surviving dependants as well as in connection with the succession in title of former subsidiaries.

As of December 31, 1991, loans granted to members of the Board of Management amounted to DM 880,000.00; as agreed, DM 20,000.00 was repaid in the year under review. These loans bear interest at up to 5.5% p.a., and they have an agreed term of up to 12 years.

The members of the Supervisory Board and Board of Management are named on pages 4 and 6.

Extract 5.32 – Bayer AG 1992 accounts, Supplementary Data.

TOTAL REMUNERATION OF THE BOARD OF MANAGEMENT AND THE SUPERVISORY BOARD, ADVANCES AND LOANS

The remuneration of the Board of Management for 1992 amounted to DM 13,171,603.00.

Emoluments to retired members of the Board of Management and their surviving dependents amounted to DM 9,969,398.00.

Bayer AG provisions for pensions for these individuals amount to DM 73,538,244.00.

Provisions for remuneration of the Supervisory Board amount to DM 1,719,037.00.

Loans to members of the Board of Management and the Supervisory Board as of December 31, 1992 amounted to DM 73,413.00 and DM 55,067.00, repayments during the year to DM 2,837.00 and DM 3,334.00, respectively. Some of these loans are interest-free, and others are at interest rates of 5.5% p.a.

Extract 5.33 – Saint Gobain Group 1991 accounts, Notes.

NOTE 27: DIRECTORS' REMUNERATION

The remuneration of directors and designated officials ("mandataires sociaux") from Compagnie de Saint-Gobain in 1991 amounts to FF 6.5 million.

Extract 5.34 – Akzo NV 1991 accounts, Notes.

Remuneration of members of the Board of Management and of the Supervisory Council of Akzo N.V.

In fiscal 1991, remuneration including pension expense amounted to Hfl 4,797,000 (1990: Hfl 7,960,000) for members and former members of the Board of Management, and to Hfl 685,000 (1990: Hfl 668,000) for members and former members of the Supervisory Council. These amounts were charged to Akzo Group income.

All parties involved in the corporate governance process should follow the same principles of conduct and be subject to the same degree of accountability and disclosure. Given that the annual audit is one of the cornerstones of corporate governance, I believe its provision should apply equally to the auditing profession, otherwise the structure proposed by the Cadbury Committee will remain fundamentally flawed.

Most UK companies do comply with the Cadbury recommendations, and do not make critical comments.

As the senior Non-Executive Director on your Company's Board, it is my privilege, on behalf of my colleagues, to address shareholders on our responsibilities to them and to ICI.

All of your Directors are, of course, accountable under law for the proper stewardship of ICI's assets and undertakings. The Non-Executive Directors have a particular responsibility to ensure that the principal operational and financial strategies and policies proposed by our Executive colleagues are examined and discussed fully and objectively. In making decisions, we consider carefully the balance of interests of our shareholders, employees, customers and the many communities in which ICI is represented.

I can confirm that, to enable your Non-Executive Directors to contribute effectively to ICI's affairs and progress, we are given full access to all appropriate information. We engage in open, constructive debate and are involved fully in ICI's strategic plans and in such things as helping to guide the extensive reshaping programme set out in this and last year's Reports. This programme provides an excellent example of a vital strategy which has been considered diligently by the entire Board and which will help us to achieve our primary objective of improving earnings quality and shareholder value.

Since ICI's foundation, the Board has had a significant representation of Non-Executive Directors, and today we have equal numbers of Executive and external Directors. We bring to all the Board's deliberations, and to strategic and financial matters, wide experience from our various business backgrounds. As befits a company with global operations and markets, half of your Non-Executive Directors are from outside the UK.

We participate in the committees of the Board listed below, ensuring high standards of financial integrity and the independent determination of the employment terms and rewards of the Chairman, Executive Directors and senior managers. We are directly concerned in planning the senior management succession, including the Chairman and other Board members.

For each of us, membership of the ICI Board is a challenging and stimulating responsibility. We look forward to continuing to serve the interests of the Company and its shareholders.

Patrick Meaney

Sir Patrick Meaney

Audit Committee
Members:
Mr T H Wyman (Chairman)
Lord Chilver
Sir Antony Pilkington
Terms of reference: To assist the Board in the discharge of its responsibilities for corporate governance, financial reporting and corporate control.

Remuneration Committee
Members:
Sir Patrick Meaney (Chairman)
The Non-Executive Directors
Terms of reference: To determine employment terms and retirement provisions for Executive Directors and the most senior management in the company. To exercise the powers of the Directors under the Senior Staff Share Option Schemes.

Appeals Committee
Members:
Mr F Whiteley (Chairman)
Mr J D F Barnes
Dr P Doyle
Sir Patrick Meaney
Sir Jeremy Morse
Terms of reference: To determine the policy and practice for the making of charitable donations in the UK.

Corporate governance as an area of concern has not yet led to major changes in reporting practice in the five other countries being examined. However, a number of companies in these countries do provide some information about the decision-making structure within the company.

Mission Statements

It has become fashionable for companies to provide in their annual report a mission statement or to make some statement about their purpose or objective. Presumably the reason for printing such statements is to enable the owners of the company to better understand what the directors are trying to achieve. It can be seen as part of the accountability exercise. If shareholders know the long-term goals being pursued by the directors they are better able to judge their success.

Unfortunately such statements are usually so general and similar in nature from one company to another as to be more or less useless. Having read such statements for a number of companies it would be difficult for an investor to decide on the basis of their contents to follow the long-term fortunes of one company rather than another.

Such statements certainly provide an opportunity for creative writing. The award must go to Elf Sanofi who start off their annual report with a poem about the colour blue (Extract 5.36). Needless to say the annual report is produced on blue paper. Following the poem they reaffirm their 'mission to serve the cause of life'. Who but a cynic could fail to be attracted by a company with such an objective?

ICI, also in the chemical industry also make reference in their 'Group Purpose' to the quality of life. But their objectives are much less grandiose and as a result more achievable (Extract 5.37). Bayer in their opening statement giving the 'Corporate Overview' also refer to having a duty to use their expertise 'to benefit mankind' (Extract 5.38).

Not all companies provide mission statements or statements of purpose, but many state their strategic goals or long-term strategies (Extract 5.39).

References

1. *Report of the Committee on the Financial Aspects of Corporate Governance* (The Cadbury Report), Gee, London, 1992.

2. Clarkham, J. (1989) *Corporate Governance and the Market for Companies: Aspects of the Shareholders Role,* Bank of England Discussion Paper, London.

3. Schneider-Lenne, E.R. (1992) 'Corporate control in Germany', *Oxford Review of Economic Policy,* **8**(3), 11–23.

4. Sheridan, T. and Kendall, N. (1992) *Corporate Governance,* Financial Times–Pitman, London, pp. 112–113.

5. Gower, L.C.B. (1992) *Gower's Principles of Modern Company Law,* 5th edn, Sweet & Maxwell.

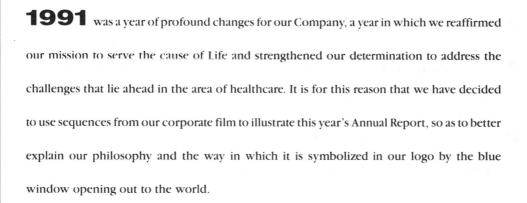

*B*lue, cerulean or midnight blue
Blue like the boundless sky, the blue serene
The projection of mankind's dreams
Blue, the symbol of our research endeavors

Blue, aquamarine or deeply blue
Great Neptune's perpetual hue
The source of being
Blue, the symbol of our commitment to serve the cause of Life

Blue, translucent or crystalline
The blue of freedom
Celestial, pelagic, terraqueous blue
Blue, the symbol of our search for transparency and of our fundamental corporate values

1991 was a year of profound changes for our Company, a year in which we reaffirmed our mission to serve the cause of Life and strengthened our determination to address the challenges that lie ahead in the area of healthcare. It is for this reason that we have decided to use sequences from our corporate film to illustrate this year's Annual Report, so as to better explain our philosophy and the way in which it is symbolized in our logo by the blue window opening out to the world.

Extract 5.37 – ICI plc 1991 accounts, Group Purpose.

The chemical industry is a major force for the improvement of the quality of life across the world. ICI aims to be the world's leading chemical company, serving customers internationally through the innovative and responsible application of chemistry and related sciences.

Through achievement of our aim, we will enhance the wealth and well-being of our shareholders, our employees, our customers and the communities which we serve and in which we operate.

We will do this by:

- Seeking consistent profitable growth;

- Providing challenge and opportunity for our employees, releasing their skills and creativity;

- Achieving a standard of quality and service internationally which our customers recognise as being consistently better than that of any of our competitors;

- Operating safely and in harmony with the global environment.

Bayer is an international, broadly diversified chemicals and health care company with operations in some 150 countries.

Its 23 Business Groups are organized within six Sectors: Polymers, Organic Products, Industrial Products, Health Care, Agrochemicals and Imaging Technologies.

Our expertise lies in research, service, technology, quality and efficiency in all our areas of activity. This forms the basis for our success and safeguards the future.

We consider it our duty to use this expertise to benefit mankind, and to play our part in solving the major problems of our time.

Moreover, it is our responsibility to ensure the safety of our operations and to minimize their impact on the environment, while efficiently utilizing natural resources.

Bayer: Expertise with Responsibility.

Long-term vision

Through conscious positioning in three strategic sectors and endeavoring to achieve maximum quality in all of our actions, BT seeks to be essential to both our customers and our suppliers, so that their market position is strengthened. For each of the Group's five divisions, this means striving for 'World-class Performance.'

Strategic goals

• *Leading market positions.* Attaining or, where appropriate, strengthening leading market positions in BT's selected geographic markets, based on productivity, market-oriented innovations, and a total quality approach.
• *Pro-active behavior.* Alert anticipation – by management at all levels – of developments that would create opportunities or avert threats.
• *Profitability.* Achieving results that are above-average in terms of return on investment, thus fostering the stability of our corporation and creating the means to finance the further growth of the Group.

Orientation

1990	1991	1992
Shaping the future	Developing management 'tools'	Increasing profitability
• Core activities	• Information systems	• Productivity
• Organization structure	• Planning systems	• Innovation
• Reward system	• Training programs	• Quality

Problems

1. Examine the annual report of a large publicly quoted company to ascertain the information disclosed on matters relating to corporate governance. Write a report based on your findings, explaining the significance/usefulness of the information disclosed.

2. Why should the shareholders of Siemens become concerned about the company's employee share purchase scheme? Are there any lessons to be learned from such dissatisfaction for those who operate executive share option schemes?

3. Does less disclosure in certain countries seriously disadvantage shareholders?

4. What arguments can be put forward to support the German approach to corporate governance, and the accounting practices followed? What are the arguments against the traditional German approach?

5. What are the causes of corporate failure? What factors should an analyst take into account in trying to predict corporate failure?

6. Compare the two-tier board structure as a form of corporate governance with the unitary board structure. Why did the Cadbury Committee emphasize the importance of non-executive directors in the UK system?

7. Extract 5.20 shows the interest of directors of Marks and Spencers in the shares of that company. How useful is such information to those shareholders who wish to determine the actual gains made by directors from holding shares and holding options in shares of the company?

8. Hanson plc and Marley plc were critical of the recommendations of the Cadbury Committee. Write a report to a user of company accounts explaining the points made by the directors of these two companies and contrasting their views with those expressed in the Cadbury Report.

9. Comment on the reply of the Czechoslovakian finance director when he had been told of the system of corporate governance in the UK. Do you believe that he was being unfair to the UK system?

10. Read the mission statements of Elf Sanofi (Extract 5.36), ICI (Extract 5.37) and Bayer (Extract 5.38). Why do you believe companies find it advantageous to include such statements in their annual report and accounts? In what way might they be useful to shareholders and potential investors?

6

Tangible Fixed Assets

Objectives

- To examine the factors affecting the accounting treatment of tangible fixed assets.

- To highlight different approaches to cost measurement, depreciation and asset revaluation adopted by companies operating in different countries.

- To illustrate the potential effect on financial results of reclassifying current assets as fixed assets.

Introduction

The term 'fixed assets' covers a wide variety of assets whose treatment in terms of both balance sheet and profit and loss account presentation can affect quite dramatically the results and financial position shown by company financial statements. In general terms fixed assets can be regarded as those assets intended for long-term use in the company's business.

Under the UK Companies Act 1985 fixed assets include intangible assets such as goodwill as well as tangible fixed assets which would include land and buildings, plant and machinery, and fixtures and fittings. Investments held for continuing use may also be included under this heading. In this chapter we will concentrate on tangible fixed assets while intangibles and permanent investments are dealt with in separate chapters.

Issues

In most countries there would be little disagreement on the broad principles of fixed asset accounting. Fixed assets would normally be capitalized at cost on acquisition and then subsequently depreciated over their useful economic life through the profit and loss account. If at any time the carrying value was thought not to be fully recoverable then this value would be written down. On the sale or scrapping of an asset the difference between written down value and any proceeds received would be treated as a gain or loss arising on disposal.

However, in practice there are a number of issues which may complicate matters. Among these will be:

- recognition of when expenditure creates a fixed asset;
- cost measurement;
- depreciation policy;
- revaluation policy.

Analysis

Unfortunately accounting standard-setters have not yet prescribed standards which deal with all of these issues. There are a number of accounting standards in the UK which deal with various aspects of tangible fixed asset accounting which include SSAP 12, *Accounting for Depreciation,* and SSAP 19, *Accounting for Investment Properties.* In addition the ASC, which predated the ASB, issued exposure drafts relevant to the treatment of tangible fixed assets: ED 49, *Reflecting the Substance of Transactions in Assets and Liabilities* and ED 51, *Accounting for Fixed Assets and Revaluations.* However, following the replacement of the ASC by the ASB there has been no further progress with these particular projects.

Recognition of Fixed Assets

The Companies Act 1985 defines fixed assets as those which are intended for use on a continuing basis in the company's activities and any assets which are not intended for such use are taken to be current assets. More useful criteria for recognizing fixed assets were provided by ED 51 as follows:

A fixed asset is an asset that:

(a) is held by an enterprise for use in the production or supply of goods and services, for rental to others, or for administrative purposes and may include items held for the maintenance or repair of such assets;

(b) has been acquired or constructed with the intention of being used on a continuing basis; and

(c) is not intended for sale in the ordinary course of business.[1]

As fixed assets investments were excluded from this exposure draft and, in addition, the definition given above was based on that in the International Accounting Standard for tangible fixed assets,[2] it provides a much better working definition of tangible fixed assets.

ED 51 also proposed criteria for recognition of fixed assets as follows.

A fixed asset should be recognized on an enterprise's balance sheet when:

(a) it is possible that any future economic benefits associated with the asset will flow to the enterprise; and

(b) the asset has a cost and where carried at a valuation, a value that can be measured with reliability.[3]

These are drawn from the general tests for the recognition of assets included in the IASC's *Framework for the Preparation and Presentation of Financial Statements*. One problem area that has arisen in practice concerns transfers between current and fixed assets. During the early 1990s several companies which had been holding properties for development and sale as current assets transferred the properties into fixed assets. The rationale for this was that, because of the state of the property market, the properties could not be sold in the immediate future and they would therefore be held as fixed assets until the property market and related disposal prices improved. From an accounting perspective the treatment of diminutions in value are significant. Later on we look at a case study relating to Trafalgar House plc where the treatment of such transfers gave rise to a number of controversial issues.

Cost Measurement

The Companies Act generally requires fixed assets to be included at their purchase price or production cost under the historical cost rules, subject to any provisions for depreciation or diminution in value. However, alternative accounting rules allow tangible fixed assets to be included at a market value or at their current cost. Many companies, while adopting historical cost, also make periodic revaluations of fixed assets. As this may also affect depreciation charges the policies of different companies must be checked so that varying policies can be considered when making comparisons.

The Companies Act defines 'purchase price' so as to include any consideration in cash or otherwise given by the company for the asset.[4] Moreover the act says that 'the purchase price of an asset shall be determined by adding to the actual price paid any expenses incidental to its acquisition.'[5]

A number of problems can arise in determining what expenses may be regarded as incidental to the acquisition of fixed assets. This can lead to what some commentators describe as 'capitalization of costs' where expense items are treated as the cost of an asset rather than being charged through the profit and loss account. For example, whether fixed assets are purchased or constructed by the company itself, overheads can present a problem. Generally non-production overheads should be excluded unless they can be reasonably attributed either to the purchase or construction or as part of the cost of bringing the asset into commission.

In France tangible fixed assets are usually carried at historical cost or legal revaluation. The impact of legal revaluation is likely to be insignificant as the last such event was in 1976. Although fixed asset revaluations are permitted they are rare because French tax law requires that capital gains recognized in the accounts are liable to taxation. Subsequent depreciation is then allowed for tax purposes.

In general, tangible fixed assets of German companies are included at acquisition or manufacturing cost. Acquisition cost includes purchase price, incidental costs and expenses necessary to get the asset ready for use. Manufacturing cost includes expenditure on goods and services including overheads.

Netherlands law identifies two bases for tangible fixed assets: historical cost and current value. Where the asset is produced by the company, cost would include purchase price of raw materials and consumables. A reasonable proportion of indirect costs (overheads) may be included in the cost of manufactured assets. The use of current value is also permitted and this is discussed later in the chapter under 'Revaluation policy'.

Capitalizing interest

This is perhaps the most significant and apparent of the costs capitalized by companies. It is also controversial in that different methods of treatment are used in different countries; it can also make a significant difference to reported profits and measures of interest cover where levels of borrowing and related interest rates are high.

The practice is most associated with property companies or where properties are constructed for business use, for example factories, supermarkets, etc. Tax legislation may be important where, for example, relief is only given for interest charged in the profit and loss account. In fact this used to be the position in the UK until the 1981 Finance Act specifically made provision for capitalized interest to be charged to income for tax purposes.[6] At the moment there is no UK accounting standard on the subject although ED 51 makes passing reference to it. The Companies Act 1985 allows the inclusion in the cost of production of an asset of 'interest on capital borrowed to finance the production of that asset, to the extent that it accrues in respect of the period of production'.[7] In the UK therefore interest capitalization is optional. This contrasts with the USA where SFAS 34 makes capitalization of interest compulsory for certain assets requiring time to get them ready for intended use.[8] The IASC has provided a more flexible approach with IAS 23 where capitalization is optional with rules to be followed where capitalization is adopted.[9]

The capitalization of interest will affect reported profit. In the year of capitalization higher profits will be shown by companies adopting capitalization; however, depreciation should be higher in later years as the asset cost is depreciated. However, as we shall see, in some situations UK companies do not depreciate their property assets.

In other European countries the policy on capitalizing interest varies according to national laws and GAAP, whether IAS policies are adopted or if US principles are adopted. In France some companies capitalize interest while others do not. Contrast the policies of Chargeurs and CMB Packaging in Extracts 6.1 and 6.2.

German legislation allows interest on liabilities to be capitalized for the period of construction but the option seems to be used only rarely by German companies.

In both the Netherlands and Spain interest on debts over the production period of the asset may be included – that is, in both countries it is optional. If it is indicated then there should be a note to this effect.

1.2 PROPERTY, PLANT AND EQUIPMENT

Property, plant and equipment is stated at cost, including capitalized interest (note 1.4) and allocated goodwill (note 1.5). The impact of the French statutory revaluation performed in 1976-1978 and revaluations by foreign subsidiaries has been eliminated from the consolidated financial statements. Property, plant and equipment acquired in connection with mergers accounted for by the purchase method is stated on the basis of the carrying value in the absorbed company's books, net of accumulated depreciation. In the case of mergers accounted for by the pooling of interests method, the historical cost before accumulated depreciation is used. Depreciation is recorded by the straight-line method over the estimated useful lives of the assets, as follows:

- Cruise ships: 20 years, based on original cost less 5% representing estimated residual value;
- Flight equipment: 15 years;
- Buildings: 15 to 40 years;
- Plant and equipment: 4 to 8 years;
- Fixtures and fittings: 5 to 10 years.

Capital leases are recorded as an asset and an obligation. The capitalized amount corresponds to the fair value of the leased property and is amortized in accordance with the above policy.

Gains on sale-leaseback operations are deferred and credited to income over the lease term. Losses resulting from under-depreciation of the underlying assets are charged against income for the year in which the contract is signed.

Extract 6.2 – CMB Packaging SA 1991 accounts, Notes.

Tangible assets

Tangible assets are shown at historical cost. Depreciation is provided, except on freehold land, on a straight-line basis over the estimated useful lives of the assets. For the major categories of assets, these are:

Buildings	10 to 50 years
Industrial plant and machinery	3 to 10 years
Other tangible assets	3 to 15 years

Capital grants are classified in provisions and credited to the profit and loss account over the estimated useful lives of the related assets.

Interest capitalization is one of the items adjusted for in comparative case study analysis, and when making comparisons between companies both within the same country and between countries this policy will need to be considered.

Depreciation

Depreciation is defined in SSAP 12 as follows:

Depreciation is the measure of the wearing out, consumption, or other reduction in the useful life of a fixed asset whether arising from use, affluxion of time or obsolescence through technological or market changes.[10]

Depreciation is regarded as a measure of consumption under this definition and not a measure of change in value. This can sometimes cause problems with users of accounts who wrongly assume that balance sheets portray asset values. SSAP 12 requires depreciation of all fixed assets except investment properties, goodwill, development costs and investments.

A number of problems can arise when making comparisons between companies because of differing depreciation policies. The most commonly used method of depreciation is the straight line method, followed by the reducing balance method, the annuity method and the unit of production method. The choice of depreciation method is left to management to select the method they regard as most appropriate to the asset type and business. There is clearly room for a great deal of subjectivity. In some countries tax may be a significant factor in determining choice. In Germany, where tax depreciation has to be included in the accounts, companies will use accelerated depreciation wherever possible. This will reduce reported profits but increase the economic value of the company by reducing the tax payment. In the UK, where profit performance is seen as important and tax depreciation (capital allowances) are adjusted for in separate tax computations, there is scope for management to adopt particular depreciation policies and change those policies to enhance reported profits.

Different managements may have different perceptions of useful life relating to similar assets. Therefore analysts will need to compare the quoted rates of depreciation and/or quoted asset lives when comparing accounts. Management may also change the useful life over which the company is expected to benefit from the asset. This may mean extending the useful life thus reducing the annual depreciation charge and increasing the reported profit figure. The information given by companies on the detail of depreciation policy can vary quite considerably. For example, Sainsbury's information is fairly non-specific – see Extract 6.3. Tiphook, on the other hand, gives quite detailed information – see Extract 6.4. In its note on accounting policy for fixed assets, Daimler-Benz includes a very detailed note, as can be seen from Extract 6.5.

Revaluation Policy

The revaluation of tangible fixed assets from cost to alternative values can be discussed from a number of viewpoints. First there may be companies which revalue to current replacement cost as part of an integrated system of current cost accounting. For example, in the Netherlands both historical cost and current cost accounting are permitted. Extract 6.6 taken from the 1991 accounts of the Dutch company VNU shows that property, plant and equipment are included at current values. Extract 6.7 shows the note on depreciation and

Extract 6.3 – J. Sainsbury plc 1993 accounts, Accounting Policies.

Depreciation

Depreciation is provided on freehold and long leasehold properties if, in the opinion of the Directors, the estimated residual value of any property will be less than its book value after excluding the effects of inflation, so that the shortfall is written off in equal annual instalments over the remaining useful life of the property.

Certain landlords' fittings, which have been capitalised as part of leasehold properties, are depreciated in equal annual instalments over the estimated useful life of the asset to the Group.

Leasehold properties with less than 50 years unexpired are depreciated to write off their book value in equal annual instalments over the unexpired period of the lease.

Fixtures, equipment and vehicles are depreciated to write off their cost over their estimated useful lives in equal annual instalments at varying rates not exceeding 15 years and commencing in the accounting year following capitalisation except for certain Subsidiaries where depreciation commences from the date of the acquisition of the asset.

Extract 6.4 – Tiphook plc 1993 accounts, Accounting Policies.

f) Tangible Fixed Assets and Depreciation

For all tangible fixed assets except rail wagons, depreciation is calculated to write down their cost to estimated residual values over their estimated useful economic lives by equal annual instalments. Rail wagons are depreciated on an annuity method (reverse sum of digits) over the period of their financing and by equal annual instalments thereafter.

The estimated useful lives and residual values of tangible fixed assets are as follows:

	Estimated Useful Lives	Estimated Residual Values
Freehold buildings	50 years	nil
Tank containers	25 years	20% of cost
Other containers	15 years	15% of cost
Trailers	15 years	10% of cost
Rail wagons	25 years	10% of cost
Plant and machinery	10 years	nil
Other fixed assets	5 years	nil

Short term leasehold land and buildings are amortised over the period of the lease. Freehold land is not depreciated.

Accounting Principles and Valuation Methods

During the year under review, we have continued to apply the same accounting principles and valuation methods. Assets and liabilities presented in the consolidated balance sheet – in identical group circumstances – are uniformly valued. In 1992, as in previous years, provisions for approved conversion, reconstruction and maintenance projects have been set up, or have been systematically updated.

Intangible assets are valued at acquisition costs and are written off over the respective useful lives. Goodwill resulting from the capital consolidation, if derived from the extension of the group, is in principle amortized over five years; goodwill relating to the restructuring of the group is charged to retained earnings. Goodwill which arose from the creation of strategic alliances, is split. The portion relating to the group's expansion is written off over the relevant useful life, the one relating to the restructuring is charged to retained earnings.

Fixed assets are valued at acquisition or manufacturing costs. The self-constructed facilities comprise direct costs and applicable materials and manufacturing overheads, including depreciation allowances.

The acquisition/manufacturing costs for fixed assets are reduced by scheduled depreciation charges. The opportunities for special tax-deductible depreciation allowances were fully utilized, i.e. in connection with Section 7d of the Income Tax Act (environmental protection investment), Section 6 b of the Income Tax Act, Section 4 of the Regional Development Law and Subsection 35 of the Income Tax Guidelines.

Scheduled fixed asset depreciation allowances are calculated generally using the following useful lives: 17 to 50 years for buildings, 8 to 20 years for site improvements, 3 to 20 years for technical facilities and machinery, and 2 to 10 years for other facilities and factory and office equipment. Facilities used for multi-shift operations are depreciated using correspondingly lower useful lives. Buildings are depreciated using straight-line depreciation rates – and where allowable under the Tax Codes – declining rates. Movable property with a useful life of four years or more is depreciated using the declining-balance method. For movable property, we change from the declining-balance method to the straight-line method of calculating depreciation allowances when the equal distribution of the remaining net book value over the remaining useful life leads to higher depreciation amounts. Depreciation allowances on additions during the first and second half of the year are calculated using the full year or half-year rates, respectively. Low-value items are expensed in the year of acquisition.

amortization which gives details of both method and rates used in the accounts. Whichever principle is chosen then it should be systematically applied. A majority of companies use historical cost principles although a substantial minority use both historical and current cost principles. In Italy, although historical cost is the dominant valuation principle, the Pirelli company in recent years has used both historical cost and current cost in preparing its published consolidated statements. In France and Spain historical cost with some statutory revaluations is the method used while in Germany tangible fixed assets are valued at cost of acquisition or construction less depreciation.

In the UK most revaluations undertaken relate to property assets. These are generally valued on the basis of the open market value for existing use as this is the generally accepted basis for property assets used in business. Other bases of valuation used are depreciated replacement cost where market value is not obtainable because of the specialized nature of the asset, open market value for alternative use where an alternative use is possible, and open market value (without qualification) which is used for investment properties.

Extract 6.6 – VNU 1991 accounts, Notes.

Property, plant and equipment

Property, plant and equipment, including items on order are reflected at current value based on replacement costs. The annual revaluation of real estate is based upon appraisals and, for other tangible fixed assets, based upon indexes taking into consideration technological developments and inflation. Revaluation of fixed assets is reflected net of deferred income taxes in the revaluation reserve section of shareholders' equity. Decreases in fixed asset valuations below historical net book value are reflected in the statement of earnings.

Property, plant and equipment not used in the production process is valued at the lower of cost or market, when replacement is not anticipated for such equipment.

Software and databases are capitalized and amortized over their estimated useful lives when the acquisition or development costs are in excess of a certain level.

UK companies have revalued tangible fixed assets (usually property assets) for a number of reasons. Directors may feel that balance sheet values are misleading and might lead to an undervaluation of the company by the market. This assumes that market participants use balance sheet valuations rather than cash flow projections in their valuation model. Revaluation is sometimes seen as a defence or deterrent to takeover raiders in an asset rich company, for example a brewery company owning valuable freehold public houses or a retailer owning valuable town centre sites. Another reason for revaluation would be to increase shareholders' funds by the amounts transferred to revaluation reserves thus improving the debt to equity ratio and perhaps increasing borrowing capacity and/or reducing the cost of new borrowing.

A consequence of revaluing assets is the subsequent effect on depreciation. In the past there was much debate between those who considered that the revalued amount should be regarded as the 'new cost' and those who argued that revaluation should relate only to the balance sheet and not affect the profit and loss account. The 'new cost' argument ties in with the ASB's draft *Statement of Principles,* Chapter 6, which proposes articulation between accounting statements and consistency of treatment.[11] In any event SSAP 12 already seems to have made this point as follows.

> *'The accounting treatment in the profit and loss account should be consistent with that used in the balance sheet. Hence the depreciation charge in the profit and loss account for the period should be based on the carrying amount of the asset in the balance sheet, whether historical cost or revalued amount. The whole of the depreciation charge should be reflected in the profit and loss account. No part of the depreciation should be set against reserves.[12]*

Extract 6.7 – VNU 1991 accounts, Notes.

Depreciation and amortization

Depreciation is based upon the assets' current value using the straight line method over its estimated useful lives. Property, plant and equipment on order is not depreciated.

Depreciation percentages for the most significant asset categories are as follows:

Industrial buildings	$2^1/_2$ –	$3^1/_3$
Office buildings		2
Printing presses	$6^2/_3$ –	8
Other machinery	10	– 20
Office machinery and equipment	10	– $33^1/_3$
Cars	25	– $33^1/_3$
Trucks		20
Databases and software	20	– $33^1/_3$

Although complying with the standard most companies have also transferred from revaluation reserve to profit and loss account reserve depreciation on the revalued amount thus reinstating distributable profits. This treatment is allowed by the Companies Act. However, despite this treatment the annual profit and earnings per share would still be reduced by increased depreciation. Some companies have therefore opted for non-depreciation of their property assets, usually arguing that a high standard of maintenance ensured that residual values were always equal to or above cost or revalued amount, or that the useful lives of assets were prolonged indefinitely. Support for this stance was provided by the press release with SSAP 12 which recognized and validated this view.[13]

The argument has been widely used so that now many companies make no provision for depreciation on their property assets. Forte plc provides an example of this treatment in Extract 6.8.

Extract 6.8 – Forte Group plc 1993 accounts, Accounting Policies.

2. Depreciation: No depreciation is provided on freehold properties or properties on leases with twenty years or more to run at the balance sheet date or on integral fixed plant. It is the Group's practice to maintain these assets in a continual state of sound repair and to extend and make improvements thereto from time to time and accordingly the Directors consider that the lives of these assets are so long, and residual values (based on prices prevailing at the time of acquisition or subsequent valuation) are so high, that their depreciation is insignificant. Any permanent diminution in the value of such properties is charged to the profit and loss account as appropriate.

Like many UK companies owning hotels and public houses, Forte does not provide depreciation on freehold and long leasehold properties. This is justified on the grounds that the properties are maintained to a high standard. It is very difficult for an external analyst to comment one way or the other on the justification given as maintenance costs are not disclosed in the accounts.

It is clear that the analyst must compare all policies which relate to the treatment of fixed assets when carrying out cross-sectional analysis. Different valuation methods will affect comparisons of profitability and gearing. Profit figures will be affected by depreciation policies adopted both in terms of whether depreciation is or is not charged on certain assets and on the assumptions made about residual value and asset life. Particular attention should be paid to significant changes relating to fixed asset accounting policies.

Case Study 6.1: Fixed Asset Valuations and Revaluations

Trafalgar House plc is a UK-based international organization engaged in construction and engineering, commercial and residential property, passenger shipping and hotels. Over time it has made many acquisitions including the Cunard Shipping Group, London's Ritz Hotel and more recently the Davy Engineering Group. In common with many companies it found trading conditions difficult in the early 1990s, particularly in its construction and property divisions.

The accounts for the year ended 30 September 1991 were the focus of a number of criticisms from both the financial press and analysts. The writer of the 'Lex' column in *The Financial Times* of 21 December 1991 was outraged enough to write:

> *Trafalgar's latest report and accounts perhaps demonstrate why the remuneration of its auditors jumped 20% this year.*

Not unnaturally Trafalgar House denied any manipulation of its figures, stating that full disclosure of what it had done and why it had adopted certain policies were fully disclosed in the financial report.

In July 1991 Trafalgar acquired Davy and with it a surplus on the Davy Corporation pension schemes. Trafalgar's actuaries assessed this surplus at acquisition on a basis consistent with Trafalgar's extant pension schemes.

The surplus of £75.4 million was used in arriving at the fair value of acquisition and included on the group balance sheet as a pension prepayment boosting the groups net assets. The group is to amortize this surplus in future periods.

Another criticism which we will discuss in more depth relates to Trafalgar's decision to transfer some UK properties from current assets where they were classified as 'developments for sale', to 'tangible fixed assets'. Details were given in the Chief Executive's Report by Sir Eric Parker who stated:

> *In view of the state of, and the short-term outlook for, the commercial property market, we decided at the beginning of the year to retain certain properties rather than selling high quality assets at unattractive prices. These properties have been reclassified as fixed assets and were revalued at 30 September 1991, resulting in a £68m writedown of wholly-owned properties and a £34.7 m writedown of associates.*

This transfer enabled the total write-down of £112.7 million to be set against revaluation reserve resulting in the previous surplus of £84 million being converted into a deficit of £18.7 million which was carried forward. If the properties had continued to be classified as current assets and included in developments for sale they would have been valued at the lower of cost and net realizable value in accordance with Note 1(i) to the accounts. The resulting write-down would have been a charge against operating profit which would have resulted in an after-tax loss and negative earnings per share compared with the reported after-tax profit (before extraordinary items) of £79 million and earnings per share excluding extraordinary items of 15.5p.

The Trafalgar accounts for the year to 30 September 1991 were referred to the Financial Reporting Review Panel in February 1992 with the main point at issue being the reclassification and revaluation of the properties. If the properties had been revalued at the end of the accounting year and then transferred, the loss would have been taken through the profit and loss account and no criticism would have arisen. It was the timing of the transfer – which seemed to have an element of backdating about it – which caused the controversy.

It is of interest that the 1990 accounts, although containing a Chairman's Statement, did not include a Chief Executive's Report. This Chairman's Statement, although dated 4 December 1990, made no mention of the property transfer although the Chief Executive's Report with the 1991 accounts quoted earlier indicates that the decision was taken at the beginning of the year. This is confirmed in Note 14 to the accounts relating to developments for sale where it specifically states:

On 1st October 1990 certain commercial properties were transferred to tangible fixed assets.

The *Accountancy* magazine, November 1992, reported that agreement had at last been reached between the Panel and the company. At the outset there had been speculation that the Panel might apply to the courts for an order requiring the company to produce revised accounts which, under the 1985 Companies Act, would have to be paid for by the company directors. After taking independent legal and accounting advice the directors initially refused to change their views on the transfer of assets and also on the recoverability of advance corporation tax carried forward on Trafalgar's balance sheet. However, faced with the threat of legal action the Panel announced:

The directors have undertaken to make the appropriate changes and adjustments in the 1992 accounts to meet the Panel's concerns.

This compromise means that in the 1992 accounts the 1991 comparative figures will show a £102.7 million deficit on revaluation of properties as a charge in the profit and loss account. In addition an extra £20 million tax charge for 1991 is expected to arise from the revised ACT policy as well as an increase in the 1992 write-off. This is an early illustration of the use of the Panel to investigate what is perceived to be inadequate financial reporting. As well as censuring the company, the auditors, Touche Ross, were reported to the appropriate regulatory body as the accounts were not qualified.

The Urgent Issues Task Force had already been moved to issue on 22 July 1992 its Abstract 5, *Transfers from Current Assets to Fixed Assets*. This abstract is reproduced in Figure 6.1 as it clearly was prompted by the Trafalgar case. It emphasizes that the problem arose from the different bases of valuation applied to fixed and current assets and illustrates the use of reserve movements to avoid taking losses to the profit and loss account even where losses caused the revaluation reserve to move into deficit.

We can also see that the existence of the new financial reporting regime enabled both early reference to the Financial Reporting Review Panel and early issue of a clarifying abstract by the Urgent Issues Task Force. What it did not do was deter a company from drawing up accounts in a form which caused it a great deal of adverse publicity and, it can be questioned, for what gain? When the 1991 accounts were issued it was clear to analysts and others with accounting knowledge what had taken place. Full disclosure was made and the accounting effects were purely cosmetic. Much time and energy were devoted both to devising the policies and to subsequently investigating and

---

Figure 6.1 – UITF Abstract 5:
Transfers from current assets to fixed assets (22 July 1992).

The issue

1. The Companies Act 1985 defines a fixed asset as one intended for use on a continuing basis in the company's activities and any which are not intended for such use are current assets (section 262(1) CA 1985. Where at a date subsequent to its original acquisition a current asset is retained for use on a continuing basis in the company's activities it becomes a fixed asset and the question arises as to the appropriate transfer value. An example is a property which is reclassified from trading properties to investment properties.

2. Of particular concern is the possibility that companies could avoid charging the profit and loss account with write-downs to net realisable value arising on unsold trading assets. This could be done by transferring the relevant assets from current assets to fixed assets at above net realisable value, as a result of which any later write down might be debited to revaluation reserve.

3. This abstract deals only with situations where current assets are included in the balance sheet at the lower of cost and net realisable value under paragraphs 22 and 23 of Schedule 4 to the Companies Act 1985.

4. The timing of the transfer of current assets to fixed assets should reflect the timing of management's change of intent and should not be backdated (for example to the start of the financial year). Since the date of the management decision is unlikely to correspond with the balance sheet date at which a full review of carrying values would be made, consideration must be given to the appropriate amounts at which such assets should be transferred at the time of transfer.

UITF consensus

5. The Task Force reached a consensus that where assets are transferred from current to fixed, the current assets accounting rules should be applied up to the effective date of transfer, which is the date of management's change of intent. Consequently the transfer should be made at the lower of cost and net realisable value, and accordingly an assessment should be made of the net realisable value at the date of transfer and if this is less than its previous carrying value the diminution should be charged in the profit and loss account, reflecting the loss to the company while the asset was held as a current asset.

Case Study 6.1

6. Whether assets are transferred at cost or at net realisable value in accordance with paragraph 5 above, fixed asset accounting rules will apply to the assets subsequent to the date of transfer. In cases where the transfer is at net realisable value, the asset could be accounted for as a fixed asset at a valuation (under the alternative accounting rules of the Act) as at the date of the transfer, at subsequent balance sheet dates it may or may not be revalued, but in either event the disclosure requirements appropriate to a valuation should be given.

Date from which effective

7. The accounting treatment required by this consensus should be adopted in financial statements relating to accounting periods ending on or after 23 December 1992, but earlier adoption is encouraged. In order to ensure consistency of treatment, corresponding amounts for preceding years should be restated where applicable.

References

Companies Act 1985 Section 221(1) and Schedule 4 paragraphs 17 to 19, 22 to 23, 30 to 34 and 43.

Northern Ireland - Companies (Northern Ireland) Order 1986, articles 229(1) and 270(1), and Schedule 4 paragraphs 17 to 19, 22 to 23, 30 to 34 and 43.

Republic of Ireland - Companies Act 1990 section 202(1) and the Companies (Amendment) Act 1986, the Schedule paragraphs 5 to 7, 10 to 11, 18 to 22, 30 and 60.

Statement of Standard Accounting Practice 6

- Extraordinary items and prior year adjustments–paragraph 33.

Statement of Standard Accounting Practice 9

- Stocks and long-term contracts - paragraph 26.

Statement of Standard Accounting Practice 19

- Accounting for investment properties - paragraphs 11 and 13.

Note on legal requirements:

The Task Force has been advised by leading Counsel that assets can be treated as having been transferred from current assets to fixed assets at a value equal to the lower of cost and net realisable value. Counsel indicated that the above advice is based on the assumption that where the transfer takes place at net realisable value, the asset will be accounted for as a fixed asset as at the date of transfer in accordance with the alternative accounting rules in Schedule 4 to the Companies Act (that is, included at a current value rather than historical cost).

defending them. The main gainers seem to have been professional accountants and lawyers representing all parties concerned; it is difficult to see how shareholders were ever expected to gain from the strategies adopted and given the costs involved must surely have been net losers.

Assignment

Obtain a copy of the Trafalgar accounts for the year ended 30 September 1991. Using the accounts and the notes thereto revise the profit and loss account and shareholders' funds to reflect current practice and comment on the differences arising.

References

1. ED 51, *Accounting for Fixed Assets and Revaluations,* ASC, May 1990, para. 57.
2. IAS 16, *Accounting for Property, Plant and Equipment,* IASC, March 1982, para. 6.
3. ED 51, op. cit., para. 66.
4. Companies Act 1985, s.262(1).
5. Ibid., Sch. 4, para. 26(1).
6. Taxes Act 1970, ss.248(5)(a), 269 as amended by Finance Act 1981, s.38 (now Taxes Act 1988, s.338(3)).
7. Companies Act 1985, Sch.4, para. 26(3)(b).
8. SFAS 34, *Capitalisation of Interest Cost,* FASB, October 1979.
9. IAS 23, *Capitalization of Borrowing Costs,* IASC, March 1984.
10. SSAP 12, *Accounting for Depreciation,* ASC, revised January 1987, para. 10.
11. The presentation of financial information, Discussion Draft of Chapter 6 of *Statement of Principles,* ASB, December 1991.
12. SSAP 12, op.cit., para. 16.
13. Technical Release 648, Statement on the publication of SSAP 12 (revised), *Accounting for Depreciation.*

Problems

1. Explain the assumptions made and any other factors determining the charge for depreciation on fixed assets. How might changes in assumptions affect the amount of depreciation charged? What are the implications for investment analysts?
2. Discuss the alternative treatment of interest and overheads incurred when fixed assets are constructed by the company itself. Explain the effect on profits disclosed and relevant ratios of the company. Give examples of companies using different policies.
3. Many UK companies periodically revalue property assets. Discuss the purpose of this policy and the extent to which such revaluations are undertaken in other European countries.
4. A policy associated with the revaluation in 3 above is the subsequent depreciation policy adopted. Discuss the possible depreciation policies adopted in connection with property assets and their effect on reported profits and leverage ratios.

7

Accounting for Groups

Objectives

- To examine the diversity in the definitions of a group and in the methods used to prepare the financial statements of groups of companies.

- To discuss the implications of the use of merger accounting for business combinations.

Introduction

The rate of adoption of group accounts as a means of reporting the results of a parent company and its subsidiaries has differed significantly between European countries. Evidence of adoption in the legislation of the United Kingdom dates from 1947, that of Germany 1965, Netherlands from 1970 and France 1985, with Spain and Italy having no requirement until very recently. The EC Seventh Directive was intended to harmonize the presentation and publication of group accounts. However, the nature of harmonization and the complexity of group accounting give rise to a situation in which there is still significant scope for accounting diversity. Indeed, Nobes[1] points out that the range of options in the Seventh Directive results in a possible 'two zillion' alternative ways of preparing group accounts. Although this is mathematically correct the Seventh Directive does, as Nobes concedes, represent substantial harmonization compared to the previous situation.

The importance of the possible diversity for analysts is, firstly, that the subjects of analysis are likely to be major companies with many subsidiary and/or other related companies and, secondly, that the possible accounting methods give scope for significant differences in reported results both within and between countries.

Evidence of the importance of changes and differences in group accounting practice can be seen in the study of Pellens and Linnhoffs.[2] They investigated the informational content of group accounts in Germany before and after the Seventh Directive changes. The tradition for analysts in Germany has been to base assessment primarily on parent company accounts rather than group accounts. The researchers examined the informational content of the parent company accounts versus the group accounts. They also examined the impact of the change in the definition of a group after the implementation of the

Seventh Directive. In the cases they examined, they found that significantly different estimates of future earnings would be given by 'new rules v. old rules group accounts' and by 'parent co. v. new rules group accounts'. They conclude (p. 119) that: 'The financial development of the overall group and thus the consolidated accounts will become increasingly significant for the share price, dividend prospects and also the creditworthiness of the parent company.' If this holds true for Germany then it should also do so for the perceptions of analysts from other member states, although the change in these perceptions will depend upon their tradition.

The principal issues

- What is the definition of a group – that is, what relationship between one company and another will form a parent–subsidiary or Investor–associate relationship? The profit and loss account and balance sheet of a group will look totally different from that of a company with an investment accounted for as a separate entity.

    What accounting methods might be adopted for group accounting? The principal potential methods are full (or global) consolidation, equity accounting and proportional consolidation (although there are potential variants of each method). These give rise, in particular, to different balance sheet representations of the group and thus affect asset-based ratios and gearing levels.
- When are subsidiaries required, or allowed, to be excluded from consolidation and how are excluded subsidiaries accounted for? The potential for manipulation of financial statements by omitting certain subsidiaries from the group accounts has been much used, particularly in the UK.
- Is merger accounting a potential alternative to acquisition accounting and, if so, in what circumstances?
- What are the potential areas of diversity in the detailed accounting methods that can be adopted in carrying out group accounting procedures?

The Definition of a Group

The existence of a parent–subsidiary relationship may be determined by establishing 'de jure' control or 'de facto' control by the parent. 'De jure' control was the UK tradition and is determined by the ownership of legal control. A form of 'de facto' control was the German tradition, this being based upon the exercise or the right to exercise actual control.

The Seventh Directive achieved a combination (and compromise) of these. Article 1.1 states that consolidated accounts are required where the parent undertaking:

(a) has a majority of the shareholders or members voting rights; or

(b) is a member and has the right to appoint or remove a majority of the administrative, management or supervisory body; or

(c) has the right to exercise a dominant influence pursuant to a control contract or provision in the memorandum and articles. Member states may require the parent to be a member;

(d) (aa) is a member, and a majority of the members of the board who have held office throughout the year, the previous year and up to the time of the issue of the accounts have in fact been appointed solely as a result of the exercise of the parents' voting rights; or

(bb) is a member and controls alone, pursuant to an agreement with other members, a majority of the members' voting rights.

Member states may opt not to apply (d) (aa) or to make it dependent on a holding of 20% or more of the voting rights. These are essentially the 'de jure' definitional rules.

Article 1.2 states that *consolidated accounts may be required by member states where the parent has a participating interest and either (a) actually exercises dominant influence over the subsidiary or (b) the undertakings are managed on a unified basis.* These are the 'de facto' definitional rules, which were optional for member states.

In implementing these provisions member states have not taken a uniform approach to the options, as demonstrated in Table 7.1.

TABLE 7.1

Approaches of member states to the Seventh Directive

	ARTICLE 1.1 (c) Parent not member	ARTICLE 1.1 (d) aa adopted	ARTICLE 1.2 adopted
United Kingdom	yes	no	yes
France	no	yes	no
Germany	yes	yes	yes
Netherlands	yes	no	yes
Italy	no	yes	no
Spain	no	yes	no

There are a number of possible exemptions from the requirement to prepare group accounts where:

1. the holding company is a financial institution;
2. the holding company is a 90% owned subsidiary and the minority shareholders agree; or
3. the holding company is a subsidiary of another company and is

included in the consolidated accounts (in compliance with Seventh Directive requirements) of an EU member state company (a further extension of this rule might allow this exemption for non-EU member state parents); or
4. the holding company is not a limited company.

A further exemption applies to small groups. Again, these rules have not been taken up uniformly.

The Seventh Directive also included definitions of associated (related) companies and joint ventures. These have been adopted in similar but not identical ways in member states and thus once more differences might occur.

Having established that differences in definition occur it might be useful to summarize the relevant accounting methods. Thus the basic Seventh Directive schema is:

Relationship to investor	Normal accounting method
1. Subsidiary	Full consolidation
2. Associate	Equity
3. Joint venture	Proportional consolidation
4. Investment	Cost or net realizable value

The adoption of methods 1 and 4 has been relatively consistent; however, there have been some minor differences in practice in the adoption of methods 2 and 3.

The result of the implementation of the Seventh Directive has been a significant change in the companies treated as subsidiaries in all member states. For example, John Swire and Sons Ltd, a UK company, changed the treatment of Swire Pacific, a company which was 27% owned, but this holding carried 49% of the voting rights.

In Extract 7.1 the change in treatment of Swire Pacific is reflected in the two balance sheets for 1989. In the Actual 1989 column (that is as published in 1989) Swire Pacific is treated as part of the investments. In the Group accounts for 1990 the 1989 figures are restated with Swire Pacific being consolidated as a subsidiary. The effect of this change on the 1989 balance sheet is enormous:

- total net assets change from £898.9 million to £2848 million;
- minority interests change from £0.5 million to £1919 million;
- tangible assets change from £274 million to £3267 million;
- borrowings change from £79.2 million to £1053 million.

These changes will have an equally important impact on the ratios which the analyst will compute and thus on the conclusions drawn.

In Germany one of the most important changes bought about by the Seventh Directive was the introduction of the requirement to consolidate foreign subsidiaries (see Extract 7.2).

	Note	1990 £m	Group (Restated) 1989 £m	Actual 1989 £m
Fixed assets				
Tangible assets	...	3,191	3,267	274.3
Investments	...	157	136	642.8
		3,348	3,403	917.1
Current assets				
Stocks	...	169	186	5.9
Debtors	...	860	949	77.7
Investments		339	342	–
Cash at bank and on deposit		423	467	105.1
		1,791	1,944	188.7
Current liabilities				
Creditors: due within one year				
Borrowings	...	(283)	(376)	(25.8)
Other creditors	...	(738)	(802)	(83.1)
Net current assets (liabilities)		770	766	79.8
Total assets less current liabilities		4,118	4,169	996.9
Creditors: due after more than one year				
Borrowings	...	(1,161)	(1,053)	(79.2)
Other creditors	...	(238)	(230)	(1.3)
Provisions for liabilities and charges	...	(51)	(38)	(17.5)
Net assets		2,668	2,848	898.9
Capital and reserves				
Called-up share capital	...	120	120	120.0
Reserves	...	810	809	778.4
Shareholders' funds		930	929	898.4
Outside shareholders' interests		1,738	1,919	0.5
		2,668	2,848	898.9

Scope of Consolidation

In addition to VEBA AG, 404 domestic and 269 foreign companies in which a majority of the shareholders' voting rights are indirectly or directly held by VEBA AG have been included in the Consolidated Financial Statements, which have been drawn up in accordance with the legal provisions of the German Commercial Code and Corporation Act.

Compared with the previous year, 55 domestic and 54 foreign companies have been included in the Consolidated Financial Statements for the first time; 44 domestic and 37 foreign companies have been eliminated.

333 subsidiaries have not been included. Of these companies, 37 have been subject to restrictions on their assets or their management. 161 companies have not been included because their influence, even combined, on the assets, financial and profit situation of the Group is of minor significance; their sales volume has been less than 1% of total Group sales. It was decided not to include the financial statements of companies either established

or acquired during the financial year, in particular Schenker & Co. GmbH (now SCHENKER-RHENUS AG) with their subsidiaries as the necessary organizational requirements for consolidation did not yet exist in these companies. As in the previous year, however, the RHENUS-WEICHELT division with its subsidiaries, which was transferred by RHENUS AG to SCHENKER-RHENUS AG, has been included in the Consolidated Financial Statements. The non-consolidated part of SCHENKER-RHENUS AG with its subsidiaries has been valued using the equity method.

The scope of consolidation and other major equity interests have been summarized on the inside front cover. The major affiliated and associated companies together with the share held, the shareholders' equity and the earnings are listed on pages 124 to 128. An itemized listing of the entire Group equity interests has been filed with the Düsseldorf Local Court, Commercial Register HRB 22 315, and the Berlin-Charlottenburg Local Court, Commercial Register 93 HRB 1647.

Extract 7.3 provides an example from Spain to illustrate by way of note, the effect of a new requirement to prepare consolidated accounts.

Thus it can be seen from these extracts that the determination of the membership of the group is of considerable importance. Analysts need to be aware of the definition and interpretations being used and to ensure that the impact of non-consolidated related companies is understood.

The data of these companies' net worth position were obtained from their financial statements as of December 31, 1991 and 1990. The 1991 financial statements have not been approved by the respective Stockholders' Meetings.

Had consolidation principles been applied in the accompanying financial statements of ENDESA, the balances of the captions shown in the table below would have increased by the amounts indicated therein. The basis of application of consolidation principles includes the following:

1. Consolidation by the global integration method of the Companies in the ENDESA Group (ENHER, ERZ, GESA, UNELCO, ENCASUR and VIESGO) whose accounts were adapted to the accounting methods applied by ENDESA in preparing its financial statements.

2. Recording by the equity method of the holdings in Red Eléctrica de España, S.A., Compañía Sevillana de Electricidad, S.A. (CSE); Unión Eléctrica Fenosa, S.A., (UEFSA); Fuerza s Eléctricas de Cataluña, S.A. (FECSA); Saltos del Nansa, S.A. (NANSA) and Empresa Nacional Eléctrica de Córdoba, S.A. (ENECO).

	Millions of Pesetas	
	1991	1990
Utility plant, net	**418,006**	283,072
Prepaid taxes	**19,506**	7,198
Current assets	**74,189**	61,746
Total assets	**511,701**	352,016
Reserves	**78,126**	76,023
Long-term debt	**94,416**	67,444
Current liabilities	**124,104**	102,786
Other liabilities	**201,669**	94,294
Income for the year, after taxes	**13,386**	11,469
Total liabilities	**511,701**	352,016
Sales revenues	**282,276**	219,830
Other revenues	**11,533**	5,013
Purchases and expenses	**(276,244)**	(209,772)
Taxes	**(4,179)**	(3,602)
Income after taxes	**13,386**	11,469

The criteria for conforming to the new legislation at ENDESA Group level, the nature of which was similar to the criteria described in Note 2-b, had to be taken into account when comparing the 1991 and 1990 figures.

Exclusion from Consolidation

Given the impact on the financial statements of consolidation it is important to understand when a subsidiary is either required (must) or allowed (may) to be excluded from consolidation. Articles 13 and 14 of the Seventh Directive sets out the reasons why subsidiaries may or must be excluded. Table 7.2 provides the interpretation of these articles in three member states.

It can be seen that the UK position is more prescriptive than that required by the Directive or than the approach adopted in other countries. However, we need to be aware of the different interpretations which might be adopted in different states. A good example is provided by the Dutch company Ahold 1988 and 1990 accounts (Extracts 7.4 and 7.5, emphasis added).

TABLE 7.2
Exclusion of subsidiaries
from consolidation

	Seventh Directive	UK		Germany	France
		C.A. 1989	FRS 2		
Immaterial	May	May		May	May
Severe long-term restrictions	May	May	Must	May	May
Undue delay or expense	May	May*	Must not	May	May
Held for resale	May	May	Must	May	May
Different activities, exclude if necessary to enable true and fair view	Must	Must**	Must**	Must	May

* if not material

** a very restricted category of company

Extract 7.4 – Ahold NV 1988 accounts, Notes.

Real estate activities

In the course of 1988 a review of real estate operating strategy took place, leading to the decision to increase the autonomy of the real estate operations and management.

Through an issue of cumulative preferred stock by the real estate companies and through the arrangement of long-term loans, the assets have been refinanced in an appropriate manner. Furthermore, a one-time write-up of the carrying value of the real estate, by an amount of Dfl 217 million, was effected so as to better align this with the market value.

The autonomous real estate activities differ considerably from Ahold's main activity selling food and other consumer goods through chainstores. In order to provide better insights into the size and composition of stockholders' equity and the results achieved by both types of activities, their financial statements are presented separately. Their combined balance sheet, statement of earnings and notes are presented in the notes to Ahold's consolidated financial statements.

Ahold Real Estate

As in previous years, the real estate companies have been excluded from the consolidation, but have been shown under unconsolidated subsidiaries and affiliates. This was done in view of the progress made by the real estate companies since the 1988 decision to increase their autonomy. The realization that business and marketing requirements necessitate a distinction between retail and real estate activities has resulted in the formation of a (real estate) group with a structure of its own. Consequently, and pursuant to section 405 of Book 2 of the Netherlands Civil Code, the real estate companies are no longer included in the consolidated financial statements of Koninklijke Ahold nv.

It can be seen that the exclusion of the real estate subsidiaries in 1988 and 1989 was on the basis of differing activities. The change in the rules to that of the exclusion being necessary to enable a true and fair view meant that Ahold had to restructure the group in order to avoid consolidation in 1990.

The treatment of financial subsidiaries may be of importance, in particular to the determination of gearing. The Dutch rules and the UK rules in FRS 2 state that the financial activities of a subsidiary are not sufficient grounds for exclusion (Extracts 7.6 and 7.7).

Extract 7.6 – Marks & Spencer plc 1991 accounts, Accounting Policies.

Basis of Consolidation

The Group financial statements incorporate the financial statements of Marks and Spencer plc and its subsidiaries for the year ended 31 March 1991. The net assets of financial activities were previously shown as a separate item in the Group's balance sheet and analysed in a note. In accordance with the new requirements of the Companies Act 1985, financial activities are now fully consolidated within the main balance sheet. Comparative figures have been restated to reflect the change in policy from last year.

Extract 7.7 - DAF NV 1990 accounts, Notes.

General

DAF N.V. considers the industrial activities as its corebusiness; the finance activities performed by DAF Finance Company N.V. are considered to be sales supportive and of a dissimilar nature. Through 1989 the accounts of DAF Finance Company N.V. were for this reason not included in the DAF N.V. consolidation and published separately. Starting 1990 consolidation of the accounts of DAF Finance Company N.V. has become mandatory, since the "Aanpassingswet 7e E.G. Richtlijn" has become effective.

In order to continue providing information to enable a sound judgement in the corebusiness and to also comply with the legal requirements, financial information is presented with respect to the industrial activities as well as the consolidated information.

The Burton Group highlights the impact on gearing levels of the inclusion of such subsidiaries by a footnote to the balance sheet (Extract 7.8).

Extract 7.8 – Burton plc Group 1991 accounts, Balance Sheet.

Capital and Reserves	1991	1990
Called-up share capital	335.1	279.3
Share premium account	113.6	8.8
Revaluation reserve	80.4	80.4
Retained earnings	185.0	372.8
	714.1	**741.3**
Gearing	43.1%	62.5%
Gearing, excluding High Street Property Investments		
Limited and property lease obligations	24.3%	44.1%

The treatment of such subsidiaries is less constrained in other countries, for example in France and Italy as demonstrated in Extracts 7.9 and 7.10.

A - Principles of consolidation

The consolidated financial statements include the financial statements of all the significant Group controlled subsidiaries, with the exception of those of the Finance Division which are accounted for in the consolidated financial statements by the equity method, due to the nature of their activities and the specific structure of their financial statements.

Nevertheless, as mentioned above, note 27 presents proforma consolidated financial statements which include the financial statements of all the companies controlled by the Group. The consolidation of the Finance Division subsidiaries has no impact on the net income and shareholders' equity of the Group.

Significant companies in which the Group has a material influence are accounted for by the equity method, except for joint-venture companies, which are consolidated on a proportional basis.

All material intercompany transactions and unrealized internal profits included in capital assets and inventories are eliminated for the consolidated statements.

(1)   BASIS OF THE CONSOLIDATED FINANCIAL STATEMENTS

The consolidated financial statements include the financial statements of the parent company, Ing. C. Olivetti & C., S.p.A., and of the Italian and foreign companies in which the former directly or indirectly holds the majority of voting rights or operating control, with the exception of a few minor subsidiaries and those companies operating in the financial services sector.

Some interesting exclusions may be found in some German group financial statements – see Extract 7.11

In conclusion, analysts need to be aware of the potential differences to the financial statements which non-consolidated subsidiaries may make as well as potential differences in the definitions of parent–subsidiary and parent–associate relationships. The treatment of non-consolidated subsidiaries may be either to include them using equity accounting or at lower of cost and NRV, together with some additional disclosures. Once more, analysts should take care to determine the exact treatment of such subsidiaries and make any necessary adjustments in their deliberations.

Extract 7.11 – RWE AG 1990/91 accounts, Notes.

The following are not consolidated: welfare funds, since significant and continuing limitations inhibit the exercise of the parent company's rights over their assets; fuel trading companies which primarily distribute goods that are manufactured within the Group itself but are already marketed on a larger scale; other companies whose assets, income and expenses, even in sum, are immaterial for the Group's net worth, financial position and results.

We refrained from including companies formed or acquired in the new federal states in the year under review in the Consolidated Accounts as their activities are still of lesser importance.

Merger versus Acquisition Accounting

It has often been suggested that the preparation of consolidated accounts using acquisition accounting may give a misleading representation of the affairs of a business combination where two firms merge in a pooling of their mutual interests. The basic premise of acquisition accounting is the purchase of control in one entity by another. This would in consequence give rise to a need to place a value on purchase consideration, to the revaluation to fair value of purchased assets, to a positive or negative value for goodwill and to the capitalization of pre-acquisition profits. None of these consequences is relevant if the combination of the entities does not involve one of the parties having control over the other in the combined entity.

A problem in the UK is that merger accounting and acquisition accounting have both been abused. David Tweedie, Chairman of the ASB, has described 'acquisition accounting' in the UK as the 'black hole' of financial reporting, and 'merger accounting' as the route to 'instant profits'. Merger accounting has long been controversial, one reason being that it does allow a company to create instant profits. If company A is having an unprofitable year, and it can 'merge' with a profitable company B before company 'A's year end, the addition of B's profits for the year to the 'combined' performance, can hide from investors the true performance of 'A'.

The resulting boosted profits are available for distribution as dividends for the year, even though the two companies may have combined only a few days before company A's year end. With acquisition accounting only the profits earned by the acquired company following the acquisition would be available for distribution to the purchasing company's shareholders.

In the UK the latest proposals – there have been many – on the subject (FRED 6), if accepted would effectively eliminate merger accounting. FRED 6 proposes to restrict merger accounting to a few, tightly defined cases. It would restrict the use of merger accounting to the situation where in substance (if not in legal form) a new reporting entity arises on a substantially equal partnership with no one company dominant. This is considered a pre-emptive response by the standard setting body to a potential increase in interest in merger accounting, expected as a result of measures being taken by the ASB against abusing reserve accounting at the time of an acquisition.

To satisfy the new criteria as to whether a merger has taken place, neither party should have or be portrayed to have a dominant role following the combination, the size of each company should be more or less equal, and the form of compensation paid to the shareholder should be mainly equity.

The concept of a merger is sound, and there may be situations where a true merger occurs, but it is rare. The difficulties of defining what is in practice a true merger is so difficult that it can be argued it is not worthwhile doing so. In the UK British Aerospace explained in their accounts that with some acquisitions they had followed merger accounting practices. They highlighted one of the advantages of this

---

Extract 7.12 – SmithKline Beecham plc 1989 accounts, Additional Information for US Investors.

	31 December	
	1989	1988
	£m	£m
Balance Sheet Data		
Shareholders' equity per U.K. GAAP	**(297)**	1,360
U.S. GAAP adjustments:		
Elimination of SmithKline equity prior to Merger	**—**	(98)
Goodwill — Beecham	**461**	441
Capitalisation of interest	**37**	7
Dividends	**50**	74
Deferred taxation:		
due to timing differences	**(66)**	(61)
due to ACT	**5**	32
Revaluation reserve	**(156)**	(108)
Other, net	**(12)**	—
Purchase accounting:		
Property, plant and equipment	**69**	—
Intangible assets	**754**	—
Goodwill	**2,665**	—
Other, net	**35**	—
Shareholders' equity per U.S. GAAP	**3,545**	1,647

method, namely that is allows the full annual profits of the acquiree to be consolidated, however late, in the acquiree's accounting year the acquisition took place. This is precisely the criticism of the technique.

With the new tougher rules in the UK by 1993 only a few companies were adopting the merger accounting approach. British Aerospace would not with the new rules have been allowed to use merger accounting when it combined with Arlington as it would have failed the size test, the equity consideration test and the market dominance test. One consolidation that did pass the merger tests was that of Elsevier and Trace Computers in 1993. This involved the merger of two companies who came together sharing the equity of the new holding company on a 50/50 basis and no cash payments were involved.

The effect of using merger rather than acquisition accounting is dramatically illustrated by SmithKline Beecham plc where merger accounting was allowed under UK GAPP but not under US GAAP (Extract 7.12).

The Seventh Directive allowed the use of merger accounting and Article 20 sets out the qualifying conditions which were similar to the then extant UK rules. This is not surprising as the UK is the member state where merger accounting has been of most importance in the past. Even then, the adoption of merger accounting is very low; in a survey (*Company Reporting*, No. 37, July 1993) of companies showing evidence of business combinations over the five years to 1993 only 1.4% of these used merger accounting. In the Netherlands a few cases of merger accounting have occurred in the past although there are no specific rules for when it may be used.

Thus the use of merger accounting is very restricted, but where it is used it has a major impact on both the profit and loss account and the balance sheet. (See also Chapter 8 on intangible assets.)

Other Group Accounting Issues

There are a number of technical accounting issues which arise in preparing financial statements for groups.

Uniform accounting policies

The issue here is whether the accounting policies used in the group accounts need necessarily to be those used in the individual financial statements. In the UK the same principles are required in all cases; however in France, Germany and Italy it is possible to use one method in the individual accounts and another in the consolidated accounts, for example with regard to stock valuation. In some cases French and Italian groups adopt a different set of accounting rules in the consolidated accounts from the domestic rules used in the individual company accounts (see Extract 7.14). The purpose of this is to achieve acceptance on the international capital markets, therefore the group accounts will either be based upon US GAAP or the International Accounting Standards (see Extract 7.13).

The overwhelming majority of German companies adopt the same accounting principles in both sets of financial statements. Thus tax

A - Basis of Consolidation

The consolidated financial statements have been prepared in accordance with current French accounting principles. These accounting principles comply with the financial and accounting methods prescribed by accounting principles generally accepted in the United States of America, which the Group uses as a reference in view of the international nature of its activities, with the exception that, since 1989, brands have not been amortized. Had accounting principles generally accepted in the United States of America been fully applied, net income for 1991 would have been FF164 million lower (1990: FF138 million), and stockholders' equity at December 31, 1991 would have been reduced by FF401 million (1990: FF237 million).

(13)   RECONCILIATION WITH THE PARENT COMPANY'S FINANCIAL STATEMENTS

The reconciliation of the net income and shareholders' equity reported in the consolidated financial statements with those shown in the parent company's financial statements as of December 31, 1990, is as follows:

(millions of lire)	Net income	Shareholders' equity
AMOUNTS SHOWN IN THE FINANCIAL STATEMENTS OF ING. C. OLIVETTI & C., S.p.A. AS OF DECEMBER 31, 1990	95,123	3,790,405
Items used by Ing. C. Olivetti & C., S.p.A. to benefit from relevant tax allowances which are treated differently for consolidation purposes:		
– reversal of the effects of accelerated depreciation charged to the parent company statement of income	(16,400)	53,900
– research contributions excluded from the parent company statement of income	695	–
Effects of the elimination of unrealized intercompany profit or loss between group companies	(109,836)	(212,169)
Results of subsidiaries and associated companies included in the consolidated financial statements, deferred taxes, translation and other consolidation adjustments	90,823	(144,931)
AMOUNTS SHOWN IN THE CONSOLIDATED FINANCIAL STATEMENTS AS OF DECEMBER 31, 1990	60,405	3,487,205

induced valuations are not eliminated in the process of consolidation with a few exceptions. When Schering AG was listed on the London Stock Exchange in 1986 they released tax-induced hidden reserves resulting in an increase in equity by 76%. In 1989 Daimler discontinued its extremely conservative accounting policies in the consolidated accounts thereby increasing equity by 32%. In the 1992 group accounts Daimler released another DM4.5 billion of hidden reserves in order to comply with the requirements of the SEC in the process of being listed at the New York Stock Exchange. This does not give the analyst any particular problems unless he or she is examining a subsidiary set of accounts where special accounting methods have been adopted and thus care needs to be taken in comparative analysis.

Fair values

The use of fair values in consolidation arises in terms of the consideration which passes on an acquisition, i.e. the value placed on the assets acquired, and thus in the determination of goodwill and the amount given for minority interests. The Seventh Directive allows some variation in the application of fair value rules. The United Kingdom has for some time required the full use of fair values on consolidation

---

Extract 7.15 – Beazer plc 1990 accounts, Notes.

A number of small acquisitions were made in the year, including the purchase by Beazer East, Inc. of the Stephens Paving Company, the purchase by Beazer West, Inc. of Partin Limestone Products, and the purchase by Beazer Australia Pty Limited of three contracting and property companies. The aggregate of these acquisitions is shown in the following table:

Assets acquired	Book value	Revaluation	Provisions for trading losses	Other provisions	Fair value
	£m	£m	£m	£m	£m
Fixed assets	8.7	1.4	–	–	10.1
Current assets	38.4	–	(5.8)	(5.5)	27.1
Liabilities	(32.8)	–	(2.5)	–	(35.3)
Net assets	14.3	1.4	(8.3)	(5.5)	1.9

Provisions for trading losses
- current assets: represents the amount by which it was considered that contracting work-in-progress was overvalued due to the additional costs that were yet to be incurred prior to sale.
- liabilities accruals sold and against the cost of refurbishing certain fixed assets.

---

together with a fair value table. Extract 7.15 is a typical example. In Germany, companies may use the 'book value method' or the 'purchase method'. The 'book value method' involves a comparison of the value of the investment with the book value of the subsidiary's assets. The resulting difference is eliminated by allocation to the individual assets and liabilities up to their market value and by the creation of goodwill. The 'purchase method' uses fair values directly in the group accounts up to the carrying cost of the investment. Although Alexander and Archer[3] assert that there are only classification differences between these two methods there are implications for the treatment of negative goodwill and the carrying value of minority interests.

Extract 7.16 – Guinness plc 1992 accounts, Notes.

Accounting for acquisitions and disposals (extract)

(c) Fair value adjustments and acquisitions provisions

The net assets of companies acquired are incorporated in the consolidated accounts at their fair value to the Group and after adjustments to bring the accounting policies of companies acquired into alignment with those of the Group. Fair value adjustments include provision for re-organization costs, anticipated future losses, and excess stocks. If the estimates on which these provisions are based prove to be in excess of actual expenditure or losses, the unutilized surplus provisions will not be taken to profit and loss, but will be credited to reserves as a recalculation of goodwill.

One controversial issue arising from the fair value exercise is the creation of provisions for future trading losses, reorganization costs or asset write-downs. These techniques all allow future costs or losses to miss the future profit and loss account and to be taken on consolidation as a part of the goodwill/reserve calculation.

In his book *Accounting for Growth*, Terry Smith[4] describes this as 'probably the area of acquisition accounting which has provided the greatest opportunity for abuse'. This has been considerably reduced in the UK by the requirements of FRS 2 (see Extract 7.16), but these opportunities may still be available in countries which have not gone further than the Seventh Directive requirements.

Other issues

There are other technical areas of interest which analysts might need to consider, and the history of the adoption of group accounting and the influence of Anglo-Saxon group accounting methods means that there is more discussion of the issues in the UK than in other countries where the Seventh Directive requires new approaches to the problem.

Analysts should in particular be aware of the following problems:

- non-coterminous year ends;
- the treatment of intra-group transactions;
- the treatment of goodwill on disposals of subsidiaries;
- the problem of quasi-subsidiaries;
- the treatment of changes in the level of shareholding by a parent;
- reorganizations and reconstructions.

References

1. Nobes, C.W. (1988) 'Seven zillion ways to prepare group accounts', *Accountancy*.
2. Pellens, B. and Linnhoffs, U. (1993) 'Financial analysis of group accounts in Germany: an empirical study', in Gray, S.J., Coenenberg, A.G. and Gordon, P.D. (eds), *International Group Accounting*, Routledge.
3. Alexander, D. and Archer, S. (1992) *European Accounting Guide*, Academic Press.
4. Smith, T. (1992) *Accounting for Growth*, Century Press.

Problems

1. Using the accounts of John Swire plc (Extract 7.1) examine the effect of the change in treatment of Swire Pacific in the 1989 and restated 1989 figures in the 1990 accounts in relationship to:
   a current ratios;
   b gearing ratios;
   c asset ratios.
2. Discuss the effect of a change from acquisition to merger accounting using the figures in Extract 7.12 to illustrate your arguments.

8 | Intangible Assets

Objectives

- To examine the items that appear in financial accounts under the classification intangible assets.

- To discuss the many issues involved with accounting for goodwill and to compare the alternative treatments adopted in different countries.

- To consider whether or not the value of brands should be included in balance sheets.

- To compare the treatment of items such as research and development expenditure and start-up costs in the accounts of companies in different countries.

Introduction

Assets are called intangible if they do not have a physical substance, but are expected to confer some future benefit to a business. For some companies intangibles are a major part of their real value. The problem is that any attempt to place a value on them can be very unreliable. The Fourth Directive allows companies to record intangibles in their accounts.

There are two classes of intangible assets. One class includes patents, goodwill, brand values, trade marks and franchises. These assets clearly have a value to a business in that they lead to future receipts. Companies are prepared to pay to acquire such intangible assets. The other class relates to deferred charges, such as capitalized research and development expenditure, advertising costs and start-up costs. These are items of expenditure which have been incurred, but have not yet been charged to the profit and loss account. The recognition of the charge has been deferred so that the costs can be matched against the income when it is earned in future periods. As with the other class of intangible they possess no physical form.

There are in fact other assets of a business which meet the criteria of 'no physical substance', which do confer future benefits beyond the current accounting period, but which do not appear in the balance sheet, for example an investment in an education and training programme or the employment contract of a particularly skilled management team or labour force. There have been suggestions that such human assets should be reported, but support for the idea is not strong, the main criticism being that there is no guarantee that the business will continue to benefit from the services of these 'assets'. The individuals involved could easily leave the business; the evidence as to the future benefits of these assets is therefore weaker (less reliable) than that for those intangible assets that are usually included in accounts.

In 1989 the International Accounting Standards Committee produced a paper entitled *Framework for the Preparation and Presentation of Financial Statements*. In this they define an asset as 'a resource controlled by the enterprise as a result of past events and from which future economic benefits are expected to flow to the enterprise'. They state, however, that the asset should only be recognized if 'the item has a cost or value that can be measured with reliability'.

There are a number of possible treatments of intangible assets in a balance sheet.

1. There is an argument that balance sheets should not include intangible assets but should only reflect tangible assets. Following this approach, if a company pays for an intangible asset it should write it off immediately against reserves or the profit and loss account. One argument for such a policy is that present practice is inconsistent. Traditionally companies have not recorded intangible assets they have created themselves. Why, therefore, capitalize purchased intangibles and exclude from the balance sheet intangibles a company has self-generated? To exclude all intangibles is at least consistent.

2. Companies should exclude from the balance sheet intangibles that do not represent a specific property right. Franchises and patents give a property right, goodwill does not.

3. Companies should enter the intangible asset in the balance sheet and write it off, either to reserves or profit and loss account, within a limited period of time. The Fourth Directive indicates goodwill should normally be written off over a period not exceeding five years.

4. Companies should enter the intangible asset in the balance sheet and write it off over its economic life. This is treating an intangible asset in the same way as a tangible asset.

This chapter will begin by examining the controversial topic of goodwill. This naturally leads to a discussion on brand values. In the final section we will examine the treatment of other items of intangibles, including research and development expenditure and deferred charges.

Goodwill

The important questions that a user of accounts would wish to consider on this topic are as follows.

- How does goodwill arise and how is it measured?
- How is it recognized in the accounts?
- If it is to be recognized, should it be left as an asset in the balance sheet (if positive) or be written off over time?
- If it is to be written off, should this be against reserves, or the profit and loss account? If it is being written off, over how many years should it be amortized?
- What happens to goodwill when the asset to which it relates is sold?

How Goodwill Arises and how it is Measured

If a business has built up its own reputation, it creates a premium in terms of value. The total value of the business will be greater than the aggregate of the fair value of the net identifiable assets. This is called 'inherent goodwill'. No accounting entries are involved, it is not shown in the balance sheet as it has not traditionally been the function of a balance sheet to show the total overall value of the business. Goodwill only enters into accounting records when it is purchased, when one business acquires all or part of another business. The price paid in terms of cash and shares normally exceeds the sum of the net assets acquired. The business is worth more than the collection of assets and the goodwill is positive. The excess is called 'purchased goodwill'. If it is a subsidiary that is being acquired, then consolidated accounts need to be prepared, and the goodwill involved is called 'goodwill arising from consolidation'. In addition the subsidiaries themselves may make acquisitions or have made acquisitions and have goodwill appearing in their own accounts. Negative goodwill can arise when the price paid is less than the book value of the assets acquired (see Extract 8.13 later).

In economic terms, there is no difference between inherent goodwill and purchased goodwill, but the accounting treatment differs. The existence of purchased goodwill is validated by a transaction but no such evidence exists for inherent goodwill.

The acquiring company pays more (or less in the case of negative goodwill) than the acquired net assets values because the assets operating together usually would have a higher value than the total of the acquired assets operating separately. One other reason why goodwill arises is because the purchase price is often based primarily on the acquiring management's expectation of future cash flows, not on asset values. There is also the possibility that if synergy results the value of the assets of the two businesses will increase.

Following the introduction of the Seventh Directive the treatment of goodwill in the different countries in the Community appears on the surface to be more or less the same. The Directive did introduce some uniformity of treatment within the Community, but still left many options. This makes it difficult for the user of accounts. Care needs to be taken to ensure that the treatment being followed is understood.

Basically the Directive says that purchased goodwill is to be recognized in the consolidated accounts. In certain circumstances, however, what is known as merger accounting will be allowed, and with this technique goodwill does not necessarily arise. The Directive also left member states options as to the method by which goodwill is to be written off and the period over which this is to take place.

In the UK, until recently, goodwill had provided an opportunity for some companies to 'manage the disclosure of earnings' and 'to increase the apparent strength of the balance sheet'. A change in company law and accounting standards, however, reduced the scope for some of the creative accounting aspects of goodwill. The financial analyst still needs to exercise care as it is still not always possible to detect from the information in the published accounts the treatment of some of the more intricate aspects of goodwill.

Since the reform of the relevant laws in Germany, a genuine computation of goodwill along the lines of British consolidation practice has to be carried out by German parent undertakings. Prior to the change there was not a policy of revaluing assets, either because it was against the law or because it had tax implications. Following implementation of the Seventh Directive there is a requirement in Germany that, if in the past in individual company accounts within a group, the valuation of assets has been based on tax considerations, this should either be disclosed in the notes to the accounts or the asset valuations be 'corrected' (revalued) in the consolidated financial statements. It should be appreciated that in Germany the calculation of how much tax is payable is not based on the consolidated accounts, but on the accounts of the individual companies in the group. To revalue assets in the consolidated accounts does not therefore have tax implications.

Bayer in their 1992 accounts provide a detailed footnote giving details of their intangible assets and explaining the change in value over the year (Extract 8.1). Bayer differentiates between goodwill arising 'from capital consolidation' and goodwill that is taken 'from the individual statements' of companies comprising the group. This is a similar layout to that appearing in other major German companies

By way of contrast no intangible assets appear in the accounts of ICI. They explain that purchased goodwill is immediately eliminated against reserves. This conservative approach to intangible assets, as will be seen in the remainder of the chapter, is not followed by all UK companies.

In Germany, following the implementation of the Seventh Directive, assets of newly acquired companies or those of companies being introduced into the consolidated accounts for the first time can be revalued. It is the difference between these revalued figures and the purchase price that is goodwill. There is no specific guidance as to how any upward revaluation should be assigned to different assets. This does give an opportunity to 'manage' profits. For example, if inventory is not revalued to its 'fair value' extra profits can quickly be obtained when the inventory is sold. Similarly some financial assets acquired may be quickly disposed of following reorganization. Again a non-revaluation results in an early surplus on sale.

The treatment of goodwill in Germany in the major companies' accounts is now similar to that of companies in the other countries in the Community, but some differences still do remain. Germany allows two methods of calculating goodwill: one is based on book value, the second on current value. With the first if book value exceeds purchase consideration, negative goodwill can arise. With the second method acquired assets are revalued to their fair value, and this cannot exceed the cost, that being the price paid. Merger accounting is allowed, but is rarely used. Goodwill can be written off to reserves or to the profit and loss account.

Extract 8.1 – Bayer AG 1992 accounts, Financial Statements.

	Gross Carrying Values (DM million)					
	Balance	Changes in companies			Transfers	Balance
	Dec. 31, 1991	consolidated	Additions	Retirements	Reclassifications	Dec. 31, 1992
Concessions, patents, licenses, trademarks, etc.	528	1	84	45	10	578
Advance payments	13	–	6	–	(10)	9
Intangibles	**541**	**1**	**90**	**45**	**–**	**587**

	Accumulated Depreciation, Amortization and Write-Downs					Net Carrying Values	
	Balance	Changes in companies			Balance	Balance	Balance
	Dec. 31, 1991	consolidated	Additions	Retirements	Dec. 31, 1992	Dec. 31, 1992	Dec. 31, 1991
Concessions, patents, licenses, trademarks, etc.	219	5	89	40	273	305	309
Advance payments	–	–	–	–	–	9	13
Intangibles	**219**	**5**	**89**	**40**	**273**	**314**	**322**

In France in 1986, a Decree and a Supplement to the 1982 Plan Comptable Général specified rules for consolidation. French law now states that normally any excess of consideration over the net book value of assets should first be allocated to asset items. Only the excess over fair values is goodwill. This exercise should take place at the time of the first consolidation of an acquisition (Extract 8.2).

Goodwill arising on acquisition can either be valued on the basis of the difference between purchase price and the fair values of net assets, the practice followed in the UK, the Netherlands, Spain and Italy, or on the basis of the difference between purchase price and book values. In Germany and France either method may be used. As well as differences with regard to valuation there are differences of opinion as to whether goodwill is a maintainable asset. There are in fact still major differences between countries in the way that goodwill is treated.

The purchase price is a definite figure, book values can be observed, but fair values involve an element of revaluation. There have been

Goodwill and intangible assets

On the acquisition of a subsidiary, goodwill representing the difference between the purchase price and the fair value of the separable underlying net assets acquired is carried as an asset in the balance sheet and amortised on a straight line basis against attributable profit over a period not exceeding 40 years.

The intangible asset arising from the MB transaction is reviewed annually to ensure that its value has not been impaired. No amortisation will be provided unless there is a structural reduction in activity or productivity which would lead to a reassessment of its value.

difficulties in deciding on what is a fair value of an individual asset. One definition that has been used in the UK was the amount that would be exchanged in an arm's length transaction. This loose definition led to companies adopting their own interpretation. They could choose between either strengthening their company's balance sheet by overstating the value of separable net assets or boosting the post-acquisition earnings figure by understating the acquired net assets' value and so reducing the depreciation charge. Other practices that have been adopted by UK companies include (a) introducing into the balance sheet a value for intangible asset such as brands that had not previously been included in the accounts of the acquired company, and (b) creating provisions at the time of acquisition for future losses and the costs of reorganization of the acquired company.

Following the adoption of such practices in some company accounts it was proposed, in the UK, that the fair value of assets and liabilities should be established using the principle of 'value to the business'. This fair value should be based on the state of affairs of the acquired business as a separate entity at the date of acquisition before control passes to the new parent company. This is an important point. It is being proposed that the fair value depends on the value in use in the acquired firm immediately before control passes to the purchasing company.

This was a significant change to the position that was previously taken, namely that fair value be based on the perspective of the acquiring company. This had provided opportunities for companies to create a favourable impression. Situations arose where some companies carried out massive write-downs of acquired companies' current assets following an acquisition (Extracts 8.3 and 8.4). The companies could justify such policies on the grounds that they were valuing such assets from the perspectives of the acquiring company. The write-downs were of course taken through reserves. If they revalued downwards current assets such as inventory, they could later sell the inventory, boost the apparent profit on the sale and take the profit to the profit and loss account. Such practices exaggerate post-acquisition performance. Valuing the assets from the point of view of the acquired business (rather than the acquiring business) should reduce the opportunities for such management of earnings. But there is much still to be settled in accounting for goodwill.

Extract 8.3 – Trafalgar House plc 1991 accounts, Notes.

25 Acquisitions and disposals

Acquisitions	Book value at acquisition £m	Fair value adjustments £m	Accounting policy alignment £m	Acquisition adjustments £m	Fair value to the Group £m
Davy Corporation plc					
Tangible fixed assets and investments	110.8	(9.6)	—	—	101.2
Goodwill	64.5	—	(64.5)	—	—
Current assets	425.6	(115.8)	—	75.4	385.2
Creditors and provisions	(442.8)	(29.4)	—	—	(472.2)
Borrowings	(122.8)	—	—	—	(122.8)
Acquisition provisions	—	—	—	(28.7)	(28.7)
	35.3	(154.8)	(64.5)	46.7	(137.3)
Other acquisitions	6.4	—	—	—	6.4
Net assets acquired	41.7	(154.8)	(64.5)	46.7	(130.9)

Cost of control	
On the acquisition of Davy Corporation plc	255.6
On other acquisitions	2.2
Consideration	126.9

Discharged by	
Cash consideration	72.7
Loan notes issued	.1
Deferred consideration	54.1
	126.9

Fair value adjustments include revisions to the accounts at 31st March 1991.

The profit/loss of Davy Corporation plc for periods prior to acquisition were as follows:

	Period ended 23rd July 1991 £m	Year ended 31st March 1991 £m
Profit/(loss) on ordinary activities after taxation	**(14.6)**	**9.1**

Adjustments to the book values of Davy's separable net assets were made to reflect the Directors' opinion of their fair values on acquisition and to bring the accounting policy of Davy in respect of goodwill into alignment with that of the Group. Further acquisition adjustments were made in respect of the surplus on the Davy UK pension schemes, as explained in Note 4, and for the costs of restructuring and integrating Davy.

Intangible Assets

3   ACQUISITIONS AND DISPOSALS

Significant acquisitions and disposals during 1992 were:

June	Acquisition of the entire issued share capital of Dowty Group PLC (comprising 250.1m ordinary shares of 50p each and 39.4m 7% convertible redeemable preference shares of £1 each) for £510m.
September	Disposal of Dowty Information Technology for £50m (equivalent to book value).
October	Disposal of Thermal Equipment for £40m (see note 6).

Other acquisitions included a further 5% of Japan Marine Technologies Ltd (formerly Dover Japan Inc).

All acquisitions were accounted for by the acquisition method.

Details of goodwill written off and net assets acquired are as follows:

Goodwill written off		£m
Acquisition of Dowty Group PLC		
Issue of 140.1m Ordinary shares of 25p		
each of the Company		488.5
Dowty shares purchased for cash		
– Ordinary shares	10.8	
– Preference shares	10.6	21.4
Total consideration		509.9
Underwriting and professional fees	24.3	
Less: share issue costs charged against share premium	(12.5)	11.8
Net borrowings acquired		137.6
Fair value of net assets acquired (see below)		(269.2)
Goodwill written off		390.1
Goodwill written off in respect of other acquisitions in the year		1.9
Total goodwill written off in year		392.0

| | BOOK VALUE PRIOR TO ACQUISITION £m | FAIR VALUE ADJUSTMENTS | | | | | FAIR VALUE OF NET ASSETS TO TI GROUP £m |
		PENSIONS AND OTHER POST RE-TIREMENT OBLI-GATIONS £m	REVALU-ATION OF ASSETS £m	CON-TRACT LOSSES £m	LEGAL AND ENVIRON-MENTAL ISSUES £m	REOR-GANIS-ATION £m	
Fair value of net assets acquired – Dowty Group PLC							
Intangible assets	6.9	–	–	–	–	–	6.9
Fixed tangible assets	200.1	–	(4.1)	–	–	(3.2)	192.8
Investments	1.6	–	1.5	–	–	–	3.1
Dowty Information Technology held for disposal	50.0	–	–	–	–	–	50.0
Stocks	113.4	–	(9.2)	(0.3)	–	–	103.9
Debtors	154.4	19.8	(3.0)	–	–	–	171.2
Creditors	(173.9)	–	(2.4)	(6.6)	(3.8)	(6.2)	(192.9)
Acquisition provisions	–	–	–	(10.4)	(1.1)	(46.5)	(58.0)
Pensions and other post-retirement obligations	(2.2)	(2.5)	–	–	–	–	(4.7)
Deferred taxation	(7.8)	(0.9)	1.2	0.6	0.2	6.2	(0.5)
Minority interests	(2.6)	–	–	–	–	–	(2.6)
Net assets	339.9	16.4	(16.0)	(16.7)	(4.7)	(49.7)	269.2

An interesting feature of the Trafalgar House treatment of the major acquisition of Davy Corporation is that they show the book value of the assets acquired as £41.7 million, for which they were prepared to pay £126.9 million (£72.7 million being in cash). By the time they had carried out the fair value and acquisition adjustments, the fair value of the acquisitions 'to the group' was negative, –£130.9 million. No wonder accounting confuses people. A company pays £126.9 million for the privilege of taking over a company with liabilities in excess of revalued assets by £130.9 million and it is the sum of these two figures (£257.8 million) that is written off to reserves. The chairman and chief executive were removed from office not long after these accounts were presented to shareholders.

Another example of a massive write-down following an acquisition was GEC's purchase of Plessey. They paid £928 million for net tangible assets which after adjustment to 'fair value' were said to be worth £110 million. This was of course after setting aside £67.5 million to provide for future trading losses, £63.2 million to provide for rationalization and £51.2 million for the mysterious item 'changes in accounting estimates'. Such provisions not only benefit the profit performance in the year following the acquisition, but also in a number of years following that. The notes to the GEC accounts show only a small amount of these provisions were utilized during the year of acquisition.

GEC's 1992 accounts show they utilized in that year £60 million of the total provisions for rationalization and £27 million of the total provisions for trading losses. It is emphasized that these figures relate to utilization of the the total provisions which had been built up following a number of acquisitions, not just that of Plessey. The 1992 accounts do mention, however, that the 'Provisions utilized relate mainly to the ex Plessey and Ferranti business and to GEC Alsthom.'

In Germany there are two methods of capital consolidation permitted by the Commercial Code, one based on book values, the other on current values. Under the 'current value' or 'purchase' method the book values of the subsidiary's net assets are directly replaced by market values, but only up to the carrying cost of the investment in the parent's books. Goodwill is the difference between the acquisition cost and either the book values or the market values.

BASF, Bayer and Hoechst all use the 'book value method'. Hoechst, from 1987 until 1990, applied a method called 'limited revaluation' which did not involve a revaluation of its subsidiaries' net assets. This method was allowed as a simplification for parent companies who adopted the new regulations of the Commercial Code earlier than 1990. In its 1991 report, Hoechst switched to the 'book value method', thus adopting the method of capital consolidation that is most widely used in Germany. The company declared that this switch did not lead to any material differences. Nobes and Parker state that the German techniques of capital consolidation under the new law are '...reasonably similar to Anglo-American practice...'.[1] This view is confirmed by observing the annual reports of major companies in Germany and the UK.

The following quote from the 1992 report of ICI illustrates the way in which UK companies compute goodwill arising on consolidations: 'On the acquisition of a business, fair values are attributed to the net assets acquired. Goodwill arises where the fair value of the consideration given for a business exceeds such net assets.'

As explained above there is more than one way of arriving at a fair value figure. Extract 8.4 shows that the TI Group paid £510 million for the Dowty Group, of which £390 million was goodwill. This goodwill figure was arrived at after a large number of fair value adjustments.

Goodwill and the Provision for Future Losses

In the late 1980s the practice developed in the UK of not only re-valuing assets acquired at the time of an acquisition but also of making adjustments to the liabilities side of the balance sheet by introducing 'new liabilities' and provisions. In particular this meant the creation of provisions to cover anticipated future losses, post-acquisition reorganization and integration costs resulting from the acquisition, the advantage to the management of the acquiring company of this practice being that it avoided charging such items against future profits. When the expenditures occurred they could be charged against the provisions that had been created at the time of the acquisition. The practice helps future profit figures although it is to the detriment of the balance sheet position immediately following the acquisition. The practice also helps distort post-acquisition performance. The case of GEC has been mentioned in the previous section.

The ASB published a discussion paper in April 1993 which indicated a wish to eliminate such practices. It is proposed that provisions for future losses in acquired businesses and for reorganization costs following an acquisition should not be accounted for as liabilities of the acquiring business and so dealt with through the goodwill figure. They should be treated as post-acquisition items in the consolidated profit and loss account of the acquirer and written off in the profit and loss account in the period following the acquisition. Post-acquisition reorganization costs should be treated as exceptional items in the period in which the expenses are incurred. This is the new proposed treatment in the U.K.

To further illustrate what on occasions has happened in the UK we will mention the case of Coloroll. In August 1986 Coloroll purchased Staffordshire Potteries whose net assets' value was £7 million. The purchase consideration of this acquisition was £14 million. In February 1987 Coloroll spent £31 million on acquiring Fogarty whose published accounts showed net assets of £12 million. For those two deals Coloroll created 'other provisions' of £11 million which comprised the costs of reorganizing the subsidiaries acquired and the closure of certain business segments. This allowed Coloroll to report its profit for the period ended March 1987 as £10 million. If Coloroll had not created the provisions and had charged reorganization costs against the profit and loss account in the period in which the expenses were incurred, they would have reported a loss in 1987.

As mentioned earlier the acquirer of a company might anticipate that in the near future it will be necessary to write down items taken over such as stock. Such items would normally be passed through the profit and loss account as a cost in subsequent accounting periods. Instead, however, many acquiring companies decided to reduce the 'fair value' of the net assets of the acquired undertaking in the year of acquisition. This diminution in the 'fair value' of the net assets led to a high goodwill figure. The resulting positive 'goodwill' figure could then be offset against reserves. Thus, the profit and loss account was by-passed. 'The significance of these pre-acquisition write downs is that they absorb costs or potential future costs, at the expense of the balance sheet (to which the write-offs are applied), and thereby boost future profits.'[2]

The 1990 report of ICI contains an example of such a 'pre-acquisition write-down'. In Note 22, 'Acquisitions, New Investments and

Disposals', the company discloses the acquisition of net assets which were originally recorded at a book value of £240 million. The 'fair value' of these net assets after revaluations and provisions is stated at £187 million. This amounts to a reduction of approximately 22%. Of this reduction, £18 million was caused by 'other provisions'. ICI's comments in Note 22 reads: '… provisions for closure are made where appropriate. Other acquisition provisions reflect the projected costs of reorganization, integration of the businesses acquired and provisions for environmental improvements.'

The new proposals in the UK on 'Fair Values in Acquisition Accounting' would not allow such accounting manoeuvres. It is proposed that provisions like the ones made by ICI should be treated as a post-acquisition item, and the cost should be recognized as an exceptional item on the profit and loss account.

British companies are not the only ones to take advantage of the opportunity to capitalize expected future costs at the time of an acquisition. In France, Alcatel Alsthom acquired three major telecommunication companies in 1991, paying in the region of FF 13.5 billion for them. In the 1991 accounts a footnote explains that the restructuring reserves of the company were increased by FF 5.2 billion, most of which was associated with the three companies acquired.

The cost of the acquisitions plus provisions for future costs was therefore in excess of FF 18 billion. What assets did the company acquire? The goodwill in the balance sheet increased over the year by FF 11 billion, most of which was the result of the three acquisitions. The net fixed assets acquired therefore were only in the region of FF 7 billion.

The financial accounts will benefit in future years as a result of this method of recording acquisitions. Some of the goodwill will be charged against reserves, with the balance of the goodwill and the annual depreciation charged against profits. Any expenditure on restructuring in future years will not be charged against profits but against the restructuring provisions/reserves. The restructuring provisions/reserves are not built up as a result of a charge against profits, but as a cost of acquisition. This is increasing the asset side of the balance sheet with goodwill, and the other side of the balance sheet with provisions.

Writing off Goodwill

One question that should be asked is does goodwill need to be eliminated at all? Can it be a permanent asset if its value is maintained? This has become a controversial issue in the UK. It has been proposed that in certain circumstances goodwill can be a permanent asset.

What lies behind the new approach is that many UK companies have chosen to introduce brand values as an intangible asset in their balance sheet, differentiating between goodwill and brand values. One reason they have chosen to do this is because brand values do not have to be written down, but goodwill does. Traditionally, in many companies brand values were treated as part of goodwill and by taking brand values out of the goodwill figure a company can avoid either a reduction in reserves or a reduction in profits.

Brand values will be discussed later in this chapter. However, the thinking behind the new UK proposal is that, if it is accepted that goodwill need only be written down when there is a permanent diminution in its value, the companies will not need to place brand values as a separate asset in the balance sheet. The brand value problem will therefore go away.

At the present time goodwill arising on consolidation is either offset against reserves at the time of acquisition or it is capitalized and written off in subsequent years against profits. As the FEE survey showed, this choice leads to a major area of difference between EC countries.[3] In the sample of companies FEE examined they found not a single case in France of an immediate write-off of goodwill against reserves. In the UK and Netherlands, on the other hand, it was the most common practice.

From a company's point of view an immediate write-off against reserves weakens the balance sheet and a write-off over time reduces reported profits. From the point of view of some companies they would rather do neither. They would like to have the opportunity to leave the intangible asset on the balance sheet and not amortize it.

The German Commercial Code allows for one of three possible treatments. The alternatives are (a) capitalization and amortization over a maximum of four years; (b) capitalization and amortization over the period of the prospective usefulness of the goodwill; or (c) offsetting against reserves. BASF capitalizes goodwill arising on consolidation and predominantly amortizes this asset within four years, whereas both Bayer and Hoechst set it off against revenue reserves directly.

In the United Kingdom, direct write-off against reserves is the dominant practice. Courtaulds is one company that refers to both writing off against reserves and against the profit and loss account. The company explains that when using the latter method, the amortization is spread '… over a number of years'. However, Courtaulds does not inform the reader of its accounts over how many years. The ASC in February 1990 issued an Exposure Draft (ED) 47, *Accounting for Goodwill*, which favoured the amortization and gradual write-off of goodwill through the profit and loss account. This provoked hostile reactions from the corporate sector. It has been suggested that the reason British companies favour reserve accounting and do not like capitalizing goodwill and writing it off against future profits is that many business people find it more convenient to weaken the balance sheet (already containing many suspicious figures) than damage the all-important EPS figure.

The accounts of the TI Group show a massive write-off of goodwill arising from the acquisition of the Dowty Group. In the USA goodwill has to be amortized against profits over a period not exceeding 20 years. The profit position of the TI Group is not strong and if a similar policy had existed in the UK (as was proposed) half the profits would disappear.

In France the 1986 Decree on the subject states that normally goodwill should be amortized, but in 'exceptional circumstances' it can be charged directly against reserves. One such exceptional circumstance is where a subsidiary is being consolidated for the first time, and it is difficult to estimate fair value. In such a situation goodwill could be written off against reserves.

A survey of published accounts in France in 1990 showed that of 100 listed companies, 76 amortized goodwill. Eight companies wrote it off to reserves even though the legislation states that only in exceptional cases should this method be used. The Decree does not recommend a particular period for amortization, but the survey found that 20- and 40-year periods were the most frequent ones used. It was also discovered that some companies simply capitalized goodwill without amortizing it, leaving it on the balance sheet at its full value. An argument French companies have used as support for such treatment is that normally a business would not be run in such a way that the value of its client base falls. Only where a fall in value is noticeable, should goodwill be written down.

Pechiney (Extract 8.5) in their accounts refer to a novel way of amortizing goodwill. Not only do they make use of the maximum period of 40 years to write it off against profits, they also charge less per annum in earlier years than in later years. They refer to a progressive charge being consistent with the long-term benefits the company expects to derive from goodwill. In fact in Pechiney goodwill accounts for a high proportion of the total assets, comprising in 1990 21%. Its amortization policy is therefore significant. The French preference for long amortization periods with a maximum of 40 years is just the opposite to the international trend towards shorter periods.

In the UK SSAP 22 indicated that the preferred treatment is for goodwill to be eliminated from accounts by immediate write-off against

---

Extract 8.5 – Pechiney Group 1990 accounts, Notes.

c) Intangible Assets

The difference arising upon acquisition between the purchase price and assumed liabilities, on the one hand, and the book value of net assets acquired, on the other, is allocated to tangible and intangible assets for which a fair value can be separately established and verified. The excess of the purchase price over fair value is allocated to goodwill.

Such goodwill is amortized systematically over a period not exceeding 40 years.

For acquisitions which have a deep and lasting effect on the Group's industrial future, goodwill is amortized over 40 years on a progressive basis. The progressive charge for the amortization is consistent with the long-term benefits the Group expects to derive, in real terms, from such investments. For other acquisitions, goodwill is amortized on a straight-line basis.

Formation costs are amortized on a straight-line basis over five years. Patents and licenses are amortized over their estimated useful lives.

Debt issue costs are amortized over the term of the debt.

Deferred costs, relating mainly to start-up and acquisition costs of new installations, are amortized over five years.

d) Long-term Investments

Long-term investments are carried at cost, after deducting appropriate provisions for permanent impairment.

reserves. The standard does, however, allow capitalization of goodwill and a write-off against profits over its useful life. The justification for this preferred treatment is to achieve consistency of treatment with non-purchased goodwill that is not allowed to be carried in a company's accounts. But such accounting treatment has some limitations. The write-off of goodwill at the date of acquisition will sharply decrease the value of the shareholders' fund. In effect, this will boost the figure of return on equity. It means that such goodwill treatment results in a distortion in the profitability figures. At the same time it causes the gearing ratio to rise. One effect of this treatment is that it could produce a negative figure of shareholders' equity. This is nonsense from one point of view, since at the same time as the accounts show negative equity the market capitalization of the company can be very high. For instance, SmithKline Beecham had a situation where they had negative shareholders' equity of £296.5 million when its market capitalization was indicating a worth of more than £2 billion.

One issue that does arise is the problem of which reserve account should be used to write off goodwill. There are a variety of practices. The share premium account cannot normally be used for this purpose. In the UK in order to do this it is necessary to obtain court approval for a capital reconstruction.

A merger reserve may be created at the time of a business combination and this account can be used for the write-off of goodwill. Unlike a merger reserve a revaluation reserve is a statutory reserve. It is created to be used for certain restricted purposes. It should not be used for goodwill write-off. In one year Grand Metropolitan did adopt the policy of writing off goodwill against the revaluation reserve – the practice was criticized and the group had to reinstate the reserve in the next year's financial statements.

Treatment of Goodwill on the Disposal of a Business

When goodwill arising on an acquisition has been written off against reserves in the year of the acquisition, the future carrying value of the investment in that subsidiary is reduced considerably. As a result, on disposal of this acquired business, a substantial surplus could easily arise. When this happens, it has been a fairly common treatment in the UK for the 'apparent' profit on the sale to be credited immediately to the profit and loss account. This is in contrast to the treatment of expected future costs which, as explained earlier, is deducted from reserves.

The ASB, through its Urgent Issue Task Force, has felt it necessary to publish a document which points out the obvious inconsistency of such an accounting procedure. Abstract 3, *Treatment of Goodwill on Disposal of a Business,* issued by the UITF in December 1991, expresses the opinion that when a business is sold the profit and loss account should be debited with the amount of goodwill which – on acquisition – had been written off against reserves. Any gain on sale shown in the profit and loss account would then be the difference between the sale price and the book value of the assets sold plus any goodwill relating to the business sold that has been written off. Owing to this UITF ruling, various British companies, for example BOC, Courtaulds and ICI, had to change their accounting policies in their 1992 reports.

In the UK, therefore, in order to prevent companies overstating profit on the disposal of a business, FRS 3 requires companies to include the amount of goodwill previously written off to reserves in the calculation of any gain or loss on the disposal of a business. One technique to achieve this result is to transfer from reserves to the profit and loss account (at the time of disposal) the amount of goodwill that was debited against reserves at the time the business was acquired.

Extract 8.6 – Saatchi & Saatchi Co.plc 1992 accounts, Principal Accounting Policies.

GOODWILL

Goodwill, including any additional goodwill arising from the contingent capital payments disclosed in Note 20, is written off directly to reserves in the year in which it arises. When a provision is made in the accounts of a company which holds a fixed asset investment in a subsidiary in respect of a permanent diminution in value of that subsidiary, a charge is recognised in the Group's profit and loss account in respect of any permanent diminution in value of the related acquisition goodwill. Any goodwill relating to a disposal or closure that has not previously been written off through the profit and loss account for a period is taken into account in calculating the profit or loss on that disposal or closure.

Charging a permanent diminution in the value of goodwill as described above to the Group's profit and loss account represents a change of accounting policy, as does the decision to no longer recognise notional amortisation of the goodwill as a reserve movement. Previously, no such corresponding entry was made in the Group accounts and the transfer of goodwill in reserves was over a 40 year period. The effect on prior year profit is immaterial. The effect of the change in policy on the 1992 reported result before tax is to charge £600.0 million to the profit and loss account.

Some companies have adopted the policy of transferring from reserves to the profit and loss account any permanent diminution in the value of goodwill that has occurred. Saatchi & Saatchi explain this policy in Extract 8.6.

Another company adopting a similar policy is Christian Salvesen. They explain in their accounts to 31 March 1993, that they have charged to the profit and loss account a proportion of purchased goodwill previously written off to reserves. During the year £5 million had been credited to goodwill reserve and charged against profits. They make this transfer 'on a disposal or closure or a permanent diminution in value' of purchased goodwill. It should be noted this policy is being adopted by companies not just on disposal of a business, but also on anticipated disposal. This policy could be seen as a way of smoothing profits. If a charge is made to the profit and loss account in a year of good profits, when the business involved is eventually sold a higher profit will be recognized (because of the reduced value of the goodwill in that business) in the profit and loss account in the year of sale.

We will now examine how the various issues discussed above are dealt with in different countries. In particular we will examine the level of disclosure in the accounts of companies from the different countries.

France

Many French companies disclose the subsidiaries to which the goodwill relates. Unisor Sacilor (Extract 8.7) show a detailed analysis of the goodwill figures, linking the goodwill to particular subsidiaries. Unisor differentiate between 'Goodwill on business combination' and 'Goodwill'. Elf do not analyse goodwill by subsidiary, but do so by business segment (Extract 8.8).

There are a number of points of interest in the accounts of Saint Gobain (Extract 8.9) relating to their treatment of goodwill.

Extract 8.7 – Unisor Sacilor 1991 accounts, Notes.

NOTE 4 – **INTANGIBLE ASSETS**

in millions of French francs	Cost at Dec. 31 1991	Accumu- lated amortization	Net at Dec. 31 1991	Net at Dec. 31 1990
Licenses, patents and other	164	106	58	58
Goodwill	5,054	966	4,088	3,430
Goodwill on business combination [1]	1,389	628	761	951
Other	283	110	173	56
Total	6,890	1,810	5,080	4,495

(1) In 1990, SFBI and CMB Aciers were acquired by Sollac and merged into the latter company. The merger gave rise to goodwill of MF 1,140 which is being amortized over 5 years.

Goodwill

in millions of French francs	Rate	Cost at Dec. 31 1991	Accumu- lated amortization	Net at Dec. 31 1991	Net at Dec. 31 1990
Alessio Tubi (Italy)	20%	158	79	79	159
Allevard (France)	20%	95	18	77	47
Ancofer Feinstahl (Germany)	20%	274	71	203	–
A.S.D. (U.K.)	20%	88	9	79	22
Edgcomb Metals (U.S.A.)	5%	705	47	658	595
Ugine SRL (Italy)	20%	142	57	85	114
Georgetown (U.S.A.)	5%	202	16	186	209
Imphy Alloys (U.S.A.)	5%	134	15	119	119
International Metal Service	20%	246	105	141	146
Interstate (U.S.A.)	5%	80	16	64	81
J & L (U.S.A.)	5%	1,587	126	1,461	1,507
Lutrix (Italy)	20%	198	66	132	39
Sidmed (Spain)	20%	456	38	418	–
Others		689	303	386	392
Total		5,054	966	4,088	3,430

Amortization of goodwill for 1991 totalled MF 544 (1990: MF 312). After deducting amortization of negative goodwill in an amount of MF 150 (1990: MF 151), the net charge was MF 394 (1990: MF 161). The goodwill arising in 1990 on the acquisition of Edgcomb Metals was increased by MF 110 in 1991 to MF 705, primarily to reflect the adoption by this company of SFAS no. 106 (Employer's accounting for post-retirement benefits other than pensions).

•2. Intangible assets

Millions of French francs	1991	1990	1989
Goodwill	3,337	3,318	2,525
Patents, trademarks and other intangibles	716	682	571
Total	4,053	4,000	3,096
Less: accumulated depreciation and amortization	(1,225)	(1,067)	(880)
Intangible assets – net	**2,828**	**2,933**	**2,216**

Following is an analysis of goodwill (see note A.2.a) (net of amortization) by business segment:

Millions of French francs	Total	Human Healthcare	Bio- activities	Perfumes- Beauty Products
1991.......................................	2,419	976	1,067	376
1990.......................................	2,528	1,033	1,103	392
1989.......................................	1,862	677	829	356

Goodwill amortization expense by business segment is as follows:

Millions of French francs	Total	Human Healthcare	Bio- activities	Perfumes- Beauty Products
1991	143	55	71	17
1990	130	52	64	14
1989	95	29	53	13

- The profit and loss account shows 'amortization of goodwill' as a separate item. It appears after the amount of net operating income from consolidated companies. This is required by French GAAP.
- The goodwill is written off to the profit and loss account over what in some countries would be regarded as a long period. The goodwill arising from the Norton acquisition is being written off over 40 years.
- The notes on goodwill explain that, in 1991, the allocations to goodwill were revised following a valuation. What appears to have happened is that certain items were transferred out of the 'other intangible asset' and 'fixed asset' categories into goodwill.

NOTE 12: INTANGIBLE ASSETS

in millions of French francs	1991	1990	1989
● At January 1,	1,716	215	188
● Changes in the composition of the Group	(184)	1,592	24
● Acquisitions	62	71	98
● Disposals	–	(5)	(4)
● Exchange rate fluctuations	17	(70)	(5)
● Amortisation for the year	(124)	(87)	(86)
● At December 31	1,487	1,716	215

In 1991, the reduction in intangible assets is mainly due to the effects of the revision of the fair values of Norton's assets amounting to FF 215 million (see note 13) and the amortisation for the year.

The increase in 1990 mainly related to the allocation of part of the purchase price of Norton and Solaglas to trademarks and patents (FF 1,298 million for Norton and FF 122 million for Solaglas) and the transfer of part of the goodwill arising on the acquisition of Générale Française de Céramique to other intangible assets (FF 170 million).

NOTE 13: GOODWILL

in millions of French francs	Goodwill			Negative goodwill		
	1991	1990	1989	1991	1990	1989
At January 1,	8,159	3,712	2,457	(261)	(273)	(287)
● Acquisitions	871	5,160	1,135	–	–	1
● Disposals	(1)	–	(2)	–	–	–
● Exchange rate fluctuations, changes in the composition of the Group and other	206	(499)	292	1	–	–
● Revision of the Norton allocation	620	–	–	–	–	–
● Amortisation for the year	(325)	(214)	(170)	13	12	13
Net book value at December 31	9,530	8,159	3,712	(247)	(261)	(273)

In 1991, the increase in goodwill mainly relates to Bicron, Covina, Glasindustrie AG, Flachglas Torgau GmbH and Norton.

The Norton Group has been consolidated from August 8, 1990. The total purchase cost amounted to FF 9,717 million. The acquisition has been accounted for using the purchase method under which the assets and liabilities acquired are recorded on the basis of estimated fair values. The purchase price was allocated to identifiable assets and liabilities for a net amount of FF 5,046 million, the balance of FF 4,671 million was recorded as goodwill and is amortised on the straightline basis over forty years.

In 1991, the allocations were revised following the completion of additional valuation and other studies during the year. The effect of the reallocations on intangible assets and fixed assets is included under the caption "Effect of changes in the composition of the Group" (see notes 12 and 14).

The increase in goodwill mainly related to Norton and Solaglas in 1990 and to VETR.I, Générale Française de Céramique and Stettner in 1989.

Negative goodwill mainly relates to Stanton.

The method of amortisation of goodwill is described in note 1.

- It can be seen from the notes that 'negative goodwill' does arise, this being when the price paid for the acquisition is less than the net book value or the assets acquired. Negative goodwill can in theory only arise when the difference is calculated on the basis of book values, not on the basis of fair values. The negative goodwill figure is not netted off in the balance sheet against positive goodwill but is shown on the liabilities side of the balance sheet under the heading 'provisions'.

Ciments Français (Extract 8.10) include an interesting reference to intangible assets. As is the French practice – and the practice increasingly common throughout Europe – the company show in the balance sheet an item 'Intangible assets' (17% of total assets) and an item 'Purchased goodwill unallocated' (4% of total assets). They explain that upon an acquisition they first assign the premium paid to specific balance sheet items, and only the balance is recorded as purchased goodwill unallocated. What then are intangible assets? The notes explain that this includes 'market shares'. This is an amount that is not written off on a regular basis, but only if there are 'major economic changes in the company or its markets'.

Extract 8.10 – Ciments Français 1991 accounts, Balance Sheet extract and Notes.

CONSOLIDATED BALANCE SHEET

(after appropriation, in millions of French Francs)

As of December 31	1991	1990
ASSETS		
Cash	569	664
Receivables, net	6,767	5,817
Inventories, net	2,186	2,060
TOTAL CURRENT ASSETS	**9,552**	**8,541**
Property, plant and equipment, net (Note 5)	13,042	11,931
Intangible assets (Note 4)	5,303	5,189
Purchased goodwill unallocated, net (Note 3)	1,332	1,182
Investments and other assets, net (Note 6)	1,909	1,778
TOTAL ASSETS	**31,108**	**28,621**

Goodwill

The difference between the cost of the group's investment and the value of its share in a company's net assets is analyzed on first consolidation to identify amounts assignable to specific balance sheet items, including minority interests. Such amounts are amortized over the same period and on the same basis as the related assets, as shown in Note C. The remaining amount is recorded as an intangible asset under "Purchased goodwill unallocated" and amortized on a straight-line basis over a period not exceeding twenty years in the general case and forty years for new acquisitions of particular long-term strategic interest for the group.

– Intangible assets:

Start-up expenses are generally fully depreciated during the year in which they are incurred. As indicated in Note 1.B, Goodwill, after analysis, is assigned to specific balance sheet items. For acquisitions since the year 1989, these items have included intangible assets which represent the value of the market shares acquired. This value has been evaluated by the computation of operating incomes before depreciation of fixed assets of the purchased companies over several years, depending upon the circumstances of the acquisitions and the specific nature of the company and its activities. This value is to be recomputed each year, and the corresponding intangible assets will be reduced if major economic changes in the company or its markets make it necessary.

NOTE 3 – PURCHASED GOODWILL UNALLOCATED

After analysis as described in Notes 1.B and 1.C, unallocated purchased goodwill changed as follows:

(in millions of French France)	1991	1990
As of January 1	1,182	1,339
Increase of the year	223	127
Amortization	(55)	(48)
Other	(18)	(236)
As of December 31	**1,332**	**1,182**

Increases for 1991 amounted to 129 million French Francs following the increase in the group's interest in Financiera y Minera; Ciments Français acquired all the new equity issued by Financiera y Minera at the end of 1991. The other significant increases in 1991 correspond to the Arena division and to additional investments made in Spain, Portugal, Greece and the United States.

Purchased goodwill unallocated as of December 31 was as follows:

(in millions of French Francs)	1991	1990
Gross amounts	1,488	1,285
Amortization	(156)	(103)
Net amounts	**1,332**	**1,182**

NOTE 4 – MARKET SHARES

(in millions of French Francs)	1991	1990
As of January 1	4,880	1,071
Acquisitions of the year	123	3,877
Other	(28)	(68)
As of December 31	**4,975**	**4,880**

Acquisitions of market shares in 1991 concerned mainly the Derudder group (Arena) and San Juan Cement Company (Puerto Rico).

In 1990, market shares amounting to 294 million French Francs were acquired in France and abroad amounting to 3,583 million (mainly market shares of CCB in Belgium and FyM in Spain).

As indicated in Note 1.C.2, the analysis of the market shares led to the conclusion that their evaluation at initial consolidation of these companies remains appropriate.

Germany

Daimler-Benz in their 1990 accounts in the section dealing with the principles of consolidation mention that 'The hidden reserves have been made active and will be written off over their useful lives in an effective manner' (Extract 8.11).

What is meant by this is that for any subsidiary which is consolidated for the first time in the group accounts (the subsidiary may have been acquired a number of years earlier) any difference between the parent company's acquisition costs and the book value of the assets is 'as far as possible allocated to the relevant balance sheet items'. It is only the remaining difference that is classified as goodwill. For subsidiaries being consolidated for the first time therefore the 'hidden' value of the assets is recognized in the revaluation. The hidden reserves are therefore made active. They explain in the accounts that such changes have made their accounts more acceptable to the international business community.

In the 1992 accounts Daimler make reference to the fact that they are seeking to have their shares introduced to the New York Stock Exchange. They did not anticipate that their valuation methods would cause any problems, stating that the results to date of their talks with the SEC 'have made us very confident that Daimler-Benz shares can already be traded in the course of this year on the world's most important stock exchange'. In fact, to obtain acceptance in the USA they needed to make additional changes. There were further 'hidden reserves' that needed to be made active.

The 1992 Daimler-Benz accounts show an interesting treatment of goodwill that arises from a 'strategic alliance' with both a write-off over time to the profit and loss account and a charge to 'retained earnings'.

> *Intangible assets are valued at acquisition cost and are written off over the respective useful lives. Goodwill resulting from the capital consolidation, if derived from the extension of the group, is in principle amortized over five years; goodwill relating to the restructuring of the group is charged to retained earnings. Goodwill which arose from the creation of strategic alliances is split. The portion relating to the group's expansion is written off over the relevant useful life, the one relating to the restructuring is charged to retained earnings.'*

Siemens adopt a similar policy. They explain that:

> *Insofar as intangible assets have been acquired for consideration, they are carried at acquisition cost and are amortized up to a maximum of five years. Any goodwill resulting from consolidation is offset against retained earnings.*

The note in the 1991 accounts dealing with retained earnings mentions that:

New Valuation Methods in Group Financial Statements Prove Beneficial

The change in the valuation methods in the 1989 consolidated financial statements, where we have more closely adapted our accounting policies to internationally accepted accounting practices, was positively received both at home and abroad. For the purpose of analyzing companies and industries, the data can now be directly taken from the Daimler-Benz consolidated financial statements. Improved comparability of our group financials with other large industrial enterprises operating worldwide has made it easier during the reporting year to list the Daimler-Benz shares on important stock exchanges such as London and Tokyo. In each instance, we were able to rely solely on the published annual financials and we were not required to submit additional computations for important key figures such as net income for the year and net equity.

The new valuation of pension provisions and inventories in the 1989 group financials had not only impacted the balance sheet but also the statement of income. For this reason, some basic figures in last year's income statements are not comparable with those of 1990. Moreover, we have, for the first time, included the accounts of MBB in the earnings statements. In order to illustrate the actual development, we are therefore partly deviating in the following analysis from the official presentation of our accounts.

Principles of Consolidation

Capital consolidation was effected according to the book value method where the parent's acquisition costs are eliminated against the relevant share capital and retained earnings at the time of acquisition or first-time inclusion in consolidation.

The differences resulting from the capital consolidation are, as far as possible, allocated to the relevant balance sheet items. For the treatment of the remaining difference (goodwill) resulting from additions in 1990, see explanation given in the caption "Accounting Principles and Valuation Methods". The hidden reserves have been made active and will be written off over their useful lives in an effective manner.

'Goodwill of DM 1016.4 million resulting from the initial consolidation of subsidiaries and from the initial consolidation of associated companies accounted for under the equity method was offset against other retained earnings.'

In German companies' accounts there is usually an explanation of which subsidiary companies have been consolidated, and those which have been excluded from consolidation. Extract 8.12 is taken from a long note in Siemens' accounts explaining the treatment of the 'Acquisition of subsidiaries and associated companies'. They explain that they adjust the policies adopted in individual company financial statements when they come to consolidation. They do this to bring about uniform valuation policies worldwide; it results, they say, in financial statements comparable to those of companies in other countries.

Other countries

Italy implemented the Seventh Directive in 1991, but the law actually did not come into force until 1994. Only for accounts with year endings after 1994 are groups required to prepare consolidated accounts. When goodwill does arise it is calculated using the book value method as opposed to the fair value method. It can be deducted immediately from reserves, or amortized over a five-year period or more if the useful life is longer. Negative goodwill is to be treated as a reserve or a provision for future losses.

Extract 8.12 – Siemens AG 1991 accounts, Notes.

In consolidating our investment in subsidiaries, we offset the purchase price against the value of Siemens' interests in the shareholders' equity of the consolidated subsidiaries at the time of their acquisition or initial consolidation. Any resulting goodwill is offset against retained earnings. The same principles are applied in consolidating associated companies under the equity method. Our share in the net income of these companies is shown in the statement of income under net income from investment in other companies.

In Spain any difference between the acquisition cost of an investment and the book value of the net assets acquired must first be allocated to those assets or liabilities whose book value is different from the market value. This practice applies to new acquisitions, and to companies at their first consolidation.

The Seventh Directive was only implemented into national law in Spain in 1989. Before 1990 consolidation was not required. Groups that existed before the end of 1990 were required to consolidate in 1991 so it would be from this date of first consolidation that the revaluation of many acquired assets and liabilities would apply. Assets and liabilities are to be revalued to their market value. If after this revaluation there still exists a positive difference, called goodwill, it will be considered as an asset in the consolidated balance sheet. It must be depreciated over a maximum of ten years, provided that the investment can be shown to produce income over this write-off period. If this is not the case the maximum period will be five years. Spain prohibits the immediate write-off of goodwill against reserves.

5.- NEGATIVE GOODWILL

The detail of the negative goodwill, classified by company, as of December 31, 1991, is as follows:

	Millions of Pesetas
FECSA	11,896
SEVILLANA	19,959
UEFSA	4,195
ENECO	4,424
	40,474

As a result of carrying the foregoing companies by the equity method because their book value, as adapted to the parent company's accounting principles, was higher than acquisition cost, a negative goodwill of Ptas. 40,474 million was disclosed in consolidation. Management of the Company believes that this negative goodwill will cover any negative development which might arise in the future.

This negative goodwill was recorded in full in 1991 as a result of the inclusion of these companies in consolidation in that year, as described in Note 2-b.

The amount relating to Compañía Sevillana de Electricidad, S.A. does not include the effect of adjusting the costs incurred by it in the construction of the Valdecabelleros nuclear power plant, since such costs are not addressed in the debt recognized by the Directorate-General of Energy and because management of the consolidated Group believes that the recovery of these costs is conditional upon future decisions by the Administration which cannot be objectively evaluated at the present time.

When the final decisions by the Administration become known, the loss recorded in consolidation will be adjusted. Nevertheless, this adjustment would not materially affect the consolidated Group's net worth.

Endesa shows a relatively large negative goodwill figure in its balance sheet. The company explains this arose because the book value of the assets acquired was higher than the acquisition cost, a situation which arose in the case of not just one acquisition but of four. It is surprising that four sets of shareholders were prepared to sell at a price below the book value of net assets. In fact Endesa explains that the negative goodwill arose after the book value of the acquired companies was 'adapted to the parent company's accounting principles' (Extract 8.13).

In the Netherlands, positive goodwill is treated in the same way as it is in the UK. The fair value method is used to calculate goodwill. The whole of the amount of acquired goodwill can be charged direct to the profit and loss account or it can be charged against reserves, charging to reserves being in practice the most common method. In a study into the 1990 accounts of companies it was round that 69% of companies charged goodwill against reserves in the year of acquisition, with only 2% charging it in full to the profit and loss account. Worryingly 26% of the 117 listed companies did not disclose their treatment of the item.

Dutch companies have had to make major adjustments when reconciling the treatment of goodwill in their accounts based on domestic

Extract 8.14 – Unilever Group 1991 accounts, adjusted for US GAAP.

	Fl million	
	1991	**1990**
Capital and reserves as reported in the consolidated		
balance sheet	**11,165**	9,373
Attributable to: **N.V.**	**6,583**	4,975
PLC	**4,582**	4,398
Adjustments, net of taxation where applicable, in respect of:		
Goodwill	**9,858**	9,693
Interest	**717**	657
Retirement benefits	**218**	254
Current investments	**(41)**	(23)
Deferred taxation	**(116)**	(131)
Dividends	**1,009**	959
Foreign currency translation	**–**	60
Net increase	**11,645**	11,469
Approximate capital and reserves in accordance		
with United States generally accepted accounting principles	**22,810**	20,842
Attributable to: **N.V.**	**14,587**	12,720
PLC	**8,223**	8,122

regulations to conform to US GAAP. As Extract 8.14 from the 1991 accounts of Unilever shows the equity according to Dutch standards is 11165 million Dutch guilders. This is after a major write-off of goodwill to reserves. In the USA such goodwill has to be capitalized and amortized over its estimated life. According to US standards, Unilever's equity is nearly twice as high.

Brand Accounting

Brand accounting is a bigger issue in the UK than in the other countries with which we are concerned. It clearly does exist in France. It is not allowed in Germany. As previously mentioned the problems arising from accounting for goodwill have led to the issue of accounting for brands. Many companies now identify and value brand names as a separable asset in the accounts instead of treating them as part of goodwill value. However, the method of valuation varies among those companies.

The Fourth Directive states that intangible assets, including internally developed assets, may be recognized in the balance sheet. It therefore does allow a company not only to capitalize acquired brands but also brand names that it has itself created. However, most countries have decided not to allow companies the option to capitalize internally generated intangibles.

When brands are purchased individually or are purchased as one of the assets in an acquisition of another business, they can be valued and brought into the accounts. It is necessary of course to be able to separately identify the asset. The UK allows a company to introduce into its balance sheet a value for a brand it has created itself or for a brand it has purchased in the past and not previously shown as an asset.

Why do companies wish to include brand value as an asset? As explained, in the UK the most common approach to writing off goodwill is an immediate charge against reserves. This method appears attractive as it enhances future reported profit figures. However, in the situation of escalating goodwill values writing goodwill off immediately to reserves may have a detrimental effect on the balance sheet. A number of UK companies therefore now include brand value on their balance sheet to avoid depletion in the value of shareholders' funds. Brand values do not have to be written off.

The issue of brand accounting in the UK partly results from the requirement of SSAP 22 to separately identify the different assets. The standard requires that identifiable intangibles should be valued at the fair value in the acquiring company's accounts even if they were not so recorded in the acquired company's accounts. Based on this statement many companies have taken the opportunity to separate the brand value from the goodwill element. They recognize brands as identifiable, separable intangible assets. When brand values are capitalized and recorded in the balance sheet there is no requirement for them to be amortized. The accounting standard concerned with goodwill only requires goodwill to be written off.

The ASB do not like brands being shown as a separate intangible asset. They believe that brands should be subsumed within goodwill and accounted for accordingly. It is their belief that the present flexible position, far from being helpful to users of accounts, is potentially dangerous to the whole basis of financial reporting and that to allow brands – whether acquired or home-grown – to continue to be included in the balance sheet is highly unwise.

The ASB argue that brands are 'seldom sold and acquired as bare rights to trade names'. The acquisition of a brand normally involves all or part of an integrated set of constituents including an established marketing operation, trading connections, as well as the product or range of products. They argue that such a combination of factors is what is generally regarded as goodwill.

The practice of valuing brands grew during the 1980s. Companies following an acquisition took the opportunity to assign fair values to brand names. Reckitt & Colman first recognized trade marks in its balance sheet in 1987.

The accounting policy on intangible assets and goodwill was explained as follows:

> ... Goodwill is deducted from reserves on acquisition. No annual provision for depreciation is made in respect of intangible assets, which are wholly comprised of trademarks, as it is considered that their useful economic lives are not limited. Their carrying value is reviewed annually by the directors to determine whether there should be a reduction to reflect any permanent diminution in value.

A number of companies decided to value brands came following the takeover of Rowntrees by the Swiss food group Nestlé. It was clear that Nestlé had been willing to pay a high price to acquire the brand names owned by Rowntrees. Subsequently, in August 1988, Grand Metropolitan announced that it had decided to capitalize acquired brands on the basis of the cost attributed to them upon acquisition. Its 1988 annual report explained the change in accounting policies: 'Significant brands acquired after 1st January 1985, which were formerly written off against reserves, are now recorded in the balance sheet as fixed intangible assets.' The note dealing with reserves accordingly showed as a prior year adjustment the capitalization of brands. Later in 1988 Rank Hovis McDougall went one step further by incorporating a valuation of both acquired and internally developed brands (Extract 8.15).

Among companies carrying brand value in their balance sheet, there are differences in the valuation methods adopted. Grand Metropolitan, Cadbury Schweppes and Guinness (Extract 8.16) value their brands on the basis of the cost attributed to brands upon acquisition. Rank Hovis McDougall in 1991 stated that brands, both acquired and created within the group, are valued at their 'current use value to the Group'. They employed Interbrand Group plc, who were referred to as branding consultants, to carry out the valuation. The WPP Group (Extract 8.17) capitalized acquired brand names using as a valuation base 'the present value of notional royalty savings arising from ownership of those brands and ... estimates of profits attributable to brand loyalty'. Those who support such valuations believe that brands can be separately identified and valued and that brand valuation is no less subjective than say property valuation.

There is no common policy with regard to brand valuation. As explained RHM were amongst the pioneers in the UK in valuing brands. It was slightly amusing therefore that when they were taken over in 1993 by Tomkins the accounting policy adopted by the new owners of the brands was not to show value for the RHM brands in the consolidated balance sheet. The management of Tomkins do not believe that brand values should appear in balance sheets.

Extract 8.15 – Rank Hovis McDougall plc 1991 accounts, Notes.

ACCOUNTING POLICIES

Intangible assets

The accounting treatment for additions to goodwill is considered on an individual basis and elimination against reserves has been selected as appropriate for the current year.

Brands, both acquired and created within the Group, are included at their 'current cost'. Such cost, which is reviewed annually, is not subject to amortisation.

NOTES TO THE ACCOUNTS

13 Intangible assets

	The Group	The Company
Brands	£m	£m
At 1 September 1990	588.0	–
Revaluation	20.0	–
As at 31 August 1991	608.0	–

The group has valued its brands at their 'current use value to the Group' in conjunction with Interbrand Group plc, branding consultants.

The basis of valuation ignores any possible alternative use of a brand, any possible extension of the range of products currently marketed under a brand, any element of hope value and any possible increase in the value of a brand due to either a special investment or a financial transaction (e.g licensing) which would leave the Group with a different interest from the one being valued.

In their accounts for the year ending May 1993, Tomkins show that they paid £990 million for RHM. The fair value of the assets acquired was £244 million. They therefore paid £746 for goodwill (including the value of the brands). They did not wish to capitalize this and so it was written off immediately against reserves, £394 million against merger reserves and £352 million against capital reserves. RHM had previously shown brand values as being worth £459 million.

Another major company reversing the trend to value brands is Lonrho (Extract 8.18). In their accounts for the year ending September 1992, they explain that 'intangible assets undoubtedly have a considerable worth to the Group'. However, they point out that 'the basis of valuing such assets for inclusion in the accounts is entirely subjective. This subjectivity has generally led the investment community and other users of accounts to ignore the value of intangible assets when considering the net assets of a business and its level of gearing.'

Extract 8.16 – Guinness plc 1991 accounts, Accounting Policies and Notes.

Accounting Policies

BRANDS

The fair value of businesses acquired and of interests taken in associated undertakings includes brands, which are recognised where the brand has a value which is substantial and long-term. Acquired brands are only recognised where title is clear, brand earnings are separately identifiable, the brand could be sold separately from the rest of the business and where the brand achieves earnings in excess of those achieved by unbranded products.

Amortisation is not provided except where the end of the useful economic life of the acquired brand can be foreseen. The useful economic lives of brands and their carrying value are subject to annual review and any amortisation or provision for permanent impairment would be charged against the profit for the period in which they occur.

Notes to the Group accounts

12. ACQUIRED BRANDS AT COST	£m
At 1 January 1991	1,375
Additions, arising on acquisition of Asbach	20
AT 31 DECEMBER 1991	1,395

The amount stated for brands represents the cost of acquired brands. Brands are only recognised where title is clear, brand earnings are separately identifiable, the brand could be sold separately from the rest of the business and where the brand achieves earnings in excess of those achieved by unbranded products.

The cost of the brands is calculated at acquisition, as part of the fair value accounting for businesses acquired, on the basis of after tax multiples of pre-acquisition earnings after deducting attributable capital employed.

The acquired brands which have been recognised include Bell's, Dewar's, Gordon's, Johnnie Walker, Old Parr, Tanqueray, White Horse and Asbach.

The Directors have reviewed the amounts at which brands are stated and are of the opinion that there has been no impairment in the value of the brands recognised, that all brands recognised could be sold for amounts substantially greater than those recognised in the balance sheet and that the end of the useful economic lives of the brands cannot be foreseen.

ACCOUNTING POLICIES

4 Intangible fixed assets

Intangible fixed assets comprise certain acquired separate corporate brand names. These are shown at a valuation of the incremental earnings expected to arise from the ownership of brands. The valuations have been based on the present value of notional royalty savings arising from ownership of those brands and on estimates of profits attributable to brand loyalty. The valuations are subject to annual review. No depreciation is provided since, in the opinion of the directors, the brands do not have a finite useful economic life.

Notes to the accounts

9 Intangible fixed assets	1991	1990
	£000	£000
Corporate brand names	350,000	350,000

Corporate brand names represent the directors' valuation of the brand names J. Walter Thompson and Hill and Knowlton which were originally valued in 1988, and Ogilvy & Mather acquired in 1989 as part of The Ogilvy Group, Inc. These assets have been valued in accordance with the Group's accounting policy for intangible fixed assets and in the course of this valuation the directors have consulted their advisers, Samuel Montague & Co. Limited.

As a result of this the directors of Lonrho decided to reverse the policy of earlier years, namely to value newspaper titles owned by the group and to include such brand values as an asset in the company's balance sheet. In the past the directors valued such titles. From 1992 the company eliminated such assets from the balance sheet (valued as at that date as £117 million).

If, as Lonhro claim and as investment analysts often state, they ignore brand values shown on the balance sheet, one wonders how companies such as Guinness with a high proportion of brands in their balance sheet are able to borrow such large amounts relative to their fixed assets.

The Lonhro brand values referred to above relate to newspaper titles. There has been a long tradition in the UK in the newspaper industry of valuing the titles of papers and entering such values on the face of the balance sheet. These have traditionally been valued based on an estimate of either the minimum market value or the realizable value of the titles. This is the approach allowed by the Companies Act. It is interesting to read therefore in the accounts of the Daily Telegraph that 'Provision for corporation tax that could arise if the titles were disposed of at the revalued amount has not been made as it is not the intention of the directors to dispose of them.' Revaluation is of course necessary as the historical cost of titles such as *The Daily Telegraph* or *The Times* is irrelevant.

The difficulty and confusion in valuing newspaper titles can be demonstrated by observing the accounts of Mirror Group Newspapers. In a flotation document they show newspaper titles valued at £625 million. This is an estimated value as at the end of 1990 prepared by Cooper & Lybrands, an 'independent expert valuer'. Before the next set of accounts were prepared, the chairman of the company, Robert Maxwell, died in strange circumstances. The accounts as at the end of 1991 show the same value for newspaper titles as a year earlier, but

---

Extract 8.18(a) – Lonrho plc 1991 accounts, Statement on Accounting Policies.

Valuation of newspaper titles

No cost was allocated to newspaper titles on the acquisition of the relevant subsidiaries concerned. Independent professional valuations of certain newspaper titles have been incorporated into the Group's accounts within intangible assets, in order to reflect more fairly their value to the Group.

Depreciation is not provided as the newspaper titles do not have a finite economic life. If there were to be a permanent diminution in value, the deficit would be charged to profit before tax.

Extract 8.18(b) – Lonrho plc 1991 accounts, Report of the Directors.

Change of Accounting Policy

Intangible assets at 30th September, 1991 comprised newspaper titles at a current cost of £117m. and development costs of £14m.

Newspaper titles were first valued in the accounts in 1988 and the resulting surplus was credited to reserves. In the year ended 30 September, 1992 the Scottish newspaper titles were realised at a profit. The Directors are of the opinion that there has been no material permanent diminution during the year in the current cost of the remaining newspaper title.

Intangible assets undoubtedly have a considerable worth to the Group but the basis of valuing such assets for inclusion in the accounts is extremely subjective. This subjectivity has generally led the investment community and other users of accounts to ignore the value of intangible assets when considering the net assets of a business and its level of gearing. The Directors have therefore concluded that there is no benefit to be gained from keeping such assets in the balance sheet. Accordingly, intangible assets have been eliminated from the accounts for the year ended 30 September, 1992 and comparatives have been adjusted accordingly as set out in Note 23 to the Accounts.

they are now referred to as being valued on a historical cost basis! What is a current value in one year will be a historical cost the next year. A note to the accounts explains the titles were sold to a 'fellow subsidiary' during 1991.

In the accounts as at December 1992 the newspaper titles remain in the accounts at £625 million, but this time this value is described as 'the directors' estimate of current cost'. This same value started as a current cost, became a historical cost, and then reverted back to a current cost. The directors say in 1992 that they have not disclosed the historical cost of these newspaper titles because 'it is not now possible to ascertain it'.

In France, many companies do show brands as an asset on their balance sheet. The BSN Group, whose products include Danone yogurt, Kronenbourg beer and Evian mineral water, include a large value for brands amongst their assets. In 1991, brand names accounted for 19% of the total fixed and intangible assets. Extract 8.19, taken from the note dealing with accounting policies, provides an explanation.This policy conforms to French GAAP. The company, however, goes on to explain that the policy differs from that in the USA.

Extract 8.19(a) – BSN Group 1991 accounts, Notes.

The valuation of these brands, determined with the assistance of specialized consultants, takes into account various factors including, particularly, their reputations and earnings. These brands, which are legally protected, are not amortized. In the event that the recorded value of the brands becomes permanently impaired, a provision would be charged to income.

Purchased goodwill ("fonds de commerce"), licenses, patents and tenancy rights are recorded at cost. Purchased goodwill is amortized on a straight-line basis over a maximum period of 40 years. Other intangible assets are amortized on a straight-line basis over their estimated useful lives.

Extract 8.19(b) – BSN Group 1991 accounts, Notes.

A – BASIS OF CONSOLIDATION

The consolidated financial statements have been prepared in accordance with current French accounting principles. These accounting principles comply with the financial and accounting methods prescribed by accounting principles generally accepted in the United States of America, which the Group uses as a reference in view of the international nature of its activities, with the exception that, since 1989, brands have not been amortized. Had accounting principles generally accepted in the United States of America been fully applied, net income for 1991 would have been FF164 million lower (1990: FF138 million), and stockholders' equity at December 31, 1991 would have been reduced by FF401 million (1990: FF237 million).

The Fourth Directive allows trade marks, patents and copyrights, licences, franchises and similar rights to be capitalized. It is quite common to see such items referred to in the accounts of companies. An important difference between these items and brand values is that brand values do not have to be amortized, but these other intangible assets have to be written off over their useful lives or to reflect a fall in value. In France, however, trade marks and these other items do not have to be written down if there is no limit to their useful life. In such situations there is little difference from an accounting point of view between a brand name and a trade mark. It is important for the analyst to know what treatment is being followed with respect to intangible assets. Unfortunately only inadequate information is usually given with respect to the valuation method used and the amortization policy being followed. For example, Saint Gobain give brief details of the items included in intangible assets other than goodwill but include little helpful information on amortization policy (Extract 8.20).

Extract 8.20 – Saint Gobain Group 1991 accounts, Notes.

Other intangible assets

Other intangible assets are mainly represented by trade-marks, patents and computer software.

Trademarks are amortised over a period not exceeding 40 years using the straight-line method. A provision for depreciation of other intangible assets is made when there is any impairment in value.

Patents and computer software are amortised over their estimated useful lives using the straight-line method.

Research and Development Expenditure

The European Community Directives allow member states to permit research and development expenditure to be capitalized but the actual practice varies from country to country. In Germany the capitalization of research and development expenditure is extremely rare, only being allowed for expenses specifically attributable to clients' orders. The result is that in German companies the amount of research and development expenditure shown as 'intangible assets' is very small. The Bayer accounts (shown in Extract 8.1) value intangibles at the end of 1991 as DM 322 million (1992 as DM 314 million). This amount has to be taken in the context that in 1991 they spent DM 3007 million on research and development. They also spent DM 9445 million on selling expenses, which includes large amounts invested in creating and maintaining such widely known brand names as Aspirin and Alka-Seltzer. The capitalization of advertising expenditure in Germany is extremely rare.

In some other countries research and development expenditure can be capitalized under certain conditions. When capitalized it will be written off over its useful economic life. The maximum period for write off is usually five years. In the UK all research costs must be written off immediately against annual revenues, but development costs may be capitalized under certain circumstances. The justification for capitalizing development costs is that they are by definition costs associated with the introduction of a new specific product or process, or the improvement of a specific product or process. Therefore applying the matching accounting principle means that the capitalized development cost is written off as future revenue is earned. It is also permitted in the UK to capitalize development expenditure where a company has contracted to do work for another party and the costs incurred will be reimbursed.

Italy, Spain and the Netherlands permit the capitalization of R&D

Extract 8.21 – EniChem SpA 1992 accounts, Notes.

— *Research and development*

Those research costs which related to non-specific research and to the improvement of existing products or production processes are expensed as incurred.

Research and development costs for new products or new processes are capitalised if they relate to projects which the Group expects to develop and which are expected to be profitable. Capitalised research and development costs are amortised over three years on a straight-line basis.

Capitalised research and development costs are written off immediately in the event that the research proves unsuccessful. When the research is completed successfully, unamortised costs are transferred to "Licenses, patents and other charges".

---

expenditure under certain conditions. In Spain such expenditure can only be capitalized if the costs are associated with a particular project with an identifiable cost and there are justifiable reasons to expect the project to be a commercial success. Similar conditions apply in other countries. STT, the Italian company, refer to the capitalization of development costs connected with large-scale new software projects of major operational importance. They capitalize these as intangible assets if they 'offer reasonable prospects of earning revenues or curbing costs in the future'. Reasonable is an interesting word. The company amortizes these costs over three or five years, but it is explained this is not five years from the time of incurring the costs – rather it is five years from when the product is brought into use.

EniChem, the Italian company, points out that its accounts conform with the principles of the International Accounting Standards Committee. In the 1992 accounts they show in the balance sheet goodwill of 243 billion lire and deferred charges of 508 billion lire, of which 120 billion lire of the latter relate to research and development. They give details of their policies with regard to such costs (Extract 8.21), referring in the explanation to the capitalization of research and development. The total expenditure on research and development in 1992 was 307 billion lire. Part of this is charged directly to the profit and loss account and some of it is capitalized, but they do not give details of how the total expenditure is divided. The footnote dealing with depreciation and amortization does, however, give some clue: 'with a high charge for amortization of research and development' (in 1992 it was 119 billion lire). They must therefore have a policy of capitalizing a high percentage of the annual expenditure.

Formation (Start-up) Costs

The Fourth Directive allows companies to capitalize formation expenses, but practice varies within the Community. In the UK such expenses must not be capitalized. In the other five countries we are concerned with they can be capitalized, but must be written off within five years.

In Germany start-up costs and expansion costs can be capitalized in certain situations. If the amounts represent expenses recoverable from another party in case of default, then they can be treated as an asset. One of the few German companies taking advantage of this capitalization option explains in the footnotes to the accounts that the expenses concern investments in internally developed intangible assets.

The Spanish company Fortmento de Comercio Exterior provide a footnote in their accounts giving brief details of their treatment of start-up expenses: 'The balance of this caption in the accompanying consolidated balance sheet basically consists of the incorporation expenses of FOCOES International de Venezuela, C.A. These expenses are being amortized by the straight-line method over five years.' The French glass-making company Saint Gobain include start-up costs for major projects in the company under the heading of 'Deferred Charges'. They explain that 'Deferred charges include start-up costs for major projects which are deferred and amortized over 5 years.'

Groupe Euro Disney include formation expenses within the heading 'Deferred charges'. But they differentiate such expenses from 'start-up costs' which is included under the heading 'Intangible assets'. They include in their 1992 accounts FF 1458 million of 'start-up costs' as an intangible asset. These costs include marketing, recruitment and training costs, and were incurred between 1 January 1992 and the opening on 12 April 1992. These costs have been capitalized and are being amortized over five years.

These are not the only costs incurred prior to the opening that have been capitalized and are being amortized. There are FF 2001 million 'Deferred charges'. These include FF 1896 million of pre-opening costs which were costs incurred before 1 January 1992, in order to 'establish the permanent organization and operating structure of the Group, primarily for personnel, relocation and professional services'. These deferred costs are being amortized over 20 years. It is pointed out in Form 10Q that reconciles US GAAP and French GAAP that these pre-opening costs would need to be amortized over five years according to US standards.

The division between 'start-up costs' and 'pre-opening costs' is important. It would be interesting to know how the decision was reached to make 1 January 1992 the changeover date. It is perhaps relevant that, in the French accounts, the one set of costs are amortized over five years and the other set over 20 years. Here is a clear example of the fact that the actual reported profits depend on management policy decisions.

Other Categories of Intangible Asset

There are other categories of intangible asset. For example, publishers usually include publication rights as an intangible, and a company that operates under a franchise arrangement will value the remaining years of its franchise and include the value in its balance sheet. We will not deal with these and the other categories in detail. The chapter has, however, dealt with the major items and the major issues involved.

References

1. Nobes, C.W. and Parker, R.H. (eds) (1991) *Comparative International Accounting*, Prentice Hall.
2. Smith, T. (1992) *Accounting for Growth*, Century Business, London.
3. Fédération des Experts Comptables Européens (1991) *FEE European Survey of Published Accounts*, Routledge.

Problems

1. Why has accounting for intangible assets become such a significant issue since the late 1980s?

2. What are the arguments for and against banks taking into consideration the value of a company's intangible assets when deciding whether or not to make a loan to the company? Examine the annual report and accounts of two large companies in order to ascertain whether or not the providers of debt finance to the companies appear to have taken into consideration the level of the companies intangibles when making the decision to lend.

3. 'In transforming its balance sheet by the valuation of brands, RHM is taking to its conclusion a process which has been bubbling along furiously … anything that tends to reinstate the balance sheet and profit and loss account as tools of analysis can only be useful.' (Quote from *The Financial Times*.)

   Comment on the above statement, taking into account the treatment of the RHM brand values by Tomkins following the acquisition.

4. Company A purchases company B for ECU 200 million. The book value of the net assets of B, in its own accounts, prior to the acquisition was ECU 120 million. It is estimated the fair value of the net assets of B is ECU 160 million. The estimated average life of the assets of company B is 10 years.

   Show four alternative methods of recording the acquisition of company B in the accounts of company A. Which method can be used in which country?

5. Discuss the arguments for and against the immediate write-off of goodwill against equity. Illustrate your answer with reference to the SmithKline Beecham case.

6. Discuss the reasons for requiring multinational companies to prepare consolidated financial statements. What are the problems with such statements from the point of view of creditors and analysts?

7. What are the arguments for and against the use of merger accounting versus acquisition accounting for business combinations.

8. Examine the extracts from the accounts of Trafalgar House and TI. (Extracts 8.3 and 8.4). Write a report explaining to a layman how the companies have accounted for the acquisitions they have made. In particular explain the logic of the fair value adjustments shown.

9. What is negative goodwill? From an economic point of view does it make sense? Discuss the issues involved using Endesa (Extract 8.13) as an example.

10. Examine the extract from the accounts of Ciments Français (Extract 8.10). What is meant by the asset 'market share'? What are the arguments for and against including such a value as an asset?

11. In their 1990 accounts Daimler-Benz refer to hidden reserves being made active (Extract 8.11). What do they mean by this statement? Comment on this policy in respect of subsequent developments.

12. Examine the treatment of goodwill in the accounts of Daimler-Benz (Extract 8.11) and Siemens (Extract 8.12). Are there any differences in the policies being adopted by these large German companies?

13. Discuss the treatment of all the pre-opening costs of Euro Disney. Why do you think they decided to divide such costs into two categories.

14. What are the arguments for and against capitalizing research and development costs? Discuss the different treatments applied by the companies for whom extracts from the accounts are included in this chapter.

15. Discuss the 'in, out, in, out' treatment of brand values by Lonhro and the Mirror Group. What explanations can be offered for such changes in policy?

9

Liabilities and Provisions

Objectives

- To examine the items that appear in company accounts under the classification liabilities and provisions.

- To attempt to define such items.

- To show that terms such as reserves and provisions can have different meanings in different countries.

- To demonstrate the differences in the level of disclosure from one country to another.

- To identify the issues concerned with liabilities with which an analyst has to be concerned when examining a company's accounts.

Introduction

The dictionary definition of the word liability is 'sums which one is bound to pay'. The amount a company is bound to pay is relatively straightforward, a problem arises over the amounts a company may have to pay.

The UK accounting definition is complicated: 'Liabilities are an entity's obligation to transfer economic benefits as a result of past transactions or events.'

A difficulty that can arise even with this definition is to decide whether an entity has an obligation. An obligation can be definite, with no chance of the entity or the creditor changing the commitment. On the other hand, an obligation can be conditional, depending on whether certain events happen, or upon a decision of the entity or the creditor. In this situation the entity might or might not have to meet the liability. The treatment of such conditional liabilities varies from country to country.

One of the postulates of accounting is prudency, therefore a company usually sets aside a sum of money out of profits to meet expenses the company might have to pay or to cover for income earned that might not be received. This is called a provision. The decision as to whether to create a provision and the sum to set aside involves an element of judgement. The practices followed on this matter vary from country to country and within a country some companies can be more prudent than others.

Issues

The questions an analyst is concerned with when examining the liabilities and provisions in a balance sheet include the following.

- How are liabilities measured?
- What is the relationship between the level of liabilities and the value of the assets of a company?
- What provisions have been made for expenses or losses that are 'likely' to occur, or crystallize, in the future?
- How have future pension payments been accounted for?
- Does the company have any contingent liabilities?
- What are the dates when the loans will need to be repaid? Are they all short term? Will repayment of a large percentage of the loans be at about the same time?
- What are the currencies that will have to be repaid? What interest rate is being paid on debt?
- Are details disclosed of stand-by credit facilities?

Balance Sheet Disclosure

Bayer show long-term debt (debentures and liabilities to banks) under the heading of 'Other liabilities' (see Extract 9.1). There is a brief footnote giving details of bonds with warrants attached, but there are no details given about the liabilities to banks, with no information about the currency of the debt and only a summary table explaining the term structure. Most of the liability to banks is short term. The 'miscellaneous liabilities' figure (Extract 9.2) is large but only very brief information is given about the details: DM 2929 million of the miscellaneous liabilities is described as 'other miscellaneous liabilities'. Of this amount an explanation is only given for DM 700 million.

The annual report of Volkswagen again only gives very brief details. Their analysis by maturity is minimal, giving the amount to be repaid in less than one year, and by implication the amount of debt of more than one year's duration. No details are given about the currency of the borrowing nor of the interest rates payable. One particularly interesting item is 'undetermined liabilities', which in total exceeds the value of stockholders' equity.

The law in Germany requires that companies disclose details of liabilities that fall due within the next twelve-month period, and that the sum of liabilities with a maturity of more than five years be stated in the notes to the accounts. It is up to the user of the accounts to compute the amount of liabilities with a maturity of between one and five years. The relevant literature in Germany is critical of the lack of disclosure of liabilities.

French companies, in contrast disclose a remarkable amount of detail. As can be seen from the accounts of Saint Gobain (Extract 9.3), the repayment schedule over each of the next five years is shown, together with details of the debt by currency and information on the extent to which risk has been hedged through interest rate swaps. Many other major French companies such as Carrefour show a similar breakdown (see Extract 9.4). Carrefour also show 'unused credit facilities'. This is clearly an important factor when liquidity ratios are calculated. Unfortunately very few companies in any country disclose their unused borrowing facilities, although it is becoming more common to do so.

Extract 9.1 – Bayer AG 1992 accounts, Financial Statements.

Stockholders' Equity and Liabilities	Note	Dec. 31, 1992	Dec. 31, 1991
Stockholders' equity			
Capital stock of Bayer AG	[8]	3,287	3,225
Capital reserves	[9]	4,065	4,125
Retained earnings	[10]	8,210	7,145
Net income		1,516	1,824
Minority interests		414	386
		17,492	**16,705**
Special item with an equity component		77	97
Provisions			
Provisions for pensions and similar conmitments	[11]	7,239	6,722
Other provisions	[12]	3,802	4,495
		11,041	**11,217**
Other liabilities			
Debentures	[13]	2,080	2,061
Liabilities to banks		2,167	2,618
Trade accounts payable	[14]	2,048	2,224
Bills payable		147	191
Payables to subsidiaries		169	140
Miscellaneous liabilities	[15]	3,005	2,518
		9,616	**9,752**
Deferred income		102	146
		38,328	**37,917**

[15] MISCELLANEOUS LIABILITIES

	Dec. 31, 1992 DM million	Dec. 31, 1991 DM million
Advance payments received	47	48
Payables to other affiliated companies	29	2
Other miscellaneous liabilities	2,929	2,468
	3,005	**2,518**

In Italy as can be seen from Extract 9.5 from the accounts of STET, very little information is given about the maturity of the debt, with no breakdown of the long-term debt. One useful piece of information is, however, the classification by interest rate. Unfortunately, this cannot be linked to the currency of the loan. It would be useful to know whether or not the high interest rate loans are in currencies which are declining in value against the home currency.

Some UK companies give a very detailed breakdown of their borrowing. A good example is Forte (Extract 9.6). The latest requirements in the UK are for an analysis of the maturity of debt showing amounts falling due:

- in one year or less, or on demand;
- between one and two years; and
- in five years or more.

Where short-term debt has been reclassified as long-term because the lender has granted a longer-term facility, the amount of the debt which has been reclassified should be disclosed, analysed by its maturity before such reclassification.

For convertible debt, the disclosure requirements are:

- the dates of redemption and the amounts payable on redemption;

the number and class of shares into which the debt may be converted, and the dates at or periods within which conversion may take place; and

· whether conversion is at the option of the issuer or the holder.

As mentioned above an important item sometimes disclosed is unused borrowing facilities. This is often as significant as balance sheet figures in evaluating liquidity. Cadbury Schweppes give useful guidance on this point (Extract 9.7).

Extract 9.3 – Saint Gobain Group 1991 accounts, Notes.

NOTE 22: LONG TERM DEBT

in millions of French francs	1991	1990	1989
Repayment five years or under			
– 1991	–	–	1,035
– 1992	–	1,991	1,574
– 1993	2,696	2,673	1,480
– 1994	1,239	807	346
– 1995	2,152	2,378	291
– 1996	1,175	599	–
– 1997	987	–	–
– Between 6 and 10 years	2,252	1,136	480
– Over 10 years	550	129	333
– Unspecified	3,094	2,460	2,318
Total debt repayable after one year	14,145	12,173	7,857
Short term portion of long term debt	2,339	4,526	1,265
Total long term debt (including short term portion)	16,484	16,699	9,122

The long term debt by currency is as follows:

in millions of French francs	1991	1990	1989
– French francs	3,169	6,514	2,901
– US Dollars	4,919	3,935	940
– Deutschemarks	4,223	3,468	2,635
– Ecus	1,301	1,014	1,221
– Spanish Pesetas	578	296	307
– Italian Lira	464	589	594
– Pounds Sterling	434	482	189
– Other currencies	1,396	401	335
	16,484	16,699	9,122
These debts include the following amounts in respect of property, plant and equipment acquired under finance leasing agreements	393	344	372

Long term debts are secured by charges (mortgages and investments pledged) on various non-current assets for a total amount of FF 2,730 million at December 31, 1991.

The Group has a Multi-Optional Financial Facility (MOFF) of $ 900 million (FF 4.7 billion) available up to November 19, 1992. None of the MOFF was drawn down at December 31, 1991 (FF 3 billion at December 31, 1990, none at December 31, 1989).

Bank overdrafts and other short term debt

in millions of French francs	1991	1990	1989
● Treasury notes (in French francs)	1,520	2,080	3,372
● Euro Commercial Paper (in US dollars)	347	477	1,505
● US Commercial Paper (in US dollars)	2,682	898	1,415
	4,549	3,455	6,292
● Bank overdrafts	9,264	9,233	7,207
	13,813	12,688	13,499

The Group has facilities to issue treasury notes for the equivalent of FF 9 billion in the French, European and American markets.

Interest rates

That part of debt subject to fixed interest rates represents 36 % of total indebtedness before taking into account the use of hedging instruments so as to provide a cover against an increase in rates. At December 31, 1991 interest rate swaps amount to FF 2,708 million and caps to FF 6,788 million. Accordingly the portion subject to fixed interest rates is 68 %. Taking into account short-term placements at variable interest rates, total indebtedness is 95 % covered. The weighted average interest rate in 1991 is approximately 9.3 % (9.5 % in 1990 and 10 % in 1989).

NOTE 14
Borrowings

In FF millions	Maturity	Effective interest rate	1991	1990
Variable rate bonds.........	1997	9.98 %	1,000	1,000
Credit National loan	2001	10.22 %	1,000	-
Equity-linked zero coupon notes	1995	9.65 %	500	-
Multi option facility..........	1994	9.69 %	600	-
Commercial paper			2,850	935
Obligations under capital leases			1,740	138
Other.......................			1,604	382
			9,294	2,455

These borrowings were contracted in the following currencies (translated into French francs at December 31 rates) :

In FF millions	1991	1990
French francs	9,245	2,334
US dollars	24	1
ECU (European Currency Unit).......	-	10
Other.................................	25	110
	9,294	2,455

These borrowings mature as follows :

In FF millions	1991	1990
1 year	5,139	1,097
2 years	644	47
3 years	796	39
4 years	401	61
5 years	1,189	28
6 to 10 years..........................	749	1,084
Over 10 years.........................	269	31
Indeterminate..........................	107	68
	9,294	2,455

At December 31, 1991, FF 83 million of these borrowings were secured by capital assets (FF 95 million at December 31, 1990).

In addition, the following unused credit facilities were available at December 31, 1991 :

In FF millions	
French francs	2,492
Spanish pesetas...	804

— *Total financial debt* comes to L. 25,441 billion
(L. 21,960 billion at 31/12/91) and breaks down as follows:

— *Classification by maturity*

	in lire	%	in foreign currency	%	Total	%	Total	%
			at 31/12/1992				at 31/12/1991	
Medium and long-term debt maturing:								
• Within 12 months	2,056	9	18	2	2,074	8	1,643	7
• After more than 12 months	17,205	71	714	58	17,919	71	17,021	78
	19,261	80	732	60	19,993	79	18,664	85
Short-term debt	4,955	20	493	40	5,448	21	3,296	15
TOTAL	24,216	100	1,225	100	25,441	100	21,960	100

— *Classified by interest rate:*

	1992	1991
up to 5%	414	332
from 5% to 10%	10,040	9,890
from 10% to 15%	13,811	11,625
over 15%	1,176	113
	25,441	21,960

Specifically, the most important items in the 5-10% band refer to loans granted by the Cassa Depositi e Prestiti (according to law no. 887 of 22/12/84) and by various banks with an interest contribution (3%) from the Treasury Ministry (according to law no. 67 of 11/3/88), as well as to loans issued in Euro-currencies out of EIB funds at market rates with practically full cover of the exchange risk by the government.

— *Classified by Foreign currency* (in millions and with exchange risk):

(in millions)

	at 31/12/1992	at 31/12/1991	at 31/12/1992	at 31/12/1991
US $	154	103	223	122
D.M.	164	3	124	2
ECU	504	91	779	140
Other			99	28
			1,225	292

NOTES TO THE ACCOUNTS

22 BANK AND OTHER BORROWINGS (continued)

Currency analysis	Company 1993 £ million	Company 1992 £ million	Group 1993 £ million	Group 1992 £ million
The outstanding loans are repayable in the following currencies:				
Sterling	423	404	441	420
US Dollar	275	338	307	395
French Franc	239	152	274	177
Deutsche Mark	25	21	46	29
Italian Lire	28	22	45	40
Dutch Florin	11	18	11	18
Spanish Peseta	–	–	18	17
Irish Punt	–	35	–	35
Other currencies	5	7	49	19
Total loans	**1,006**	**997**	**1,191**	**1,150**

Repayment analysis	Company 1993 £ million	Company 1992 £ million	Group 1993 £ million	Group 1992 £ million
Repayable otherwise than by instalments:				
in five years or more	163	203	174	221
between two and five years	387	377	397	379
between one and two years	135	283	136	285
within one year or on demand	321	134	391	200
Repayable by instalments:				
in five years or more	–	–	56	34
between two and five years	–	–	23	19
between one and two years	–	–	8	5
within one year or on demand	–	–	6	7
Total loans	**1,006**	**997**	**1,191**	**1,150**

The Group has a committed £350m multiple option facility expiring in 1994 and committed revolving credit lines of £455m and US$60m, of which £15m expires in 1995, £220m in 1996, £70m in 1997 and the balance thereafter, which may be used to refinance existing borrowings.

The repayment analysis shown above includes bank loans of £263m (1992 – £79m) repayable within one year which are backed by the above facilities and also Sterling Commercial Paper of £39m (1992 – £281m), Eurodollar Commercial Paper of £nil (1992 – £38m), US Dollar Domestic Commercial Paper of £7m (1992 – £202m) and French

Loans from banks included in the table above were £738m (1992 – £238m) for the Group of which £30m (1992 – £16m) was secured and £708m (1992 – £128m) for the Company of which none was secured.

*These loans include certain borrowings on which rates of interest vary in accordance with market rates. The rates quoted are those prevailing at the end of the period.

Secured loans are secured by mortgages on a small number of hotel and other Group properties.

Subsequent to the balance sheet date, the Group issued on 18 February 1993 a £200m 10% First Mortgage Debenture Stock 2018, the proceeds of which were used to refinance existing borrowings.

Loans from banks included in the table above were £738m (1992 – £238m) for the Group of which £30m (1992 – £16m) was secured and £708m (1992 – £128m) for the Company of which none was secured.

*These loans include certain borrowings on which rates of interest vary in accordance with market rates. The rates quoted are those prevailing at the end of the period.

Secured loans are secured by mortgages on a small number of hotel and other Group properties.

Subsequent to the balance sheet date, the Group issued on 18 February 1993 a £200m 10% First Mortgage Debenture Stock 2018, the proceeds of which were used to refinance existing borrowings.

Interest rate exchange agreements
The interest rates on loans shown above have been varied by the use of interest exchange agreements which alter interest rates as follows:

	Interest rate shown above	Varied interest rate	Expiry date
† Sterling £180m	Variable	11.9%	Between six and seven years
† Sterling £69m	Variable	10.9%	Between three and four years
US Dollar US$50m	Variable	8.7%	Between one and two years
Sterling £100m	8.375%	Libor + 1.0%	Between four and five years
Sterling £19m	10.6%	Libor + 3.9%	Between three and four years

† These interest exchange agreements were reversed with effect from the end of January 1993. Payments will be made at the rate of £8m and £3m per annum respectively until the agreements expire.

Extract 9.7 – Cadbury Schweppes plc 1992 accounts, Notes.

Borrowing facilities
At 2 January 1993, the Group had substantial amounts of undrawn committed borrowing facilities analysed as follows:

	Expiring within one year £m	Extending beyond one year £m
Multiple Option Facility	–	200.0
Revolving Credit Facility	–	185.0
Other facilities available to the Group		
– in support of commercial paper	21.9	10.6
– for other purposes	34.7	11.4
	56.6	407.0

The Multiple Option Facility totals £300m which represents £200m committed until 7 September 1994 and £100m subject to availability. The Revolving Credit Facility is committed until 20 September 1997. The other facilities available to the Group include £34.7m expiring within one year, which represents annual facilities subject to review at various dates during the year. There are in addition substantial uncommitted facilities available to the Group.

Short-Term v. Long-Term Borrowing

One problem that emerged in some company accounts in the late 1980s was the classification of borrowing. Traditionally it was always thought that borrowing that had to be repaid within a year was short term and was classified as a current liability, or, to be more exact, as 'Creditors due within one year'.

In the UK overdrafts were thought to be short-term borrowing as the bank could ask for repayment at short notice. The accounts of Ellis & Everard (Extract 9.8) show that the picture has become confused. This company refers to 'Bank loans and overdrafts repayable after 5 years'. A note explains that these are 'drawn down under the Group's evergreen facilities', and the amount is shown in the balance sheet under the title 'Creditors due after one year'. So overdrafts can also be long term?

Extract 9.8 – Ellis & Everard Group 1993 accounts, Notes.

	GROUP		COMPANY	
	1993	1992	**1993**	1992
12 Finance debt	**£m**	£m	**£m**	£m
Secured loans:				
Repayable by instalments:				
US dollar bank loans (4.5% to 11.5%) 1991/1997	**0.1**	0.1	–	–
Obligations under finance leases	**0.3**	0.4	–	–
	0.4	0.5	–	–
Unsecured loans:				
Bank loans and overdrafts wholly repayable within one year	**1.0**	0.8	–	–
Bank loans and overdrafts repayable within 2 to 5 years	**1.3**	–	–	–
Bank loans and overdrafts repayable after 5 years (LIBOR +1/2%)	**9.4**	3.6	**1.5**	5.5
Repayable by instalments:				
US dollar loan notes repayable in equal instalments between 2001/2011 (9.6%)	**16.0**	14.1	–	–
Other	**0.4**	0.2	–	–
Total finance debt	**28.5**	19.2	**1.5**	5.5

Repayable:

Within 1 year	**1.2**	1.0	–	–
1–2 years	**0.3**	0.1	–	–
2–5 years	**1.3**	0.7	–	–
5 years and over: by instalments	**16.0**	14.1	–	–
in full	**9.7**	3.3	**1.5**	5.5
	27.3	18.2	**1.5**	5.5
Total finance debt	**28.5**	19.2	**1.5**	5.5

The US dollar bank loans and other loans are secured on certain of the Group's properties.

The bank loans and overdrafts repayable after 5 years are drawn down under the Group's evergreen facilities.

The US dollar loan notes, which have been guaranteed by the Company, are due to mature on 30 April 2011.

Extract 9.9 – Reed International plc 1992 accounts, Notes.

19 Creditors – Amounts Falling Due after more than 1 year

£ million	CONSOLIDATED		PARENT	
	31 Dec 1992	31 March 1992	**31 Dec 1992**	31 March 1992
Loan capital note 20				
– within 1 to 2 years	**82.8**	0.6	–	0.4
– within 2 to 5 years	**235.1**	209.4	–	30.0
– due otherwise than by instalment after 5 years	**216.5**	276.1	–	–
Promissory notes and bank loans – within 1 to 2 years	**103.9**	0.3	–	–
– within 2 to 5 years	**308.6**	364.1	–	93.2
Amounts owed to group undertakings	–	–	**61.4**	578.9
Other creditors	**15.7**	13.5	–	–
Taxation	**23.8**	25.8	–	–
Accruals and deferred income	**1.8**	1.5	–	–
Total	**988.2**	891.3	**61.4**	702.5

Promissory notes and bank loans include short-term US commercial paper borrowings and other short-term borrowings to the extent that they are supported by available medium-term facilities, according to the maturity of the facilities, and where there is an intention to renew them as they fall due. Of these borrowings, **£103.9m** (£nil) are included within 1 to 2 years and **£308.6m** (£363.9m) within 2 to 5 years.

Extract 9.10 – Forte Group plc 1992 accounts, Notes.

Repayment analysis	COMPANY		GROUP	
	1992 £ million	1991 £ million	1992 £ million	1991 £ million
Repayable otherwise than by instalments:				
in five years or more	**203**	372	**221**	391
between two and five years	**377**	187	**379**	189
between one and two years	**283**	85	**285**	88
within one year or on demand	**134**	214	**200**	275
Repayable by instalments:				
in five years or more	–	–	**34**	33
between two and five years	–	–	**19**	5
between one and two years	–	–	**5**	2
within one year or on demand	–	–	**7**	2
Total loans	**997**	858	**1,150**	985

The Group has a committed £350m multiple option facility expiring in 1994 and committed revolving credit lines of £425m and US$60m expiring in 1995 and later which may be used to refinance existing borrowings.

The repayment analysis shown above includes bank loans of £79m (1991 – £72m) repayable within one year which are backed by the above facilities and also Sterling Commercial Paper of £281m (1991 – £201m), Eurodollar Commercial Paper of £38m (1991 – £115m), US Dollar Domestic Commercial Paper of £202m (1991 – £148m) and French Franc Commercial Paper of £141m (1991 – nil) which are repayable within one year but can be replaced by further borrowings under the Commercial Paper programmes or refinanced under the above facilities. These amounts have therefore been classified as long term borrowings.

A similar practice is followed by Reed International with respect to promissory notes and bank loans. The footnote to the relevant note explains, however, that included in the longer-term promissory notes is £364 million short-term commercial paper borrowing (Extract 9.9). The justification is that although the notes are short term the company has medium-term back-up borrowing facilities which it could use if it had to repay the short-term notes. It is saying that although the notes are short term they have medium-term finance available should they wish to use it. The fact that the actual borrowing used is short term does not seem to matter.

The Ellis & Everard justification is similar to that of Reed. Although they are actually using finance obtained through an overdraft arrangement, they have longer-term stand-by funds ('evergreen') should they wish to use them. It seems a bit like 'Alice in Wonderland' – 'Ignore what I am actually doing; the accounts are based on what I could do.' Forte offer a similar explanation for reclassifying short-term borrowing (Extract 9.10).

Certainly the analyst should no longer rely on simple tests such as the current ratio or the acid test as these reclassifications have a favourable 'cosmetic' effect on such liquidity measurements. FRS 3 tries to clarify the position on this question of the maturity of debt. It allows companies to take account of committed (stand-by, back-up, evergreen) facilities available to them at the balance sheet date. The standard allows the companies to reclassify short-term debt into longer period debt, providing certain conditions are met. One condition is that the debt and the back-up facilities are with the same lender or group of lenders. The sale by a company of short-term commercial paper in the financial markets backed by facilities with a bank fail to meet this condition as the funds obtained are not from the same lender as the back-up facilities. The Reed International classification of 1992 would not be allowed in future.

Reserves and Provisions

The countries with which we are concerned all have similar definitions of reserves and provisions, but the situation in which it is considered desirable to create a provision varies from country to country. On occasions a 'provision' in one country is called a 'reserve' in another country.

Before analysing the actual reporting practices with regard to provisions, it is necessary to try to distinguish between what is a reserve and what is a provision. 'Reserves' normally represent funds set aside out of after-tax profits either to provide finance for future growth or to be able to assist in meeting unknown future financial difficulties. A transfer of funds to reserves represents an appropriation of after-tax profits – it is not an expense. A 'provision' is an expense.

Reserves belong to shareholders. They are classified in the accounts as shareholders' funds, and they are part of the equity of the business for the purpose of gearing calculations. Provisions are not part of the equity: they are funds set aside to meet an expense. A provision can be defined as either:

- an amount written off profits to allow for the depreciation or diminution in the value of assets; or
- an amount written off profits to provide for any liability or loss which is either reasonably certain to be incurred, or certain to be incurred but there is uncertainty as to the amount or as to the date when the actual payment will be made.

Unfortunately there is a grey area between reserves and provisions. It is not always easy to agree on what is reasonably certain. What is reasonably certain to a person who is prudent by nature is not reasonably certain to a more adventurous person. The fact that terms like 'reasonable', 'possible', 'almost certain' and 'seems probable' are subjective gives rise to different interpretations. This can lead to what are called 'secret reserves' or to 'underprovisions'.

The above definitions represent the position according to generally accepted accounting principles. In fact in practice the situation can differ. For example, if a company deliberately overprovides for the diminution in the value of assets or for possible future expenses, it is creating a reserve but calling it a provision. It is hiding shareholders' money (what should be called reserves) amongst so called liabilities (provisions). This is a secret reserve. It results in the understating in the accounts of the true value of the company. As will be explained below there can be logical reasons why a company may wish to do this.

The situation can also happen in reverse. If a company under-provides for depreciation and for future possible expenses, it is over-stating its assets. It is not making a high enough provision in the profit and loss account and so is overstating profits. It is hoping to create a favourable impression of its profitability. It is up to the analyst to assess the true position.

In Germany there has long been a tradition of creating provisions with one of the objectives being to smooth profits over time. These excess provisions are made out of profits – some are tax deductible some are not. One further reason for creating such provisions is the requirements in publicly listed companies (AGs) relating to the payment of dividends. The supervisory boards and management boards of such companies are allowed to retain in the company up to 50% of the profits that are available for distribution without seeking the approval of the AGM. They could retain a higher percentage but would require the approval of the AGM to do so. Provisions are of course a way of reducing distributable profits, and so of retaining funds without shareholder approval.

In Germany, provisions (accruals) may be made for uncertain obligations, anticipated losses and certain other expenses. Uncertain obligations include tax and pension accruals. As long as the tax and pension provisions are calculated according to tax rules they are allowed as tax deductible expenses. The majority of companies choose to follow the tax approved method of arriving at such estimates. As will be shown it is not always easy for the user of accounts to determine how some of the provisions have been calculated, or to determine their size.

In France in the past there has also been a tradition of creating general provisions to allow for risk, with the object of smoothing profits. Such a practice has not been allowed in the UK where provisions must only be made for specifically identifiable future events (not general provisions). We will return to the subject of provisions shortly.

Secret Reserves

German companies have had a reputation in the past for possessing secret reserves. By this has been meant that the true value of the company was in excess of the net asset value of the company as represented in the financial accounts. This has been due partly to the fact that German companies are not allowed to revalue assets, partly to accounting practices such as depreciating assets more quickly than the true decline in their value, and partly to the practice of setting aside excessive provisions for other items.

Daimler-Benz wished to build a factory in the USA. They therefore wished to obtain a listing in the USA. They were the first German company to apply to have shares listed on the New York Stock Exchange, and they ran into problems. To obtain a listing in the USA companies need to satisfy SEC requirements with regard to accounting practices, but there is a big difference between what is acceptable in Germany and what is acceptable in the USA.

So in 1992 Daimler's attempt to have their shares listed on the New York Stock Exchange meant complying with the demanding requirements of the SEC. The Chairman of the SEC made some very critical remarks about the quality of Daimler accounts in particular and German company accounts in general. In the end Daimler responded to pressure from the SEC and, in order to have their shares quoted in the USA, amended their accounts, revealing secret reserves of DM 4 billion. As they explained these resulted from a policy over many years of high depreciation expenses and setting aside undefined provisions, with the provisions having being written off as if they were a cost. To bring these overprovisions back into the profit and loss account meant the company introducing a credit, as extraordinary profits, of this amount in the 1992 profit and loss account.

Any non-US company wishing to be listed needs each year to file a form 20F, which gives a reconciliation of the accounts produced according to the standards of the company's home country and the accounts according to US GAAP. When Daimler-Benz produced such a statement it exploded the myth that German company accounts are always conservative. They are only conservative in years when the company performs well – in such years they understate profits. In years of poor economic performance they are able to use the secret reserves to boost reported profits. Daimler showed that, contrary to what most analysts would have expected, the profits in the year before listing according to German principles were much higher than according to US principles.

An interesting aspect of this case is that the unamended accounts of Daimler had been accepted in Europe for some time; they were good enough for a listing in London. As Daimler pointed out in their accounts, they could obtain a listing in London and Tokyo, based on the content of their 1989 and 1990 accounts in which the size of the secret reserves were not disclosed. The existence of secret reserves was mentioned in the 1990 accounts, but no clue was given to the amount involved.

Were analysts in Germany in 1992 aware of the size of such secret reserves? The case illustrates the dangers of attempting to analyse accounts from a country with which one is not familiar. It also shows the dangers of mutual recognition. London had accepted the accounts but the SEC was not prepared to accept the accounts as first presented.

Germany is not the only country in which excess provisions lead to secret reserves. In Italy, Benetton, through the use of over-generous allowances for bad debts, have achieved similar results. In their 1991 accounts they reported an 18.4% increase in selling, general and administrative expenses. They revealed in a note that this was 'mainly caused by increased provisions, primarily to the allowance for doubtful accounts'. The company states that as a result of the increased annual charge the accumulated provisions for bad debts and other provisions equalled 3.3% of total revenue. This was very much higher than was normal in Italy. By reducing profits in 1991 they had built up provisions which they could use in future years should they need to boost profits.

Germany – 'Special Item with an Equity Component'

It is possible, but difficult, to try to measure the size of a German company's secret reserves. An estimate of one element of secret reserves can be made from an item that appears in the balance sheet of most German companies. Bayer have an entry in their balance sheet, placed between stockholders' equity and provisions, entitled 'Special item with an equity component'. The note in the 1992 accounts explaining the item is not particularly helpful.

Allocations to the special item with an equity component were made by domestic consolidated companies under Arts. 6b and 52, para 8, Income Tax Act, Section 35, Income Tax Regulations, and Art. 1, Taxation Act for the Promotion of Investments in Developing Countries, and by foreign companies under comparable tax regulations.

The appropriate note in the Bayer accounts for the two earlier years 1990 and 1991 differs in only one word.

The value to an analyst of the disclosure of this 'special item' is limited because of an inadequate breakdown in the accounts of the total figure. Allocations to this account can be made as a result of a number of articles in the Taxation Acts, the result being that different categories of items are lumped together under this one title. One reason 'special items' arise is in order to prevent hidden reserves leading to a taxation liability. When an asset which has been depreciated more than is justified on economic grounds is sold, then a large capital gains tax liability could arise. Special provisions of the Income Tax Act allow for the taxation on such items to be postponed if the capital gain is reinvested in qualifying assets. This policy of course encourages German companies to invest. The 'special item with an equity component' is where such capital gains on undervalued assets are entered in the accounts until the money is spent on new investments.

These 6(b) income tax allocations have to be placed in 'special items with an equity component', where they are lumped together with other transactions which have different origins. A second category of 'special items' arise as a result of government economic policies which are devised to stimulate investments in certain regions of Germany or in developing countries. These policies offer companies various investment incentives in the form of accelerated depreciation on such investments. These incentives can also be included in special items.

Interpreting this 'special item' is made even more difficult by the fact that this second category of tax benefit does not have to be recorded under this heading. A company can choose either to record the

(15) Special reserves

Special reserves of the BASF Group and BASF Aktiengesellschaft include reserves for gains from retirements of fixed assets according to §6 b EStG (income tax law) and reserves for replacements according to section 35 EStR (income tax regulations), reserves for capital investments in developing countries as permitted under §1 EntwLStG (developing countries tax law), reserves for losses of foreign subsidiaries according to

§3 AuslInvG (foreign investment law) and value adjustments on non-interest bearing loans granted prior to January 1, 1955 according to §7c EStG. In addition, the BASF Group financial statements include reserves for changes in interest rates applied for the valuation of pension provisions according to §52, section 8 EStG, according to §6 FGG (area improvement law), and from the deferral of investment grants.

transaction under this special item heading (where it becomes visible) or it can reduce the carrying value of the asset to which the tax incentive relates.

BASF name their account 'Special reserves' and give brief details of the many items that are covered by this heading (Extract 9.11). Hoechst name theirs 'Special reserve items subject to future taxation'. As explained above, tax will not have to be paid on the special items as long as the funds are invested in qualifying assets. The size of the 'special items with an equity element' account varies considerably from one company to another. Both BASF and Bayer have in recent years reduced the amount which is recorded under this heading. Whereas in the late 1980s Bayer's 'special items with an equity element' exceeded DM 100 million, this figure had dropped to DM 77 million by 1992.

In the company reports of Hoechst, 'special reserves' play a more important role. For instance, in 1989 the amount exceeded DM 1 billion, this amounting to nearly 6% of Hoechst's balance sheet total.

Consequently, the corresponding notes to Hoechst's accounts go into more detail than those of Bayer and BASF. Hoechst even quantifies the possible future tax burden.

As explained, where companies are allowed (under section 254 of the Tax Laws) to set aside special additional tax depreciation charges, these amounts can either be taken to the 'special items' account or they can be taken to accumulated depreciation. When they choose to adopt the second of these policies and so reduce the carrying value of the assets, the tax incentive becomes invisible – it becomes a truly hidden reserve.

Kaufhof provide an example of a company using the special depreciation allowances in this way. It has been estimated that the difference between the amount of annual depreciation which would have been charged in the company's 1991 accounts under the normal accelerated declining balance method, and what was charged with the special depreciation allowances, was DM 50 million. It is explained in the company's accounts that extra allowances were the result of investment in East Germany and other areas of special assistance. This was the difference in just one year.

BASF refer to additional special depreciation permitted by the tax regulators. They also make reference to the fact that gains from the sale of fixed assets can be deferred as special reserves in the balance sheet. BASF point out that such additional depreciation and the special reserves result in funds being made available which are 'retained in the Group financial statements'.

Bayer in a note under the heading 'supplementary data' refer to write-downs for tax purposes. They differentiate between depreciation (write-downs) due to a permanent loss of value (DM 43 million) and amortization, depreciation and write-downs for tax purposes of (DM 154 million). The relative size of the two amounts might surprise non-German users of accounts. Does it imply that this DM 154 million is a 'secret reserve'? Not necessarily – an item of DM 17 million is shown in the account as going through other operating expenses into special items. This leaves a balance of DM 137 million as 'disclosed' secret reserves.

Legal Reserves

Reserves in a company can arise for a number of reasons. In some countries it is necessary to create 'legal reserves'. The reason this is thought necessary is to limit the amount the directors of a company can pay out of capital funds as dividends. Before profits can be distributed as dividends, a buffer of reserves needs to be established. In France, for example, it is necessary for a company to maintain a legal reserve which is equal in amount to at least 10% of its issued share capital. The company has to make provisions out of profits each year until the reserve reaches the required level.

In Germany the law requires that capital reserves plus the legal revenue reserve must equal at least 10% of the subscribed share capital in AG companies. Spain has a very complex system for building up reserves and restricting the use of these reserves. Cementos Portland explain in their accounts the role of legal reserves (Extract 9.12).

Legal reserve

Under the Corporations Law, as amended, 10% of income for each year must be transferred to the legal reserve until the balance of this reserve reaches at least 20% of capital stock.

The legal reserve can be used to increase capital provided that the remaining reserve balance does not fall below 10% of the increased capital stock amount. Otherwise, until the legal reserve exceeds 20% of capital stock, it can only be used to offset losses, provided that sufficient other reserves are not available for this purpose.

As of December 31, 1991, the legal reserve of the controlling company amounted to Ptas. 1,078 million (20% of the capital stock).

RESTATEMENT RESERVE

Approximately Ptas. 3,464 million of the controlling company's total capital as of December 31, 1991, arose from appropriations from the following restatement reserves:

	Thousands of Ptas.
Restatement reserve Law 76/1961	354,375
Restatement reserve Decree-Law 12/1973	397,266
Restatement reserve Law 50/1977	63,225
Restatement reserve law 1/1979	2,134,021
Restatement reserve law 9/1983	515,538
	3,464,425

On January 23, 1992, the Shareholders' Meeting of the controlling company resolved to increase capital stock by Ptas. 269,435,000 through the issuance of 538,870 shares of Ptas. 500 par value each, to be subscribed by the present shareholders at a rate of one new share for every twenty existing shares. The Shareholders' Meeting also resolved to transfer Ptas. 53,890,000 (equal to 20% of the capital increase) from the restatement reserve account to the legal reserve.

The balance of the controlling company's 'Restatement Reserve 1983 Budget Law' account can be used to offset book losses and, through December 31, 1992, to increase capital at one of several times. Thereafter, the uncapitalised balance must be taken to restricted reserves. As of December 31, 1991, the balance of this reserve amounted to Ptas. 13,924 million.

Share Premium Reserve/ Additional Paid-in Capital

This represents the difference between the actual amount paid by investors to purchase shares off the company, and the par (nominal) value of the shares. If a company issues additional shares and sells them for FF10 each when the nominal value is only FF6, the difference of FF4 per share will be credited to this reserve account. There are usually restrictions as to how this capital reserve can be used.

Revaluation Reserve

In Spain these are sometimes called 'restatement reserves'. The reserves arise because at different times Spanish companies were allowed to revalue their assets, the asset value being increased on the one side of the balance sheet with the corresponding entry on the other side being to the restatement reserve. Cementos Portland explain that until 1992 this reserve could be used for a number of purposes, for example to increase capital or to offset book losses. They also explain that the controlling company had over time appropriated amounts from this revaluation reserves to capital reserves (Extract 9.12). After 1992 the restatement reserves needed to be transferred to restricted reserves.

Extract 9.13 – Pirelli SpA 1991 accounts, Notes and Supplementary Notes.

The *Legal reserve* amounts to Lire 199,592 million and includes the appropriation of Lire 25,686 million from net income of 1990 as approved by the shareholders in the preceding year.

The *Share premium reserve* amounts to Lire 1,034,971 million, an increase of Lire 15 million, due to the conversions which were made during the year.

The *Revaluation reserve* Law No. 72/1983 of Lire 124,469 million, the *Reserve for mergers* of Lire 43,490 million, the *Reserve for grants* of Lire 1,694 million, the *Provision for nonrecurring items* DPR 917/1986, art. 55 of Lire 2,729 million and the *Provision for dividends* of Lire 11,500 million have remained unchanged.

The *Revaluation reserve* Law No. 413/1991 amounts to Lire 6,235 million and derives from the aforementioned revaluation of land and buildings.

Retained earnings of prior years amount to Lire 55,703 million, after appropriation of the remaining net income of 1990 of Lire 24,521 million as resolved by the shareholders in the preceding year.

8. Revaluation reserves and sundry reserves

The revaluation reserves include the revaluation reserves relating to Laws No. 72/1983 and No. 413/1991, and the consolidation reserve arising from the difference between the net book values and the net equities of the companies (excluding results for the year which are shown separately).
These reserves comprise the following:

		(in millions of lire)
	December 31, 1991	December 31, 1990
Laws No. 72/1983 and No. 413/1991	130,704	124,469
Consolidation reserve	(11,840)	(104,302)
	118,864	**20,167**

The legal reserve was increased to Lire 200 billion.
The other reserves, which increased from Lire 124 billion to Lire 126 billion, comprise retained earnings of prior years, extraordinary reserves, grants, and also include the differences deriving from the application of the Group accounting principles in the Pirelli S.p.A. financial statements.

Such revaluation reserves exist in other countries. In France they are no longer of significance. As in Spain, they arose from the legal revaluation that took place over a decade ago. Such reserves also arise in the accounts of companies in Italy. Extract 9.13 from Pirelli's accounts show a number of different reserve accounts.

Provisions

The Fourth Directive requires an item 'Provision for liabilities and charges' to be shown in the balance sheet. This is a provision for liabilities and charges that are almost certain to arise, but the amount and timing is uncertain. The events or transactions to which these relate are known about at the balance sheet date. In the financial accounts the provisions figure is usually divided into the following items:

- provisions for pensions and similar obligations;
- provisions for taxation;
- other provisions.

A provision must be distinguished from a contingency. The latter arises when a condition exists at the balance sheet date, the outcome of which is uncertain, i.e. an actual liability will only be confirmed as the result of some future event So whether or not a contingency will result in a charge to the company is uncertain – it depends upon the outcome of a future event which is beyond the control of the company.

A provision is not dependent upon a future event. For example, a company employs people and as a result it has a liability to pay a pension. It has to put money aside to provide for this. Another example is a company that has sold goods on credit: it knows from experience that a certain percentage of its customers will not pay, so it makes a provision against bad debts.

One problem that arises with a provision is what amount should be set aside. The Fourth Directive, in prescribing a standard layout for a balance sheet was not trying to dictate what specific provisions should be made or the methods that should be used to determine the size of provisions. The result is that a wide variety of practices exists across European countries.

A company can adopt conservative accounting practices and place large sums of money aside as provisions. This will reduce current profits and increase the underlying financial strength of the company. Alternatively a company could make only small provisions show high profits, pay out high dividends, and reduce its underlying financial strength. The practices adopted by German and UK companies represent the two extremes. German companies like provisions because they can be used to lower the dividends that have to be paid and smooth profits.

The attitude towards provisions in Germany differs to that in other countries. Due to the possibly favourable tax implications (lower taxable profits) most German companies do not ask whether or not a provision needs to be set up but whether or not one can be set up. Due to this wish to create provisions the accounting regulations in Germany restrict the list of permissible provisions whereas in most other countries accounting regulations are formulated with the intention to force companies to set up provisions. As a consequence, amounts disclosed under provisions in German financial statements are high in comparison with elsewhere.

In Germany there is a tradition of making healthy provisions in years of good profits. The idea is to build up provisions in good years, so that when less successful years arise these provisions can be utilized to smooth profits. These provisions are often undefined, not being linked to any future events. The smoothing of profits is useful if investors are looking at long-term performance. It might be thought that reserves not provisions should be used for this smoothing purpose, and indeed in the UK they can be. But, as already explained there is an important difference in theory between reserves and provisions. Reserves are an allocation of profit – they are deducted 'below the bottom line'. Provisions are an expense – they are deducted above the 'bottom line,' are a charge against profits, and they reduce the tax bill.

As explained earlier in the chapter, one reason why German companies would rather make a provision than allocate from reserves is because the former policy reduces profits, and so possibly reduces the distribution to shareholders. In the UK on the other hand there are no requirements with regard to payout ratios but there is pressure on companies to show high profits in the short run. Therefore it is better for a UK company to limit its 'provisions' and show a high annual profit figure, and, if it wishes to retain funds in the business, to create reserves out of declared profits.

One obvious way of understating reported earnings is to channel a substantial part of a year's income into provisions (accruals). Nobes and Parker state that in Germany 'Accruals are usually made as large as possible...'[1] Alexander and Archer add to this statement by explaining a distinct feature of the way in which the prudence principle is interpreted by German companies. With regard to optional accruals they point out that '... the amounts accrued for need not be probable ... but only possible. This leaves considerable scope for conservative accounting.'[2]

A look at the provisions included in the financial reports of BASF, Bayer and Hoechst makes clear that the warning on conservative practices is not completely out of place, especially if the item 'other provisions' – which is meant to cover miscellaneous liabilities – is analysed in detail. As the name implies, the item 'other provisions' in the annual reports of German companies deals with amounts of money which are set aside for a whole array of obligations. In the notes to the accounts of BASF, Bayer and Hoechst, items such as 'environmental protection measures', 'risks in conjunction with sales and purchases' and 'various personnel obligations' are listed under 'other provisions'.

Due to the fact that the biggest German chemical companies keep a fairly high profile in public as far as the protection of the environment is concerned, they, of course, have to set up provisions for this purpose. What is striking is that over the last three years, provisions amount to, on average, 10% of the balance sheet total of Bayer and Hoechst and to around 15% of the respective figure for BASF. The possible overstatement of the extent of potential liabilities is merely one feature of the conservatism of financial accounting in Germany.

Bayer show two sets of provisions in their accounts, one for pensions and similar commitments, and one for 'other' which includes provisions for taxes, profit-related bonuses, environmental protection measures, discounts and other uncertain liabilities. The total provisions in 1991 stood at DM 11217 million which represents 30% of total assets. The notes to the accounts explain that provisions for pensions are made on the basis of actuarial valuations. The 'other provisions' established to provide for foreseeable risks and uncertain liabilities are based on the opinions of the directors, who have taken advice. Daimler-Benz accounts reveal that they follow a similar policy, and point out that provisions are a matter of reasonable business judgement.

VEBA shows an interesting note on 'other provisions'. It refers to a DM 6.5 billion provision as at 31 December 1991 for nuclear waste disposal. This incidentally was larger than the pension provision at the time. BASF in 1991 also included in other provisions obligations in connection with the refilling of mines and shafts, the clearing of oil fields, refilling wells and provisions in connection with environmental protection measures. They stated with confidence 'the provisions are adequate'.

There is a difference in practice from one country to another over provisions. In the UK, the Netherlands and Italy, provisions are only made for specifically identified likely future events. Germany, France and Spain are not so restrictive.

In the ICI accounts 'provisions for liabilities and charges' amounts to only 5% of total assets. The reason for the big difference in the size of provisions between ICI and Bayer is largely explained by the different approach to pensions in the two countries. This is explained in the following section. The ICI provisions are for tax, unfunded pension costs, and reshaping and environmental costs.

In the Netherlands provisions are made for specific future events. In 1990 Philips made large provisions for restructuring with the result that they made a loss in the year. The note explains that the balance of the provision 'relates to the costs of projects which have not yet been carried out'. Not a great deal of information is provided to share-holders, however, as to what these events are. The provision described is for a 'wide range of risks and obligations'. The provision in the balance sheet increased from DFl 323 million to DFl 3315 million. These provisions were in fact used in the following periods to write off over-valued assets, obsolete inventories, severance payments and early retirements. In Akzo, provisions represent 18% of total assets. The items included in provisions include the same as listed above for ICI and Bayer, with the largest item representing pension rights. Their footnote gives a brief indication of their approach to pensions.

Provision for Pensions

For most companies the major item for which provision has to be made is for the payment of pensions. The system of providing for pensions, and hence the accounting treatment, varies very much from country to country.

The level of disclosure also varies dramatically from country to country. Contrast the information provided by Glaxo in their 1993 accounts (Extract 9.14) with that provided by Daimler Benz (Extract 9.15) in their 1992 accounts.

professionally qualified actuaries, and the assets of funded schemes are generally held in separately administered trusts or are insured. In certain cases, overseas Group undertakings hold assets with the specific purpose of matching the liabilities of unfunded schemes, both in terms of maturity and value.

The Group makes contributions to and provision for the various pension arrangements as shown in the following table:

	1993 £m	1992 £m
UK funded defined benefit schemes	55	42
UK unfunded defined benefit scheme	–	1
UK funded defined contribution schemes	3	3
Overseas funded defined benefit schemes	21	13
Overseas unfunded defined benefit schemes	7	8
Overseas defined contribution schemes	12	10
	98	77

The funds of the UK defined benefit schemes are administered by Trustee Companies and are kept separate from those of the Group. Independent actuaries prepare valuations of the schemes at least every three years and, in accordance with their recommendations, annual contributions are paid to the schemes so as to secure the benefits set out in the rules. At 31st March 1992, the date of the last actuarial valuation of the UK funded defined benefit schemes, the market value of the assets was £626m. The actuarial value of those assets represented 97 per cent of the actuarial value of all benefits accrued to members at that date after allowing for future salary and pension increases. The shortfall in the principal scheme is being funded by an increase in the level of employer contributions over seven years from 1st April 1992; the shortfall in the second scheme has been funded by additional contributions. The actuarial valuations used the projected unit method and assumed an investment return of 9 per cent per annum, increases in pensions of 5½ per cent per annum, increases in salaries of 7 per cent per annum (plus an allowance for promotion) and UK equity dividend growth of 3½ per cent per annum. The Group has provided an indemnity to the Trustees of the UK funded defined benefit schemes, undertaking to reimburse the schemes for any assets misappropriated.

The UK unfunded defined benefit scheme is administered by a Trustee Company. The charge against profits in respect of this scheme is the aggregate of the increase over the year of the assessed liabilities for members still in service and the net movement in the provisions set up in respect of the pensions in payment. The liabilities are assessed annually in accordance with the advice of independent actuaries based principally on the expected rates of increase in salary and benefits payable on an individual basis for each member of the scheme.

The largest overseas scheme is the funded defined benefit scheme operated by the Group's principal subsidiary undertaking in the USA. At 31st March 1993, the date of the last actuarial review of the scheme, the market value of the scheme's assets was £44m and represented 67 per cent of the actuarial value of all benefits accrued to members at that date after allowing for future salary increases. The shortfall, which reflects the fact that only a small minority of current scheme participants are retired or deferred beneficiaries, is being funded in accordance with limits applicable under US fiscal law. The actuarial review used the projected unit method and assumed a long term asset return of 8 per cent per annum, a discount rate of 7¾ per cent per annum and increases in salaries of 6½ per cent per annum (plus an allowance for promotion).

Several overseas Group undertakings operate unfunded defined benefit schemes; the most significant scheme in terms of the pension obligation of the Group is operated by the Group's principal subsidiary undertaking located in the USA, which also holds assets to match against these obligations. Other overseas schemes vary according to local requirements but are generally provided by contributions to government, insured or self-administered schemes.

In addition to providing pension benefits to the majority of employees, several Group undertakings, in countries where it is local employment practice, provide healthcare benefits to former employees during their retirement. Approximately 8,000 current employees, mainly in North America, are potentially eligible for such benefits. Currently, the cost of providing these healthcare benefits is recognised as an expense in the year in which payments are made. The amount charged to the profit and loss account in the year was £338,000 which is less than the charge would have been on an accruals basis. The Group estimates that, at 30th June 1993, the actuarial liability in respect of these healthcare benefits was approximately £22m. Amounts payable under these schemes are deductible at the taxation rate applicable in the countries in which payments are made.

	1993 £m	1992 £m
Selling, general and administration	**19,376**	17,535
	40,024	37,083

The aggregate employment costs of these persons amounted to:	1993 **£m**	1992 *£m*
Wages and salaries	**969**	766
Social security costs	**120**	101
Other pension costs	**98**	77
	1,187	944

> **Extract 9.15** – Daimler-Benz AG 1990 and 1992 accounts, Balance Sheet and Notes.

1990 accounts

Extract from balance sheet

		December 31, 1990 In Millions of DM	December 31, 1989 In Millions of DM
Provisions			
for Old-Age Pensions and Similar Obligations	(16)	10,831	10,086
Other Provisions	(17)	16,536	16,624
		27,367	26,710

Accounting Principles and Valuation Methods

Provisions for old-age pensions and similar obligations are actuarially determined on the basis of an assumed interest rate of 6% using the Entry Age Actuarial Cost Method. The regulations of the 1992 Pension Reform Act have, for the first time, been taken into account in calculating the provision amounts.

Note

(16) Provisions for Old-Age Pensions and Similar Obligations

When the assets of the provident funds are added to the provisions for old-age pensions, the company's pension obligations are fully covered.

Finance

Group Valuation Methods Standardized Extensively

With the changes in valuation methods made in 1989, Daimler-Benz adapted its accounting policies more closely to internally accepted accounting policies because capital markets only rely on financial statements thus prepared. The valuation methods traditionally applied in the automobile business has been continued in the individual accounts of both Daimler-Benz AG and Mercedes-Benz.

In 1992, we have adapted the valuation methods for pension provisions and for inventories to the practices used in the consolidated accounts. We are thus applying the same accounting principles and valuation methods at the different levels and within each area of the Daimler-Benz group. This will increase comparability of the individual corporate sectors among themselves and of other companies with the Daimler-Benz group as a whole. At the same time, we thus improve our information by segments, which is an important part of U.S. publication requirements.

Note

17 Provisions for Old-Age Pensions and Similar Obligations

Pension provisions rose to DM 12,217 million (1991: DM 10,790 million). DM 499 million of the DM 1,427 increase pertains to the change in the circle of consolidated companies.

When the assets of the provident funds are added to the provisions for old-age pensions, the company's pension obligations are fully covered.

UK

A pension fund is legally owned by a separate company from the company which employs the people who will benefit from the fund. Payments are made by the employer and employees into this separate enterprise, a trustee-administered fund that is supposed to be operated for the benefit of existing and future pensioners. Legally it is a different board of directors that run the employing company to those who run the pension fund. However, some of the main company board executive directors are also the directors (the trustees) of the pension fund. Whether through voting power or power of personality, it is often board directors from the main company who control what happens with the resources of the pension fund.

In the 1980s it unfortunately became not uncommon for some company boards of directors to think of the resources of the pension fund as funds for them to use for the purposes of the company. It was argued that when the pension fund was in deficit it was the employing company which needed to put extra cash into the pension fund. Why not, therefore, when the pension fund was in surplus should it not be the employing company that took out the cash surplus?

One particular time of concern over the treatment of funds belonging to a pension fund is when the employing company is taken over. If the acquired company has a pension fund for its employees, what happens to any surplus that might exist in that fund as at the date of takeover? It cannot be argued that the new owner of the company contributed to the resources in the pension fund, but the new owner is in a position to decide what will happen to those resources. It has been claimed that in the late 1980s and early 1990s a number of acquisitions were partly motivated by the acquiring company's desire to gain access to the cash in its new subsidiaries' pension funds. Indeed, it has been shown to be the case that a number of acquirers have taken cash out of newly acquired subsidiaries' pension funds.

ED 53 in the UK states that when valuing a newly acquired subsidiary's pension fund, the fair value of the assets and liabilities of the fund should be measured using the acquirers methods and actuarial assumptions, and that no provision should be made for changes in benefits or number of employees following the acquisition. What this means is that if a company operating a 'conservatively' managed pension fund, whose valuations are based upon relatively low assumptions about the rate of return to be earned on the fund's assets and high expectations about future increases in salaries and pension payments, is taken over by a company that operates a more 'adventurously' managed fund, with high expectations about future rates to be earned on investments and low expectations about future payment increases, then instant valuation surpluses will be produced. The acquiring company will be in a position to take cash out of the pension fund of its newly acquired subsidiary.

An example of this happening took place in July 1991 when Trafalgar House took over the Davy Corporation. A careful reading of the Trafalgar House 1991 accounts reveals that included in the Debtors figure (Note 16) is an amount of £75.4 million referred to as a 'Pension prepayment'. What is a payment of pensions in advance? The reader is referred to Note 4, which gives an explanation of the treatment of pension costs. This is reproduced in Extract 9.16.

The point has been made that the assets of the pension schemes are separate from the finances of the group. In the last paragraph it is made clear that after the pension schemes operated by Davy had been measured on a basis consistent with that being used by Trafalgar House, a surplus of £75.4 million resulted. It is this amount that was owed to Trafalgar House at September 1991. It represents funds put aside by Davy to meet pension costs that in the opinion of Trafalgar House need not have been put aside. According to Trafalgar House calculations the funds have been put aside earlier than was necessary, i.e. they are a prepayment.

The pension cost note in the Trafalgar House accounts explains that the 'surplus will be amortized in future periods'. To appreciate this particular point being made one has to distinguish between the cash flows of a company and the accrual accounting approach to measuring profit. Although all the cash from the surplus of the Davy pension fund can be taken out of the fund by Trafalgar House at one time, the reduction in future employer pension costs resulting from the prepayment (the surplus) will not all benefit the profit and loss account in one year. The benefits will be spread over time.

It is interesting that the cost to Trafalgar House of acquiring the Davy Corporation is shown in the accounts as £255.6 million, of which £72.7 million was paid in cash. Strange that a few months later the Davy pension fund was to pay £75.4 million cash to Trafalgar House! The cost of acquiring consists of the actual payments of cash, loan notes and deferred consideration plus the liabilities of the company acquired.

Extract 9.16 – Trafalgar House plc 1991 accounts, Notes.

4   Pension costs

	£m	£m
UK defined benefit schemes	—	4.1
UK defined contribution schemes	**2.7**	2.7
Foreign schemes	**3.6**	2.8
	6.3	9.6

The Group operates a number of pension schemes throughout the world under which contributions are paid by Group companies and employees. The assets of the schemes are held in trustee administered funds separate from the finances of the Group.

The rates at which the Group accounts for the main UK pension schemes are assessed in accordance with the advice of qualified actuaries. The projected unit method was used for all but the three smaller UK schemes, for which the attained age method was used, and the latest valuations of the various schemes were as at April 1988, 1989 and 1990. The valuations of the two principal UK schemes assumed an investment return of 2 per cent. or $1\frac{1}{2}$ per cent. higher than the rate of inflationary salary growth and 5 per cent. higher than the rate of increase of present and future pensions.

At the date of the latest actuarial valuations, all the main UK schemes were in surplus. The market value of their assets was £646 million which is a significant increase as a result of the acquisition of Davy Corporation plc. The actuarial value of the assets was sufficient to cover 126 per cent. of the benefits that had accrued to members, after benefit improvements made following the valuations. £75.4m of the surplus, relating to Davy schemes, has been dealt with as described below and the remaining surplus is to be spread over the service lives of employees in the relevant schemes.

The three UK pension schemes operated by Davy have been assessed at the date of acquisition by the Company's actuaries on a basis consistent with that being used for Trafalgar House pension schemes. As part of the adjustments to arrive at fair value set out in Note 25 a sum of £75.4m has been included on the balance sheet, representing the funding surplus in respect of the Davy schemes. This surplus will be amortised in future periods.

Germany

German companies are not required by law to transfer the contributions made by employees towards their future pension to a legally independent pension fund. Over two-thirds of the total funds accumulated in Germany to pay pensions to employees is to be found in 'Pension reserves' on the liabilities side of companies' balance sheets.

Only about one third of the total funds is invested outside the company via independent pension fund companies.

The funds accumulating for the benefit of pensioners are a source of finance for the employing company, and are part of the resources of the company to invest as it chooses. They are similar to a long-term loan to the company made by the employee – money which the company can use. The company does, of course, have a commitment to pay the employee a pension in the future.

The company is required by law to allocate actuarially calculated amounts to its pension reserves as and when required. The method for determining the present value of pension liabilities is prescribed in Income Tax Law. No provisions need to be made for the future pension of employees below the age of 30 – this is in some indirect way to allow for the rate of staff turnover. The approved method of arriving at future pension payments also disregards future pay increases. It is based on current levels of pay. To allow for pay increases would increase the company's liability. The weaknesses in this method of estimating the pension liabilities generally lead to an underestimate of the true liability.

In Germany, in most cases, the pension liability has to be honoured by the company and not by a separate pension fund. This means that the assets which will be employed to generate funds to pay pensions, as well as the pension liabilities, are included in the group balance sheet. This has an effect on the gearing ratios which are higher than they would be if the pension assets and liabilities were excluded.

This effect on gearing ratios is further aggravated by the method of calculating the pension liability. German companies are required to use the vested benefit method for tax purposes and most companies choose to use the same approach in their commercial financial statements. The minimum discount rate for obtaining the present value of future pension payments is set at 6% in the tax law. This rate is the standard rate used also in the commercial financial statements. If the appropriate market interest rate is above 6%, the German approach can overstate the pension liability. It should further be noted that the assets designated for future pension payments are also valued according to the conservative German valuation rules. If the current market value of pension plan assets exceeds the original cost of acquiring the assets this is not recognized and not reported in the accounts.

Before the enactment of recent German accounting legislation pension accounting could be based on a flow-through basis as opposed to the accruals approach. This meant that no provision had to be made to pay future pensions. As pensions became payable the company just paid the cash out of general funds. This is still permissible for pension obligations incurred before 1987, but the amount of pensions not provided for in the pension provision now has to be disclosed in the notes to the accounts. In the case of the Bayer Group all pension obligations to be honoured are now covered by the pension provision in the consolidated balance sheet. It should be noted, however, that there are still many German companies retaining the flow-through method of accounting for pensions for obligations incurred before 1987.

The funding of pensions through separate pension funds is a policy chosen by some German companies. This is not usually the preferred method, as it leads to certain tax disadvantages. If a company chooses to fund pensions through a separate pension fund neither the amount of the pension obligation nor the market value of the assets have to be disclosed in the company accounts. In a situation where underfunding arises only the deficit amount has to be disclosed in the notes. Bayer operates several separate pension funds for pension obligations not reflected in the group balance sheet. No information as to the values of these separate schemes and the pension obligations is disclosed.

It should be appreciated that due to the German system of social security and health insurance – which is generous by the standards of most countries – there is no need for major provisions by companies for post-retirement benefits for employees working in Germany. Most German companies with foreign subsidiaries are fully aware of the need to set up provisions for post-retirement benefits in other countries, and many of them have for a long time provided for such expenses in their group accounts.

In the accounts of Daimler-Benz there is a very uninformative footnote explaining the provision for old-age pensions (see Extract 9.15 earlier). It is in line with the level of disclosure on this issue by most other German companies. Bayer give slightly more information, but disclose nothing that would be of value to users of accounts. It refers to the 6% discount rate used in arriving at the present value of liabilities under the tax-approved estimating approach.

France

In France the large companies usually operate funded pension schemes for their employees in a similar way to UK companies. There are, however, some companies that rely mainly on the state pension scheme to look after their employees, and there are those who rely on industry-wide schemes run by external pension fund specialists or insurance companies. As in the UK the externally funded schemes rely on contributions from employers and employees and contributions are tax deductible. Sometimes French companies provide a retirement bonus or a supplementary retirement scheme. The companies fund such 'extras' themselves.

French companies provide a remarkable amount of information on their pension costs and schemes compared with most companies in other countries – see, for example, the detail given by Thomson-CSF in Extract 9.17. As note (b) explains, no liability arises with regard to the main schemes as such costs will be 'borne by outside organisations'. It is an externally funded scheme.

BSN discusses its supplementary retirement scheme (Extract 9.18). It also gives details of the assumptions used in arriving at the present value of the liability of the externally funded scheme. It will be noted future payments are discounted at only 2% to bring them to their present value, and unlike in Germany allowance is made for a growth in salaries between the present time and for the estimated date of retirement of members of the scheme.

11 - RESERVE FOR RETIREMENT INDEMNITIES

a) Changes in the period

	Total	Pension plans	Contractual retirement indemnities	Plan asset
Balance as of December 31, 1989	40	13	404	(377)
Utilization of plan asset	32	–	–	32
Revaluation of plan asset	(26)	–	–	(26)
Allowance	13	–	13	–
Reversal / utilization	(32)	(9)	(23)	–
Changes in exchange rates, reporting entity and other	112	73	39	–
Balance as of December 31, 1990	139	77	433	(371)
Utilization of plan asset	**29**	**–**	**–**	**29**
Revaluation of plan asset	**(30)**	**–**	**–**	**(30)**
Allowance	**59**	**1**	**58**	**–**
Reversal / utilization	**–**	**–**	**–**	**–**
Changes in exchange rates, reporting entity and other	**(30)**	**(20)**	**(10)**	**–**
Balance as of December 31, 1991	**167**	**58**	**481**	**(372)**

b) Pension plans

Upon retirement Thomson-CSF employees receive such benefits as funded by pension plan arrangements; these plans conform with local regulations of the countries in which the group operates. The related benefits are accounted for on the basis of I.A.S.C. pronouncement n° 19 principle.

For Thomson-CSF and its French subsidiaries, no liability has been recognized as almost all of the cost of retirement benefits is borne by outside organizations which receive contributions from the Group; such contributions are charged to expenses as incurred.

c) Contractual retirement indemnities

Contractual retirement indemnities are payable upon retirement of the employees and are due only if the employee is on the Company's payroll when he retires. Such indemnities are based on the employee compensation at retirement date and on his/her seniority at that date. Effective January 1, 1985 Thomson-CSF and its French subsidiaries began accruing for these contractual retirement indemnities.

Analysis of allowances	1991	1990	1989
Service cost	25	22	23
Interest cost on projected benefit obligation	33	40	35
Amortization of unrecognized prior service cost	–	5	6
Impact of changes in actuarial assumptions	–	(54)	(11)
Total	**58**	**13**	**53**

Weighted average discount rate and rate of increase in future compensation levels used in determining the actuarial present value of the projected benefit obligation are respectively 10% and 4.7% in 1991 and 1990, against 9% and 3.7% in 1989.

Reserves for retirement indemnities and commitments relating to these contractual indemnities	12/31/91	12/31/90
Accumulated benefit obligation	293	265
Effect of future salary increases	189	172
Projected benefit obligation	**482**	**437**
Reserve for retirement indemnities, end of period	109	62
Plan asset	372	371
Unrecognized retirement benefit obligation	1	4
Projected benefit obligation	**482**	**437**

d) Early retirement indemnities

Those are paid upon early retirement of employees and are accrued in the period in which the decision of early retirement is made.

> **Extract 9.18** – BSN Group 1991 accounts, Notes.

Note 14

Provisions for retirement indemnities and pensions

On retirement, employees receive pensions based on pension schemes in conformity with the laws and customs of the countries where the Group operates. As a result of contributions paid under such schemes to private or state sponsored pension funds, no actuarial liability exists to the companies.

The Group is also responsible for supplementary retirement schemes and termination indemnity contractual commitments. The corresponding actuarial commitments are taken into account either in the form of contributions paid to externally managed funds, or in the form of provisions.

French companies

French companies' commitments are calculated in conformity with FAS 87. The actuarial assumptions taken into account to value these obligations are:

- personnel turnover and mortality
- retirement age between 60 and 65 years according to each employee's category
- discount rate applied, net of inflation: 2%
- growth rate for salaries between 3% and 5% according to the age and category of each employee.

Foreign subsidiaries

The present value of foreign subsidiaries' obligations was determined based on recent actuarial valuations using actuarial assumptions which take into account the legal, economic and monetary aspects of each country.

The following table reconciles the funded status of the companies' plans with amounts recognised in the Group's consolidated balance sheet at December 31, 1991.

(millions of French Francs)	French Companies	Foreign Companies	Total
Projected benefit obligation	**1,130**	**1,652**	**2,782**
Funded status			
• Plan assets at fair value	274	134	408
• Pension liability recognised in the consolidated balance sheet	784	1,500	2,284
• Unrecognised net losses*	72	18	90
	1,130	**1,652**	**2,782**

* Changes in actuarial assumptions and experience different from that assumed resulted in a FF101 million increase in the projected benefit obligation. This amount is being amortized over a 10 year period. Accordingly the net periodic pension cost for 1991, amounting to FF145 million, includes an amortization charge for this item of FF11 million.

Italy

In Italy pension schemes vary greatly from one company to another. There are internally funded schemes, as with the German model, and there are externally funded schemes as with the UK model. In fact in Italy traditionally state pensions have been the main provider for those who retire. This, however, is changing.

The FEE European Survey found that all of their sample of 30 Italian companies showed in their balance sheets evidence of pension provisions. These provisions are not, however, to cover an employee's main pension, which as mentioned is paid out of state funds. The company provisions are to provide for 'deferred salaries' which accrue to an employee whilst he or she works for the company. They are paid to the employees when they leave the company, whether as a result of resignation, redundancy or retirement. The rate at which such deferred salaries accrue is determined by a precise legal formula.

Pirelli shows in its consolidated balance sheet for 1991 a 'provision for pension and similar obligations' of 272 billion lire, and a 'provision for employees leaving indemnity' of 553 billion lire. This latter figure is the 'deferred salary' referred to above.

Spain

As a result of the changes introduced by the 1990 Companies Act Spanish companies have changed the way they provide for pensions

12. Pension plan for employees and collective insurance plan:

The employees of the Group, except for those of Standard Telecomunicaçoes, are covered by a pension plan complementary to that of the Social Security. This plan provides for the payment of complementary monthly retirement pensions to those employees that retire at the reglamentary age, to their widows or to their offspring who are not yet adult. There is no requirement for the employees to contribute to the pension plan, since all costs are on the Group's account.

To have the right to receive pension payments, the employee has to have reached the age of 65, the normal retirement age envisaged by the plan, or 60, for the case where he is included within the Reconversion Plans. The amount of the pension received depends on the employee's salary, the age of retirement and the years of service.

Additionally, as well as the pension plan, the majority of employees in the Group subscribe to a collective life and survivor insurance policy, formalized in an annual renewable policy contracted with the insurance company Metropolis, S. A. Based on the conditions established in this policy, the contributing employee, on completing 65, has the right to receive 125% of the subscribed capital. The cost of this insurance is shared between the employees and the Group Companies.

The movement of these provisions during 1991 has been as shown in the following table:

		(Thousands of pesetas)	
	Pension Plan	Collective Insurance	Total
● Balance at 1-1-91	9,860,736	2,704,056	12,564,792
● Additions to provision	3,898,155	2,746,646	6,644,801
● Earnings of funds tied to the Pension Plan (*)	1,213,120	—	1,213,120
● Disposals	(630,245)	(1,550,629)	(2,180,874)
Balance at 31-12-91	**14,341,766**	**3,900,073**	**18,241,839**

(*) Note 6.

and the way the cost is introduced into their financial accounts. Prior to the reform pensions were simply charged as an expense in the period when the pensions were paid to the retired employees, that is on a flow-through basis. No provisions were made for future pension payments, and the liability was not usually recognized in the accounts.

Following the changes in the law a provision now has to be made in the accounts of companies. As Extract 9.19 from the annual report of Alcatel mentions, company pension plans are complementary to those paid through Social Security. The company, as well as contributing towards a pension plan, also makes contributions towards a collective insurance policy for employees. The company now has to make provisions for pensions but, as in Germany, the funds put aside are a source of finance for the company. They are not transferred to a legally independent fund. The balance sheet of Alcatel as at 31 December 1991 lists financial investments, and under this heading is an item 'Funds affected to pension plan' which shows a balance of 13772 million pesetas. It is explained that 'funds tied' to the pension plan are, in general, placed in fixed interest securities and have accrued an average interest of 12%'.

Netherlands

There are no specific rules in the appropriate Dutch Acts concerning pensions, except that provisions for pension commitments must be stated separately in the financial statements. When future pension commitments have to be valued to obtain the present value, the actuarial rate of interest used for such calculations is usually 4% or 5%. This is not linked to the actual market rate of interest. Again normally no allowance is made for the effect of expected salary increases on future pension payments.

Other Post-Retirement Benefits

This could become an important accounting issue in the future. Some companies, in addition to providing pensions for employees, also provide for post-retirement health care and other post-retirement benefits. Under such arrangements, once the employee retires, any health care bills relating to the former employee will be paid by the company. Such schemes are more common in some countries than others; they are particularly important in the USA where the lack of a national health care programme makes private-funded insurance an important issue.

Until recently companies offering such schemes to employees did not make provision in the accounts for the possible future costs of these post-retirement benefits. They were accounted for on a 'cash paid' basis – as costs arose, they were paid by the company and charged to the current years profit and loss account.

The position is changing. In the UK the statement on the subject (UITF 6) points out that such post-retirement benefits are liabilities and should be recognized as such in the accounts. They are similar in nature to pensions and therefore the same principles are applicable to their measurement and disclosure. Extract 9.20 from the 1992 ICI accounts dealing with commitments and contingent liabilities mentions that this new approach has to be adopted in the UK by 1994. They estimate that they will have to make a provision of £279 million to cover for the 'unprovided initial liability'. In addition to this new 'catching up' provision, they will in future have to set aside £34 million per annum out of profits. Tesco adopt a different approach (Extract 9.21). They explain that the 'previously unrecognized liability' is being spread forward over the service lives of various employees.

In the UK the size of the liabilities involved is not usually of major importance. It could, however, be of significance to a UK company that has large operating subsidiaries in the USA. It is important to appreciate that for many multinationals such new accounting requirements can have a large impact on profits. General Motors in the USA in 1993 announced that they would need to make an initial $21 billion after-tax charge against profits to catch up on past obligations. In addition they would have an annual ongoing charge against profits of $1.4 billion, their initial charge being equivalent to $33 per share, and a continuing annual charge of $2 per share.

This is clearly another issue for the user of accounts to be aware of. It also shows the potential impact of changes in accounting standards. As a result of this new accounting reporting requirement, it is expected that many companies (particularly in the USA) will attempt to renegotiate their post-retirement benefit schemes. Such responses are what are known as 'the economic consequences of accounting standards'.

Extract 9.20 – ICI plc 1992 accounts, Notes.

34COMMITMENTS AND CONTINGENT LIABILITIES

	Group		Company	
	1992	1991	**1992**	1991
	£m	£m	**£m**	£m
Commitments for capital expenditure not provided for in these accounts (including acquisitions)				
Contracts placed for future expenditure	**401**	365	**66**	40
Expenditure authorized but not yet contracted	**304**	431	**96**	157
	705	796	**162**	197

Contingent liabilities existed at 31 December 1992 in connection with guarantees and uncalled capital relating to subsidiary and other undertakings and guarantees relating to pension funds, including the solvency of pension funds. The maximum contingent liability in respect of guarantees of borrowings and uncalled capital at 31 December 1992 was £28m (1991 £24m) for the Group: the maximum contingent liability for the Company, mainly on guarantees of borrowings by subsidiaries, was £1,537m (1991 £1,157m).

The Group is also subject to contingencies pursuant to environmental laws and regulations that in the future may require it to take action to correct the effects on the environment of prior disposal or release of chemical substances by the Group or other parties. The ultimate requirement for such actions, and their cost, is inherently difficult to estimate, however provisions have been established at 31 December 1992 in accordance with the accounting policy noted on page 37. It is believed that, taking account of these provisions, the cost of addressing currently identified environmental obligations is unlikely to impair materially the Group's financial position.

The Group is also involved in various other legal proceedings, principally in the UK and US, arising out of the normal course of business. The Group does not believe that the outcome will have a material effect on the Group's financial position.

Other guarantees and contingencies arising in the ordinary course of business, for which no security has been given, are not expected to result in any material financial loss.

A subsidiary company has entered into a take-or-pay contract to purchase electric power commencing 1 April 1993 for fifteen years. The subsidiary is obliged to make monthly payments including a fixed capacity charge and a variable energy charge. The present value of the commitment to purchase electric power over the period of the agreement is estimated at £559m.

In North America, and to a lesser extent in some other countries, the Group's employment practices include the provision of healthcare and life assurance benefits for retired employees. Some 10,931 retired employees currently benefit from these provisions, and 29,387 current employees will be eligible on retirement. The benefits are currently accounted for on a cash paid basis which resulted in a charge to profits of some £7m in 1992. In both the US and the UK accounting standards are moving to a requirement to accrue the present value of such retiree benefit obligations over the working life of the employee. This approach has to be adopted in accounts filed in the US for 1993 onwards, and for UK accounts by 1994. It is estimated that the unprovided obligation for the Group at the end of 1992, calculated in accordance with the new standards, amounts to some £279m. It is also estimated that, leaving aside the accounting for this unprovided initial liability, the implementation of accrual accounting will reduce profit before tax by some £34m per annum. Tax relief on these charges will be deferred until cash payments are made.

At 31 December 1992, the Group had outstanding forward foreign exchange contracts to purchase £154m (1991 £236m) equivalent and to sell £934m (1991 £950m) equivalent. These contracts are taken out with commercial banks for the purpose of hedging currency exposures. The majority of the contracts had a maturity of six months or less from the balance sheet date. The Group also had outstanding currency option contracts to sell £731m equivalent to hedge anticipated foreign currency transactions for 1993.

The Group has entered into currency swap, interest rate swap, and forward rate agreements to manage the interest rate and currency exposure of its borrowings. At 31 December 1992, the Group had agreements outstanding with commercial banks which had principal amounts of £1,228m (1991 £601m) equivalent at the exchange rate on that date. The principal amounts under the cross-currency agreements are revalued from contract rates to balance sheet rates with any exchange gains or losses arising treated in accordance with the Group's accounting policy on foreign currencies.

Note 22 Post-Retirement Benefits other than Pensions

The company operates a scheme offering post-retirement healthcare benefits. In previous years the cost of providing these benefits was accounted for on the basis of cash payments made. This year the accounting basis has been changed to a basis similar to that used for defined benefit pension schemes.

The previously unrecognised liability as at 27th February 1993 of £7.5m, which was determined in accordance with the advice of qualified actuaries, is being spread forward over the service lives of the relevant employees. A provision of £0.7m is being carried In the balance sheet reflecting £1.0m charged to the profit and loss account in the year less cash payments made. Comparatives have not been adjusted. It is expected that payments will be tax deductible, at the company's tax rate, when made.

Provision for Deferred Charges

Deferred tax

The major deferred charge is usually deferred tax. This occurs most often in a company when a particular item of tax is not yet legally a liability and has not been paid to the tax authorities but the amount has been deducted in the accounts in arriving at the profits of the company. Such situations can occur where the depreciation policy of a company for financial accounting purposes differs from the policy of the tax authorities with regard to the wear and tear of the particular asset. This could happen when the tax profit and loss account will be higher than the amount actually paid to the authorities allow a rapid write-down of an asset's value an accelerated depreciation policy, and the company decides to adopt a different write-down policy for its financial accounting purposes. The tax charge in the profit and loss account will be higher than the amount actually paid to the authorities. The cash not paid is set aside–it is like a transfer to provisions or to reserves. The funds can be used by the company, until they have to be paid to the tax authorities.

The 1991 ICI accounts show deferred tax of £103 million and also disclose that they have paid advanced corporation tax of £80 million. They also show on the liability side of the balance sheet deferred in-come, that is grants they have received from the tax authorities of £52 million; these have not yet been credited to the profit and loss account but will be spread out over the life of the asset to which they relate.

It is an interesting question whether or not deferred tax should be regarded as debt or equity. From the perspective of the tax authorities it could be seen as debt. The authorities have in certain circumstances the right to ask for reimbursement if, through going into liquidation, the company has not provided what the tax authorities expected.

Bayer's 'other provisions' in their 1992 accounts includes DM 819 million as 'provisions for taxes'. These are taxes that will have to be paid at some future date on profits earned in the current accounting year and in earlier years. Bayer also show on the assets side of the balance sheet 'deferred charges' of DM 981 million. A note explains that deferred charges includes 'net' deferred taxes of DM 574 million. In this year the grants received from the tax authorities not credited to the profit and loss account exceed deferred tax payments.

A provision for taxation is therefore included on both sides of Bayer's balance sheet, once as a provision for taxes payable and once as deferred tax netted against grants received in advance of their recognition in the accounts. This treatment of tax, with entries on both sides of the balance sheet and with one figure netted, will of course affect financial ratios. The non-German user of German accounts has to be very careful to ensure that this tax treatment is similar to that which he or she is used to.

Deferred payments

Deferred taxes can be seen as an example of payments deferred to future periods caused by events or transactions in the current or in former accounting periods. Other examples of deferred 'payments' are expenses for future repairs and expenses relating to guarantees. One common feature of such deferred payments is that they will only actually be paid if the business continues to exist. From the perspective of those analysing accounts it could be argued that such payments are not liabilities and thus provisions for deferred payments can be classified as part of equity.

Deferred payments are tax deductible only in specific circumstances. Provisions for deferred payments that are tax deductible can be thought of as having an equity component and a tax liability component. Setting up the provision causes a reduction in profit before taxes thereby reducing taxes payable now and retained earnings. Releasing the provision in future causes a rise in profit before taxes resulting in a rise of taxes payable and of (retained) earnings.

Another item that might be included in deferred charges is discounts on liabilities. As explained earlier in the chapter some companies value liabilities at redemption value, which is usually equal to the par (nominal) value. If the proceeds from issuing a liability are less than the redemption value the difference may be included as a deferred charge. The discount could be charged to the profit and loss account immediately or written off over the life of the security. The latter policy is the one recommended in most countries. The discount disclosed in the notes to the balance sheet of the Bayer group in the 1992 accounts (DM 175 million) results from the issue of deep discount bonds with warrants attached.

Although this chapter is concerned with liabilities, brief reference will be made to deferred income and prepaid expenses. These can be items of income received where the credit has not been taken to profits or prepayments entitling the reporting company to receive services or to use rights or facilities over a specified future period. Whether or not prepaid expenses should be classified as assets depends on the circumstances. If in case of default the rights can be sold or are reimbursed, then the recoverable amount should be shown as an asset.

Contingent Liabilities

At the end of a company's financial year there are many transactions and activities in which it is engaged that are incomplete. Some of these could lead to liabilities. The reader of financial accounts needs to be made aware of any transactions and activities that could lead to possible claims on the business. The analyst would expect to know if the amounts involved are large enough to affect future liquidity and profitability.

Examples of contingencies include:

- guarantees given;
- obligations under warranty;
- legal claims for damages and litigation;
- performance bonds.

For future costs where the expectation of their arising is high and where the amount can be estimated reasonably accurately, an accrual (provision) should have been made in the financial statements. If a loss is probable but the amount cannot be assessed with reasonable accuracy then a note should be given in the financial statements explaining the position. There is obviously a degree of judgement involved. What is probable? There are different levels of probability. At the two extremes, if the likelihood of a certain outcome of an event is **remote** then no disclosure is required in financial statements. If, on the other hand, the likelihood of the event is **reasonably certain** then we are not considering a contingency. In this latter case as mentioned the company should make a provision. Remote has been defined as an outcome that has less than a 5% chance of occurring. Reasonably certain has been defined as an event that has a 95% or better chance of occurring. Between the two extremes the likelihood of a certain outcome can be described as probable or possible and covers the range of probabilities above 5% and below 95%.

Contingent gains (as opposed to contingent liabilities) should only be accrued in the actual accounts if 'reasonably certain'. If realization is probable but not reasonably certain, the item should be dealt with by way of disclosure in a footnote to the accounts.

In the UK rules governing disclosure requirements in respect of contingent liabilities are detailed in SSAP 18 and in the Companies Act 1985. SSAP 18 states that certain details should be given relating to contingencies, namely:

- nature of the contingency;
- uncertainties that may affect the final outcome;
- a prudent estimate of the financial effect.

All estimates should be made before taking account of taxation.

Two main criticisms have been aimed at the standard. First, it has been said that the standard gives the opportunity for companies to use off-balance sheet financing by stating words to the effect that 'Guarantees have been given in respect of third parties and joint ventures.' Without more details (which few companies give) it is impossible to tell if this is a genuine statement relating to a contingency or if an off-balance sheet financing exercise has occurred. Second, terms used in the standard are ambiguous. How do directors decide what is 'probable' or 'reasonably certain'? Different interpretations may give rise to different treatment and different results.

UK companies typically include a note in the accounts in the form of a paragraph of explanation or a brief table and a few sentences of explanation. Few companies comply strictly with the standard. Most give no details of uncertainties which may affect the final outcome and some do not provide previous year's figures.

Extract 9.22 – Royal Dutch/Shell Group of Companies 1992 accounts, Notes.

31 Contingencies and litigation

Contingent liabilities of Group companies, arising mainly from guarantees for third party indebtedness and customs duties, amounted to £1,166 million at December 31, 1992 and £889 million at December 31, 1991.

Two production joint ventures, in which the Group has an interest and which are based in the Netherlands and in Germany respectively, have co-operated to extract gas on an equal basis from a common border area. In the process of the final redetermination of gas reserves in the common area it has emerged that the German venture has in good faith received considerable quantities of gas in excess of its entitlement from the operator.

In 1991 the two joint ventures reached an agreement on the quantities, which was subsequently approved by their respective governments. Due to differences of opinion between the parties involved relating to compensation in respect of the over-delivery, arbitration proceedings were commenced in Zurich under the rules of the International Chamber of Commerce with respect to that issue. Since the ultimate Group interest in the ventures and the tax regimes applicable to them are different, this over-delivery could lead to a net cost to the Group for which a provision has been made. However, the ultimate cost cannot be established with reasonable certainty.

An associated company in Japan has an exposure at December 31, 1992 on substantial open foreign currency exchange positions (see Note 7). That company has initiated a programme to limit the amount of any further losses that might be incurred through exchange rate movements occurring prior to the various foreign currency positions being closed out. As of March 11, 1993 the after tax cost of the programme and the unrealized losses arising since January 1, 1993 amounted to approximately £65 million which could eventually change depending on future programme costs and exchange rate movements.

In the judgment of the Directors of the relevant Group Holding Companies, no losses which are material in relation to the Group financial position are likely to arise in respect of the foregoing matters.

The operations and earnings of Group companies continue, from time to time, to be affected to varying degrees by political, legislative, fiscal and regulatory developments, including those relating to environmental protection, in the countries in which they operate. The industries in which Group companies are engaged are also subject to physical risks of various types. The nature and frequency of these developments and events, not all of which are covered by insurance, as well as their effect on future operations and earnings, are unpredictable.

Shell Oil Company in the United States is subject to a number of possible loss contingencies. These include actions based upon federal, state and local environmental laws involving present and past operating locations, including the US Army's Rocky Mountain Arsenal near Denver, Colorado and the McColl waste site in Southern California; and product liability actions relating to the manufacture, sale or use of polybutylene and other chemical products.

The United States filed a civil action against Shell Oil alleging environmental damage and other liabilities resulting from Shell Oil's operations through 1982 at the Rocky Mountain Arsenal. The State of Colorado has also filed an action against the United States, the US Army and Shell Oil alleging that the State is trustee of the natural resources in question. The United States and Shell Oil have entered into an administrative settlement whereby Shell Oil would pay 50% of amounts expended for remedial costs and natural resource damages up to $500 million; 35% of expenditures between $500 million and $700 million; and 20% of expenditures in excess of $700 million. In 1988, Shell Oil provided $180 million, and in 1992, an additional $105 million, both amounts before tax, for its share of related costs. Shell Oil's share of expenditures through December 31, 1992 was approximately $166 million.

Shell Oil has had liability insurance in force over the period of operations at the Rocky Mountain Arsenal, but a Superior Court jury in California decided that the insurance companies were not liable for federal and state claims for clean-up and contamination control and natural resource damages arising out of such operations. However, the California Court of Appeals has granted Shell Oil a new trial that provides Shell Oil the opportunity to establish insurance coverage for certain occurrences at the Arsenal in periods prior to 1970. Shell Oil is also seeking a declaratory judgment that it has insurance coverage at the McColl site in Southern California. Shell Oil's assessment of these actions is continuing. Future provisions may be required as the scope and nature of remediation programmes and related cost estimates are clarified.

In addition, federal, state and local income, property and excise tax returns are being examined and certain interpretations by Shell Oil of complex tax statutes, regulations and practices are being challenged.

While the ultimate effect of the foregoing matters reported by Shell Oil cannot be ascertained at this time, based on developments to date, the management of that company does not anticipate that any of the foregoing contingencies will materially adversely affect Shell Oil's financial position.

Glaxo state that: 'No provision has been made for the UK or Overseas tax that would be payable in the event of distribution being made out of profits retained in overseas subsidiaries or associated undertakings.' This disclosure seems a little unnecessary as no disclosure is required of remote events. The note for ICI is shown in Extract 9.20. It includes details of forward foreign exchange contracts and currency and interest rate swaps. Extract 9.22 from the financial accounts of the Royal Dutch Shell Group gives details of litigation in progress against the company, particularly over environmental issues.

Extract 9.23 – Saint Gobain Group 1991 accounts, Notes.

NOTE 23: CONTINGENT LIABILITIES, COMMITMENTS AND PLEDGES

in millions of French francs	1991	1990	1989
Pensions (note 21)	150	173	186
Retirement indemnities (note 21)	10	11	12
Mortgages and investments pledged as security	2,730	3,421	2,793
Other commitments given	2,182	2,346	5,100
Foreign currency operations	1,791	2,190	2,014
Pledges received	(805)	(883)	(921)
	6,058	7,258	9,184

Apart from the commitments summarised above, swaps and caps are described in note 22 and recourse to foreign currency options and swaps are described below.

The Group covers its exchange risks on imports and exports by forward purchases and sales of foreign currencies.

The currencies of the covers at December 31, 1991 are as follows:

in millions of French francs	
● US Dollars	594
● Ecus	181
● Deutschemarks	157
● Other currencies	859
	1,791

As a complement to the forward purchases and sales of foreign currency, the Group also uses foreign currency options and swaps. In 1990 a strategy of foreign currency options was implemented at Divisional level. Total foreign currency options at December 31, 1991 amounted to FF 2,101 million and foreign currency swaps to FF 4,796 million.

All foreign exchange covers have a counterpart representing economic operations made by the Group. Accordingly, the Group avoids exposure to exchange risks by the use of forward exchange contracts.

Disclosure by most French companies is less detailed than [...]
companies. BSN give no information regarding contingent li[...]
only a note on financial commitments. Saint Gobain link con[...]
liabilities with commitments and pledges (Extract 9.23). Often with
French companies no distinction is made between these two
categories.

Extract 9.24 – Daimler Benz 1992 accounts,
Notes.

In millions of DM	12/31/1992	12/31/1991
Collateral	1,383	1,557
Discounted notes	221	218
Contractual guarantees	536	261
Pledges for indebtedness of others	9	7

In addition, we are liable for non-estimable compensatory payments, guaranteed by Deutsche Aerospace AG for 1993 and future years. For outside shareholders of AEG Aktiengesellschaft and of Daimler-Benz Luft- und Raumfahrt Holding AG, there exist claims for non-estimable compensatory payments.

Moreover, there exist contractual performance guarantees that could not reasonably be estimated.

German companies by law have to disclose contingent liabilities relating to the issuance and transfer of bills of exchange, guarantees, bills and cheque guarantees, warranties and the granting of security for third-party liabilities. Practice by German companies is much more uniform than that in the UK or France – all companies supply a table. The note in the Daimler-Benz accounts for 1992 is shown in Extract 9.24.

One problem that has arisen in the UK that affects contingent liabilities is the off-balance sheet issue of whether funds obtained by a company under certain conditions are the result of a genuine sale or whether they might need to be repaid and are therefore a form of borrowing. The problem is illustrated in the contingent liabilities footnote to the accounts of Barratt Developments. Barratts had clearly built some houses which it had sold to a third party. The third party planned to sell the houses when Barratts had stopped using them as show houses. Barratts would have entered the sale in its accounts.

The note, reproduced in Extract 9.25, discloses that Barratts have a 'potential commitment to repurchase the portfolio of unsold showhouses' off the third party. The cash received by Barratts from the third party could in certain circumstances turn out not to be so different from loan funds. This issue is discussed in Chapter 10 but is mentioned here in the context of what constitutes a contingent liability.

24 Contingent liabilities

The company has guaranteed certain bank borrowings of its subsidiary undertakings amounting to £22.6m (1990 £22.2m). In addition there are contingent liabilities in respect of guarantees relating to certain subsidiaries entered into in the normal course of business.

Certain of the showhouses utilised by the group are owned by a third party under an agreement which provides that any of those show houses not sold by 31st January 1992 may be required to be repurchased by the group at that time at a predetermined value. At 30th June 1991, the potential commitment to repurchase the portfolio of unsold showhouses amounted to £30.8m. The group has facilities in place to finance this commitment which at 4th October 1991 had reduced to £20.2m. The directors expect that the commitment will be fully extinguished by the end of December 1991. Adequate provision has been made for the shortfall between the market and committed value of individual showhouses. The directors consider that the possibility of any further material loss is remote.

The US subsidiary undertaking has a number of sites being developed through joint venture agreements. In the normal course of business these joint venture partners are jointly and severally liable for, inter alia, bank loans to finance the developments of the joint ventures. The total external finance in US joint ventures under these arrangements at 30th June 1991 was £18.2m (1990 £37.0m). Adequate provision has been made in respect of the group's interest in the joint ventures as at 30th June 1991 and the directors consider that the possibility of any material loss accruing to the subsidiary undertaking as a result of these arrangements is unlikely.

There is an unprovided potential charge to Californian unitary tax in the sum of £3.3m (1990 £2.7m). Opposition to this tax continues in the U.S.A. and it is uncertain whether or not this liability will arise.

References

1. Nobes, C.W. and Parker, R.H. (eds) (1991) *Comparative International Accounting,* Prentice Hall.
2. Alexander, D. and Archer, S. (1992) *The European Accounting Guide*, Academic Press.

Problems

1. Compare the difference between the reporting of debt securities by German and French companies. Why do you believe it is possible for German companies to be able to satisfy users of accounts with such low levels of disclosure?

2. What are the alternative approaches to accounting for deep discounted bonds and bonds to be redeemed at a premium? What are the advantages of the alternative methods?

3. In Euro Disney's accounts they make reference to a premium on convertible bond redemption. What is meant by Euro Disney's policy of amortizing this at a rate 'depending on the probability that the premium will be paid'?

4. Reckitt & Colman in their 1992 accounts express the view that their convertible capital bonds are 'more in the nature of equity share capital than borrowings'. They believe that in order to show a true and fair view the accounting entries relating to these bonds should be closer to the treatment of equity finance than to debt finance. What are the arguments against such a policy? What would be the current practice in your own country with regard to the treatment of such bonds?

5. In Forte's 1992 accounts (Extract 9.10) certain bank loans repayable within one year have been classified as long-term borrowing. What are the arguments for such treatment? What are the arguments against? What is the current policy in your own country with regard to the classification of this type of finance?

6. Why is it important for financial analysts to have knowledge of the currency of borrowing of a company? What further information would an analyst need to be able to access the riskiness of foreign currency borrowing?

7. When should a company make a provision as opposed to create a reserve? When should a company make a provision as opposed to mentioning an item as a contingent liability in the notes to the accounts?

8. Examine the note from the Glaxo accounts for 1993 concerning retirement benefits (Extract 9.14). Write a report suitable for a layman explaining the method adopted by the company to fund its liabilities to UK pensioners and to account for the pension costs. Why might a surplus arise in a pension fund? How should it be treated in the accounts?

9. Compare and contrast the different methods of funding pension schemes and accounting for pension costs in two of the countries with which this book is concerned. What is the significance to profitability and long-term financial health of a company of the alternative approaches?

10. What is the relationship in the UK between the management of the company pension fund and the management of the employing company? How does a possible conflict of interest arise? How might this be overcome?

11. Analyse the information given by Thomson-CSF in their accounts on the subject of pensions and retirement obligations (Extract 9.17). Write a report explaining the policy and practices of this company.

12. What are secret reserves? What practices adopted by companies in Germany and in other countries lead to the creation of such

secret reserves? What are the reasons why directors of companies in Germany might choose to make excessive provisions to cover possible future liabilities and losses?

13. Daimler-Benz in their 1991 accounts make the (following statement when explaining the treatment they have adopted for goodwill:

'The hidden reserves have been made active and will be written off over their useful lives in an effective manner.'

What do you think they mean by this statement?

There is much talk of secret reserves when discussing German company accounts. What are secret reserves? Could they exist within companies in countries other than Germany?

14. What is the difference between the German and British methods of funding pension schemes? Demonstrate with a hypothetical example the effect on gearing ratios of the two different approaches. What is the flow-through method of providing for pensions? What are the weaknesses of the method that have led to it being abandoned in some countries

15. Examine the extracts in the chapter concerned with pension liabilities. How do the companies value their liability for pension payments? What is the significance of the discount rate that is used in the calculations?

16. What does the expression 'the economic consequences of accounting standards' mean. In this chapter at least one example is described. Give two further examples where changes in accounting standards might have economic consequences.

10

Capital Instruments and Off-Balance Sheet Finance

Objectives

- To examine how issues of financial securities are shown on company financial statements and the significance of this for financial analysts.

- To illustrate the effect on gearing/leverage ratios of treating complex capital issues as equity rather than debt.

- To examine the use of finance not fully disclosed on the company balance sheet.

- To illustrate the different treatment of similar items by companies

Introduction

The accounting treatment of shares and debt securities by issuing companies has, until comparatively recently, been non-controversial. Because of this it was not until December 1993 that the ASB issued FRS 4 *Capital Instruments*.[1] This was the first UK accounting standard issued on this topic and followed a period of increasing unease with the creative financing methods adopted by many companies.

The 1980s saw the introduction of a variety of new and complex instruments used by companies to finance their activities. The originality and complicated structure of these instruments present a major challenge to company managers, first in computing the true cost of the instruments then in deciding on the appropriate accounting presentation. Investors also need to be able to assess the impact of such issues on the risk profile of the company and also any potential equity dilution.

From an issuer's perspective the aim should be to obtain funds at the lowest cost possible given the risk of the instrument. Market efficiency would seem to suggest that it is very difficult to add value by using different types of financial instruments. Although one may be in broad agreement with this sentiment there nevertheless may be imperfections and distortions in capital markets both domestically and internationally which allow companies to obtain cheaper funds while at the same time offering investors the prospect of superior returns. Another, perhaps more dubious, reason for the growth in alternative forms of finance has been the desire by management to reduce leverage ratios by making new issues which will be regarded as equity rather than debt. Another way in which company managements have sought to improve this aspect of their finances has been by structuring borrowing so that it does not appear on the consolidated balance sheet. This so called off-balance sheet finance will be discussed later in the chapter.

One major capital market imperfection which many issues seek to exploit is that of taxation. For example in the UK and other countries while interest payments on debt are tax deductible for corporate tax purposes, dividend payments are regarded as appropriations of after-tax profit. Asymmetric treatment of payments for tax purposes in different tax regimes may also give scope for structuring issues accordingly. The aim, therefore, of many of the complex issues is to be viewed as debt for tax purposes, to obtain the tax advantage of interest deductibility, and as equity for accounting purposes to reduce leverage ratios.

The UK is by no means the only country to indulge in innovative forms of financing. French companies have produced new issues which have sometimes been more ingenious than UK or US issues and the French banking house Société Générale is one of the leaders in advising on these types of issue.

Complex Capital Issues

Issues

The problems which complex capital issues raise for the analyst are:

- to identify whether the issue should be regarded as debt or equity and the relative risk of the issue on the financial structure of the company;
- to discover how payments of dividend/interest have been treated, including in this any interest accruing on discounted issues.
- to verify whether calculations of leverage and interest cover have been affected by the way in which these items are interpreted.

Analysis

Convertible bonds, often with puts attached allowing holders to require redemption by the company at a premium, is a typical example and a very popular form of finance during the mid-1980s stock market boom. Issuing companies were able to set conversion terms at substantial premiums on current share prices while paying low coupon rates on the face value of the bonds. The sting was in the put attached to the bond which required buy-back by the company at a premium price should conversion not take place. This premium buy-back increased the effective interest cost of the bond. Because conversion into equity was assumed in many cases no provision was made for the potential extra interest payable. Thus both liabilities and interest charges were understated. The counter-argument justifying treatment as equity was that growth in share price (or current levels of share price) would make conversion fairly certain. Of course the end of the bull market in October 1987 and subsequent recession meant that for many companies faced with a collapsing share price conversion was not even a remote possibility and repayment clauses in bond contracts were enforced. This meant that additional interest had to be provided which increased the interest charge in the profit and loss account and also the liability shown on the balance sheet.

The types of capital instruments used were many and varied including: convertible preference shares, redeemable preference shares; convertible or redeemable preference shares; auction market preferred stock; convertible debt; deep discount bonds; stepped interest bonds and convertible capital bonds.

Extract 10.1 – Lucas Industries plc 1991 accounts, Notes.

	1991	1990	**1991**	1990
			Parent	Parent
	Group	Group	**company**	company
	£ million	£ million	**£ million**	£ million
Note 17: Loans other than from banks due after more than one year				
10 3/4% Unsecured Loan Stock 1992/97	**18.0**	18.0	**18.0**	18.0
5 1/4% Convertible Bonds 2002 US$51.3 million (1990 – US$65.8 million)	**30.6**	35.6	–	–
10 7/8% Eurosterling Bonds 2020	**100.0**	100.0	**100.0**	100.0
	148.6	153.6	**118.0**	118.0

The 5 1/4% Convertible Bonds may be converted at any time before 20 April 2002 at the rate of 415.9 ordinary shares of Lucas Industries plc per Bond of US$1,000 unless previously redeemed. The bondholders have the option to require redemption of the Bonds on 28 April 1994 at a premium of 18% over par which gives rise to a contingent liability of US$9.2 million.

Many of these capital instruments are hybrids in that they have qualities of both equity and debt. In fact there is nothing new about these issues as the earliest reported was an issue of £3000 5% convertible promissory notes in 1798 by the 'Company or Proprietors of the Canal Navigation from Manchester to or near Ashton-Under-Lyme and Oldham'. The use of basic convertible bonds has continued, sometimes being associated with takeover activity where they have been used as part or whole consideration. Their surge in popularity in the 1980s has been coupled with an increasing sophistication with put options emerging in 1987. Developments then continued with convertible redeemable preference share issues in 1988, convertible capital bonds in 1989 and auction market preferred stock (AMPS) in 1990.

Extract 10.2 – Lucas Industries plc 1993 accounts, Notes.

	1993 **Group** **£ million**	1992 Group £ million	**1993** **Parent** **company** **£ million**	1992 Parent company £ million
Note 15: Loans other than from banks due after more than one year				
10 3/4% Unsecured Loan Stock 1992/97	–	18.0	–	18.0
8.57% Unsecured Loan Notes 2004	**67.1**	52.1	–	–
5 1/4% Convertible Bonds 2002 US$51.3 million				
(1992 – US$51.3 million)	**34.5**	26.7	–	–
10 7/8% Eurosterling Bonds 2020	**100.00**	100.0	**100.0**	100.0
US$20,000,000 6.43% Guaranteed Senior Notes	**13.4**	–	–	–
US$81,000,000 6.98% Guaranteed Senior Notes	**54.4**	–	–	–
US$15,000,000 7.46% Guaranteed Senior Notes	**10.0**	–	–	–
	279.4	196.8	**100.0**	118.0

The 10 3/4% Unsecured Loan Stock 1992/97 was repaid at par on 10 June 1993.

The 5 1/4% Convertible Bonds may be converted at any time before 20 April 2002 at the rate of 415.9 ordinary shares of Lucas Industries plc per Bond of US$1,000 unless previously redeemed. The bondholders have the option to require redemption of the Bonds on 28 April 1994 at a premium of 18% over par. The potential premium arising is accrued evenly over the period to the redemption date.

The Guaranteed Senior Notes totalling $116 million were issued in June 1993 and have a range of maturities from 1998 to 2005.

Initially there was little official guidance on the accounting treatment of these instruments. However, in 1987 the Institute of Chartered Accountants in England and Wales (ICAEW) published Technical Release 677, *Accounting for Complex Capital Issues.* Because the recommendations in TR 677 were not widely adopted in practice, a further, more specialized, paper was issued as TR 827, *Convertible Bonds* in February 1991. The Urgent Issues Task Force of the ASB enlarged the scope of TR 827 in UITF Abstract 1, *Convertible Bonds – Supplemental Interest/Premium* issued in July 1991. This recommended that supplemental interest/premium on convertible bonds should be charged to the profit and loss account annually from inception along with the coupon rate, regardless of the probability of conversion. Together these laid the foundations for the Discussion Paper, *Accounting for Capital Instruments* issued by the ASB in December 1991 which itself was the basis for Exposure Draft FRED 3, *Accounting for Capital Instruments*, issued in December, 1992. This has now been confirmed by the issue of FRS 4, *Capital Instruments* in December 1993. Prior to these developments it was usual for companies to disclose only the details of conversion and redemption terms treating any potential redemption premium as a contingent liability. Extract 10.1 from Lucas Industries plc accounts for 1991 shows this treatment. However, Extract 10.2 from the 1993 accounts shows that the potential premium is now accrued evenly over the period to redemption date. The purpose of these adjustments is to ensure that an accurate economic picture is presented both in terms of finance charges in the profit and loss account and liabilities shown on the balance sheet.

FRS 4 seeks to remove the confusion and clarify the capital position which arises from including as equity securities with the characteristics of debt. The way this is done is illustrated in Table 10.1, taken from the standard.[2]

TABLE 10.1
FRS 4 Capital Instruments

ITEM	ANALYSED BETWEEN	
• Shareholders' funds	• Equity interests	• Non-equity interests
• Minority interests in subsidiaries	• Equity interests in subsidiaries	• Non-equity interests in subsidiaries
• Liabilities	• Convertible liabilities	• Non-convertible liabilities

The standard seeks to provide a clear distinction between equity and liabilities including those situations where issues may have taken place through a subsidiary (often overseas) but guarantees are provided by the parent company. Paragraph 24 of the standard states:[3]

Capital instruments (other than shares, which are addressed at paragraphs 37–45 below) should be classified as liabilities if they contain an obligation to transfer economic benefits (including a contingent obligation to transfer economic benefits). Capital instruments that do not contain an obligation to transfer economic benefits should be reported within shareholders' funds.

Differentiation between convertible and non-convertible liabilities on the face of the balance sheet is another requirement. Conversion should not be anticipated and the finance cost should be calculated on the assumption that debt will never be converted.

While acknowledging that certain kinds of shares have features which make them economically similar to debt, the standard stresses the requirement that all shares be reported within shareholders' funds. However, a distinction is made between equity and non-equity shares so that preference shares and redeemable shares of any type will normally be regarded as non-equity shares. The characteristics of non-equity shares are those possessing:[4]

- limited rights to receive dividends or redemption payments not linked to assets or profits;
- an immediate right to redemption or an option for redemption at a later date.

Minority interests too have to be analysed between equity and non-equity interests in subsidiaries. The thrust of this treatment is to limit the shifts between debt and equity which have been taking place with hybrid securities and try to ensure that financial statements present a clearer and consistent treatment of capital instruments.

The foregoing discussion, of course, relates to the UK position. What about other European countries? In these other countries, apart from their own company laws and GAAP, strong influences as far as larger companies are concerned are international and US standards. This reflects the need for credible accounting policies where securities are quoted in international markets. The requirements of FRS 4 are consistent with existing international accounting standards. However, the IASC has in issue an exposure draft (ED 40); this proposed standard differs from the UK standard in two main areas:

- the IASC draft requires that certain preference shares be accounted for as liabilities, for example where the holder has the right to require redemption;
- the IASC draft requires that the proceeds of instruments with both equity and liability rights, e.g. convertibles, should be allocated between the component parts. FRS 4 requires such instruments to be accounted for wholly as a liability unless the debt and equity components are capable of being transferred, cancelled or redeemed independently of each other. An example of such a financial instrument is loan stock with detachable warrants. The warrants can be transferred separately and in the UK the proceeds from such an issue can be split between the two components for accounting purposes.

FRS 4 is also consistent in many respects with current US GAAP. Redeemable preference shares are included in an intermediate category between liabilities and stockholders' equity, similar to the proposed UK equity/non-equity classification. The entire proceeds of convertible debt issues are credited to a liability account and any redemption premium on convertible puts has to be provided over the life of the bond regardless of the likelihood of conversion. This again is in broad agreement with the UK proposals.

The discussion so far has concentrated on balance sheet presentation without saying much about balance sheet carrying amounts and allocation of finance costs. FRS 4 advocates that immediately after issue debt should be stated at net proceeds of issue. Subsequently this value should be increased by the finance cost for the period less payments made for the period. Finance costs should be allocated to accounting periods over the term of the debt at a constant rate on the carrying amount with finance costs being charged to the profit and loss account. This means, for example, that a zero coupon bond would initially be stated as proceeds received. Each period a finance charge based on the redemption yield would be charged to the profit and loss account with the balance sheet value increased by this amount. The idea behind the requirements is that the effective cost of finance should be charged rather than the contractual coupon rate. Similar provisions apply to non-equity costs of finance. This again ties in with IASC and FASB requirements.

Many companies issue discounted bonds where either no interest is paid or the interest coupon rate is below the market rate and repayment is at a premium on issue price. For example, Tate and Lyle plc have in issue $5\frac{1}{4}\%$ guaranteed bonds repayable in 1996 at £163.8 million or in 2001 at £190.5 million. In the 1992 balance sheet the liability is shown as £118.l million. Clearly the cost to the company is not just the annual interest payment but also the additional amount to be repaid on redemption. Tate & Lyle's note in the 1992 accounts is shown in Extract 10.3.

The company provides each year for the discount by treating it as an extra interest payment each year and increasing the balance sheet liability. The provision is made based on the interest rate implied by the cash flows receivable and payable on the bond. For example, a five-year zero coupon bond issued at £620 and repayable at £1000 would have an imputed interest rate of 10%. In the first year £62 interest would be charged to the profit and loss account and the liability would be increased to £682. In the following year £68 (10% of £682) would be charged against profit and the balance sheet liability increased to £750, and so on for following years. Similar treatment should also be used where interest rates vary. For example Whitbread Investment Company uses this approach as indicated by Extract 10.4 from its 1992 accounts. Unfortunately not all companies may use these approaches and may charge interest on the basis of amounts paid or make some simple average calculation of interest paid.

An alternative treatment is to disclose in the balance sheet as a liability the amount to be repaid to the bondholders (gross) with the bond discount capitalized and amortized to the profit and loss account over the life of the bond. Thomson-CSF (1991) explain in their accounts that at the time the bond is issued they credit the full amount to be repaid to liabilities; the discount is initially debited to assets

17 Borrowings – due after more than one year	1992 Group £ million	1991 Group £ million	1992 Tate & Lyle PLC £ million	1991 Tate & Lyle PLC £ million
Debentures, loans and overdrafts				
4% bonds 1993 (Swiss Francs 140,000,000)	63.0	55.2	63.0	55.2
Industrial revenue bonds 1992/2005 (US$41,890,000)[1]	24.4	26.3	–	–
12⅓% medium term notes 1992/95 (US$34,925,000)	20.4	33.4	–	–
9⅝% Eurobond 1992 (US$100,000,000)	58.3	57.6	58.3	57.6
Variable unsecured bond 1996 (US$50,000,000)	29.2	28.8	29.2	28.8
7.96% notes 1999 (US$50,000,000)	29.2	–	–	–
5¼% Guaranteed Bonds 2001 (£190,500,000)[2]	118.1	113.7	–	–
Other secured loans	2.3	2.3	2.0	2.0
Other variable unsecured loans	0.9	0.2	–	–
Other fixed unsecured loans	21.6	51.2	1.7	5.5
Obligations under finance leases	0.4	3.3	–	–
	367.8	372.0	154.2	149.1
Bank loans and overdrafts				
Variable unsecured 1992 (US$70,000,000)	–	40.3	–	40.3
Variable unsecured 1994 (US$50,000,000)	29.2	28.8	–	–
Variable unsecured 1995 (US$75,000,000)	43.7	43.2	–	–
Fixed secured other	1.3	1.3	–	–
Variable unsecured other	136.8	122.5	–	–
Fixed unsecured other	39.5	29.5	–	–
	250.5	265.6	–	40.3
Owed to subsidiary undertakings	–	–	156.5	92.8
Less portion of borrowings due within one year	(91.3)	(77.1)	(58.3)	(40.3)
	527.0	560.5	252.4	241.9

[1] $23.7 million held at variable interest rates, the balance is held at fixed interest rates from 5.9% to 13.0%.

[2] Redemption of the bonds is at the option of the issuer from 21st March 1996. The redemption price from that date is £163.8 million increasing in annual increments to the par value of £190.5 million.

(intangible), and then amortized over time against profits using the effective interest rate method. Bayer (1992) explain in a note dealing with the asset deferred charges that the item includes 'unamortized debt discounts of DM 136 million'.

Extract 10.4 – Whitbread Investment Co. plc 1992 accounts, Notes.

5 Debenture loans

Stepped interest debenture stock

Interest was payable on the stock at the rate of 12 per cent per annum for the year to 31st March 1992 and amounted to £1,800,000. The rate of interest will remain fixed at the rate of 12 per cent per annum until final redemption. The gross yield to redemption, actuarily calculated at the issue price of £95,543 is 11.171 per cent.

The interest charged to revenue account has been averaged over the life of the stock and results in an addition to revenue for the year ended 31st March 1992 amounting to £28,691, as opposed to a charge for the year ended 31st March 1991 of £46,359.

If not previously repaid or purchased by the Company or any subsidiary the stock will be redeemed at par plus accrued interest on 30th September 2010.

Groupe Euro Disney is a highly geared French company. Included in their long-term borrowing figure in the balance sheet are convertible bonds. A footnote in the accounts explains that 'unless previously converted, redeemed or purchased by the company', the bonds will be redeemed at a premium. They explain that this represents a contingent liability. They are not waiting until the final redemption date to recognize the liability, but are making a provision for the future possible payment. Each year a charge is made against profits, at a rate 'depending on the probability that the premium will be paid' (see Extract 10.5).

A company might also buy its own bonds in the market when the price is above the amount of the liability in the balance sheet. It pays a premium to repurchase its debt. This would happen when interest rates have fallen since the time the bonds were issued. In the UK the UITF (No.8) has concluded that with only a few exceptions the difference on repurchase should be taken to the profit and loss account in the year of repurchase. British Telecom in their 1993 accounts show a charge of £56 million against profits for the 'premium on repurchase of bonds' (see Extract 10.6). Prior to this UITF statement a number of companies in the UK were deferring the difference and amortizing it over the term of the original borrowing. This deferring of the premium is common in a number of the countries we are considering.

With regard to issue costs UK companies are recommended to net issue costs against proceeds; however, other treatments are possible. Groupe Euro Disney, for example, in their 1992 accounts show FF 100 million debt issue costs as an asset under the heading 'deferred charges'.

Convertible bonds

On July 15, 1991, the Company issued 28,350,000 unsecured convertible bonds at par with a FF 140 principal value, primarily to finance part of the future development of the Euro Disney Resort, notably the second theme park, and to strengthen the financial position of the Company. Each bond is convertible on or after April 12, 1992, into one share of the Company. During 1992, 7,308 bonds were converted. The bonds bear interest at the rate of 6.75% per annum, payable annually beginning October 1, 1992. At September 30, 1992 and 1991, the above amounts include accrued interest of FF 328 million and FF 57 million, respectively. Unless previously converted, redeemed or purchased by the Company, the bonds will be redeemed at 110 per cent of their principal amount on October 1, 2001, which represents a contingent liability of FF 397 million (of which FF 47 million was provided and included above at September 30, 1992).

CONVERTIBLE BOND REDEMPTION PREMIUM

The liability for the convertible bond redemption premium is provided for on a straight-line basis over the term of the bonds, depending on the probability that the premium will be paid.

Convertible capital bonds were first introduced in the late 1980s; this is another issue with features of both debt and equity. The bonds are debt instruments often issued by a special-purpose company incorporated outside the UK. Prior to maturity they may be exchanged for shares of a subsidiary which are then either immediately redeemed or exchanged for ordinary shares of the parent. The issue from the outset is guaranteed by the parent.

Because conversion into shares is mandatory except for default, it has been argued that the liability to repay can be ignored and the bonds treated as convertible preference shares. In this case the analyst has to decide whether they are debt or equity as the impact on gearing ratios can be significant.

The accounts of Reckitt & Colman indicate that the company wishes its convertible capital bonds to be seen as 'capital plus reserves'. The notes to the accounts explain the nature of the bonds and concludes 'the bonds are more in the nature of equity share capital than borrowing' (see Extract 10.7). The layout of the company's balance sheet does not include such bonds as creditors, but lists them under capital and reserves. There is no sub-total for this later term and the user of the accounts has to be careful not to be misled by such a balance sheet layout. The amount involved can be relatively large as it is for Reckitt & Colman. If the bonds are included with long-term creditors the gearing ratio alters significantly

In fact the profit and loss account indicates even more clearly that the company wants the bonds to be seen as equity. The interest (coupon) on these items is deducted after profits on ordinary activities. But surely such payments are an expense, not an appropriation of profits? Again, care must be taken to ensure the ratio linking interest payments to profits available is correct.

FRS 4 now requires that these be treated unambiguously as liabilities both from subsidiary and group viewpoints. As the liabilities are convertible they should be included in convertible debt which should be shown on the face of the balance sheet separately from other liabilities.[5]

Extract 10.6 – British Telecommunications plc 1993 accounts, Accounting Policies.

IV Interest

Interest payable, including that related to financing the construction of tangible fixed assets, is written off as incurred. Discounts or premiums on the issue of debt securities are amortised over the term of the related security and included within interest payable. Premiums payable on early redemptions of debt securities, in lieu of future interest costs, are written off when paid.

Capital Instruments and Off-Balance Sheet Finance

29 Convertible capital bonds

In March 1990 Reckitt & Colman Capital Finance Limited, a wholly-owned subsidiary undertaking of the parent company, made an issue of £200,832,954 9.5% Convertible Capital Bonds 2005.

The terms of the bonds allow the holders to convert into Reckitt & Colman ordinary shares on 31 July in each of the years 1993 to 2004 and at the initial exchange price of 505p per share (equivalent to 19.802 Reckitt & Colman ordinary shares per 100 bonds of £1 each). In so far as this right is not exercised, remaining bondholders may be required to convert their bonds into Reckitt & Colman ordinary shares at maturity, such shares to be sold in the market on their behalf. Only if the proceeds of such sales are less than the issue price of the bonds, does Reckitt & Colman have to fund any deficit from its own resources. There is no put option under which bondholders can require early redemption and there are no cross default provisions or financial covenants.

With the approval of shareholders and in compliance with the terms of the bonds, Reckitt & Colman can, at any time, require bondholders to exchange all bonds outstanding for convertible redeemable preference shares of Reckitt & Colman plc on a one-for-one basis.

Because the terms of the bonds are such that the company will issue shares either on redemption of the bonds or on their earlier conversion, the bonds are more in the nature of equity share capital than borrowings. The Companies Act 1985 permits the directors to depart from the accounting provisions otherwise required by the Act where they believe it is necessary to do so to show a true and fair view. The directors have therefore chosen to disclose the bonds as an additional category to the balance sheet format prescribed by the Act, after capital and reserves, rather than as borrowings. In order to reflect the equity nature of the bonds and to achieve consistency with the treatment adopted in the balance sheet, the coupon payable, net of taxation, has been separately disclosed in the profit and loss account as a deduction from profit after taxation rather than as part of interest.

		1992 Group £m	1991 Group £m
	Total assets less current liabilities	**1,296.31**	1,220.10
17	Creditors due after more than one year	**(379.46)**	(421.05)
18	Provisions for liabilities and charges	**(88.02)**	(71.17)
	Minority interests	**(10.17)**	(8.27)
	Total net assets	**818.66**	719.61
	Capital and reserves:		
30	Called up share capital	**41.91**	41.85
	Share premium account	**116.88**	115.47
31	Other reserves	**459.04**	361.46
29	**Convertible capital bonds**	**200.83**	200.83
		818.66	719.61

Financial Instruments Issued by Subsidiaries

If a subsidiary issues debt securities, these are consolidated as debt in the group accounts and so the total borrowing of the group is disclosed on the face of the balance sheet. If, however, a subsidiary issues equity shares to investors, other than to the parent company, these are classified as minority interests in the consolidated accounts. What happens if a subsidiary issues redeemable preference shares? It could be argued that preference shares are equity, therefore this issue should be classed as equity in the consolidated accounts. But what is the position if these preference shares are issued by a subsidiary located in an offshore financial centre and the subsidiary does not have wealth of its own but the payment of dividends and the possible redemption is guaranteed by the parent company? Is it still equity of the subsidiary and minority interest of the group? Further, what is the position if the dividend rate is similar to the current interest rate at the time of issue? The security is very close to being debt.

Extract 10.8 – Coats Viyella plc 1992 accounts, Balance Sheet, Notes and Statement of Accounting Policies.

Extract from Balance Sheet

| | | GROUP | |
		1992	1991 (Restated)
Creditors – amounts falling due after			
more than one year		£m	£m
Other creditors	18	(289.3)	(268.6)
Redeemable convertible preference			
shares in Coats Viyella Finance NV	18	(115.8)	(109.9)
		(405.1)	(378.5)

NOTE

18 Creditors (amounts falling due after more than one year) continued

Note

On 14 June 1989, Coats Viyella Finance NV, a subsidiary company incorporated in the Netherlands Antilles, issued 98,000 7.25% Guaranteed Redeemable Convertible Preference Shares with a paid up value of £1.000 per share. The shares are guaranteed on a subordinated basis by Coats Viyella Plc and are convertible into its Ordinary Shares at a price of 196p per Ordinary Share at any time prior to 7 June 2004. The shares then outstanding will be redeemed on 14 June 2004 at their issue price or in certain circumstances upon earlier revocation of the guarantee. The preference shareholders may require the shares to be redeemed on 14 June 1994 at a redemption price of 128.5% of the paid up value thereof subject to the issuer's right to seek deferral of the redemption by electing to pay dividends at a higher level. Provision is made for the possible premium on redemption. At 31 December 1992 the amount accrued was £17.8m (1991: £11.9m). This is now included along with the paid up value of the shares.

Statement of accounting policies

Changes in accounting policies and presentation of financial information

Since the previous Annual Report, the Accounting Standards Board issued two Financial Reporting Standards: FRS2 – Accounting for Subsidiary Undertakings and FRS3 – Reporting Financial Performance. In addition the Accounting Standards Board issued an exposure draft FRED3 – Accounting for Capital Instruments. These financial statements comply with both Standards and the Exposure Draft. Comparative figures have been restated accordingly including reconsolidation of Yarns businesses for the whole of 1990 and 1991.

FRS3 prescribes a new format for the profit and loss account, virtually eliminates extraordinary items and changes the basis of calculation of earnings per share. The definition of a discontinued operation is restricted to a business the sale or termination of which has a material effect on the nature and focus of the Group's activities. In addition, a statement of total recognised gains and losses and a reconciliation of movements in shareholders' funds are required.

In addition, FRS3 requires that provisions for losses on sale or termination of operations are only created where the Group is demonstrably committed to the sale or termination and, in the case of a sale, this should be evidenced by a binding sale agreement. Comparative figures have therefore been restated to eliminate certain provisions for losses on anticipated disposals (principally Yarns businesses) totalling £11.5m originally created in 1989 and 1990 and released in 1991.

FRED3 requires the redeemable convertible preference shares issued by Coats Viyella Finance NV and guaranteed by Coats Viyella to be treated as debt and not as minority interest.

The effect of these restatements on the comparative figures for 1991 can be summarised as follows:-

	As published £m	FRS3 Reconsolidate Yarns £m	FRS3 Extraordinary items £m	FRS3 Exceptional items £m	FRS3 Eliminate provisions for losses on disposals £m	FRED3 Euroconvertible financing £m	As restated £m
Turnover	1,947.5	33.1	–	–	–	–	1,980.6
Operating profit	126.4	1.0	1.5	(6.8)	–	–	122.1
Profit on sale of fixed assets	–	–	–	10.2	–	–	10.2
Losses on sale and termination of operations	–	–	–	(2.1)	–	–	(2.1)
Profit before interest	126.4	1.0	1.5	1.3	–	–	130.2
Associated companies	5.5	–	–	–	–	–	5.5
Net interest	(20.5)	(0.9)	(4.0)	(1.3)	–	(12.3)	(39.0)
Profit before taxation	111.4	0.1	(2.5)	–	–	(12.3)	96.7
Taxation	(36.9)	–	0.3	–	–	–	(36.6)
Minority interests	(16.1)	–	–	–	–	12.3	(3.8)
Extraordinary items	9.4	(0.1)	2.2	–	(11.5)	–	–
Profit for the financial year	67.8	–	–	–	(11.5)	–	56.3

20 Capital and Reserves

(a) Share capital of Cadbury Schweppes plc

	1992 £m	1991 £m
Authorised Share Capital:		
Attributable to equity interests:		
Ordinary shares (949 million of 25p each)	**237.3**	237.3
Attributable to non-equity interests:		
US$ Preference shares (750 of US$ 1,000 each)	**0.4**	0.4
Can$ Preference shares (150 of Can$ 1,000 each)	**0.1**	0.1
	237.8	237.8
Allotted and called up Share Capital:		
Attributable to equity interests:		
Ordinary shares (741.5 million of 25p each fully paid) (1991 – 702.4 million)	**185.4**	175.6
Attributable to non-equity interests:		
US$ Preference shares (455 of US$ 1,000 each)	**0.2**	0.2
Can$ Preference shares (150 of Can$ 1,000 each)	**0.1**	0.1
	185.7	175.9

(b) Movements on capital and reserves – Company

	Preference shares £m	Ordinary shares £m	Share premium £m	Revaluation reserve £m	Retained profits £m
At beginning of year	0.3	175.6	393.8	1.7	236.1
Exchange rate adjustments	–	–	–	–	(3.1)
Share options exercised	–	1.0	9.8	–	–
Share dividends	–	0.2	3.3	–	–
Share placing*	–	8.6	136.5	–	–
Profit for financial year	–	–	–	–	24.5
Dividends to ordinary shareholders	–	–	–	–	(98.0)
Realised on disposals	–	–	–	(0.1)	0.1
Other	–	–	(0.3)	–	–
At end of year	0.3	185.4	543.1	1.6	159.6

The profit for the financial year for the Company was £24.5m (1991 – £161.4m).

Total recognised gains and losses – Company	1992 £m	1991 £m
Profit for the financial year	24.5	161.4
Currency translation differences	(3.1)	–
Total recognised gains and losses for the year	21.4	161.4

The analysis of movements in shareholders' funds is given in table (b) above. The net increase in shareholders' funds was £82.5m.

(c) Ordinary shares

During the year 39,138,677 Ordinary shares of 25p each were allotted and issued as follows:

- Share placing*   34,400,000
- Share dividends   764,141
- Share options exercised   3,922,366
- Irish Share Scheme   14,100
- Bond conversions   38,070

*Share placing: on 20 March 1992, the Company issued, by way of a placing with institutional shareholders, 34.4m Ordinary shares of 25p at a price of 425p, raising £145.1m (net of expenses).

20 Capital and Reserves (continued)

The nominal value of Ordinary shares issued during the year was £9,784,699.25. There were no other changes in the issued Share Capital of the Company during the year. During the year options were granted over Ordinary shares of 25p in accordance with the Rules of the various schemes and at 2 January 1993 taking account of options exercised, cancelled and lapsed, options to subscribe for the following Ordinary shares of 25p each were outstanding:

Scheme	No. of Shares	Exercise Price Range	Exercisable until
Savings-Related Share Option Scheme	14,150,308	122.4p – 344p	30 June 2000
Share Option Scheme 1984 for Main Board Directors and Senior Executives	7,412,000	175p – 452p	13 October 2002
Share Option Scheme 1986 for Senior Management Overseas	8,375,820	270p – 452p	27 October 2002
Irish Savings-Related Share Option Scheme	326,876	266p – 412p	23 July 1999
Irish AVC Savings-Related Share Option Scheme	342,380	239p – 371p	23 July 1997
US Stock Option Plan 1987	133,900	US$ 2.39 – US$ 3.95	17 February 1997

(d) Cumulative Perpetual Preference Shares

In 1990 the Company issued 105 US$ Cumulative Perpetual Preference Shares (Series 1) and 150 Can$ Cumulative Perpetual Preference Shares (Series 2) at a price of US$ 500,000 and Can$ 500,000 respectively. For the first five years the dividend rate on the Series 1 shares is a floating rate set at 75% of 3 month US$ LIBOR, and that on the Series 2 shares is a floating rate set at 75% of 90 day Canadian Bankers' Acceptance rates.

At the end of the five year period the dividend rate is subject to re-negotiation.

Also in 1990 the Company issued 350 US$ Auction Preference Shares (Series 3 to 6) at the same issue price. The dividend rate on each of Series 3 to 6 is reset at auctions normally held every 28 days.

For the US dollar shares the rates of dividend paid during 1992 ranged between 2.54% and 4.14% and at 2 January 1993 the weighted average rate payable was 2.98%. For the Canadian dollar shares the rates of dividend paid during 1992 ranged between 3.64% and 5.64% and at 2 January 1993 the weighted average rate payable was 6.23%. The preference shares are redeemable at any time only at the Company's option and at 2 January 1993 the redemption value was £189.5m (1991 – £155.4m).

(e) Movements on reserves – Group	Revaluation Reserve £m	Retained Profits £m	Share Premium £m
At beginning of year	99.9	207.1	393.8
Restatement	–	(1.8)	–
As restated	99.9	205.3	393.8
Exchange rate adjustments	5.2	67.4	–
Premiums on shares issued in year	–	–	149.3
Retained profit for year	–	97.6	–
Goodwill on acquisitions	–	(119.7)	–
Realised on disposals	(0.7)	0.7	–
Other	–	(0.4)	–
At end of year	104.4	250.9	543.1

Goodwill written off

The total goodwill written off on businesses continuing within the Group amounts to £882.0m of which £753.0m has been written off since 3 January 1988.

In the UK before the issue of FRS 4 such securities were treated in consolidated accounts as minority interests, but FRS 4 changes the position. The standard accepts that if the parent company issues redeemable preference shares they should be classified as equity, one reason being the legal position. However, if a subsidiary company issues such securities they should in certain circumstances be regarded from the group's point of view as equivalent to debt and they should be treated as such in the consolidated accounts. One situation in which such redeemable preference shares should be treated as debt is when the parent company guarantees the redemption of the subsidiary's redeemable preference shares. They are in such situations a liability, as the group has an obligation to transfer economic benefits to those minority shareholders who hold these securities.

One company that was affected by this change in definition was Coats Viyella. As Extract 10.8 shows, they needed to restate their balance sheet and profit and loss account.

Preference shares which form part of shareholders' equity may nevertheless be quite similar to fixed interest borrowings where there are provisions for repayment and/or renegotiation of dividends payable. Cadbury Schweppes has issued preference shares with an initial floating dividend renegotiable after five years; the shares are redeemable at the company's option. The note shown in Extract 10.9 shows full details of the terms of the issue.

In fact when we look at the company's issued capital we find that these preference shares are only a very small amount of the total nominal value of issued capital shown. This is because the shares were issued at a huge premium with the share premium account being boosted accordingly. Although the preference shares are shown in share capital as 'non-equity interests' totalling £0.3 million they are dwarfed by ordinary shares of £185.4 million. However, it is estimated that approximately £160 million is included in the share premium account relating to these preference shares. In fact the company shows the redemption value of the preference shares in its summarized statements covering the past five years but has effectively improved its gearing (leverage) ratio for 1990 and later years by excluding the redemption value of the preference shares from both numerator (net borrowings) and denominator (ordinary shareholders' funds and minority interests) in calculating the ratio. In 1989 prior to issuing the preference shares gearing was 62.5%; in 1990 following issue the company calculated gearing at 49.8%. If the preference shares were treated as debt this would have raised the 1990 ratio to 70.8%. In the 1992 accounts gearing is shown as 36.9%; again if preference shares were treated as debt this would raise gearing to 55.4%.

Another company which includes preference shares issued through an overseas subsidiary in minority interest is SmithKline Beecham; however, the company does show the shares separately from other minority interests on the face of the balance sheet. The note to the financial accounts shown in Extract 10.10 gives details about the terms and conditions of the issue.

In computing its own financial ratios SmithKline Beecham includes the preference shares as part of equity. It could be argued that at the very least they should be excluded from equity (as does Cadbury

16. Called up share capital

	Number of shares	1992 £m	1991 £m
Authorised			
The Company			
A Shares of 12·5p each	2,500,000,000	**313**	313
B Shares of 12·5p each	1,500,000,000	**187**	187
	4,000,000,000	**500**	500
SB Corp			
Participating Preferred Shares of $0·025 each	2,000,000,000	**33**	27
Issued			
The Company			
A Shares of 12·5p each	1,360,710,886	**170**	169
B Shares of 12·5p each	1,309,504,490	**164**	164
	2,670,215,376	**334**	333
SB Corp			
Participating Preferred Shares of $0·025 each	1,310,008,670	**22**	18
		356	351

	A Shares of 12·5p each '000	B Shares of 12·5p each '000	Nominal value £m	Share premium £m	Consideration £m
The Company					
At 31 December 1991	1,353,022	1,309,504	333	23	356
Issue of shares on exercise of options	7,380	—	1	17	18
Shares issued at par in lieu of dividends	309	—	—	1	1
At 31 December 1992	**1,360,711**	**1,309,504**	**334**	**41**	**375**

	Participating Preferred Shares of US$0·025 each '000	Nominal value £m	Share premium £m	Total £m
SB Corp				
At 31 December 1991	1,310,009	18	—	18
Exchange movement	—	4	—	4
At 31 December 1992	**1,310,009**	**22**	—	**22**

One B Share is paired with one SB Corp Participating Preferred Share to form an Equity Unit. B Shares cannot be transferred separately from the paired Participating Preferred Shares.

The SB Corp Participating Preferred Shares may be redeemed in whole for cash at the option of the SB Corp Board of Directors. The amount payable would be $0·225 per share (total — $295 million) plus any accumulated and unpaid Preference Dividends. On redemption of the Participating Preferred Shares, the dividend equalisation arrangements for the holders of A and B Shares would continue to apply.

On 13 July 1992 the A and B shares were split into two and the Equity Units were split into ten. In the US five new Equity Units were combined to create an Equity Unit ADR and five new A Shares were combined to create an A Share ADR. The 1992 opening amounts of shares have been restated.

Schweppes) or alternatively that they be included in borrowings rather than equity. By including them in equity the gearing ratio is reduced to 24%; if they were excluded from equity, gearing would rise to 35.4%, while if the preference shares were included in borrowings the gearing ratio would be 83.4%. Even within the same country we can see that there are differences in presentation and interpretation. The accounting ratios shown in the reports of Cadbury Schweppes and SmithKline Beecham are computed, in some cases, on different bases using different assumptions. In this case we were able to make adjustments from the information given. However, it is possible that in other cases the analyst will have to probe further, particularly when comparing companies operating under different legal jurisdictions.

Off-Balance Sheet Finance

Unease with the use of off-balance sheet transactions grew during the 1980s as the financial services industry produced a seemingly endless stream of schemes involving off-balance sheet transactions. In many cases it became difficult to fully comprehend the trading results and financial position of a company from the financial statements produced.

Off-balance sheet finance is often discussed in disparaging terms as a means by which companies may hide the true extent of their borrowings. However, there may be occasions where innovative forms of financing may provide companies with cheaper debt or allow risk to be isolated and managed more effectively. A formal definition of off-balance sheet finance was provided by ICAEW Technical Release 603 as 'the funding or refinancing of a company's operations in such a way that, under legal requirements and existing accounting conventions, some or all of the finance may not be shown on its balance sheet'.[6]

As with many controversial areas of accounting what finance can be taken off-balance sheet will change as both the statutory requirements and accounting standards change over time. A further factor will be the imagination of financial engineers producing even more exotic forms of capital instrument. But why bother to spend time and money in producing exotic schemes if the net effect is to have the same total borrowing and risk spread among a number of companies rather than being contained in a single entity?

Issues

A number of reasons have been suggested for the growth in off-balance sheet finance. Some of these reasons appear to have good commercial justification while others seem to suggest that users of financial statements cannot see behind the figures on the statements and identify the commercial rationale that lies behind them. Reasons in the latter category would include the following:

- Where companies are increasing borrowing levels the use of off–balance sheet finance enables leverage ratios to be maintained at or near existing levels thus reassuring investors and analysts. This should help in keeping the cost of borrowing down and protect share price performance.

- Where a company carrying out a number of related activities begins what is regarded as a completely different type of activity it is often contended that the new activities should be placed off-balance sheet. A typical example is the provision of financial services by a retailing group where a common practice was to exclude the financial services company from the group accounts.
- By taking the development stage of a large new venture off-balance sheet until positive profits start to be produced, at which stage the assets and related borrowings can be brought on balance sheet. In this way profitability and other ratios may be sustained during the initial stages of the venture.

It could be argued that all these justifications assume that readers of financial statements cannot understand the significance of the transactions involved. If information is withheld or suppressed then readers may be misled; however if disclosure is made elsewhere than on the face of the accounts then the implication is that readers should be able to interpret the information and its significance for the accounting statements.

As stated earlier not all new forms of finance are aimed at achieving cosmetic accounting effects; some have clear financial implications. They may enable finance costs to be reduced and risk managed more effectively. For example proponents of securitization transactions would argue that it is possible to achieve both the objectives in a properly structured deal. Whatever the stated or implied motive for taking financing off-balance sheet a problem arises where disclosure, by note or otherwise, is not sufficient to allow a proper assessment of the company's results or financial position. It is this situation which has led to disquiet both among users and the accounting profession.

Analysis

An early example of off-balance sheet finance was the use of leasing transactions. Legally the lessor owns the asset and rents or leases it to the lessee. Taking a legal view the asset would appear in the lessor's balance sheet and lease payments would be charged through the lessee's profit and loss account and appear as income in the lessor's financial statements. However, SSAP 21 issued in 1984 was the first UK standard to require economic substance to take precedence over legal form.[7] This is because finance leases, or capital leases as they are also known, are structured in such a way that the risks and rewards of ownership of an asset are transferred to the lessee. This is accomplished by using a non-cancellable lease agreement where the lease payments cover both the full cost of the asset and the financing charges of the lessor. The commercial reality of the transaction is that the lessee assumes all the risks of ownership including potential obsolescence; it is a way of gaining use and control over the asset by paying set periodic instalments. It is very difficult to distinguish this type of transaction from a borrow and buy transaction and SSAP 21 requires that lessees should capitalize and depreciate finance leases and recognize a corresponding obligation to creditors. Lessors on the other hand should treat finance leases to customers as receivables and include them as debtors rather than fixed assets.

Extract 10.11 – British Airways plc 1992 accounts, Notes.

---

11 TANGIBLE ASSETS [extract]

£ million	Group		Company	
	1992	1991	**1992**	1991

I LEASING COMMITMENTS [extract]

The aggregate payments, for which there are commitments under operating leases as at the end of the year, fall due as follows:

i) Fleet

Within one year	**232**	220	**232**	220
Between one and five years	**497**	517	**497**	517
Over five years		2		2
	729	739	**729**	739

Amounts payable within one year relate to commitments expiring as follows:

Within one year	**27**	35	**27**	35
Between one and five years	**205**	180	**205**	180
Over five years		5		5
	232	220	**232**	220

The fleet leasing commitments include the balance of rental obligations under operating leases in respect of 13 Boeing 747-400s, eleven Boeing 767-300s, five Boeing 747-200s, one Boeing 757-200, 20 Boeing 737-200s, four Boeing 737-400s, two DC10-30s and 13 BAe ATP aircraft, but exclude six Boeing 757-200s which were converted from operating leases to finance leases during the year ended 31 March 1992 following an extension of the original lease periods. In the case of most of these obligations, the Company may be required to meet a small share of any loss on resale if options to extend the lease are not exercised.

The capitalization refers to finance leases only as defined in SSAP 21. Other leases falling outside the definition of finance leases are termed operating leases. The latter do not require to be capitalized and the operating lease rentals are charged to the lessee's profit and loss account on a straight line basis. A number of potential problem areas exist in accounting for leases. In certain circumstances lessees may prefer leases to be categorized as operating rather than financial because of the apparent beneficial effect this may have on their leverage position. This could lead to leasing deals being structured in such a way that they can be treated as operating leases. For example, if the residual value of a lease is significant and is not guaranteed by the lessee or a related party it is likely to be classified as an operating lease. British Airways is one company which has entered into this type of operating lease whereby the leased assets can be returned at certain times without incurring material residual liabilities. This has been the position since privatization although the 1992 accounts showed that some of the leases had been converted into finance leases. Extract 10.11 shows the notes to the accounts covering these items.

Although the capitalization of finance leases has long been established in the UK and USA it would be wrong to assume that this is the case in other countries. If there is a strong legal influence on accounting practice as is the case with many other European countries then all leases may be treated as pure rental agreements with payments being charged to the profit and loss account and no balance sheet entries at all. In France the capitalization of finance leases in group accounts is at the discretion of the company; analysts will need to consult policy notes to verify treatment. Alexander and Archer suggest that the majority practice is to follow IAS 17[8] which has similar basic requirements to SSAP 21. However, Groupe Euro Disney which prepares accounts using French GAAP, does not capitalize leases and instead accounts for them as operating leases. The appropriate note taken from the 1992 accounts is shown in Extract 10.12.

The company has managed to avoid disclosing in the group accounts the true level of borrowing associated with the theme park activity. This has been achieved through the use of a sale and leaseback arrangement. The Group operate the theme park and a number of the adjacent hotels but it does not own the assets involved. The assets 'were sold on an ongoing basis by the company to Euro Disney SNC and are being leased back to the company' (page 19 of 1992 annual report). It is explained that 'The Group has no ownership interest in these SNCs'. A number of SNCs were established as financing companies. It is these financing companies that borrow, own the assets, and lease them to the quoted company. Because the quoted company does not have an ownership interest in the finance companies they do not have to be consolidated.

Who owns Euro Disney SNC and the other financing companies? They are under the indirect control of the Walt Disney Corporation. Who then owns Euro Disney SCA (the quoted company)? The answer is that the largest shareholder, with 49% of the shares is the EDL Holding company, which is described in the Euro Disney SCA accounts as a 'wholly owned, indirect subsidiary of the Walt Disney Group'. So the result is the Walt Disney Group effectively controls the company that

25 ★ LEASED ASSETS

The Company has a leaseback agreement with Euro Disneyland S.N.C. for the Theme Park, and in conformity with French accounting principles, accounts for it as an operating lease. The rental expense under this lease approximates Euro Disneyland S.N.C.'s related debt service payments, which fluctuate with variable interest rate changes and principal repayments.

This lease commenced April 12, 1992 and ends when the underlying borrowings and interest are repaid in full by Euro Disneyland S.N.C. or, at the latest, December 31, 2030.

Rental expense for the year ending September 30, 1992 was FF 564 million. The following amounts are stated at nominal value. Rental commitments are based on an estimated interest rate of 10%.

	Rental Commitments FF millions
1993	1,207
1994-98	6,184
After 1998	19,217
Total	26,608
Purchase Option	1

(1) This information is not analyzed by asset category as the lease comprises the Theme Park as a whole and not its specific assets.

As an operating lease, the cost and depreciation of the assets and underlying borrowings are not included in the Company's financial statements. These amounts, which are carried by Euro Disneyland S.N.C., are as follows:

September 30, 1992	Cost	Depreciation	FF millions Net Book Value
★ Land and Infrastructure	294	(7)	287
★ Buildings	3,477	(95)	3,382
★ Rides and attractions	4,731	(94)	4,637
★ Furniture, fixtures & equipment	2,168	(108)	2,060
	10,670	(304)	10,366

These assets are depreciated using the straight-line method over their estimated useful lives from the date they are placed in service, as follows:

* ★ Buildings — 20 to 33 years
* ★ Infrastructure — 10 to 25 years
* ★ Rides and attractions — 25 years
* ★ Furniture, fixtures & equipment — 4 to 10 years

At September 30, 1992, borrowings and accrued interest specific to these assets were FF 12.1 billion, including FF 2.5 billion due to the Company.

The Company has other operating leases primarily for office space, office and computer equipment and vehicles, for which total rental expense was FF 152 million and FF 51 million in 1992 and 1993, respectively, of which FF 57 million and FF 51 million were capitalized as start-up or pre-opening costs.

Future minimum rental commitments under non-cancelable operating leases are as follows:

1993	1994	1995	1996	1997	FF millions thereafter
102	85	55	31	24	51

operates the theme park and the major hotels and indirectly controls the finance companies that own the park and hotels.

The result is that in the 1992 Consolidated balance sheet of the Groupe Euro Disney SCA (the quoted company) the long-term borrowings are shown as FF 6222 million and the total assets as FF 17230. If, however, the financing companies used to fund the development (including Euro Disney SNC) are consolidated with those of Groupe Euro Disney SCA, the long-term borrowing becomes FF 18813, and the total assets FF 27541. The gearing ratio (long-term liabilities/total assets) changes from 36% to 68%. One can see why off-balance sheet financing seems so attractive to the managers of some companies.

The quoted company does not disclose the total borrowing, but it does not hide its future financial obligations. The company is leasing the assets and does disclose its future lease payments (page 34 of the 1992 Annual Report).

The impact of this policy can also be gauged from the statement adjusting the loss as reported under French GAAP, to US GAAP, for the Form 10-K required by the US regulatory authorities. Using French GAAP, a loss of FF 188 million was reported for the year ended 30 September 1992; however, this loss was increased to FF 699 million in the adjustment statement of which FF 350 million related to additional charges arising on the capitalization of leases originally treated as operating leases.

In Germany lease accounting, like a number of other reporting issues is influenced by the laws of taxation. Assets leased under financial leasing contracts are typically not included in tangible fixed assets but recorded in the notes under the heading 'Other financial commitments'. Extract 10.13 from Bayer's 1992 accounts shows the present value of future payments broken down between amounts due in the following year, the next four years and after five years.

In Italy, although capitalization of finance leases is permitted in group accounts it is not commonly used; this may be because tax law forbids its use for individual companies. However, major companies, because they raise funds in international financial markets, may adopt capitalization to reflect international reporting standards. Pirelli does in fact capitalize its finance leases as shown in Extract 10.14.

Extract 10.13 – Bayer AG 1992 accounts, Notes.

OTHER FINANCIAL COMMITMENTS

In addition to provisions, other liabilities and contingent liabilities, certain other financial commitments exist. Those arising from long-term leasing and rental agreements, stated at the present value of future payments, amount to DM 1,002 million, including DM 212 million due in 1993, DM 507 million due in 1994-1997, and DM 283 million due after 1997. Those existing under purchase agreements related to capital expenditure projects amount to DM 751 million.

Extract 10.14 – Pirelli SpA 1992 accounts, Accounting Policies.

Leased assets

All existing lease contracts in the Group are in the nature of financial leases. Consequently, these assets are recorded in fixed assets, in accordance with international accounting practice. Leased assets are therefore capitalized and depreciated over their estimated useful lives; the major part of the lease payment is considered as a financial expense and residual lease payments are recorded as a financial liability.

In the Netherlands similar provisions exist for the treatment of leases as in the UK with a distinction being drawn between finance and operating leases. The terms of the contract as a whole determine whether the leases should be accounted for as finance or operating. General guidelines are given for determining the existence of economic owner-ship and the requirements are broadly in line with IAS 17. In Spain leased assets are required to be capitalizsed when there is no reasonable doubt that the purchase option will be exercised. This seems to be a legal approach and it is not clear, for example, what the position would be if the rental period was extended on payment of a nominal annual rental. Where capitalization takes place the value of the asset and associated liability are included on the balance sheet. The interest element in the lease payments is allocated to appropriate accounting periods and the depreciation provision is on the basis of the useful life of the asset.

Special-Purpose Financial Transactions

In the UK the above term was used to refer to specially structured deals where the full impact of the transactions did not affect the group accounts. They could include instances where companies were effectively subsidiaries but consolidation was avoided or where netting off of liabilities against assets was achieved to avoid full disclosure of liabilities.

With this form of transaction, the account entries do not disclose the commercial reality of what has taken place. The legal position may be captured by the bookeeping entries, but not the commercial reality. For example, a transaction may be entered as a sale, but the 'purchaser' has the opportunity to resell the goods back to the 'original seller'. In effect the purchaser has a put option on the goods. What is in reality a long-term arrangement may be entered as a series of short-term trans-actions. Such transactions cause particular problems for the user of published financial reports whether they be banks or equity investors. In fact in the UK the banks themselves become involved in such trans-actions, and so their own accounts can become as 'managed' as those of their clients.

Part of the problem arises because new forms of financial transaction and financial instruments keep arising, and the accounting rules and procedures are not designed to cover them. Part of the problem is that there is a fundamental disagreement between lawyers and accountants as to how many transactions should be handled. The lawyers claim the accounting treatment should reflect the legal position in the contract. The accountants argue the treatment should reflect the commercial reality. The accountants argue for 'substance over the legal form'.

In this section a number of special-purpose transactions will be con-sidered. It must be remembered, however, that the subjects of finance and accounting are continually changing. In financial circles new and imaginative schemes are continually being created. Accounting standard-setting committees have been examining special purpose transactions that have resulted in off-balance sheet situations. Leasing was once one of the major off- balance sheet techniques, but in a number of countries there are now standards on the subject which have reduced the opportunities for the non-disclosure or limited disclosure of such financing deals. However, as we illustrated earlier, there is no consistency of treatment despite the existence of national and international accounting standards.

It must be remembered that nobody is forcing the parties involved to enter into these transactions: they do so presumably because it is in their financial interests. From an accounting point of view, off-balance sheet financing distorts gearing ratios and return on capital employed calculations. The accounting profession has for some time been considering the matter. In the UK a technical release issued in December 1985 gave guidance on the subject and expressed the opinion that substance should triumph over form in situations of window-dressing and off-balance sheet financing.[9] It is argued that assets and liabilities should be brought together on the balance sheet if this is necessary to give a true and fair view, whether or not the information involved is specifically required by legislation. The Department of Trade and Industry backed this interim guidance given by the profession on the subject.

The preliminary considerations of the ASC on this topic resulted in support for four basic principles. The first is that of global consolidation, which means the consolidation of all entities that are effectively controlled, whatever their main activities. The second is a reiteration of the fact that accounting for transactions should be in accordance with their substance, not their legal form. The third relates to the point that no amount of disclosure in the notes can make up for misleading figures on the balance sheet, and the fourth stipulates that accounting effects should be consistent with economic effects.

Many lawyers, however, were not happy with the guidance that had been given. They believe that the detailed requirements of the Companies Act should not be modified just because accountants believe that to follow the Act would not result in a true and fair view. Following this argument, if the provision of additional information by way of note is sufficient to give a true and fair view, then it is not necessary, in the opinion of the legal profession, to show the transaction on the face of the balance sheet.

In March 1988 the ASC issued an exposure draft (ED 42) on the subject.[10] There were at least three novel aspects about this draft, which is entitled *Accounting for Special-Purpose Transactions*. One is that the ASC attempted to lay down general principles that should be applied to all special-purpose transactions. It made recommendations on the rules that are applicable and should be applied to all off-balance sheet type transactions and financial instruments. It did this rather than attempting to prescribe the accounting treatment for each specific type of special-purpose transaction that at present exists and may be created in the future.

The ASC stated that 'the accounting treatment of a transaction should fairly reflect its commercial effect'. 'It is analysis of the commercial effects flowing from the form of special purpose transaction that will lead to an understanding of their substance.' In other words it is the substance of the transaction that is to be reported. The draft points out that this does not imply that 'accounting measurements should necessarily portray economic values such as current costs or discounted cash flows'. Measurement should not always be based on economic values.[11]

A novel aspect of the draft was in its definitions of an asset and liability. It stated that an asset should be recognized in financial statements if, as a result of past transactions and events, an enterprise will receive and control economic benefits.[12] The important point is that it is not so much the physical asset that is being recognized as the economic benefits that are expected to accrue from it. The benefits must of course be capable of reasonably reliable measurement. This is an important concept, which if accepted as an overall concept in accounting would mean that other accounting standards need to change, for example those dealing with goodwill and merger accounting. A number of parties might have an interest in the benefits; the important issue from the point of view of recognizing the asset in the financial accounts is who controls the benefits. As we have discussed with leasing, one test of who controls the asset is who carries the risks.

'The existence or otherwise of the assets have to be determined by reference to the rights and obligations (including rights and obligations taking effect in the future) resulting from the transaction as a whole and which exists at the balance sheet date.' For example, if a company engages in a transaction with another company and legally the title to an asset is transferred but if the prospects of future benefit, the exposure to inherent risks and the control that is exercisable over the asset are not affected to any significant degree, then it is to be regarded as a refinancing arrangement, and the asset remains in the balance sheet of the controlling company. Such a situation can arise when a manufacturer supplies goods to a dealer 'on consignment', whereby the dealer can return the goods without incurring a loss. Control implies the ability to obtain future benefits or to restrict others' access to them. It may take a variety of forms, and does not have to imply legal control

The same accounting concept can be applied to liabilities. A liability is defined in the draft as 'present obligations of a particular enterprise entailing probable future sacrifices of economic benefits by transferring assets or providing services to other entities in the future'.[13] The term 'present obligations' embraces legal liabilities, but is wider in scope. It includes commitments that may be inferred from its dealings or its general business policies. The event giving rise to the obligation must have already taken place, although the obligation may result in a legal liability only on the happening of some future event.

Accounting has had success in reducing the opportunities for 'managing earnings disclosure'. With leasing, if the lessee is obtaining substantially all the rewards (and risk) that would result if he owned the asset, then the leased asset is to be capitalized. It is only with operating leases that the lease payment is charged to the profit and loss account, with no recognition of the use of the asset in the balance sheet.

The non-consolidation of some subsidiaries and what are known as controlled non-subsidiary companies were a problem in the UK for much of the 1980s. The Companies Act 1985 and the relevant accounting standard recognized that, in certain circumstances, subsidiaries need not be consolidated in group accounts. In addition there was the problem of companies, which in reality are controlled by a parent company, but did not meet the legal definition of a subsidiary. This type of 'off-balance sheet' activity has been restricted by the Companies Act of 1989, which changed the UK definition of a subsidiary. The UK adopted the definition of subsidiary used in most other

EC countries, namely whether one company has effective control of the other company. The previous definition was based on ownership of more than 50% of the shares.

With this old definition one company could control the decisions of another company, but because it did not own over 50% of shares it did not have to consolidate the assets and – more importantly – the debts.

There are many 'creative' techniques. Some of the better known ones include the following.

- **Sale of inventory to a bank,** with the seller having an option to buy the inventory back at a future date. This is a way of speeding up sales – it can be used particularly by companies that have to hold inventory for a length of time before it is ready for sale. It is an alternative to the manufacturer borrowing from a bank on the security of the inventory.
- **Assignment of work in progress.** This technique might be used by a construction company. The company agrees to assign irrevocably all the accounts they will receive on a long-term construction project, and in return the bank would make regular periodic payments to the company.
- **Goods on consignment** – with goods being supplied by a manufacturer to a dealer, on a sale or return basis. In whose accounts does the stock appear? Is the dealer a debtor?
- **Discounting of bills of exchange.** Does a contingent liability arise?
- **Factoring of debts.** A company sells its debts to a factor. Is there a right of recourse? Is a contingent liability disclosed?
- **Securitization.** Similar to the above, is a contingent liability shown?
- **Interest rate and currency rate swaps.** To show the importance of this one item, in 1987 it was estimated that the amount of this business in the major UK banks was £200 million. Of this amount the banks disclosed as contingent liabilities only £20 million, one tenth of the total. The rest of the transactions were not being disclosed. The banks have a contingent liability in that they bring the parties to the transaction together, and if one of the parties defaults, the bank is liable.

Although ED 42 was in the main supported by respondents, two years passed before the ASC progressed further. In fact they were waiting for the finalization of the Companies Bill as this had a significant impact on the subject. As noted above, in the bill the definition of a subsidiary to be included in group accounts was changed from one based on de jure control to one based on de facto control. This affected the treatment of 'non-consolidated subsidiaries'. Because of the time delay the ASC issued a further exposure draft ED 49, *Reflecting the Substance of Transactions in Assets and Liabilities,* in May 1990. The significant changes from ED 42 were to enhance the definition of assets and liabilities, to introduce a new section on control following the Companies Act 1989, and to add detailed mandatory notes setting out the accounting treatment of a number of forms of off-balance sheet finance. Although the exposure draft no longer referred to 'special purpose transactions' and the title of the paper changed, the object remains the same. In defining assets and liabilities ED 49 used wording taken from the IASC's conceptual framework document as follows:

> The essential characteristics of an asset are that it is a resource controlled by the enterprise as a result of past events and from which future economic benefits are expected to flow to the enterprise.[14]

> The essential characteristics of a liability are that it is a present obligation of the enterprise arising from past events the settlement of which is expected to result in an outflow from the enterprise of resources embodying future benefits.[15]

ED 49 also required that assets and liabilities should be accounted for individually with right of set-off only allowed for monetary assets and liabilities. Although the Companies Act 1989 allowed for easier recognition of de facto controlled subsidiaries, ED 49 still found it necessary to include provision for inclusion of 'quasi-subsidiaries' where this was needed to give a true and fair view.

However, the major change from ED 42 was the inclusion of specific 'application notes' intended to be mandatory for the transaction specified and to give guidance on the treatment of similar items. The topics covered were consignment stock, sale and repurchase agreements, factoring of debts, securitized mortgages and loan transfers.

Although it was hoped that ED 49 would quickly produce a standard the ASB which succeeded the ASC shortly after its issue, did not do so. This was probably related to the need for the eventual standard to be consistent with the ASB's *Statement of Principles* and the opposition to the proposals on securitization from the banking industry.

In February 1993 the ASB issued FRED 4 *Reporting the Substance of Transactions.* This contained the general thrust of ED 49 provisions with two major changes. The first introduced linked presentation for particular types of non-recourse finance including securitizations. With the linked presentation for securitization, finance is deducted from the gross value of securitized assets. Thus both total income earning resources and financing are shown, although the presentation emphasizes the limited exposure to loss of this type of transaction. The other change related to the inclusion of detailed situations where items could be offset in the accounts. For example, the offset of amounts denominated in different currencies or bearing interest on different bases was prohibited on the basis that any two offsetting items should exactly eliminate each other.

It was not until April 1994 that FRS 5, *Reporting the Substance of Transactions,* was issued as this book was going to press. The FRS covers four main areas and is drafted in general terms. It seeks to determine the substance of transactions, whether resulting assets and liabilities should be included on the balance sheet, what disclosures are necessary and whether any special-purpose vehicle companies should be consolidated. The FRS also contains the application notes previously referred to covering five specific types of transactions. The FRS broadly carries through the proposal of FRED 4 relating to linked presentation. Where the securitization is carried out through a quasi-subsidiary , then linked presentation should be used in the group accounts. However, if a subsidiary is involved then linked presentation may not be used and the items should be treated as normal assets and liabilities of the group. With regard to offset, FRED 4's proposal to prohibit offset of amounts denominated in different currencies or bearing interest on different bases is relaxed.

The Board has emphasized that it is determined to ensure that the spirit of FRS 5 is applied and to come down heavily on any abuses. To this end the FRS is framed in terms of general principles rather than detailed rules; in this way it can be applied to new schemes as they are produced. However, should new schemes be developed which are beyond the scope of the FRS then the Board has stated that they will be referred to the Urgent Issues Task Force or, if considered necessary, the FRS will be revised. In the UK then, the days of off-balance sheet finance seem numbered. It is difficult to say whether this also applies to other EU countries.

References

1. FRS 4, *Capital Instruments,* December 1993.
2. Ibid., p. 3, para. b.
3. Ibid., p. 10, para. 24
4. Ibid., p. 7, para. 12.
5. Ibid., p. 26, para. 89.
6. TR 603, *Off-Balance Sheet Finance and Window Dressing,* ICAEW, December 1985, para. 5(i).
7. SSAP 21, *Accounting for Leases and Hire Purchase Contracts,* August 1984.
8. IAS 17, *Accounting for Leases,* IASC, September 1982.
9. TR 603.
10. ED 42, *Special Purpose Transactions,* ASC, March 1989.
11. Ibid., para. 57.
12. Ibid., para. 14.
13. Ibid., para. 22.
14. ED 49, *Reflecting the Substance of Transactions in Assets and Liabilities,* ASC, May 1990, para. 53.
15. Ibid., para. 54.

Problems

1. Obtain copies of Cadbury Schweppes and SmithKline Beecham accounts for their latest financial year. Analyse the accounting treatment of equity and debt comparing it with the treatment outlined in the chapter for earlier years. How has the treatment changed? What effect if any, has it had on the calculation of return on equity calculation and gearing ratios?

2. In recent years banks have been securitizing receivables such as mortgage loans and credit card debts. Explain why banks and other financial institutions may wish to follow this policy and the effect it will have on capital ratios.

3. Explain why companies might wish to issue new types of financial instrument and give two examples of new types of issue made in the last few years.

   What problems do these types of issues bring to the measurement of the gearing (leverage) ratio? How has the UK FRS 4, *Capital Instruments*, changed the way in which these capital issues are reported? Comment on whether you think FRS 4 has completely clarified the distinction between debt and equity.

4. Discuss the use of finance and operating leases and the reporting of such leases in the financial statements of European companies. Comment on the problems facing a financial analyst where companies adopt different policies for lease accounting.

11

Revenue Measurement and Extraordinary Items

Objectives

- To examine the nature of revenue and profit in the company context.

- To outline the different approaches to revenue recognition and their significance for profit measurement.

- To discuss the issues concerned with the reporting of corporate profits and their impact on the work of the financial analyst.

- To review how different reporting regimes approach the disclosure of extraordinary/exceptional items.

Introduction

The profit which an enterprise reports each year and the trend in annually reported profits is seen by analysts as a significant figure in assessing the value and future prospects of the enterprise. The FASB's Concepts Statement No I. states:

> The primary focus of financial reporting is information about an enterprise's performance provided by measures of earnings and its components. Investors, creditors and others who are concerned with assessing the prospects for enterprise net cash inflows are especially interested in that information.[1]

Over the lifetime of a business enterprise its total income will be the difference between its cash receipts and cash expenditure. Valuation models would focus on this cash flow stream to arrive at the present value of the enterprise. However, this information is notoriously difficult to estimate and analysts focus on year-by-year profits to confirm their forecasts and as indicators for the future.

Because of the need to focus on annual or shorter trading periods two major accounting issues must be considered. In the first instance it is necessary to allocate the effects of transactions which are not concluded in a single accounting period between the periods concerned. The fundamental accounting concepts of matching and prudence will be used to develop appropriate policies. Examples of these transactions would include inventories and long-term contracts dealt with in Chapter 12. In this chapter we will first of all discuss aspects of revenue recognition and how the revenue derived from activities such as franchising, software licences, etc., should be treated. The second issue examined relates to whether all period transactions should be included in the computation of net profit or loss for the period. One view is that all recorded transactions should be included in the net profit or loss figure while others argue that this figure should not be distorted by abnormal, unusual or non-recurring items. These conflicting views are mirrored in two alternative views of income, the all-inclusive concept and the current operating performance concept. For many years the treatment of so-called extraordinary and exceptional items has been critical as analysts focused on the bottom line profit. Significant changes are now under way in the UK following the issue of FRS 3.

Revenue Recognition

Issues

In many cases revenue will be recognized when a sale has been made and delivery of the goods takes place. In most circumstances these two events will be simultaneous (or almost so) and there will be little doubt in anyone's mind as to when the sale occurs and should be treated as such. However, there are a range of transactions where there is less certainty, for example where goods are sold with after-sales service or long-term contracts which take a number of years to complete. In both these cases some basis for apportioning revenue over a number of years will be used and clearly the methods used will significantly affect the profit profile reported over the extended contract period. In the next section we discuss alternative approaches to revenue recognition.

Analysis

The basic accounting concept relating to revenue recognition is that of realization. As noted above the most common recognition of this is on sale and subsequent delivery to customers. However, where the transaction does not fit the simple trading model of sale and delivery various bases have been adopted to recognize revenue. It should be stressed that there are no universally agreed rules covering all types of transactions. There are different, and not always wholly consistent, rules covering different situations which themselves rely on three approaches to revenue recognition which we will briefly review.

The critical event approach to revenue recognition takes the view that revenue is earned when the most significant decision is made or act performed. The time of sale is the most common basis for recognizing revenue where goods are sold. The time of sale is usually assumed to be when delivery of the goods takes place and thus sale and delivery forms the critical event for most sales of goods and services. In some cases completion of production may be viewed as the critical event, for example where construction contracts are recognized on completion.

On the other hand an accretion approach to revenue recognition recognizes revenue during production (broadly defined) rather than on completion. Long-term contracts where profit is taken on the basis of the proportion of the contract completed would be an example. The accretion method is also applied to royalty and interest income receivable.

The revenue allocation approach combines aspects of both the critical event and accretion approaches. Some transactions are difficult to classify because the ramifications of the sale may extend beyond the original date of sale. Goods are sometimes sold with warranties attached to them for future replacement and/or servicing; an alarm system may be sold on the basis of an initial installation charge and subsequent annual maintenance agreements, or franchise fees may be received covering present and future services to be provided. One way of dealing with these transactions would be to recognize the revenue at the point of sale and make provisions based on estimates of future costs. Another approach would be to allocate revenue over the periods involved based on the matching of revenue with costs and services provided. This approach to revenue recognition probably causes the most problems for the analyst as it involves the use of more subjective methods of revenue allocation than the two previous methods discussed.

Extract 11.1 – BOC Group plc 1993 accounts, Accounting Policies.

Turnover

Turnover is based on the invoiced value of sales and includes the sales value of long-term contracts appropriate to the state of completion. It excludes sales between Group undertakings, VAT and similar sales-based taxes.

It is sometimes very clear from the accounting policy dealing with turnover how a company is recognizing revenue. For example, Extract 11.1 from the BOC Group states that turnover is based on 'invoiced value of sales'.

This extract can be contrasted with the Tiphook policy shown in Extract 11.2 which seems less specific.

Somewhat similar wording is used by Sherwood Computer Services PLC which provides software services, as shown in Extract 11.3.

Where the basis of revenue recognition may not be entirely clear the analyst should examine current assets carefully to check the level of trade debtors, work in progress and similar items. If these are high compared with turnover shown in the profit and loss account it may indicate that some anticipation of revenue is taking place.

Extraordinary Items

Issues

For a number of years the treatment of so-called extraordinary and exceptional items in UK accounts was a matter of some controversy. It seems likely that this matter has been solved as far as the UK is concerned by the introduction of FRS 3, *Reporting Financial Performance*, which became part of standard practice for accounting periods ending on or after 22 June 1993.[2]

As the terms suggest they relate to ways of accounting for unusual transactions. Prior to the introduction of SSAP 6 in 1974 it was common practice for unusual items to be treated as a movement on reserves. In this way companies could exclude from profits calculations unfavourable items on the justification that they were unusual or non-recurring and would be misleading if included in current profits. There was clearly much subjectivity in defining what was unusual and non-recurring and different companies treated similar items in different ways. Examples of the types of items which caused problems were profits and losses on the sale of fixed assets, reorganization costs and termination costs.

SSAP 6, *Extraordinary Items and Prior Year Adjustments*,[3] required, with only a few exceptions, all extraordinary and prior year items to be included in the profit and loss account. It was therefore moving towards a comprehensive income concept of financial reporting. However, so that current performance could be shown separately extraordinary items had to be disclosed separately after profit after tax on ordinary activities. The latter figure was that used to calculate earnings per share and the associated price earnings ratio; these are arguably the most significant figures from the viewpoint of analysts. Earnings per share growth is seen as a key indicator of success and growth in share price and hence there was an incentive to show as good a performance as possible. Unfortunately SSAP 6 did not end the subjectivity and inconsistencies in reporting these items as companies sought to take unfavourable hits below the line as extraordinary items thus not affecting current operating performance and earnings per share. Even after SSAP 6 was revised in 1986 the inconsistencies remained. This may have been thought surprising as definitions were given as follows:

> ***Extraordinary items:*** *are material items which derive from events or transactions that fall outside the ordinary activities of the company and which are therefore expected not to recur frequently or regularly…*

> ***Exceptional items:*** *are material items which derive from events or transactions which fall within the ordinary activities of the company, and which need to be disclosed separately by virtue of their size or incidence if the financial statements are to give a true and fair view[4].*

However, these definitions, which were supported by examples failed to cut out the variety and subjectivity between individual companies. In his book, *Accounting for Growth,*[5] Terry Smith includes two revealing tables reproduced below. Table 11.1 shows companies where more than half of reported profits is represented by extraordinary costs; in some cases these costs are much more than reported profits. These companies reported positive earnings per share figures which in some cases would have been losses, if extraordinary items were taken into account.

TABLE 11.1
Exceptional costs as a percentage of profits

Company	Year	Pre-tax profit £m	Extraordinary costs as % pre-tax profits
Costain Group	1990	5.5	245.5
Saatchi & Saatchi	1990	35.6	216.0
Storehouse	1991	6.2	180.7
Unigate	1991	75.5	125.8
Greenhall Whitley	1990	62.2	91.6
Tootal Group	1990	23.2	67.4
Burton Group	1990	133.1	63.0
Amstrad	1990	43.8	55.3

Source: Smith, Terry, Accounting for Growth, p.66

Revenue Measurement and Extraordinary Items

Table 11.2 shows companies where a high proportion of profits have been contributed by exceptional items. In this case exceptional profits taken above the line have increased reported current operating profits and earnings per share.

TABLE 11.2
Exceptional profits as a percentage of profits

Company	Year	Pre-tax profit £m	Exceptional profits as % pre-tax profits
Stakis	1990	30.6	60.4
Storehouse	1991	6.2	58.1
George Wimpey	1990	43.3	44.1
Daily Mail & General Trust	1990	44.2	40.5
Sears	1991	146.9	37.0

Source: Smith, Terry, Accounting for Growth, p.67

Credibility was also strained by companies including similar items as extraordinary over a considerable number of years. Smith illustrated this with the example of RHM shown in Table 11.3 which showed extraordinary closure costs each year for eight years. How could these costs be regarded as extraordinary?

TABLE 11.3
RHM - extraordinary closure costs

£m	1984	1985	1986	1987	1988	1989	1990	1991
Extraordinary closure costs (£m)	14	15	12	20	21	14	24	11
Post-tax profits (£m)	45	44	59	74	105	125	93	105
Ratio %	31	34	20	27	20	11	26	10

Source: Smith, Terry, Accounting for Growth, p.68

Analysis

The introduction of FRS 3 in the UK has made a major change to accounting reporting practice and in particular to the treatment of extraordinary items and earnings per share. It has superseded SSAP 6 (Revised), *Extraordinary Items and Prior Year Adjustments* and amended SSAP 3, *Earnings per Share.*

In future extraordinary items will be very rare. FRS 3 states:

Extraordinary items are extremely rare as they relate to highly abnormal events or transactions that fall outside the ordinary activities of a reporting entity and which are not expected to recur. In view of the extreme rarity of such items no examples are provided.[6]

It seems that the authors of FRS 3 could not envisage an extraordinary item and in an early article two practitioners conclude:

We have not yet come across any transactions or other events that we believe should give rise, under FRS 3, to extraordinary profits or losses in the profit and loss account, and like the ASB we are unable to envisage any. We believe that the ASB has, in effect, abolished the extraordinary item – a move that we support.[7]

FRS 3 has introduced a layered format to be used in the profit and loss account so that important components of financial performance are given prominence This approach, which is illustrated in Figure 11.1, emphasizes:

(i)   the results of continuing operations (including the results of acquisitions);

(ii)   the results of discontinued operations;

(iii)   profits or losses on the sale or termination of an operation, costs of a fundamental reorganization or restructuring and profits or losses on the disposal of fixed assets;

(iv)   extraordinary items.[8]

FIGURE 11.1

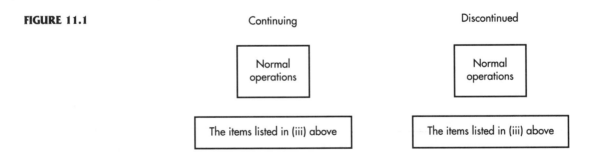

Continuing

Discontinued

Normal operations

Normal operations

The items listed in (iii) above

The items listed in (iii) above

Extraordinary items - being unusual
items outside ordinary activities

The major change to the presentation of financial performance arises in part from the failure of SSAP 6 to achieve the objective of narrowing the difference and variety of accounting practice in this area. As the previous tables suggest preparers seemed on occasion to be using the extraordinary classification to charge expenditure so that it would not adversely affect the reported earnings per share. The ASB also wished to get away from what may have been seen to be an over-preoccupation with a single performance indicator.

The Board believes that the performance of complex organisations cannot be summarized in a single number and has therefore adopted an information set approach that highlights a range of important components of performance.[9]

No serious analyst of accounts would disagree with these sentiments but as the Board also noted:

This approach inevitably means that financial statements will sometimes appear more complex than under the former standard.[10]

Although the new approach does mean that inconsistencies inherent in the subjectivity allowed by the SSAP 6 approach will no longer apply, it seems likely that the all-inclusive approach to earnings per share calculation will lead to greater volatility in its value over time. It could be said that a major discretionary source of income smoothing available to corporate management has been removed. This view was confirmed by the chairman of GKN plc in his report with the 1992 accounts. When discussing the implications of FRS 3 he suggests:

It is certain that under the new format the figures disclosed as pre-tax profits and earnings will be more volatile in the future .

While the provisions of FRS 3 can be regarded as realistic and constructive there are difficulties in using the resulting all-inclusive earnings per share figure for making comparisons over time and between companies and as a basis for calculating price/earnings ratios. The significance of information provided for and on the various databases will also be an issue.

What is the position with regard to the reporting of extraordinary items in other countries? In the financial reports of French companies the extraordinary items sections present some problems for the analyst. One difficulty is that the French have one word 'exceptionnel', which is used to describe both extraordinary and exceptional items. Items appearing as 'exceptionnel' may include tax depreciation in excess of economic depreciation and profits and losses on sales of non-financial. assets such as property, plant and equipment. Unfortunately the degree of analysis of 'exceptional' items is variable with some companies giving full details and explanations and others giving little more than a single figure for income and expense. However, earnings per share calculations use income after allowing for any 'exceptionnel' items. Extract 11.4 shows the profit and loss account of L'Oréal and the earnings per share calculation. Although no specific reference is made to the term 'extraordinary', earnings per share is calculated on 'net profit before capital gains and losses after minority interests'. Below the line are capital gains and a charge for restructuring costs; this would be similar to the UK position before FRS 3.

The German Commercial Code (HGB) defines extraordinary income or expense as those amounts incurred outside the regular activities of a company (s.277(4),HGB.) This is a rather loose definition and a com-

CONSOLIDATED PROFIT AND LOSS ACCOUNT FOR THE YEARS ENDED DECEMBER 31, 1991, 1990 AND 1989

(FF thousands)	1991	1990	1989
Net sales	**33,444,638**	**30,359,549**	**27,169,787**
Variation in stocks of finished products	133,944	55,751	290,752
Production converted into fixed assets	49,457	64,262	50,105
Production for the year	33,632,039	30,479,562	27,510,644
Purchases	8,583,973	8,189,130	7,587,828
Variation in stocks of finished products, raw materials and supplies	60,988	– 188,709	– 121,696
External charges	11,918,591	10,693,798	9,750,942
Purchases used in production	20,563,552	18,694,219	17,217,074
Added value	**13,068,487**	**11,785,343**	**10,293,570**
Taxes	– 557,466	– 553,333	– 483,479
Personnel costs	– 7,369,971	– 6,787,801	– 6,102,111
(Charges to)/reversals of provisions - net	– 356,883	– 67,287	+ 15,186
Depreciation	– 1,192,543	– 1,153,844	– 878,812
Royalties from patents and trademarks (paid) received	+ 1,301	– 43,363	– 13,269
Other operating income - net	+ 24,766	+ 213,851	+ 98,001
Operating expense - net	– 9,450,796	– 8,391,777	– 7,364,484
Operating profit	**3,617,691**	**3,393,566**	**2,929,086**
Group's share of profit/(loss) of joint ventures	– 7,691	– 2,398	– 742
Interest expense - net	+ 331,974	– 181,711	– 95,165
(Charges to)/reversals of financial provisions - net	– 32,450	+ 6,389	– 53,657
Exceptional expense - net	– 79,485	– 83,126	– 54,195
Charges to exceptional provisions - net	– 473,384	– 87,358	– 48,424
Group's share of profits of associated companies	+ 98,866	+ 47,404	+ 34,878
Profit before tax, employee profit-sharing and capital gains and losses	**3,455,521**	**3,092,767**	**2,711,781**
Employee profit-sharing	– 155,108	– 136,162	– 119,932
Company taxation	– 1,137,292	– 1,128,349	– 1,050,169
Net profit before capital gains and losses and minority interest	**2,163,121**	**1,828,256**	**1,541,680**
Gains on disposals of fixed assets - net	+ 407,513	+ 5,246	+ 747,086
(Charge to)/reversal of provision for tax claim	–	+ 272,081	– 388.000
Restructuring costs	– 186,394	– 87,674	–
Net loss - Lanvin	–	– 61,600	–
Net profit before minority interests	**2,384,240**	**1,956,309**	**1,900,766**
Minority interests	– 228,871	– 140,206	– 96,054
Net profit	**2,155,369**	**1,816,103**	**1,804,712**
EARNINGS PER SHARE			
Net profit before capital gains and losses, after minority interests (FF thousands)	**2,018,483**	**1,686,524**	**1,464,390**
Number of shares outstanding (adjusted for investment certificates and convertible debentures)	58,190,305	58,148,682	58,136,970
Earnings per share (FF)	**34.7**	**29.0**	**25.2**

mon interpretation and practice of what exactly is to be understood by extraordinary has not yet been achieved. However, there seems to be an increasing acceptance of the Anglo-American view of extraordinary, although in the UK case FRS 3 has caused a complete rethink of extraordinary items. As we have seen they have in effect virtually been abolished! In Germany extraordinary items are characterized by non-recurring events resulting in significant amounts. Results of a recurring nature, for example gains or losses from the disposal of fixed assets, would be regarded as ordinary items unless they were very high amounts. There is, therefore, a degree of subjectivity which the user must be aware of when analysing German accounting statements. Extract 11.5 shows the Consolidated Statement of Income for Daimler-Benz. Although there is no extraordinary figure for 1992 there is for 1991. Presumably Daimler-Benz's headline earnings is the 'Results from Ordinary Business Activities'. We say presumably because there is no reference to earnings per share in the report. There is a section in the report on the performance of the Daimler-Benz share but although details of share price, dividend and return are shown and discussed in some detail no reference is made to earnings per share. There is also a ten-year summary of results which also contains no reference to earnings per share. This would not be the case in the UK and other countries where prominence is given to growth in earnings per share over time. It is also not possible to identify what items are treated as extraordinary; the relevant note for 1991 merely shows extraordinary income of DM490 million and expenses of DM1034 million to give the charge of DM544 million shown in the income statement.

Italian accounting statements are probably the least familiar to those used to dealing with UK or US statements. Pirelli, for example, discloses substantial extraordinary items before taxation; in fact there is no calculation or indeed mention of earnings per share in the financial report. The extraordinary items for 1991 include substantial charges for non-recurring expenses, reorganization expenses and costs of the abortive link up with Continental. Disclosure of the extraordinary item is automatic following the profit and loss account format of both the former and new law. The major difference with UK presentation prior to FRS 3 is that in Italy extraordinary items are above the line. Extract 11.6(a) shows Pirelli's 1991 income statement and 11.6(b) the note on extraordinary items.

Under Dutch law income and expenses arising from extraordinary activities are required to be shown separately from those arising from ordinary activities. Extraordinary income and expenses are defined as those items arising otherwise than in the ordinary course of the company's business; this may include income and expenses arising from transactions and events which are of a non-recurring nature and which also fall outside the company's ordinary activities. Examples of extraordinary items would be gains or losses on the disposal of interests in other companies or assets, charges arising from reorganizations or discontinued business. In Holland earnings per share calculations are based on net income after taking into consideration extraordinary items. Extract 11.7 shows the 1991 statement of earnings and note relating to extraordinary items for VNU, a Dutch publishing company. This company also includes a ten-year financial summary which shows earnings per share based on the bottom line net earnings figure. Extraordinary items include losses on discontinued operations and gains on sales of assets.

Extract 11.5 – Daimler-Benz AG 1992 accounts, Consolidated Statement of Income.

	Notes	1992 In Millions of DM	1991 In Millions of DM
Sales	(22)	**98,549**	**95,010**
Increase in Inventories and Other Capitalized In-House Output	(23)	2,330	3,556
Total Output		**100,879**	**98,566**
Other Operating Income	(24)	4,506	3,545
Cost of Materials	(25)	(49,084)	(49,456)
Personnel Expenses of which for Old-Age Pensions DM 1,539 million (1991: DM 1,511 million)	(26)	(32,003)	(29,372)
Amortization of Intangible Assets, Depreciation of Fixed Assets and of Leased Eqipment	(27)	(7,085)	(5,977)
Other Operating Expenses	(28)	(15,254)	(13,824)
Income from Affiliated, Associated and Related Companies	(29)	118	56
Interest Income	(30)	577	623
Write-Downs of Financial Assets and of Securities	(31)	(121)	(134)
Results from Ordinary Business Activities		**2,533**	**4,027**
Extraordinary Result	(32)	–	(544)
Income Taxes	(33)	(586)	(1,039)
Other Taxes	(33)	(496)	(502)
Net Income	(34)	**1,451**	**1,942**
Profit Carried Forward from Previous Year		2	8
Transfer to Retained Earnings		(816)	(1,275)
Income Applicable to Minority Shareholders		(184)	(99)
Loss Applicable to Minority Shareholders		151	29
Dividend (1991: Unappropriated Profit) of Daimler-Benz AG		**604**	**605**

Under disclosure requirements in Spain extraordinary items are shown after computation of the operating or trading income but before any taxation charge. The tax charge is shown as a single item without distinguishing between the ordinary and extraordinary contribution. Extraordinary items include gains or losses in selling fixed assets, extraordinary profits or expenses that are not reasonably expected in relation to the ordinary activity of the firm and asset revaluation adjustments. Once again earnings per share are calculated on the net income after tax which is also after allowing for any extraordinary items.

Consolidated statements of income

(historical cost)

(in millions of lire)

	notes	Year ended Dec. 31, 1991		Year ended Dec. 31, 1990	
Value of production		10,519,262		10,603,816	
– Revenues from sales and services	13		10,023,763		10,139,469
– Other revenues and operating income			269,494		222,115
– Stock change in semifinished, work in progress, finished products and additions to fixed assets	14		226,005		242,232
Production costs		(9,716,192)		(9,677,010)	
– Costs of raw materials, supplies and goods for resale including stock change	15		(4,778,986) f		(4,721,726) f
– Cost of services and other expenses	16		(2,044,906)		(2,164,912)
– Personnel costs	17		(2,892,300)		(2,790,372)
Operating profit before depreciation, amortization and write-downs		**803,070**		**926,806**	
Depreciation, amortization and write-downs		(585,176)		(456,924)	
– Amortization of intangible assets			(40,059)		(37,297)
– Depreciation of fixed assets			(470,595) g		(416,707) g
– Write-downs of current assets			(17,206)		2,906
– Provision for risks and other expenses			(57,316)		(5,826)
Gross operating profit		**217,894**		**469,882**	
Financial income and expenses	18	(337,300)		(300,515)	
– On investments			11,637		14,196
– Other financial income			219,434 h		196,693 h
– Interest and other financial expenses			(568,371)		(511,404)
Valuation adjustments to investments		5,779		13,685	
Extraordinary items	19	(567,538) i		64,773 i	
Income before income taxes		**(681,165)**		**247,825**	
Income taxes		(48,128)		(143,982)	
Net income (loss) for the year		**(729,293)** l		**103,843** l	
Group's share		**(622,471)** m		**99,753** m	
Minority interest's share		**(106,822)** n		**4,090** n	

Current value data

Production costs					
– Costs of raw materials, supplies and goods for resale including stock image			(4,749,081) f		(4,689,530) f
Depreciation, amortization and write-downs					
– Depreciation of fixed assets			(525,247) g		(486,315) g
Financial income and expenses					
– Other financial income			261,981 h		304,048 h
Extraordinary items		(575,457) i		43,845 i	
Net income (loss) for the year		(719,412) l		152,858 l	
Group's share		(618,648) m		139,436 m	
Minority interest's share		(100,764) n		13,422 n	

19. Extraordinary items

These comprise the following:

	(in millions of lire)	
	1991	**1990**
Nonrecurring income	17,580	10,853
Nonrecurring expenses	(89,177)	(50,649)
Reorganization expenses*	(240,433)	–
Continental costs*	(336,796)	–
Other non-operating expenses	(32,518)	(16,742)
Other non-operating income	45,315	40,432
Miscellaneous expenses/income (net)	38,491	80,879
Utilization of provision for risks and expenses	30,000	–
	(567,538)	**64,773**

* Reorganization expenses regard operational rationalization programs to eliminate business areas which are in a loss position, in order
to strengthen other areas and reduce general expenses. They may be analyzed as follows:

	(in billions of lire)
— Tyre Sector	166
— Cable Sector	56
— Diversified Products Sector and other activities	18

The costs relating to the Continental operation - of which Lire 299 billion were incurred by the subsidiary Sipir Finance N.V. (The Netherlands) and
Lire 38 billion by Pirelli Tyre Holding N.V. (The Netherlands) - may be analyzed as follows:

	(in billions of lire)
— losses, options and legal, consulting and financial fees (of which Lire 68 billion recorded in the first half 1991)	168
— indemnities to investors	138
— write-down of the Continental investment held by Pirelli Tyre Holding N.V. (The Netherlands)	31

The indemnities to investors may be analyzed as follows:

— Finstahl S.A. (Falck Group)	8.4
— Italmobiliare International B.V.	13.0
— Inverban S.A. (Rocca Group)	47.6
— Mediobanca S.p.A.	55.7
— Sal. Oppenheim Jr. & Cie	12.8

The reorganization expenses and the expenses relating to the Continental operation attributable to minority interests are Lire 54.0 billion and Lire
11.8 billion, respectively.

Nonrecurring income relates to grants from government agencies, insurance reimbursements, accounting adjustments for
accruals, etc.
The other non-operating expenses and income include expenses concerning environmental protection, entertainment,
association dues, benefits, sundry losses, sundry revenues, utilization of various provisions, sundry gains and other
non-operating items.

The miscellaneous expenses/income (net) include gains or losses on the disposal of fixed assets (including the gain of Lire
10.5 billion relating to the sale of land in St. Maurice/Pirelli Cables France). The utilization of the provision for risks and
expenses of Lire 30 billion relates to nonrecurring expenses of Fintrasporti S.p.A. in particular; the balance of this account
after utilization is Lire 93 billion.

i) - **Current costs** - The balance of gains on the disposal of fixed assets when calculated on the current costs of the assets disposed of, is Lire 7,919
million lower compared with the historical costs of such assets (in 1990 Lire 20,928 million). Therefore, the balance of nonrecurring income and
expenses at current cost amounts 14,1991 is a negative figure of Lire 575,457 million, whereas in 1990 the amount of Lire 43,845 million was a
positive figure.

YEARS ENDED DECEMBER 31, 1991 AND 1990
Thousands of guilders

	1991	in %	1990	in %
Net revenues	2,734,830		2,717,545	
Change in stocks of work-in-process inventories	(3,404)		(3,939)	
	2,731,426	100.0	2,713,606	100.00
Raw materials	927,867	34.0	904,991	33.4
Purchased services	191,940	7.0	213,065	7.9
Personnel costs	863,695	31.6	833,400	30.7
Depreciation and amortization	122,671	4.5	97,622	3.6
Other operating expenses	434,703	15.9	440,777	16.2
Total operating costs and expenses	2,540,876	93.0	2,489,855	91.8
Operating income	190,550	7.0	223,751	8.2
Interest income	39,318	1.4	39,031	1.5
Income of non-consolidated subsidiaries	11,819	0.4	6,072	0.2
Interest expense	(46,580)	(1.7)	(32,995)	(1.2)
Results of financial income and expenses	4,557	0.1	12,108	0.5
Results of ordinary activities before income taxes	195,107	7.1	235,859	8.7
Income taxes	(75,038)	(2.7)	(84,745)	(3.1)
Results of ordinary activities after income taxes	120,069	4.4	151,114	5.6
Extraordinary items before income taxes	(3,938)		(27,760)	
Income taxes	505		22,739	
Extraordinary items after income taxes	(3,433)	(0.1)	(5,021)	(0.2)
Net earnings	116,636	4.3	146,093	5.4

EXTRAORDINARY ITEMS
Thousands of guilders

	1991	1990
Provision for discontinued operations	(7,540)	(54,032)
Gain on sale of real estate	3,211	147
Gain on sale of subsidiaries	391	1,372
Transfer from equalization account investment premiums	—	24,753
	(3,938)	(27,760)
Income tax effects	505	22,739
	(3,433)	(5,021)

We can see that in some countries the problems of classifying items as extraordinary may have been less acute because of the way in which earnings per share has been calculated, or indeed because less attention is paid to this figure. An all-inclusive approach to profit measurement has been used in some cases with earnings after extraordinary items used as a basis for computing earnings per share. Perhaps in some countries, for example Germany, there were other ways of smoothing income through the adjustment of reserves and provisions; perhaps also headline indicators such as earnings per share are less important in countries where the stockmarket has less significance and informal channels of communication exist between companies and their financiers.

However, in many countries the final earnings per share figure is used as a key indicator and along with the allied price earnings ratio figures prominently in published financial data. This continues to be the case despite attempts by accounting regulators to play down the significance of these figures.

These potential problems were recognized by the Institute of Investment Management and Research (the UK professional organization for investment analysts). The Institute identifies two purposes of reported earnings which they consider are of most practical importance to most users of financial statements:

- as a measure of the company's maintainable earning capacity, suitable in particular as a basis for forecasts and for inter-year comparisons, and for use on a per share basis in the calculation of the price/earnings ratio;
- as a factual 'headline' figure for historic earnings which can be a benchmark figure for the trading outcome for the year.[11]

The Institute considers that the calculation of maintainable earnings requires judgements and estimations by analysts and, because of this subjectivity, attempts to standardize its calculation are bound to fail. Indeed it is the skill with which analysts exercise the necessary judgments which makes their work of value to clients.

On the other hand the desirability of an unambiguous and standardized 'headline' earnings figure which was acceptable to and understood by users was considered possible and desirable. The revised 'headline' earnings figure could be used in addition to the bottom line figure required by FRS 3; the value of such a figure lies in the consistent and unambiguous method of calculation which is important where markets will often be reacting rapidly to new information. In fact some UK companies are now providing this additional earnings information which is being published in databases and is also used in the calculation of published P/E ratios in *The Financial Times* and other important sources of information. The main characteristics required of the headline figure are that it should measure trading performance, be capable of consistent and straightforward calculation and be based on facts.

These main points which the Institute has sought to cover in its recommendation are as follows.

1. All trading profits and losses for the year (including interest) should be included in earnings; abnormal trading items should be included but identified separately in a note if significant.
2. Profits and losses of operations discontinued or acquired during the year should be included in earnings.
3. Profits or losses on the sale or termination of a discontinued operation should be excluded.
4. Any profits or losses on the sale of fixed assets or businesses or arising on their permanent diminution in value should be excluded. However, this does not apply to any assets acquired for resale, such as marketable securities.[12]

Appendix 11.1 to this chapter gives an example of a calculation of headline earnings in line with IIMR recommendations.

In fact similar recommendations were published earlier in both Germany and Italy. The German financial analyst group (DVFA) have been issuing recommendations for a number of years. The latest advice published in 1991 was the result of cooperation between the DVFA and the working group on external company accounts of the Schmalen-bach-Gesellschaft (SG.)[13]

The calculation of earnings according to the DVFA method has been extensively applied by German companies and financial analysts as a basis for comparing earnings since 1968 and has become part of their information policy. The new German accounting law incorporating the provisions of the Fourth and Seventh Directives came into effect in the FRG on 1 January 1986. For financial years beginning after 31 December 1989 the new regulations are mandatory and this has resulted in significant changes in German accounting practice. The DVFA and SG have now joined together to publish revised joint recommendations for determining earnings, the objectives of which are to:

- take into account the knowledge gained from the practical application of the new accounting law;
- integrate the new regulations for consolidated financial statements to an increased extent; and in particular
- remove the coexistence of different recommendations for the determination of earnings.

The adjustments seek to make allowance for factors which are extraordinary, exceptional or which relate to the application of accounting options. In this way it is hoped that the adjusted earnings figure will provide a better basis for identifying a single company's earnings trends over time, making comparisons between companies and providing a starting point for estimating future earnings. Uniformity in the calculation of the net profit disclosed is seen as the main aim of the recommendation. Despite the adjustments it is recognized that international comparability will still be impaired by different national accounting regulations and practices; the interrelation of commercial accounts and tax accounts in Germany is an example.

The Italian Analysts Association (AIAF) recommendations have a shorter history than the German. A project was started in 1988 but it was not until November 1992 that a paper emerged.[14] This paper was to a large extent derived from the earlier work undertaken by the German analysts' association. The actual recommendations and pro forma adjustment statements are very detailed and it must be asked whether they may be perhaps too ambitious. The report states that:

> The AIAF earnings can be obtained in part from the published annual report and mostly from the additional information that the company may supply on request.[15]

Will companies be willing to supply this extra information? If not then we are left with the published reports and the analysts' skills.

Although the rationale of FRS 3 is supported, reporting UK companies are by no means convinced that the resulting EPS figure is useful either as a performance indicator or for use in the P/E multiple. If **all** companies were to publish headline EPS figures in line with the IIMR recommendations and these figures were used in **all** databases then consistency should be achieved. However, early indications show that only one third of large UK companies are providing EPS figures additional to the FRS 3 figure. Additionally many of these are based on companies' own adjustments, presumably to bring the EPS more in line with previous years' reported figures. In view of the current variation in policy, earnings per share and their associated P/E ratios will need to be treated with caution by analysts. It could be that in the short term at least there will be less consistency in the production of these figures than the position prior to the introduction of FRS 3.

In addition to specifying how the profit and loss account information should be presented, FRS 3 requires three additional pieces of information to be included in the financial statements as follows.

- **Note of historical cost profits and losses.**[16] This note is required where there is a material difference between the result disclosed in the profit and loss account and what the result would have been on a pure historical cost basis. The note should be presented immediately after the profit and loss account or the statement of total recognized gains and losses (see below.) The purpose of this note is to show the effect of past revaluations on the current year's results and what they would have been had those revaluations not occurred.
- **Statement of total recognized gains and losses.**[17] This is referred to as a 'primary statement' which should be given the same prominence as other primary statements. The information to be shown is the total recognized gains and losses attributable to shareholders showing the individual gains and losses. It should be noted that the immediate write-off to reserves of purchased goodwill is not a recognized loss. The aim of this statement is to highlight the change in shareholders' funds arising from all gains or losses recognized during the period including items not passing through the profit and loss account. This would include revaluation surpluses taken directly to reserves and similar items.

- **Reconciliation of movements in shareholders' funds**.[18] This shows a complete summary of changes in shareholders' funds for the period under review. It will include the final result shown in the profit and loss account and information contained in the statement of total recognized gains and losses; in addition items such as new share issues, goodwill written off against reserves and any other items affecting shareholders' funds will be disclosed.

These additional statements along with the revised format and disclosures of the profit and loss account aim to provide financial analysts and other users with a broader range of information on which to base an assessment of the company under review. A positive by-product might be the de-emphasizing of the 'bottom-line' profit figure. This could lead to less attention being given by both preparers and users to short-term changes in earnings per share and more attention being given to the longer-term effects of investment and other policy decisions.

Earnings per share continues to be a significant accounting number in many countries with the associated P/E ratio and dividend yield being the financial ratios given most prominence in the financial press worldwide. In this section we have tended to concentrate on this aspect because of its continuing importance. Although FRS 3 has introduced important changes to financial reporting in the UK other countries remain unchanged in their treatment of extrordinary items.

Categorization of certain items

Appendix 11.1. Extract from IIMR Recommendations

	Headline earnings – in or out	Tax and minority information required by FRS 3 or not
Profit or losses on the sale or termination of an operation	Out	Yes
Profits or losses on the disposal (including expropriation) of fixed assets	Out	Yes
Amortization of goodwill	Out	See note above
Costs of reorganizing or restructuring having a material effect on the nature and focus of the reporting entity's continuing operations	In	n/a
Costs of non-fundamental reorganization	In	n/a
Abortive bid costs	In	n/a
Bid defence costs	Out	No
One-off costs of complying with major new legislation	In	n/a
Litigation costs (whether a hazard of normal business or abnormal)	In	n/a

Diminution in value of fixed assets	Out	No
Diminution in value of current assets	In	n/a
Profit or loss on capital reorganization of long-term debt	Out	No
One-off charge or credit relating to a pension fund deficiency or surplus	In	n/a
Profits or losses on disposal of trade investments	Out	No
Profits or losses on disposal of investments held for resale	In	n/a

IIMR headline earnings – an example

This appendix first of all sets out an example of a published profit and loss account; this is an extension of the example set out on page 43 of FRS 3. This extract includes a figure for earnings per share according to the rules laid down in FRS 3.

Companies are permitted to show an additional earnings per share figure if they wish, providing it is reconciled to the FRS 3 figure. In this example it is assumed that the company has chosen the IIMR headline figure for this calculation. The table of adjustments on page 28 provides the elements for the necessary reconciliation.

Extract from published accounts

	Continuing Operations	Acqui-sitions	Discontinued Operations	Total	Total
	1993	1993	1993	1993	1992 as restated
	£ million	£ million	£ million	£ million	£ million
Turnover	550	50	175	775	690
Cost of sales	(415)	(40)	(165)	(620)	(555)
Gross profit	135	10	10	155	135
Net operating expenses	(85)	(4)	(25)	(114)	(83)
Less 1992 provision			10	10	
Operating profit	50	6	(5)	51	52
Loss on disposal of discontinued operations			(17)	(17)	
Less 1992 provision			20	20	
Provision for loss on operations to be discontinued	(1)			(1)	(30)
Restructuring costs	(2)			(2)	
Profit on sale of properties	12			12	6
Profit on ordinary activities before interest	59	6	(2)	63	28

Interest payable	(18)	(15)
Profit on ordinary activities before taxation	45	13
Tax on profit on ordinary activities	(14)	(4)
Profit on ordinary activities after taxation	31	9
Minority interests	(2)	(2)
Profit for the financial year	29	7
Dividends	(8)	(1)
Retained profit for the financial year	21	6
Earnings per share (74 358 974 shares in issue)	**39p**	**10p**
Adjustments for IIMR calculation (as in the following reconciliation)	(19p)	xp
IIMR headline earnings per share	**20p**	**yp**

IIMR Headline earnings – adjustments for 1993

	Notes	Profits on ordinary activities	Tax	Minority interests	Profit
		£ million	£ million	£ million	£ million
Per accounts	(1)	45	(14)	(2)	29
Adjustments					
Less 1992 provision	(2)	(10)	3	–	(7)
Exceptional items:					
Loss on disposal of discontinued operations	(3)	17	(5)	–	12
Less 1992 provision	(4)	(20)	6	–	(14)
Provision for loss on operations to be discontinued	(5)	1	–	–	1
Profit on sale of properties	(6)	(12)	3	1	(8)
Goodwill amortization	(7)	2	–	–	2
Total adjustments (per share 19p)					(14)
IIMR headline earnings	23	(7)	(1)		**£15m**
IIMR headline earnings per share					**20p**

Notes

1. Figures as shown in the published profit and loss account as 'profit on ordinary activities'.
2. This adjustment is in respect of the provision made in the 1992 accounts in respect of loss on operations to be discontinued and relates only to the operating losses of the operations in the 1993

financial year up to the date of the termination/sale (and not the direct costs of termination/sale).

3. As shown in the published profit and loss account.
4. This adjustment is similar to that described in Note 2 above: in this case it relates to a provision made in the 1992 accounts in respect of the loss on disposal of operations discontinued in 1993.
5. This adjustment relates to the provision made in the 1993 financial year in respect of loss on an operation to be discontinued in the next financial year – 1994. This provision, when released in 1994, will be adjusted for in arriving at 1994 IIMR headline earnings.
6. As shown in the published profit and loss account.
7. It is assumed that this charge to the profit and loss account is disclosed in the notes to the accounts.
8. It is assumed that the associated tax credit or charge and also the minority charge in respect of each adjustment are disclosed in the notes to the accounts as required by FRS 3.
9. It is assumed that a review of the remaining exceptional items (i.e. those other than those disclosed on the face of the profit and loss account) do not necessitate any further adjustment to the headline earnings figure.

The reference to IIMR headlines earnings

The IIMR headline earnings as calculated in the example above can include in the total certain abnormal items disclosed by the company under paragraph 19 of FRS 3. These items are not, in the example above, shown on the face of the profit and loss account (although FRS 3 requires their presence on the face of the profit and loss account if they affect the true and fair view). For the present purposes, it is assumed that several such abnormal items are included in the notes, of which one – the cost of company reorganization on the creation of the Single European Market (£1.2 million or £0.8 million net of tax) – is of significant size. In addition, of the items disclosed on the face of the profit and loss account in accordance with paragraph 20 of FRS 3, one (restructuring costs of £2 million or £1.3 million net of tax) is included in IIMR headline earnings and is of significant size.

Earnings should then be referred to as follows:

The company's IIMR headline earnings for the year were £15million after abnormal items of £1.3 million in respect of the restructuring of certain continuing operations and £0.8 million in respect of company reorganization on the creation of the Single European Market.

Such a reference might appear in a research department's report on a company, or in the report provided by a statistical company. Such a reference could also appear in a company report or preliminary statement, should the company choose to adopt the IIMR headline earnings figure.

Note that the **prominent display** of the abnormal items is only of those items included in the earnings calculation. The amounts excluded from the headline figure on grounds of principle are not mentioned in this immediate context, as it will not be supposed that they are included. If they are important, they will be mentioned as a separate part of the report or analysis.

References

1. SFAC No. 1, *Objectives of Financial Reporting by Business Enterprises.*
2. FRS 3, *Reporting Financial Performance,* October 1992.
3. SSAP 6 *Extraordinary Items and Prior Year Adjustments,* revised August 1986.
4. Ibid., paras. 28–30.
5. Smith, T. (1992) *Accounting for Growth,* Century Business, London.
6. FRS 3, p. 29, para. 48.
7. Wild, K. and Woodhead, C. (1993) 'Between the lines of FRS 3', *Accountancy,* July, 92–94.
8. FRS 3, p. 3, para. b.
9. Ibid., p. 5l, para. lll.
10. Ibid., p. 5l, para. iii.
11. *The Definition of Headline Earnings,* Statement of Investment Practice No. 1, Institute of Investment Management and Research, September 1993, p. 5, para. iv.
12. Ibid., p. 7, para. x.
13. Earnings according to the DVFA/SG method, 1991.
14. Calculation of adjusted earnings according to the AIAF method, November 1992.
15. Ibid., p. 2.
16. FRS 3, p. 16, para. 26
17. Ibid., p. 16, para. 27.
18. Ibid., p. 16, para. 28

Problems

1. Both companies, as suppliers of information, and financial analysts, as users of information, have been criticized for putting too much emphasis on the 'bottom line' earnings figure. Discuss the reasons for this and whether the introduction of FRS 3 *Reporting Financial Performance* in the UK will change this situation. Your answer should include reference to the information FRS 3 requires to be given.

2. Use Extracts 11.4, 11.5, 11.6 and 11.7 to compute in each case the profit figure on which a meaningful earnings per share might be based; you should try and achieve consistency in your approach. Comment on the extent to which your approach might differ from FRS 3 and draw attention to any assumptions made and further information you would require to achieve greater accuracy and consistency.

3. Obtain a copy of a quoted UK company's financial report. (You can do this either by writing to the company or using the service offered by *The Financial Times*.) Analyse the information given by the profit and loss account and the other statements included. Comment on how an analyst might use the information in forecasting future earnings of the company.

4. Compare the income statements shown in Extracts 11.4, 11.5, 11.6 and 11.7 with a UK company's profit and loss account (obtained as in problem 3 above). What are the main differences in presentation and information given? Devise a uniform statement which would enable you to present the statements together for comparative purposes.

5. Advanced Information Design (AID) plc market computer systems. The company offers their customers a comprehensive service, providing the computer hardware, preparing software to meet the customers' specific IT requirements, installing the equipment and the system, and carrying out all the necessary maintenance activity. Although specific contracts vary with the scale of the customers' needs a typical contract is made up as follows:

Hardware costs	£39 600
Software costs	£30 800
Installation costs	£48 400

Annual maintenance costs £33 000 p.a. after the first year.*

* Note that maintenance costs of £33 000 in the first year are included in the installation costs.

In addition, the company has to meet its administrative overhead, currently £600 000 but expected to rise in line with total business activity.

In order to keep arrangements with customers simple, AID uses a standard legal agreement, which for a typical contract would require the customer to pay £132 000 in the first year and £44 000 in the second year. The customer would be guaranteed the option of extending the contract for up to two further years at an annual fee of £44 000. At the end of this time, subsequent fees would be negotiable but AID's experience had shown that nearly all customers are ready to undertake a substantial update at that time.

Following a sales campaign, operations have risen to the current level of 100 contracts per annum and further expansion at 30% per annum compound is anticipated. The success of the business was a major consideration in deciding to go ahead with the flotation and public quotation.

The company considers that its published results will play an important part in its future success and is giving attention to a number of alternative accounting policies which may be used in reporting the resulting operating leases. These have been described as follows:

a recognizing turnover as payment from the customer becomes due and all initial costs except maintenance as the cost of fixed assets with a four-year life;

b recognizing turnover as in **a** above but only hardware as fixed assets;

c recognizing costs and revenues on a straight line basis over a four-year period;

d recognizing costs as in **b** above but matching revenue to cost.

You are required to discuss the problems of revenue recognition raised as a result of franchise fees and initial fees, making use of the example of AID plc above and their proposed policies to illustrate your discussion.

12

Accounting for Inventories and Long-Term Contracts

Objectives

- To examine the implications for analysts of different methods of inventory valuation.

- To discuss the problems of recognition of profits and losses on long-term contracts.

Introduction

The valuation of inventories, work in progress and long-term contract work in progress is essentially a problem of profit allocation and is therefore a potential source of income management. The Fourth Directive contained general principles as to valuation and income measurement and some more detailed rules as to their application to inventories. However, as we might expect, these still give scope for some diversity.

Principal issues

- What is the basis of valuation? There are several cost formulae available which might be used to deal with the allocation and valuation of fungible assets. The basis on which production, post-production or other overheads, in particular interest paid, are allocated to inventories is another problem area.
- To what extent has cost allocation based upon historical cost accounting principles been rejected in favour of some form of current value accounting by using market values or replacement cost of inventories?
- What is the basis of profit recognition on long-term contracts? This issue involves a more than usual level of subjectivity and the interpretation of the requirements may lead to considerable differences in reporting profits and assets.

Valuation and Allocation of Inventories

Article 40 of the Fourth Directive states that *'Member States may permit the purchase price or production cost of stocks of goods of the same category and all fungible items including investments to be calculated either on the basis of weighted average prices, or by the first-in, first-out (FIFO) method or by the 'last-in, first-out (LIFO) method, or **some similar method**'* (emphasis added), and in Article 39.1 (b) that *'value adjustments shall be made in respect of current assets with a view to showing them at the lower market value or, in particular circumstances, **another lower value** to be attributed to them at the balance sheet date'* (emphasis added). Thus, the basis 'lower of cost or market value' rate is adopted but with some room for choice of method. The 1991 FEE Survey of published accounts found evidence of the use of weighted average, LIFO, FIFO, specific identification, latest purchase price and 'other', in those cases where the method was disclosed but also found that in 48% of the cases examined, there was no disclosure of the method adopted. It is clear that in companies with significant levels, or change in levels of inventory, analysts need to be aware of the potential income effect of the use of different methods. The quantification of the effect of a change in method is illustrated in Extract 12.1 from Ford-Werke 1990 accounts.

Extract 12.1 – Ford-Werke AG 1991 accounts, Notes.

(5) Inventories

The inventories were stated at the lower of cost or market value. The acquisition production cost calculation was changed, in the business year, from FIFO to LIFO method according to the changed regulation of the tax reform. This lead to a valuation reduction of inventories amounting to DM 58.4 million. Costs included direct material and direct labor as well as variable and fixed manufacturing overheads as required by tax law. The general risks in inventories of lower market prices and of obsolescence were covered by adequate provisions.

This example might also illustrate the requirement in Article 32 that 'if exceptional value changes are made for taxation purposes alone the amount of ... and the reasons for the adjustments must be disclosed'.

Extract 12.2 from the Cookson Group plc 1991 accounts is an example from the UK of a company which uses a different method in the balance sheet from that used in the profit and loss account. This group also invokes the true and fair override to adopt the base stock method which is not allowed by SSAP 9.

Extract 12.2 – Cookson Group plc 1992 accounts, Notes.

11 Stocks

	1992 £m	1991 £m
Raw materials	**76.9**	64.5
Work in progress	**38.3**	30.3
Finished goods	**97.4**	85.2
Total stocks	**212.6**	180.0

Certain metals and minerals stocks held by Group subsidiaries are valued in the profit and loss account on the Base Stock or, for certain overseas subsidiaries, the last in first out (LIFO) method. As market prices of the materials involved can fluctuate widely over a period, and because these companies are processors and not traders, the effects of such variations in stock values are not operating profits or losses. The use of the Base Stock and LIFO methods, together with covering arrangements for quantities in excess of Base Stock levels, causes the profit and loss account to be charged with the current cost of the materials consumed. The stock valuation for the balance sheet is at the lower of cost and net realisable value on the first in first out (FIFO) method. The difference between the Base Stock or LIFO valuations, where these methods are used, and the FIFO valuation is included in reserves. This amounted to a charge of **£4.1m** in 1992 (1991: £7.5m).

The directors believe that this method of accounting is more appropriate for these stocks than that required by Statement of Standard Accounting Practice No 9.

Further examples of the range of methods are illustrated in Extracts 12.3, 12.4 and 12.5.

Extract 12.3 – Carrefour SA 1991 accounts, Note on Accounting Principles.

Inventories

Inventories are valued on the basis of the latest cost, because of their fast turnover. If necessary, they are reduced to their market value at year end.

Extract 12.4 – FOCOEX SA 1991 accounts, Notes.

e) Inventories

Inventories relating to product supply contracts are stated at the lower of cost (specific identification method) or estimated net realizable value.

Accounting for Inventories and Long-Term Contracts

> **Extract 12.5** – ASW Holdings plc 1991 accounts, Principal Accounting Policies.

Stocks and Work in Progress

Stocks and work in progress are stated at the lower of cost and net realisable value. In general, cost is determined on a weighted average basis and includes transport and handling costs; in the case of manufactured products, cost includes all direct expenditure and production overheads based on a normal level of activity. Net realisable value is the estimated price at which stocks can be sold in the normal course of business after allowing for the costs of realisation and, where appropriate, the cost of conversion from their existing state to a finished condition. Provision is made, where necessary, for obsolescent slow moving and defective stocks.

Rolls, which are used in the production process and have a finite useful life, are included in stocks and work in progress at net book value. This net book value is based on the original cost of the rolls, depreciated on a straight line basis over their estimated useful lives.

The other major problem in inventory valuation is the allocation of overheads and other costs. Articles 39(2) and 35(3) of the Fourth Directive state (*inter alia*) that:

> 'Production cost shall be calculated by adding to the purchase price ... the costs directly attributable to the product.
>   A reasonable proportion of the costs which are only indirectly attributable to the product in question may be added into the production cost ...

Member states may allow interest on capital borrowed to finance production of current assets to be included in production cost. Distribution costs may not be included. Thus, the fairly obvious issue of direct costs is dealt with positively whilst the more subjective issues of indirect costs and interest is open to interpretation and choice.

The 1991 FEE survey revealed some considerable differences in application for countries where the Fourth Directive had been adopted. These may be summarized as in Table 12.1.

TABLE 12.1
Disclosure of recognized costs

Disclosure of costs recognized in sample cases examined	% of sample*	
	Raw Materials	Work-in Progress (not long term)
Purchase price	75	39
Expenses incidental to purchase	36	30
Direct costs	13	45
Indirect costs	7	59
Interest on capital	-	2
Profit	-	3
Other	2	6
Non disclosure	20	15

*More than one answer possible

Even in this summarized form this data is difficult to interpret as accounting policy disclosures may often be vague or confusing. However, it illustrates the range of possible values and emphasizes the importance of careful reading in cases where stocks are an important part of a company's assets. An example of a particularly informative policy is given in Extract 12.6 from the 1991 accounts of VEBA. Disclosure is often less informative, as in, for example, the accounts of Tarmac 1991 (Extract 12.7).

Extract 12.6 – VEBA AG 1991 accounts, Notes.

The valuation of inventories is based on average acquisition or production cost or on lower current values. Taking advantage of the possibilities under tax law, major raw materials, products, and commodities were valued using the LIFO method. The production costs comprise all costs which must be capitalized for tax purposes; general administrative costs, expenses for voluntary fringe benefits, company pensions, and interest rates on borrowings are not capitalized. Inventory risks arising from the duration of storage and reduced usability are taken into account by appropriate write-downs.

Extract 12.7 – Tarmac plc 1991 accounts, Notes.

Stocks

Stocks are valued at the lower of cost and net realisable value. Cost includes appropriate overheads.

The measurement of net realizable value gives rise to similar problems of diversity and interpretation of accounting policy. Once more the level of disclosure is often poor.

The Current Value Basis for Inventory

The Fourth Directive permits member states to allow the use of replacement costs or other valuation methods which are designed to take inflation into account. This reflects the history of the use of current value methods in some states. For example, both the Netherlands and the UK have in differing degrees recognized the relative weakness of historical cost accounting in times of changing prices and the advantages of some form of current value accounting. In others, Germany in particular, the recognition of other than historical cost has been viewed as unacceptable. The actual use of current values, even where member states have allowed it is, however, fairly restricted. In the Netherlands the Dutch Institute of Chartered Accountants (NIVRA) found that only 15% of listed companies with inventories used current values and in a later survey in 1991 found only 10% using them.

The Fourth Directive recognizes that some form of current value disclosure for inventories does have informational value, requiring in Article 40 that *'Where the value shown in the balance sheet … differs materially … from the value on the basis of last known market value prior to the balance sheet date, the amount of that difference must be disclosed …'* An example of such disclosure is to be found in the British Petroleum 1991 accounts, shown in Extract 12.8.

Extract 12.8 – British Petroleum plc 1991 accounts, Notes.

19 Stocks

		£ million
	1991	1990
Petroleum	**1,990**	2,463
Chemicals	**307**	353
Nutrition	**272**	239
Other	**87**	105
	2,656	3,160
Stores	**337**	316
	2,993	3,476
Replacement cost	**3,036**	3,494

Companies which are exposed to volatile commodity price changes may in times of rising prices wish to reflect the effect of price level changes on their inventories and thus profits. British Petroleum Co. plc in their 1991 accounts give such information in the Directors' Report and also in a supplementary group income statement (Extract 12.9).

Extract 12.9 – British Petroleum plc 1991 accounts, Report of the Directors.

Our historical cost profit for 1991, after stock holding losses of £620 million, amounted to £415 million whereas 1990's historical cost profit of £1,676 million was boosted by stock holding gains of £472 million.

Our replacement cost profit for the year, which excludes stock holding losses, amounted to £1,035 million. Within this result, net after-tax divestment profits amounted to £147 million. By comparison, the replacement cost result for 1990 was £1,204 million and included after-tax divestment profits of £311 million. Underlying replacement cost results, excluding divestment profits, were therefore similar at around £890 million in each year.

GROUP INCOME STATEMENT

			£ million
For the year ended 31 December	Note	1991	1990
Turnover	2	32,613	33,039
Replacement cost of sales		25,117	24,655
Production taxes	3	1,001	1,348
Gross profit		6,495	7,036
Distribution and administration expenses	4	4,068	4,140
Exploration expenditure written off		425	460
	6	2,002	2,436
Other income		553	526
Replacement cost operating profit		2,555	2,962
Stock holding gains (losses)		(629)	477
Historical cost operating profit		1,926	3,439
Interest expense	7	723	671
Profit before taxation		1,203	2,768
Taxation	9	820	1,042
Profit after taxation		383	1,726
Minority shareholders' interest		(32)	50
Profit before extraordinary items		415	1,676
Extraordinary items	10	–	12
Profit for the year		(490)	827
Distribution to shareholders			
Earnings per ordinary share	12	7.7p	31.3p

Accounting for Inventories and Long-Term Contracts

This information will be particularly useful to the analyst where other current value information is also available. Companies often disclose only that the difference between the balance sheet value and replacement value is not material (Extract 12.10).

Extract 12.10 – British Airways plc, 1992 accounts, Notes.

£ million	Group		Company	
	1992	1991	1992	1991
Raw materials, consumables and work in progress	34	37	31	28

The replacement cost of stocks is considered to be not materially different from their balance sheet values.

However, it is sometimes the case that companies are silent as to replacement values, leaving us to guess whether the difference is or is not material or if the company considers the disclosure to have less benefit to the user than the cost of computing it!

Long-Term Contracts

The Fourth Directive contains no requirements concerning the accounting treatment of long-term contracts thus IAS 11, *Accounting for Construction Contracts*, is the only guidance. This standard recognizes two methods of dealing with the recognition of income on long-term contracts, that is the percentage of completion method whereby profits are taken over the life of a contract, and the completed contract method where profits are not recognized until the completion.

Extract 12.11 – Boskalis NV, 1991 accounts, Notes.

Work in progress

Works in progress are valued at cost (wages, materials, other direct costs and charges for plant employed), excluding a surcharge for general overhead costs. If losses on works in progress are anticipated, provisions for these are made. On large long-term contracts (with a contract value of 50 million guilders or more) results are accounted for as the work proceeds. The result thus calculated is included in the valuation of work in progress. Progress payments invoiced and advance payments are deducted from the work in progress.

The choice of method under IAS 11 and the lack of any harmonization requirements has given rise to a mixture of approaches, which might be summarized as:

- all/mainly percentage of completion: UK, Spain, Ireland;
- little uniformity – either one or both methods may be used in a single set of accounts : France, Spain, Italy, Netherlands;
- all/mainly completed contract: Germany.

Illustrations of both methods are taken from Dutch companies in Extracts 12.11 and 12.12.

A more complete policy disclosure may be useful in giving an analyst a feel for the assessment approach adopted by a company. An example is given in Extract 12.13 from the BICC 1990 accounts.

Extract 12.12 – Volker Stein NV 1991 accounts, Notes.

Profits on works are taken into account only when these are completed or virtually completed; account is taken of anticipated losses.

Where works are invoiced and paid for on the basis of production, the profit or loss arising from production is taken into account in the year concerned.

In the case of projects which span a number of years, the various phases, for which payment is received on completion and which therefore cease to involve any risk, are treated as separate works.

Extract 12.13 – BICC plc 1990 accounts, Principal Accounting Policies.

5 Profit recognition on contracts

Profit on contracting activities is taken as work progresses. Unless a more conservative approach is necessary, the percentage margin on each individual contract is the lower of margin earned to date and that forecast at completion, taking account of agreed claims. Profit is recognised on property developments when they are subject to a substantially unconditional contract for sale and on housebuilding on completion of the sale of individual houses. Full provision is made for all known or expected losses at completion immediately such losses are forecast on each contract. Profit is not taken on contracts in certain overseas territories where it is considered that restrictions on repatriation may arise. Profit for the year includes settlement of claims arising on contracts completed in prior years.

There are a number of technical considerations which might enable analysts to better appreciate the results of accounting for-long term contracts. These include,

- determination of contract cost and overhead allocations;
- treatment of relevant interest;
- provisions for penalties and rectification work;
- treatment of changing price levels.

However, in general the level of disclosure of accounting policy for contracts is poor and explanation of the technical considerations used in determining profit allocations is rare.

The degree of diversity in accounting policy and disclosure in the area of long-term contracts makes this a problem area for analysts where there are significant amounts involved. Indeed, the lack of quality disclosure may mean that the analyst is sometimes unaware of the effect on income and the potential for income management.

Problems

1. Using the information given for British Petroleum (Extracts 12.8 and 12.9) in the text, compile three accounting ratios using the two stock valuation methods. What are the implications of your results?

2. Identify three construction/civil engineering companies in your country. Do they use the same accounting method for long-term contracts? Is there sufficient disclosure to enable you to appreciate the effect on current year profit of such contracts?

13

Foreign Currency Translation and Exchange Rate Risk

Objectives

- To discuss the effect on the financial statements of transactions in foreign currencies.

- To discuss the issues involved in incorporating financial statements of related companies into consolidated financial statements.

- To ascertain the extent to which information provided in the accounts can be used to determine the level of foreign exchange risks of a company.

- To consider the accounting implications of hedging techniques employed by companies to reduce exchange rate risk.

Introduction

The most obvious and important omissions from the Fourth and Seventh Directives are the problems of accounting for transactions in foreign currencies and the consolidation of financial statements expressed in foreign currencies. This lack of a harmonizing framework is evidenced by the different degrees of prescription in the legislation and standards of European states. Surprisingly, the 1991 FEE survey shows that there exists a significant de facto level of harmonization with many companies in different countries arriving at very similar accounting treatments.[1] 'This is probably due to two reasons. The first is the influence of IAS 21 (which was itself influenced by US standard FAS 52); however, the approach of these two statements has not received universal acclaim (see Busse Von Colbe, 1993[2]) and we might have expected more diversity if this were the only reason. The second (more cynical) reason is that in times of volatile currency relationships there are preferred methods of accounting if companies wish to minimize the impact of foreign currency exposure on their income statement and balance sheet.

The degree of de facto harmonization might, however, hide the fact that there are still potential areas of difference and, perhaps more importantly, significant differences in the level and usefulness of disclosures.

With companies becoming increasingly multinational in their operations and with floating exchange rates leading to increased volatility in exchange rate movements, the foreign exchange risk of companies has increased dramatically. Unfortunately very few companies provide enough information to their shareholders and other users of accounts to enable them to assess the significance of such risks.

At present existing standards in European countries do not cover this issue. This is unfortunate because companies can adopt different policies towards such risks. A company could decide to hedge against the risks, or at least against a certain percentage of the risk. It could try to minimize its foreign exchange rate risks. Alternatively, the company could take no action and just absorb whatever gains or losses result from movements in foreign exchange rates. Another strategy would be for the company to speculate. That is to take action that it hopes will lead to gains in its foreign currency dealings. The company would be relying on its own managers being more successful than dealers operating in the foreign exchange markets in forecasting future exchange rates.

Exchange rates have an impact on the financial management and accounting reports of a company in a number of ways. The issues that need to be considered include:

- the determination of gains or losses arising on transactions where more than one currency is involved, for example production costs incurred in one currency, with the goods sold on credit and payment to be made In another currency;
- the translation into the currency of the parent company of the financial statements of a foreign subsidiary – this is necessary in order to prepare consolidated financial statements;
- the segmental information provided in accounts on the geographical location of assets, on where sales take place, and where profits are made;
- the analysis of debt by currency – in order to form an opinion on the level of foreign exchange risk it is important to know the extent to which assets and liabilities are matched in terms of currency;
- what steps are taken by the management of a company to avoid exchange rate risks (or to gain from exchange rate movements) – there are now many hedging (and speculating) techniques;
- the statements made in the annual report and accounts relating to the effect of exchange rate movements on the activities and future financial position of the company.

The remainder of the chapter is divided into two main areas. The first is concerned with foreign currency translation issues which arise in order to produce accounts in units of a single currency. It will cover such questions as:

- If a company enters into transactions involving foreign currencies how and when are gains and losses on these recognized and how are these reflected in the financial statements?
- A company which has foreign subsidiaries (associates or branches) needs to translate their financial statements for consolidation purposes. What method is adopted and how are gains and losses reflected?
- The translation of financial statements of subsidiaries in countries with hyper-inflation gives rise to difficulties in producing meaningful results. What methods are used to deal with this?

The second area considered in the chapter concerns foreign exchange risk.

Foreign Currency Translation

Individual company-level transactions

The basic rule is that a foreign currency transaction is translated into domestic currency at the rate of exchange at the date that the transaction occurs. If the settlement of the transaction takes place at a different rate of exchange then the resultant gain or loss (that is the difference between the translated domestic currency amount at transaction date and the amount at settlement date) should be treated as part of the operating results of the period. This treatment of gains and losses reflects the fact that they arise as a normal part of operating activities.

If at the balance sheet date a company has unsettled transactions, that is debtors and creditors, it might be supposed that such monetary items would be restated at the rate at the balance sheet date (the closing or current rate). The gains and losses arising from this restatement would be recognized as part of the operating results of the period. However, the prudence concept could be applied to this procedure which may lead to a distinction being made in the treatment of long-term and short-term monetary items, and a more restricted approach to the recognition of gains at the year end. This might be summarized thus:

1. Distinction between long-term and short-term:
   (a) no difference in treatment;
   (b) short-term treated differently to long-term items.
2. Recognition of gains and/or losses:
   (c) all gains and losses recognized;
   (d) all losses recognized but gains recognized on short-term items only;
   (e) as for (b) but long-term gains and losses deferred and recognized in current and future income on a systematic basis;
   (f) only unrealized losses recognized.

The treatment adopted in various countries is illustrated with reference to the above in Table 13.1.

TABLE 13.1

Treatment of unsettled transactions at balance sheet date

	1. Short-term vs. long-term	2. Recognition of gains and/or losses
IAS21	(b)	(e)[1,2]
United Kingdom	(a)	(c)
France	(a)	(e/f)
Germany	(b)	(f)
Spain	(b)	(c/f)
Netherlands	(a)	(c/f)[3]

1. E44 would probably change this to 2a
2. Recognition may be restricted where there are doubts as to the convertibility of the relevant currency
3. It is possible to allocate gains over the period to maturity

Examples of differing timing distinctions and recognition are illustrated in Extracts 13.1, 13.2 and 13.3.

Extract 13.1 – EDF 1990 accounts, Notes.

I. Translation of accounts in foreign currencies

Receivables and payables and forward transactions in foreign currencies are translated into francs in the balance sheet at exchange rates prevailing at year-end. Exchange gains and losses determined in this manner are recognized in the Statement of Operations for the year, except that unrealized gains on long-term items are deferred and individual translation losses are amortized on a straight-line basis over the remaining life of the related long term transactions.

Unamortized translation losses and gains deferred have been as follows :

Losses (in millions)		Gains (in millions)	
	FF		FF
1989	2,428	1989	5,779
1990	2,224	1990	7,517

EDF defers realized gains and losses on premature debt repayments and amortizes those amounts over the remaining portion of the original repayment schedule. Such amounts deferred as of December 31, were as follows :

Losses (in millions)		Gains (in millions)	
	FF		FF
1989	1,736	1989	1,303
1990	1,293	1990	3,415

Receivables in foreign currencies which are not hedged and payables in foreign currencies are translated at the rate of exchange as of the recording date or the current or an earlier balance sheet date, whichever yields an amount that is lower for receivables and higher for payables.

Foreign currencies Assets and liabilities in foreign currencies on which there is exchange risk exposure are valued according to the exchange rates ruling on the balance sheet date. Resultant exchange differences are taken to the profit and loss account.

A further complication arises where the 'transaction exposure' has been avoided by an agreement as to the rate to be used at the settlement date by the parties to the original transaction (a contracted rate), or where a company has entered into forward contracts or future currency options or swaps. Again the problem is one of recognition of gains and losses. Should the forward/contracted rate be used to record the transaction at its inception or should the difference (gain or loss) between spot and forward/contracted rate be allocated over the life of the transactions? There is little specific guidance on this issue in most countries and this is compounded by low levels of useful disclosure. For example, Reckitt & Colman give little useful information (Extract 13.4) whereas Fokker and SmithKline Beecham take differing views on recognition (Extract 13.5 and 13.6).

The net cost of hedging transactions will to a large degree represent the relative interest rates operating in the countries of origin of the relevant currencies. The theory of interest rate parity (or the Fisher effect) is used to explain the relationships of exchange rates and interest rates. Further discussion of these relationships is beyond the scope of this text but will be of importance to those concerned with the workings of the international forex and money markets.

Extract 13.4 – Reckitt & Colman plc 1991 accounts, Accounting Policies.

Foreign currency translation

Transactions denominated in foreign currencies are translated at the rate of exchange on the day the transaction occurs or at the contracted rate if the transaction is covered by a forward exchange contract.

Assets and liabilities denominated in a foreign currency are translated at the balance sheet date at the exchange rate ruling on that day or if appropriate at a forward contract rate.

Extract 13.5 – Fokker NV 1991 accounts, Accounting Policies.

Results on forward exchange transactions entered into to hedge exchange risks on purchases and sales in foreign currencies are included in the operating result in the year of delivery.

Extract 13.6 – SmithKline Beecham plc 1991 accounts, Accounting Policies.

Currency translation

The costs and benefits arising from hedging transactions taken out to mitigate the effect of exchange rate fluctuations on profits are dealt with in profit and loss account in the year in which the related exposure arises.

The consolidation of foreign subsidiaries

It is clear that in preparing the accounts of a group of companies it is only possible to do so if they are all expressed in the same currency. Thus, it is necessary to translate the profit and loss accounts and balance sheets of foreign subsidiaries into the reporting currency of the parent company.

There are several theoretical approaches which may be taken to this translation. However, in practice there are two dominant methods which are operated.

The closing rate/net investment method (current rate method)

The rationale for this method is that the parent's interest in the subsidiary is in its net investment and that this should be restated to reflect current exchange rates. Thus, all of the assets and liabilities are translated at the closing rate. The income for the year might arguably be translated at the average for the year or the closing rate.

A difference on exchange arises which reflects the impact of the restatement on the opening net investment and the profits (if average rate is used), and as this restatement difference does not reflect any impact on the parent company's expected cash flows it should normally go through the reserves and not the income statement.

The temporal method (monetary/non-monetary method)

The rationale for this method is that the parent company and the subsidiary are one single entity, therefore the subsidiary's activities, assets and liabilities are simply an extension of those of the parent company. The translation method, therefore, should be consistent with the individual company-level treatment in the previous section. Thus, monetary assets and liabilities are translated at the closing rate but non-monetary assets at the historical rate (the rate at the date of the transaction). Income should be translated at either the actual rate or the average rate for the year. Any difference on exchange is put through the operating income of the current year.

In most European countries companies may use either accounting method as there are either no specific requirements or the rules do specifically allow the choice. The International Standard IAS 21 allows either method to be used.

In deciding which accounting policy is relevant, the following factors should be considered:

- the interlinking of the affairs of the parent and subsidiary;
- the extent to which the cash flows of the subsidiary impact directly on the parent; and
- the extent to which the subsidiary is dependent upon the parent company's currency rather than its own reporting currency.

The choice of policy may, of course, have a significant impact on both the balance sheet and income statement of the group. However, as most companies would wish to avoid the effect of foreign currency losses on their current year income a large majority of companies will operate the closing rate method. This is illustrated by Table 13.2 taken from the 1991 FEE survey.[3]

TABLE 13.2
Method of translation of foreign subsidiaries' results into consolidated accounts

	F*	D	I	N	UK	Total
Sample size	40	49	38	40	50	341
Evidence of foreign operations	18	36	22	28	36	161
Incorporation of entire balance sheet at:**						
Closing rate	14	19	18	26	33	129
Historical rate	–	2	–	1	3	8
Temporal method	–	9	1	–	–	10
Other	3	–	1	–	–	4
Different bases for individual items	1	3	–	–	–	4
No disclosure of translation basis	–	3	2	2	–	7

*Answers for France are based on the 22 consolidated accounts surveyed
**More than one answer possible

As described above the translation of the current year income under the closing rate method may give rise to diversity of treatment. In 1991, for example, *Company Reporting* found a range of methods being used, as listed in Table 13.3.[4]

Extract 13.7 – Chargeurs 1992 accounts, Notes.

Assets and liabilities denominated in functional currencies other than the French franc are converted at year-end exchange rates and income statement items are converted at weighted average exchange rates. The resulting translation difference is recorded as a separate component of stockholders' equity, "Foreign currency translation adjustments". In the case of foreign subsidiaries whose functional currency is the French franc, assets and liabilities denominated in foreign currency are converted according to the monetary/non monetary-concept. Exchange differences resulting from transactions in currencies other than the functional currency are recorded in the consolidated statements of income, with the exception of those relating to long-term intercompany financing transactions and the hedging of specific net foreign currency commitments, which are recorded in stockholders' equity under "Foreign currency translation adjustments".

TABLE 13.3
Foreign currencies
translation method used
for profit and loss
accounts and balance
sheets

	Total
Number of companies	685
	%
Evidence of foreign operations	60
No evidence of foreign operations	40
	100

Translation method used for profit and loss accounts*	
	%
Closing rate method	32
Historical rates:	57
average rate approximation method	
actual	1
Temporal	1
Other method(s)	1
No disclosure	8
	100

Translation method used for balance sheets*	
	%
Closing rate method:	89
throughout	9
except where rates are fixed by contract	1
Temporal	
No disclosure	100

* The percentage figures below are based on the number of
companies with evidence of foreign operations.

The analyst will, therefore, find it necessary to examine and interpret
the note to the financial statements to discover the methods being
operated, a typical note is that in the accounts of Chargeurs for 1992
(Extract 13.7, p. 327).

As can be seen from the above companies may apply both methods
to different subsidiaries within the same set of financial statements.
Thus, the importance of analysts carrying out a detailed review of the
notes to the accounts is to be emphasized when dealing with groups
having material foreign operations.

Operations in hyperinflationary countries

The dominance of the historical cost accounting convention in most
European countries means that analysts have to a greater or lesser
degree developed a tolerance for the limitations of this convention in
normal conditions. However, in situations where the levels of inflation
are abnormal, accounting which ignores the impact of changing price
levels will be misleading.

The condition of hyperinflation is described in the international
standard IAS 29, *Financial Reporting in Hyperinflationary Economies*, by
identifying a number of economic factors. The most obvious of these is
where the cumulative rate of inflation over three years is approaching
or exceeds 100%. In recent European history (in the market economies)

          Foreign Currency Translation and Exchange Rate Risk

this level of inflation has, thankfully, not been reached. Companies, however, may well carry on operations in countries which will meet the criteria for hyperinflation (information on national inflation rates is available in *International Financial Statistics* which is published monthly by the IMF). When countries suffer from hyperinflation the depreciation of the purchasing power of the domestic currency will be accompanied by a change in the exchange rate of that currency, that is the condition called purchasing power parity. The implications of this for financial reporting may be illustrated as follows:

MNC plc, a UK company, invests in a subsidiary in a South American country in 19X0 when the exchange rate was then £1 sterling to 2.0 cruzados. In 19X9 the exchange rate is £1 to 50 cruzados.

The domestic accounts of the subsidiary show assets purchased in 19X0 of 10 million cruzados. If we ignore depreciation the closing rate method of translation would give the following sterling values

19X0 accounts $\dfrac{10\ m}{2.0}$ = £5 000 000

19X9 accounts $\dfrac{10\ m}{50.0}$ = £200 000

Thus, the effect of the exchange rate movement adjusted for without some compensating purchasing power adjustment will give rise to misleading financial information.

The effects on the group accounts of using the closing rate on unadjusted historical cost information in these circumstances will normally be:

- the balance sheet asset values will be unrealistically low and there would be a significant debit to group reserves; and
- the profit and loss would include inflated profits caused by either high interest on local currency deposits or unrealistically 'profitable' local operations.

There are three possible solutions to this problem:

1. to adopt the temporal method of translation;
2. to adjust the local currency financial statements to reflect current price levels before the translation process is undertaken; or
3. to use some other relatively stable currency as the functional currency. Thus, the foreign operations would be measured at the temporal rate in this functional currency and then translated into the reporting currency using the closing rate method.

The accounts of Elf 1991 illustrate the first method (extract 13.8), whereas Akzo use the second method in their 1990 accounts, (Extract 13.9)

An exception to this general rule is made for subsidiaries located in countries where the cumulative rate of inflation exceeds 100% over a 3-year period. In those instances, inventories, property, plant and equipment and other long-term assets are translated at the rates of exchange in effect at the date of acquisition, and related Statement of Income items, such as depreciation expense, are translated on the same historical basis. The resulting translation gains or losses are recorded in income under 'Other income and expense'.

However, before being translated into guilders, the financial statements of affiliated companies established in hyperinflationary countries are adjusted to reflect the effects of changing prices.

and Chargeurs use the third method in their 1992 accounts (Extract 13.10).

The accounts of foreign subsidiaries are stated in the functional currency used in their operations. Effective from January 1, 1991, the accounts of subsidiaries operating in countries with highly inflationary economies based in part on the U.S. dollar (Argentina, Uruguay) are prepared in dollars. Prior to January 1, 1991, the accounts of these subsidiaries were stated in French francs.

A rather less satisfactory approach is to sidestep the problem as we can see in the accounts of CEP Communications for 1991 (Extract 13.11).

Foreign Currency Translation and Exchange Rate Risk

Certain Group investments meeting the above criteria are not consolidated, as follows:

Certain foreign subsidiaries belonging to the Publishing Division, either because their financial statements are not published in time for the closing of the consolidated accounts or they operate in highly inflationary economies, making it difficult to determine the exchange rate at which their accounts should be translated, or local legislation imposes restrictions on the repatriation of capital.

Foreign Exchange Risk

The financial management literature divides foreign exchange risk into three categories. These are explained in the following sections.

Transaction risk

This is the risk that the rate of exchange between two currencies will vary from the time when a transaction begins to when it is finished. For example, a company might agree at one date to sell an item to another company at a price fixed in the purchaser's currency. The risk is that by the time the actual cash is received the rate of exchange will have changed. This involves the risk of an actual cash loss.

A company faces transaction exposure in a number of situations. These include:

- normal trade with countries with different currencies;
- repaying foreign currency loans;
- sale of fixed assets or of subsidiaries in foreign countries;
- repatriation of profits, and payment of royalties and management charges by foreign subsidiaries to parent company.

Most companies have a policy towards hedging against such risks. A few companies tell their shareholders about this policy.

Translation risk

This is sometimes referred to as accounting risk; it has already been referred to in the previous section. It is necessary for the user of accounts to appreciate the difference between translation exposure and transaction exposure.

Translation exposure refers to the translating of subsidiary company accounts, both the balance sheet and the profit and loss account, into the currency of the parent company. Translation exposure does not result in any cash gains or losses. It can, however, result in accounting gains and losses which will have an impact on the reported financial result for a year. There is a disagreement in the international financial management literature as to whether or not a company should hedge against the translation exposure of its net assets.

Economic risk

This is the most complex of the three. It is concerned with the impact of future exchange rate movements on the future cash flow of a company. There are many ways in which such movements will affect future cash flows. These include the impact on production costs, raw material costs, selling prices, transfer prices and dividends. The impact of changes in the exchange rate on the position of competitor companies also has to be considered. It is not easy to measure economic risks.

Most companies do not use hedging instruments to minimize such risks; rather they adjust their borrowing policies and their international diversification policies to minimize the effects.

Issues

On matters concerned with foreign exchange risk a financial analyst would like answers to the following.

- In which countries are overseas assets located? What is the value of the net assets in each country?
- Which currencies have been borrowed? In what amounts?
- What would be the effect on future trading activities of a devaluation/upward revaluation of the home country currency (i.e. economic risk)?
- What would be the effect on the translation of overseas earnings and the effect on the net value of overseas assets of a devaluation/upward revaluation of the home country currency (i.e. translation risk)?
- What is the company's policy with regard to hedging transaction risk?
- What is a company's policy with regard to hedging translation risk?
- Does the company speculate in the foreign exchange market?
- What percentage of the shareholders' funds is exposed to fluctuations in foreign exchange rates? What percentage in what currency?
- What use is made of swaps, future and option contracts?
- What is the policy with regard to interest rate risks? Is use made of interest rate swaps?

These topics are dealt with in the remaining sections of the chapter.

Dealing with Foreign Exchange Risk

Information on geographical distribution of assets

The first step a shareholder or other interested user of accounts can take to determine the foreign exchange risk of a company is to ascertain the geographical breakdown of activities. How active is the company outside its home country? To answer this question it is important to know the location of the company's assets, and where sales are made and profits earned. The level of disclosure on these matters varies very much from country to country and company to company.

Extract 13.12 – Lonrho plc 1992 accounts, Notes.

Turnover represents sales of goods and services outside the Group net of discounts, allowances and value added tax and includes commissions earned.

Turnover by origin is analysed by activity and geographical area below:-

	1992 Total £m	1992 Associates £m	1992 Group £m	1991 Total £m	1991 Associates £m	1991 Group £m
United Kingdom	1,839	43	1,796	1,919	90	1,829
Europe and Other	941	731	210	1,554	1,397	157
East, Central and West Africa	492	88	404	532	80	452
Southern Africa	400	10	390	439	10	429
The Americas	194	71	123	402	271	131
	3,866	943	2,923	4,846	1,848	2,998

An analysis of Group net non-interest bearing operating assets and of associates' net assets by activity and geographical area is given below:-

	1992 Total £m	1992 Associates £m	1992 Group £m	1991 Restated Total £m	1991 Restated Associates £m	1991 Restated Group £m
United Kingdom	756	13	743	897	10	887
Europe and Other	272	34	238	221	80	141
East, Central and West Africa	376	68	308	372	63	309
Southern Africa	678	16	662	694	54	640
The Americas	300	25	275	427	66	361
	2,382	156	2,226	2,611	273	2,338
Net interest bearing liabilities	(842)			(1,092)		
Proposed dividend and ACT	(28)			(73)		
Net total assets	1,512			1,446		

The comparative figures have been adjusted to reflect the change of accounting policy for intangible assets as described in the Report of the Directors on page 59.

An analysis of Group profit on ordinary activities before interest and taxation and of associates' profit before taxation by activity and geographical area is given below:-

| | 1992 | | | 1991 Restated | | |
| | Total | Associates | Group | Total | Associates | Group |
	£m	£m	£m	£m	£m	£m
United Kingdom	31	5	26	51	2	49
Europe and Other	19	8	11	44	21	23
East, Central and West Africa	95	26	69	123	27	96
Southern Africa	31	2	29	86	3	83
The Americas	3	2	1	13	(1)	14
	179	43	136	317	52	265
Net interest payable	(99)			(112)		
Profit before tax	80			205		

An analysis of profit on ordinary activities before taxation by activity and geographical area is given below:-

| | 1992 | 1991 Restated |
	£m	£m
United Kingdom	12	17
Europe and Other	6	33
East, Central and West Africa	50	85
Southern Africa	17	65
The Americas	(5)	5
	80	205

Central finance charges have been allocated over the various activities and geographical areas in proportion to profit contribution.

Dividends from associates amounted to £19m. (1991 – £10m.)

The 1991 comparative figures have been adjusted to reflect the change of accounting policy for intangible assets as described in the Report of the Directors on page 59.

First it should be appreciated that the balance sheet itself gives no guidance on currency exposure. It does not differentiate between assets owned in the home country and those held in foreign countries. It does not disclose the currency of debt. A big multinational, such as Lonrho, owns assets in many countries. As with all companies the assets in each country are first valued in the local currency, and this value is then translated at official exchange rates into the currency of the home country.

UK companies are required to show a version of a geographical breakdown of assets The segmental information given in most company accounts is, however, inadequate; it does not give the user any idea about the extent of currency exposure or the political risks involved. For example, Lonrho, in the segmented information it provides, divides the world into what it calls 'geographical areas', one being Southern Africa and another the Americas (see Extract 13.12). The reader does not know how the assets in Southern Africa are divided between, say, South Africa, Botswana and Zimbabwe. The political risk and the foreign exchange risk of the currencies of each of these countries is very different. A geographical breakdown into broad geographical regions does not help in determining foreign exchange risk.

Another problem is that the consolidated balance sheet gives an aggregate figure for assets. There is an implication that all these assets are available for creditors and shareholders. This is in fact not the case. If Lonrho, for example, sold one of its mines in Zimbabwe for Zimbabwe dollars there is no certainty it could take those dollars out of the country. This is a risk in addition to foreign exchange risk, which is concerned with the movement of the Zimbabwe dollars against pounds sterling.

Lonrho is far from being the only company to provide an inadequate breakdown of activities by geographical area. Shell divide the world into four regions, namely

- Europe;
- Other Eastern Hemisphere;
- USA;
- Other Western Hemisphere.

One hopes the users of the accounts know where one hemisphere begins and another ends! Or perhaps it does not really matter. Shell do show in a footnote that of their £4630 million long-term debt, £3108 is denominated in US dollars.

Hanson, although a UK registered company, has more of its assets and activities in the USA than the UK. In 1993, 49% of their sales were in the USA, and 44% in the UK. They provide an interesting statement in their accounts, dividing the assets and liabilities by currency (Extract 13.13). Wolseley is another UK company that provides details of the assets and liabilities in other currencies (Extract 13.14).

Pirelli do not provide a geographical breakdown of their assets. They do, however, give information on the book value of their investment in each of their foreign subsidiaries. They show in a footnote details of the

Extract 13.13 – Hanson plc 1993 accounts, Notes.

Assets and Liabilities by Currency
at September 30, 1993

	Sterling £ million	US Dollars £ million	Total £ million
Fixed assets			
Tangible	1,496	10,699	12,195
Investments	38	188	226
	1,534	10,887	12,421
Current assets			
Stocks	656	1,090	1,746
Debtors	585	1,238	1,823
Listed investments	21	27	48
Cash at bank (see note below)	6,190	1,829	8,019
	7,452	4,184	11,636
Creditors – due within one year (see note below)			
Debenture loans	443	2,673	3,116
Bank loans and overdrafts	576	502	1,078
Creditors and taxation	1,351	1,385	2,736
Dividend	135	–	135
	2,505	4,560	7,065
Net current assets	4,947	(376)	4,571
Total assets less current liabilities	6,481	10,511	16,992
Creditors – due after one year (see note below)			
Convertible loans	500	–	500
Debenture loans	1,826	2,090	3,916
Bank loans	1,242	1,563	2,805
	3,568	3,653	7,221
Provisions for liabilities and charges	606	5,212	5,818
	4,174	8,865	13,039
Shareholders' funds	2,307	1,646	3,953
	6,481	10,511	16,992

Note: Subsequent to September 30, 1993, £1,500mn of sterling cash at bank was utilised to reduce sterling current and long term debt of £234mn and £1,266mn respectively Additionally, £500mn of sterling deposits were invested in dollar deposits, increasing dollar shareholders' funds and reducing sterling shareholders' funds each by that amount.

sales by geographic area of destination. They do not give a breakdown by geographic area of profits. What they do provide that is unusual is information on capital expenditure by country, and of research and development expenditure by country. They show this in the detailed analysis of the performance of each of the industrial sectors in which they operate. In 1991, 40.6% of its sales were in the cable sector and 40.1% in tyres. The rest were in diversified products. Taking the cable sector as an example they show the sales by country, and the capital expenditure and research and development by country (Extract 13.15).

Extract 13.14 – Wolseley plc 1992 accounts, Notes.

---

19. Foreign assets and liabilities

The group balance sheet includes the following assets and liabilities denominated in foreign currencies:

(i) US Dollars

	1992		1991	
	US$000	US$000	US$000	US$000
Tangible fixed assets		111,325		113,825
Stock		249,350		242,630
Construction loans		1,092		1,058
Debtors		247,575		215,925
Creditors and provisions		(212,686)		(193,521)
Taxation		(8,063)		(1,003)
		388,593		378,914
Net borrowings:				
Short term	(110,263)		(42,697)	
Long term	(11,399)		(103,331)	
		(121,662)		(146,028)
		266,931		232,886

(ii) French Francs

	1992		1991	
	FF'000	FF'000	FF'000	FF'000
Tangible fixed assets		168,737		—
Stock		608,008		—
Debtors		994,009		—
Current asset investments		36,374		—
Creditors and provisions		(1,589,042)		—
Taxation		(12,203)		—
		205,883		—
Net borrowings:				
Short term	(1,030,262)		—	
Long term	(141,904)		—	
		(1,172,166)		—
		(966,283)		—

Goodwill amounting to FF1,004m has been written off to reserves.

If many UK companies are poor at giving details of foreign currency assets and a geographical breakdown of activities, German companies are far worse. Most, even major, companies do not provide a geographical breakdown as such. What they do provide is a list of major subsidiaries and affiliated companies. Bayer show the sales, net income (in host country currencies) and employees in each of these affiliates, but not the value of the investment in each (Extract 13.16). Bosch, in contrast, show the equity capital of each affiliate, and the profit or loss of the affiliates (Extract 13.17). The German companies do show some information by country as opposed to by some broad geographical breakdown.

Extract 13.15 – Pirelli SpA 1991 accounts, Group Performance and Cable Sector.

Total sales revenue analysed by geographic area

Geographic area	1991	1990
Europe (of which Italy 23.9%)	68.3%	66.6%
North America	13.8%	14.5%
Central and South America	13.-%	14.6%
Australia, Africa and Asia	4.9%	4.3%

Cable sector

Research and development activities

Research & Development activities are closely coordinated and are based on an integrated structure consisting of five research centers located in Italy, France, the United Kingdom, the United States and Brazil, and of development and engineering units within all our Affiliates.

Total employees engaged in research activities numbered 830.

R&D expenditures amounted to Lire 118 billion, equivalent to 2.9% of total sales. The distribution of expenditures and employees by country is as follows:

	Number of employees	R&D expenditures
Italy	40%	57%
France	14%	11%
United Kingdom	13%	12%
Brazil	14%	10%
United States	6%	3%
Other countries	13%	7%

Sales revenue distribution of cable sector (41% of total) by country

	(in billions of lire)	
	1991	1990
Argentina	117.7	124.1
Australia	122.-	124.2
Brazil	407.-	507.2
Canada	186.9	205.2
Ivory Coast	9.2	8.3
France	926.6	918.1
United Kingdom	560.6	460.3
Italy	1,273.-	1,281.7
Peru	23.9	38.-
Spain	217.2	375.3
United States	384.7	435.8
Eliminations and other	(155.9)	(164.2)
Total sector	4,072.9	4,314.-

Over the last two years, the distribution of production, of workforce and of capital expenditures by country was as follows:

	Prod. tons 000		No. of employees		Capital expend. billions of lire	
	1991	1990	1991	1990	1991	1990
Argentina	14.4	10.9	1,436	1,449	4.2	2.3
Australia	15.6	17.4	557	631	3.4	3.9
Brazil	63.2	66.5	2,913	3,159	15.8	29.4
Canada	32.4	34.5	542	724	16.4	11.6
Ivory Coast	1.5	1.4	65	67	0.3	0.3
France	163.-	169.7	4,222	4,492	80.6	93.-
United Kingdom	56.5	51.2	3,087	2,746	26.4	37.9
Italy	171.5	182.8	4,819	4,942	73.4	100.4
Peru	4.9	8.-	136	184	0.1	0.5
Spain	39.1	38.2	874	1,319	16.-	12.4
United States	48.5	54.6	1,023	1,265	15.6	13.3
Total sector	610.6	635.2	19,674	20,978	252.2	305.-

French companies do usually give a geographical breakdown, although, as the extract from the accounts of Thomson-CSF show, again information is only provided on a broad regional basis (Extract 13.18). Thomson have an interesting note explaining that their manufacturing operations are located in Europe, and therefore all operating profit is generated in Europe.

Extract 13.16 – Bayer AG 1992 accounts, Major Affiliated Companies.

	Currency	Exchange rate	Sales (million)	Net income (million)	Employees
Other European Countries					
Agfa-Gevaert N.V., Belgium	bfrs 100	4.87	50,038	3,268	7,625
Bayer Antwerpen N.V., Belgium	bfrs 100	4.87	25,456	371	2,769
Agfa-Gevaert S.A., France	FF 100	29.36	2,731	(16)	1,530
Bayer S.A., France	FF 100	29.36	2,242	75	587
Bayer Pharma S.A., France	FF 100	29.36	1,136	52	710
Bayer plc, U.K.	£ 1	2.44	417	2	1,551
Agfa-Gevaert Ltd., U.K.	£ 1	2.44	164	(4)	754
Bayer S.p.A., Italy	Lit 1,000	1.09	1,061,770	19,902	2,365
Agfa-Gevaert S.p.A., Italy	Lit 1,000	1.09	322,389	1,146	494
Bayer Polysar International S.A., Switzerland	sfrs 100	110.38	522	17	74
Bayer Hispania Comercial, S.A., Spain	Ptas 100	1.41	37,067	210	596
Química Farmacéutica Bayer, S.A., Spain	Ptas 100	1.41	28,051	2,283	1,063
Agfa-Gevaert, S.A., Spain	Ptas 100	1.41	26,552	325	774

Extract 13.17 – Robert Bosh GmbH 1992 accounts, Shareholdings.

Name and location of the company	Currency	Exchange rate 100 units of local currency	Owned[1] %	Equity Capital millions in local currency	Profit or Loss millions in local currency
Germany					
Anlagenvermietung GmbH, Stuttgart	DM		50	32.5	17.2
ANT Nachrichtentechnik GmbH, Backnang	DM		100[2]	322.9	45.0
ANT Nachrichtentechnik Radeberg GmbH, Radeberg	DM		100	10.0	EAV[3]
Blaupunkt-Werke GmbH, Hildesheim	DM		100	183.4	EAV
Bosch-Siemens Hausgeräte GmbH, Munich[4]	DM		50	812.8	74.1
Bosch Telecom Öffentliche Vermittlungs-					

technik GmbH, Eschborn	DM		100	50.8	16.0
Hans Feierabend GmbH, Einbeck	DM		40	4.6	−2.4
MB Video GmbH, Peine	DM		35	37.4	3.0
MotoMeter GmbH, Leonberg	DM		100	25.1	EAV
Robert Bosch Elektronik GmbH, Salzgitter	DM		100	22.8	EAV
Robert Bosch Elektrowerkzeuge GmbH, Sebnitz	DM		100	14.7	EAV
Robert Bosch Fahrzeugelektrik Eisenach GmbH, Eisenach	DM		97	38.0	EAV
Robert Bosch Industrieanlagen GmbH, Stuttgart	DM		100	91.0	EAV
Signalbau Huber AG, Munich	DM		100[5]	73.9	3.1
Teldix GmbH, Heidelberg	DM		100	19.7	EAV
Telenorma GmbH, Frankfurt am Main[4]	DM		100	507.3	11.4
VB Autobatterie GmbH, Hannover	DM		35	237.4	2.5

Foreign Countries

EUROPE

Austria					
Robert Bosch AG, Vienna	ö.S.	14.21	100	650.9	104.1
Belgium					
Robert Bosch Produktie NV, Tienen	B.Fr.	4.87	100	2,864.8	506.9
NV Robert Bosch SA, Anderlecht (Brussels)	B.Fr.	4.87	100	650.5	8.2
Denmark					
Robert Bosch A/S, Ballerup	D.Kr.	25.88	100	183.7	25.1
Finland					
Robert Bosch Oy, Helsinki	Markka	30.88	100	19.4	−11.6

Extract 13.18 – Thomson–CSF 1991 accounts, Notes.

---

20 - SALES BY GEOGRAPHIC AREAS

Thomson-CSF sales by geographic areas (directly or indirectly as a subcontractor) are analyzed below:

	1991	1990	1989
France	14,822	14,513	12,577
Western Eurpe	6,604	5,673	3,326
North America	3,398	3,126	2,384
Africa and Latin America	1,327	1,150	1,236
Middle East	6,679	9,668	12,088
Far East	1,362	1,597	1,015
Other	986	1,297	1,067
Total	**35,178**	37,024	33,693

Thomson-CSF manufacturing operations are principally located in Europe. Operating profit is almost fully generated by European operations and consequently information by geographic areas is limited to the above tabulation.

Analysis of foreign borrowing

One basic hedging technique to avoid the effect of a fall in the translated value of overseas assets, if the host country currency falls against the home currency, is to borrow funds in the host country currency. The translated value of the debt will then also fall.

In total year-end net borrowings increased to £404.8m. This includes an exchange effect of £48.6m. Year-end borrowings including the convertible debt were split between currencies as follows:

(£m)	1992	1991
Sterling	(9.9)	18.4
US dollar	194.8	122.6
Deutschmark	57.1	52.8
Other	47.0	70.2
Sub total	289.0	264.0
Sterling convertible debt	115.8	109.9
Total	404.8	373.9

It is the Group's policy that its subsidiaries do not unnecessarily expose their revenues or assets to fluctuations in foreign exchange rates. This means that net trading cash flows in the subsidiaries' non-base currency are hedged to 100% of their value in the base currency wherever possible.

The Group's translation exposure in the income statement is not hedged as it is not felt that this necessarily adds to shareholder value in the longer term. However, some 30-35% of shareholders' funds are exposed to fluctuations in the pound/US dollar exchange rate. To mitigate these fluctuations the Group has a policy to hedge some 60% of the effective US dollar and dollar related net assets of the Group by financing these assets with US dollar borrowings in the UK.

The policy on interest rates is to minimise exposures by ensuring the appropriate balance of longer term fixed and shorter term floating rates.

The Group's debt is predominantly in US dollar and dollar related currencies, sterling, deutschmarks and other European currencies. Interest rate exposure is managed through the use of interest rate swaps and forward rate agreements with the Group's bankers.

Coats Viyella give details of their policy on this issue, stating that they borrow locally approximately 60% of the value of the net assets in a country (Extract 13.19). Lonrho do not give details of their policy. The Lonrho 1992 balance sheet shows 'Creditors: Amounts falling due after more than one year' of £783 million. One footnote explains that £754 million of this amount is 'loans' and another footnote (Extract 13.20) gives some details of these loans. With the exception of the unsecured bonds no details of the currency of these loans is given. The note explains that with some loans hedging arrangements have been entered into, and the balances are matched against cash and equity investments in related currencies. No further details are provided. What exactly matching loans with equity investments means is unclear. If the currency in the host country rises in value against that in the home country, the loan (when translated) will rise in value, but so will the assets and the equity investment. It could be therefore that the extra cost (in home currency terms) of a loan is matched by the increase in the value of the equity investment (in home currency terms) in that country. As well as longer-term loans Lonrho also have loans falling due for repayment within one year (£348 million) with no details of the currency provided.

Lonrho do provide an analysis of net borrowings, 'analysed by geographical area'. What the information provided means is uncertain. If it means that operations in each of the areas mentioned (say Southern Africa = £135 million) has borrowed the equivalent in local currencies of the amount shown in sterling, then it is not very helpful. It tells the reader nothing about the amount that has been borrowed in each currency. Risk is associated with a currency, not a region. Indeed the largest amount in the analysis is shown as being borrowed by 'UK Central Finance', which tells the reader nothing about the currency.

A British company that does provide information on both the currency of its borrowings and the location of its assets is Wolseley. This information assists the reader of the accounts to determine foreign exchange risk (see Extract 13.14).

Sometimes the chairman's or directors' report and the financial review give information which helps in understanding the company's policy on hedging against foreign exchange risk. As Coats Viyella explain they have a policy of hedging 60% of the assets in a country by means of borrowing in that country. De La Rue in a very informative commentary on the 'Effect of exchange rates' explain that they have a similar policy of matching assets with borrowing (Extract 13.21). They show by means of charts the effectiveness of their policy of hedging against US dollar related assets.

Major French and Spanish companies show an analysis of debt by foreign currency – see Extracts 13.22 and 13.23. Such disclosure is required by the accounting standards of the respective countries. A practice that has developed in a few companies is to include in the annual report and accounts a version of the financial statements expressed in a currency other than that of the home country, for example in US dollars or ECUs. The apparent purpose here is to give additional information to the international investment market – see, for example, Extracts 13.24 and 13.25.

The usefulness of this data is, however, questionable as the result neither represents a meaningful account of transactions in this alternative currency nor does it reflect the accounting methods of the home country of the potential investor. Thus it may well be misleading for potential international investors.

LOANS

	Group		Company	
	1992	**1991**	**1992**	**1991**
	£m	£m	£m	£m
Secured listed debenture 10¼% 1997/2002	5	5	5	5
Other secured loans	191	46		
Finance lease obligations	34	55		
	230	106	5	5
Deduct instalments repayable within one year	(18)	(14)		
	212	92	5	5
Unsecured bonds:				
Deutsche Mark 7¼% 1985/1992		28		
Luxembourg Francs 9⅝% 1991 – 1996	17			
Swiss Franc 6⅜% 1984 – 1994	40	37		
Swiss Franc 6¼ per cent. 1985 – 1995	24	28		
US Dollars 6⅝ per cent. guaranteed 1994	98	97		
	179	190		
Confirming bank loans		2		
Other unsecured loans, acceptances and finance facilities	376	633	79	138
	555	825	79	138
Deduct instalments repayable within one year	(13)	(29)		
	542	796	79	138
Total	754	888	84	143

Forward exchange contracts and currency swap arrangements have been entered into in respect of some of the above loans, the balance being matched against cash and equity investments in related currencies.

Interest on other secured and unsecured loans was paid at the current prevailing market rates in the countries in which the loans were taken out. The rates paid on the majority of loans ranged from 4 per cent. to 18 per cent. per annum.

Secured loans are secured on various assets of the Group.

Effect of exchange rates

The Group's policy is generally to protect the Sterling value of assets denominated in foreign currencies by arranging borrowing in those currencies so that the value of the Group's net assets measured in Sterling does not fluctuate significantly as a result of changes in exchange rates. Exceptions are made to this policy for certain currencies when it is considered impracticable or uneconomic.

A comparison of the assets by currency before and after the associated hedging is shown in the charts below. A much higher level of hedging was maintained for US Dollar related assets than for European assets as there has, until recently, been greater volatility in the Sterling/US Dollar exchange rate than between Sterling and other European currencies. As a result of our hedging policy changes in exchange rates during the year resulted in a movement on the net assets of only £3.9m as shown on the Statement of Recognised Gains and Losses on page 37.

The Group also generally protects against transaction risk by ensuring that, once a sale or purchase is confirmed in a currency other than the domestic currency of the business undertaking the transaction, equal and opposite commitments are made in the foreign exchange markets to protect against subsequent movements in exchange rates. Again exceptions are made to this policy where it is considered impracticable or uneconomic to operate it. At the year end the Group had sold forward US$63m at an average rate of US Dollar 1.54/Sterling.

The Group does not seek to protect the Sterling value of overseas earnings from the translation effect which may arise as a result of movements in exchange rates.

The overall effect of these policies is, first, that the movement on reserves as a result of changes in exchange rates is kept to a reasonably low level. Secondly, the forward sale and purchase of foreign currency tends to smooth the effect on earnings of movements in exchange rates over time whilst providing our operating companies with a stable environment in which to do business. Thirdly, the fact that De La Rue generates profits in US Dollars, Deutschmarks and, to a lesser extent, other currencies as well as Sterling, means that Group profits do tend to increase when these currencies strengthen against Sterling and decline when they weaken. The average exchange rates gave an improvement of £2m, compared with using 1992 average rates.

Taking an overview of our cash flows, before the effects of any transaction hedging, the currency of our earnings is approximately 50% in the US Dollar, 30% in Sterling and 20% in the Deutschmark. These percentages may change.

For the current year, based on present information, and taking account of hedging actions already in place, the full year effect on earnings of each of a movement of 10% in the US Dollar/Sterling exchange rate from 1.55, and a movement of 10% in the Deutschmark/Sterling exchange rate from 2.50, would be some £1m.

These numbers are provided to give an indication of the sensitivity of current year earnings to changes in exchange rates but may alter during the year.

ASSETS BY CURRENCY

Other 6%
US Dollar 15%
Other Europeans 35%
UK 44%

Post-hedging

Other 5%
Other Europeans 22%
UK 73%

Restructuring Expense and Other Non-current Liabilities

In accounting for the acquisition of American National Can, reserves had been established, net of future tax benefits, for restructuring expense and certain other liabilities. Of these net-of-tax reserves, FF 1,185 million remain as of December 31, 1990 (FF 1,907 million at December 31, 1989), of which FF 205 million are classified in current liabilities as of December 31, 1990 (FF 457 million at December 31, 1989).

Note 14—Long-Term Debt

In millions of French francs	1990	1989
Shareholders' loans	252	270
Limited recourse loans	—	174
Debentures	2,268	2,831
Other long-term debt	14,712	16,420
	17,232	19,695
Less: reimbursement premiums	(23)	(27)
Total	17,209	19,668
Other debt includes lease obligations amounting to	463	709

Analysis of long-term debt by major currency:

In millions of French francs	1990	1989
U.S. Dollars	11,603	11,537
French Francs	4,466	6,428
Deutsche Marks	811	852
Spanish Pesetas	83	—
Irish Pounds	78	178
Belgian Francs	56	61
Pounds Sterling	8	384
Other currencies	127	255
	17,232	19,695

The weighted average interest rate of long-term debt amounted to 9.5% in 1990 (9.7% in 1989).

15. Distribution of debt in foreign exchange

In addition to the foreign currency loan from Alcatel Finco, with exchange risk coverage for «swap» operations

(note 18), the breakdown of the debts held in foreign exchange (expressed in thousands of pesetas), is as shown below:

	U.S.$	ECU	FF	DM	BF	S₤	Cruzeiros	Others
● Debts with A.N.V.								
Group companies	204,546	5,086,255	196,056	20,892	34,339	38,166	87,755	7,872
● Trade payables	994,746	129,503	113,931	372,454	3,678	123,765	148,487	63,115
● Prepayments	1,359,833	–	–	–	–	–	–	233
● Bank loans	3,555,737	–	–	–	–	–	6,869,795	–
● Other liabilities	68,235	66	256,943	–	–	–	6,645,274	–
Total	**6,183,097**	**5,215,824**	**566,930**	**393,346**	**38,017**	**161,931**	**13,751,311**	**71,220**

Independently, the Group holds debit balances in foreign currency for a total of 20,240 million pesetas, of which 6,608 million are in US dollars and 12,703 million are in cruzeiros.

Financial Statements and Information Expressed in ECU – The consolidated financial statements are prepared in Italian Lire. In order to present the principal results of the Sector in the European currency, the 1990 financial statements have also been presented in ECU by applying to each financial statement caption the Lira/ECU exchange rate as of December 31, 1990 (ECU 1 equals 1,546.5 lire).

Basis of presentation

The consolidated financial statements are presented in Italian lire, the primary currency in which EniChem S.p.A. and its subsidiaries, (the Group) conduct their business. The financial statements for the year ended December 31, 1990 are also expressed in United States dollars for the readers' convenience based on the exchange rate at December 31, 1990 of Lire 1,130.15 = US$ 1. This convenience translation should not be construed as a representation that the Italian lire amounts could be converted at that rate.

Transaction exposure

It is generally accepted that a company should hedge against foreign currency borrowing but not on whether it should hedge to protect the value of its equity investment in a foreign country. SmithKline Beecham in the financial review appearing in their 1992 accounts explain that, as is normal practice they do hedge to protect 'the translation of its overseas profits'. They also explain that they hedge to minimize exposure arising 'on the translation of the Company's balance sheet'. Options and forward contracts are used to limit the impact of exchange rate fluctuations on overseas profits. The company does not tell us what techniques are used to protect the balance sheet – it just refers to hedging arrangements. Matching the currency of assets with the currency of loans is clearly one such arrangement. Tompkins plc, a large multinational, point in their 1993 accounts to a danger in this 'natural hedge' of borrowing in the same currencies as non-sterling assets. They indicate that it can distort the balance sheet. The solution they adopt is currency swaps, which as they point out can have a positive interest rate effect.

The statements by SmithKline Beecham and Tompkins are helpful to readers of accounts. They are indicative of a new level of disclosure on such issues by UK companies. *Company Reporting* found that in 1993, 89% of the top 100 UK companies were providing information on the function of their Treasury departments, borrowings or foreign currency exposure.[5] This is not yet as common in the other countries we are concerned with.

There are a variety of hedging techniques a company can employ to avoid transaction risk ranging from forward contracts to currency swaps. A few companies provide information on the hedging techniques they have used.

Glaxo, in their 1993 accounts, state that 'trading transactions in foreign currencies are not normally hedged, except in specific circumstances'. In contrast Coats Viyella explain that 'net trading cash flows in the subsidiaries' non-base currency are hedged to 100% of their value in the base currency wherever possible' (see Extract 13.19). De La Rue's policy is generally to protect transaction risk by matching sales or purchases in a currency by equal and opposite commitments in the foreign exchange markets (see Extract 13.21). At De La Rue's year end they had outstanding forward sales of $63 million.

Daimler-Benz inform shareholders in their 1990 accounts that the objective of their foreign exchange management department, with respect to risk prone currencies, is 'to protect through continuing hedging measures a proportion of the delivery volume'. In their 1992 accounts they provide further details (Extract 13.26).

Elf explain that as a rule they systematically hedge all short-term transactions (Extract 13.27). Saint Gobain not only show the currency of the debt, but also give details of foreign currency hedging operations in which they have been engaged. They show details of dealings in the forward foreign exchange market, and some information of the foreign currency swaps and options in which they have been engaged. The footnote dealing with 'contingent liabilities and commitments' lists an

Activities of the Group Treasury

During the year under review, we have continued to further develop, both objectively and instrumentally, our "cash-management" in connection with the inclusion of Deutsche Aerospace Airbus GmbH and the establishment of a foreign-currency based domestic "cash-pooling". We were able to increase the flexibility and efficiency of our treasury activities through more intensive use of the commercial-paper-programs, particularly in Germany and the U.S.A.

Through active portfolio management we have again invested long-term funds – depending on interest rate and interest income expectations – primarily in fixed-interest instruments of first-class issuers. Investments in stocks represent a small portion of our portfolio.

The continued growth of our leasing and sales financing business has further increased the demands placed on our centrally managed refinancing tasks.

In order to enlarge our investor basis, we floated a Euro-Medium-Term-Note-Program in 1992, with a volume objective of two billion U.S. dollars. This instrument, which can be used by Daimler-Benz International Finance B.V., Daimler-Benz of North America and Daimler-Benz United Kingdom plc – companies already well known and active in the Euromarket – allows us to use the capital markets to the fullest extent.

As in prior years, the task of the foreign exchange management consisted in limiting the currency risks of the operating sectors, particularly with regard to the USD, JPY, GBP, CHF and ESP, through suitable foreign exchange hedging measures. Also in the future, we will be guided by continually updated currency rate expectations and then employ the financial instruments individually depending on the currency and business field.

Within the scope of the above-mentioned treasury activities, we also avail ourselves of derivative capital market instruments. They serve the purpose of limiting the group's financial risks overall and of optimizing results of operations.

item 'foreign currency operations FF1791 million'. It is this amount that is analysed in terms of currencies. They point out that such forward covers are not speculative in nature, but are a counterpart to the economic operations of the group. Presumably therefore if a forward contract is to purchase US dollars at a certain price, it is counter-balanced by a transaction to deliver dollars at that date.

Unisor Sacilor give details of the amounts involved in forward currency transactions, and in currency swaps (Extract 13.28). Groupe Euro Disney point out that they employ a variety of financial instruments to reduce their exposure to foreign currency exchange risks (Extract 13.29). Thomson explain the role of their finance department including the hedging of certain currencies. They also briefly explain the accounting treatment of gains and losses on futures contracts and other financial instruments. This is an issue that is not often discussed in European company accounts. There are accounting standards on the subject in the USA, but not yet in European countries.

Extract 13.27 – Elf Group 1992 accounts, Consolidated Results and Outlook.

EXPOSURE TO MARKET RISKS

Like all multinational corporations, the Elf group faces a variety of market-related risks, particularly fluctuations in the price of crude oil.

Elf adopts a systematic hedging strategy to protect itself from the effects of price fluctuations in the financial markets.

The Group faces two types of foreign exchange risks:
– At the operating level, the effects of exchange rate fluctuations on the competitiveness of products priced directly or indirectly in foreign currencies. The financial impact depends on the readiness of clients to absorb price increases and on the relative pricing of competitive products. This risk, reflected in lower margins or volumes sold, cannot be easily quantified, due to the lack of precise data concerning the effects of pricing on demand.

– At the financial level, the impact of exchange rate fluctuations on capital and money market operations. As a rule, the Group systematically hedges all its short-term transactions.

The only currency risk affecting long-term operations concerns the Group's debt, a substantial portion of which is denominated in US dollars. These borrowings are designed partly to protect margins from oil and gas production, which are affected favorably when the value of the French franc rises against the dollar, while only a part of the cost of producing the oil is dollar-based.

The Group's exposure to the effects of fluctuations in interest rates and stock markets is insignificant, given its financial structure and investment policies (cf. Note 15 to the Consolidated Financial Statements).

NOTE 24 – **FINANCIAL INSTRUMENTS**

a) Currency hedges

Outstanding positions in foreign currencies were as follows at December 31, 1991:

forward currency transactions	
forward purchases of foreign currencies	4,394
forward sales of foreign currencies	12,255
currency swaps	
purchases of foreign currencies	1,033
sales of foreign currencies	1,422

The foreign exchange exposure of the individual subsidiaries is managed by the Group. The net foreign exchange exposure on commercial transactions, after netting off buy and sell positions, amounts to MF 9,272.

b) Long-term interest rate hedges

	Commitments given	Commitments received
Interest rate swaps in French francs	1,537	1,537
Interest rate swaps in foreign currencies	3,102	3,217
Purchases and sales of caps	–	870
Total	4,639	5,624

All currencies combined:
Fixed rates paid are primarily included in the range of 7.7% to 9.5%
Fixed rates received are primarily included in the range of 7.2% to 13.4%
Final maturities of swaps are between 1992 and 2001.

Economic exposure

Economic exposure is very important – it is concerned with the future cash flows of a company and therefore with the present value of the company. The future cash flows of an MNC will be in a variety of currencies. These currencies, translated into home currency terms and discounted, give the present value of the company. Economic exposure measures the effect of changes in exchange rates on this present value of the company. Changes in exchange rates will affect the future trading position of the company, in relation to its competitors, as well as actual exchange transactions.

Economic exposure is an indication of how future movement in exchange rates will affect all aspects of future cash flows. It is very hard to measure. In some countries companies comment on this exposure. Elf explain that at the operating level their product, oil, is priced in a foreign currency. They buy oil at dollar prices and sell worldwide in many different currencies.

The financial impact of fluctuating exchange rates 'depends on the readiness of clients to absorb price increases and on the relative pricing of competitive products'. As Elf mention, the risk 'cannot be easily quantified' (see Extract 13.27).

De La Rue refer to the fact that the currency of their earnings is 50% in US dollars, 30% in sterling and 20% in deutschmarks. They provide estimates of the sensitivity of cash flow and earnings to changes in exchange rates (see Extract 13.21).

Cadbury Schweppes explain in their 1992 accounts that changes in exchange rates have reduced reported profits for the year (Extract 13.30). They also refer to the effect of exchange rate movement on the current year's exports and imports. Coats Viyella in their 1992 financial review mention that 'The significant devaluation by 19% of sterling between year-end 1991 and year-end 1992 increased the value of net dollar assets by £26.8 million. The overall exchange effect on the balance sheet was an increase in net assets of £43.2 million.'

Interest rate swaps

Companies engage in interest rate swaps for a number of reasons. One is because swaps can reduce the cost of borrowing to the companies involved. Another reason is to avoid risk. A company may become concerned that too much of its debt is in fixed rate borrowing and that if interest rates fall the company will be paying unnecessarily high interest charges. The company might decide in such circumstances to swap fixed rate borrowing for floating rate borrowing.

Forté give details of their borrowing with a note explaining that the interest rate being paid on a number of the loans has been changed as a result of swaps (Extract 13.31). Not many companies provide this amount of detail. De La Rue explain that the Group 'continuously reviews its exposure to interest rate movements' (Extract 13.32). Hanson also provide some details of interest rate protection agreements they have entered into (Extract 13.33). They also give details of a specific currency/interest rate swap and of the impact of their interest rate swap policy.

Extract 13.30 – Cadbury Schweppes plc 1992 accounts, Financial Review.

Exchange Rates

The third column of the analysis of results table shows how changes in exchange rates have slightly reduced pre-tax profits and earnings per share by about 1%. These are translated at average rates. Exchange rate movements have significantly increased shareholders' funds and borrowings (which are translated at year end rates).

The chart above shows how the values of the principal currencies which affect the Group's results have changed. The strength of the dollar and fall in the value of the pound following sterling's departure from the Exchange Rate Mechanism in September 1992 have enhanced the value of our overseas earnings. The full effect of this will not be seen in the Group's results until 1993. If the December 1992 rates were to prevail through 1993, the benefit to operating profit would be £21m. There is also some benefit as regards exports from the UK. On the other hand, the devaluation of the pound raises the sterling price of sugar and milk purchased in the UK.

The Group manages foreign exchange risks in a strictly controlled way. As part of this, we aim to keep the ratio of income to financing costs broadly similar by currency group.

During the year Hanson announced the issue of $1.25 bn of notes in a US debt offering, comprising $500 mn nominal 5 1/2% notes due 1996 and $750 mn nominal 7 3/8% notes due 2003. The Group entered into currency swap agreements to swap the fixed rate $1.25 bn into floating rate sterling with six month LIBOR-based rollovers.

Alcatel Alsthom explain that their policy is to hedge risks 'without taking any speculative positions' (Extract 13.34). They also explain that they link interest rate risk to metal price risk – a note that whets the appetite but does not provide much of a meal!

Extract 13.31 – Forte Group plc 1993 accounts, Notes.

Interest rate exchange agreements

The interest rates on loans shown above have been varied by the use of interest exchange agreements which alter interest rates as follows:

	Interest rate shown above	Varied interest rate	Expiry date
† Sterling £180m	Variable	11.9%	Between six and seven years
† Sterling £69m	Variable	10.9%	Between three and four years
US Dollar US$50m	Variable	8.7%	Between one and two years
Sterling £100m	8.375%	Libor + 1.0%	Between four and five years
Sterling £19m	10.6%	Libor + 3.9%	Between three and four years

† These interest exchange agreements were reversed with effect from the end of January 1993. Payments will be made at the rate of £8m and £3m per annum respectively until the agreements expire.

Extract 13.32 – De la Rue plc 1993 accounts, Financial Review.

Sterling balances being held on short maturities and the effect that a significant reduction in Sterling interest rates would have had, the Group purchased an interest rate floor in February 1992 covering the 1993 financial year at 9% on £100m. Subsequent reductions in Sterling interest rates resulted in payments being received under this arrangement which terminated at the end of the financial year. The graph below compares the rates achieved on our Sterling balances, including the cost and benefit of the floor, with a rolling average 3 month market rate.

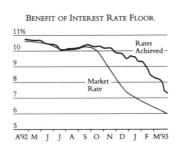

BENEFIT OF INTEREST RATE FLOOR

Foreign Currency Translation and Exchange Rate Risk

Debenture loans include £2,658mn relating to amounts borrowed under a US dollar commercial paper programme and £428mn under a sterling commercial paper programme.

Bank loans, overdrafts and debenture loans bear interest at rates ranging from 3.13% to 7% per annum. Interest rate protection agreements have been entered into which effectively fix interest payments at an average 3.73% on $1,450mn of floating rate debt due within one year. Hanson is exposed to loss in the event of non-performance by banks under such agreements. No single bank is party to more than $150mn nominal value of such agreements. Hanson does not anticipate non-performance by any of its counterparties. These agreements expire at various dates to April 1994. Hanson has unused lines of credit for short term borrowing of approximately £2.0 billion at September 30,1993.

> **Extract 13.34** – Alcatel Alsthom 1992 accounts, Notes.

Note 25 Market related exposures

Market transactions are entered into in order to manage and reduce the risks related to foreign exchange positions and interest rate and metal price exposure. The sole purpose of these transactions is to hedge risks, without taking any speculative positions.

a) Currency risk

With respect to sales, the Group's policy is to hedge all currency risks, using any appropriate means, whether these risks correspond to firm or anticipated positions. The hedging instruments most frequently used are exchange rate guarantees obtained from insurance companies (such as COFACE), forward exchange contracts and occasionally the purchase of currency options.

Where financial transactions are concerned (i.e. loans and borrowings), the Group's policy is to hedge systematically all transactions denominated in a currency other than the currency of each local operation. Currency swaps are most frequently used for this purpose.

The impact of exchange rate fluctuations of subsidiaries' and affiliates' net assets is included in the translation adjustment in Consolidated Shareholders' Equity (see the summary of accounting policies in note 1b).

b) Interest rate risk

The Group's general policy is to achieve a balance between fixed and floating rate positions, in both the short-and long-term, by using interest rate instruments if necessary. This balance may, however, be adapted to take into account projected market conditions and economic trends.

c) Metal price risk

The Group enters into future contracts operations on the London Metal Exchange in order to reduce its exposure to market fluctuations on its copper and aluminium firm positions.

References

1. Fédération des Experts Comptables Européens (FEE) (1991) *European Survey of Published Accounts,* Routledge, London.

2. Busse Von Colbe, V. (1993) 'Foreign currency translation', in Gray, S.J., Coenenberg, A.G. and Gordon, P.D. (eds), *International Group Accountancy,* Routledge.

3. FEE, op. cit.

4. *Company Reporting,* June 1991, Company Reporting Limited, Edinburgh.

5. *Company Reporting,* June 1994.

Problems

1. Using the information relating to the French company EDF (Extract 13.1) calculate the effect on profits of the alternative approaches to the recognition of gains and losses outlined in the text (make any necessary assumptions).

   Discuss the impact on these alternatives of:

   a a strengthening domestic currency, and

   b a weakening domestic currency.

2. The accounts of Chargeurs for 1992 (Extract 13.7) illustrate the use of both methods of translating the accounts of foreign subsidiaries. Using this as an example, discuss the circumstances in which each of the methods is most appropriate.

3. It might be suggested that the normal characteristics of a foreign investment is that the net investment (total assets less total liabilities) will tend to be positive but that monetary liabilities will exceed monetary assets. In these circumstances what will be the effect on the consolidated accounts of the following situations:

   a strong foreign currency/temporal method of translation;

   b strong foreign currency/closing rate method of translation;

   c weak foreign currency/temporal method of translation;

   d weak foreign currency/closing rate method of translation?

   What are the implications of the above for accounting policy choice?

4. Analyse the segmental information in the Lonrho 1992 accounts (Extract 13.12) in order to determine the profitability of the different geographical areas. What conclusions can you draw from such analysis? What are the limitations of segmental analysis?

5. Compare the level of disclosure of Pirelli with that of Lonrho (Extracts 13.12 and 13.15). What are the strong points and weak points of the approaches of each company? Examine the accounts of another company from either the UK or Italy to determine how representative of disclosure practice in their own country are either Lonrho or Pirelli.

6. Compare the level of disclosure on foreign affiliated companies of Bayer and Bosch (Extracts 13.16 and 13.17). Discuss the usefulness to an analyst of the German approach to disclosure on this issue and compare it to that of the UK approach.

7. Compare the hedging policies of Coats Viyella (Extract 13.19) with that of De La Rue (Extract 13.21). How do hedging transactions affect the amounts appearing in the profit and loss account and the balance sheet?

8. Observe the comments of Daimler-Benz (Extract 13.26) Elf (Extract 13.27), Unisor Sacilor (Extract 13.28), Groupe Euro Disney (Extract 13.29) and Cadbury Schweppes (Extract 13.30) with regard to attempts to minimize foreign exchange risks. How helpful do you believe such comments are to a reader of the accounts who wishes to obtain an impression of the level of foreign exchange exposure of these companies?

9. What is interest rate risk? Observe the comments of De La Rue (Extract 13.32), Hanson (Extract 13.33) and Alcatel (Extract 13.34) on this issue. How helpful do you believe such comments are to the reader of the accounts who wishes to obtain an impression of the exposure of these companies to interest rate movement?

14

The True and Fair View

Objectives

- To examine the concept of the true and fair view and to illustrate the application of the true and fair override.

- To discuss the harmonization of the true and fair view within the European Union.

Introduction

Article 2 of the Fourth Directive (English version) sets out the fundamental requirements for the annual accounts of companies as follows:

(1) The annual accounts shall comprise the balance sheet, the profit and loss account and the notes on the accounts. These documents shall constitute a composite whole.

(2) They shall be drawn up clearly and in accordance with the provisions of this Directive.

(3) The annual accounts shall give a true and fair view of the company's assets, liabilities, financial position and profit or loss.

(4) Where the application of the provisions of the Directive would not be sufficient to give a true and fair view within the meaning of paragraph 3, additional information must be given.

(5) Where in exceptional cases the application of a provision of this Directive is incompatible with the obligation laid down in paragraph 3 that provision must be departed from in order to give a true and fair view within the meaning of paragraph 3. Any such departure must be disclosed in the notes on the accounts together with an explanation of the reasons for it and a statement of its effects on the assets, liabilities, financial position and profit or loss. The Member States may define the exceptional cases in question and lay down the relevant special rules.

This lengthy extract from the Fourth Directive has been given in order to provide a reference for the discussion below. The use of the English language version is not merely an anglocentric view of the issues but is used as a starting point for discussion because of the long history of the true and fair view in UK accounting. The introduction in the Fourth Directive of the true and fair view as the overriding principle of financial reporting was, with the exception of the United Kingdom and the Netherlands, a significant change for most EC member states. The idea that legally determined accounting rules and practices might be abandoned in favour of an alternative based upon a vague notion of truth and fairness was difficult for auditors and accountants in these countries to come to terms with. Even in the UK the prominence given to the true and fair view in the EC legislation focused attention on the concept. Using the British model as a starting point for explication exposes the problematic nature of the concept. Walton puts it well;

> On the surface the true and fair view towers over British accounting but with the curious characteristics that no-one knows what it means, and very little academic analysis has been done on its role in accounting. As regards its meaning it is a legal term in origin and yet the Companies Acts have never defined it (nor has the Fourth Directive, or course)and there is little jurisprudence which bears upon it. There is no definition of it in accounting standards, auditing standards or other professional pronouncements. Most tellingly, a television broadcast in 1992 included interviews with senior British accountants: when asked to define the true and fair view, one (partner in Ernst and Young)laughed, another (senior partner of a major non big 6 firm)would say nothing and a third, the finance director of an Anglo-American multinational asked for time to think about the question.[1]

The analyst, however, cannot ignore the issue of true and fair as com-panies might appeal to the concept in order to deviate from accounting principles laid down in legislation. Thus, they need to have at least considered what it means in their own country and whether this is the same view as that taken in other countries.

Issues

- Is the true and fair view a concept which is consistently translated, understood and applied throughout Europe? That is, is there a European true and fair view or separate French, German, British, etc., true and fair views?
- If it is the overriding principle, what is the likelihood that legal accounting rules will be departed from and how will this be done?

Analysis

In an attempt to shed some light on the concept of true and fair in the European setting it seems logical to start with the UK experience. We will firstly examine the practical effect of true and fair and secondly discuss its operational and symbolic meanings.

The Application of the True and Fair View in the UK

The application of the true and fair view in the UK is best evidenced by two situations. The first is the situation in which the Companies Act legislation is in conflict with accounting standards and the true and fair override is used to justify this departure from law (as allowed by Article 2(5)). This might be illustrated by the UK standard SSAP 19, *Accounting for Investment Properties* which requires that investment properties should not be depreciated. This conflicts with paragraph 18 of Schedule 4 to the Companies Act 1985 (which follows the Fourth Directive), in which the requirement is that all assets with a finite useful life must be depreciated. As Alexander points out this type of override is curious as it is not an 'exceptional case' but is now a 'normal' one.[2] It is interesting to debate whether this is acceptable under the provisions of Article 2 as given above. Other examples of a standard giving rise to a 'normal' override to law are found in SSAP 9, *Stocks and Work in Progress*, and SSAP 20, *Foreign Currency Translation*. The general application of the true and fair override is illustrated by the Daily Mail accounts shown in Extract 14.1.

Extract 14.1 – Daily Mail and General Trust plc 1992 accounts, Notes.

Investment Properties

In accordance with SSAP 19, (i) investment properties, which are those held for their investment potential and which are not occupied by any Group company, are revalued annually and the aggregate surplus or deficit is transferred to a revaluation reserve, except that any deficit in aggregate against original cost is charged to the profit and loss account and (ii) no depreciation or amortisation is provided in respect of freehold investment properties and leasehold investment properties with over 20 years to run. The directors consider that this accounting policy results in the accounts giving a true and fair view. Depreciation or amortisation is only one of many factors reflected in the annual valuation and the amount which might otherwise have been shown cannot be separately identified or quantified.

This second situation is where an individual company claims an exceptional case and thus it will depart from both law and standards in its accounting policies. One example of a company using such an exceptional case override, is to be found in the 1991 accounts of Ladbrookes, shown in Extract 14.2. In this case the treatment of the bonds as equity has a beneficial effect on the company's gearing – a rather fortuitous result of the true and fair view! The ASB in FRED 3, *Accounting for Capital Instruments*, do not accept this treatment and it will be interesting to see the result of the debate on this issue.

If a number of companies adopt the true and fair override on the basis of the same exceptional case, then the standard setters need to respond. They may either forbid the exceptional treatment or convert the exceptional override into a normal one as in the first situation.

Convertible capital bonds

The £83m 9% convertible capital bonds due 2005, issued at par by Ladbroke Group Finance (Jersey) Limited, are guaranteed on a subordinated basis by Ladbroke Group PLC and are convertible at the option of the holders of the bonds into 2% exchangeable redeemable preference shares of Ladbroke Group Finance (Jersey) Limited, which in turn are immediately exchangeable into fully paid ordinary shares of Ladbroke Group PLC at 364p per share. On the maturity of the bonds Ladbroke Group PLC has the ability to deem conversion and exchange rights to have been exercised and to place the resulting ordinary shares. The proceeds from such placing up to the amount which would have been paid on redemption of the bonds would be paid to the bondholders and any shortfall would be payable by Ladbroke Group PLC. In addition, Ladbroke Group Finance (Jersey) Limited has the ability on the maturity of the bonds to deem the maturity of the bonds extended and to procure the purchase by a third party or parties of such bonds at a price not less than par.

It is considered highly probable that the bonds will be exchanged into ordinary shares of Ladbroke Group PLC and, therefore, in order to present a true and fair view the balance sheet format specified by the Companies Act 1985 has been modified to include the convertible capital bonds under capital and reserves.

A further example of an exceptional case can be seen in the 1992 accounts of Morgan Grenfell where the normal group accounting rules are overridden (Extract 14.3, p. 362).

The use of the true and fair override of both types is not uncommon in the United Kingdom. In the March 1993 issue of *Company Reporting* a review of 450 UK listed companies found evidence of its use in 10% of them. The reasons given are analysed in Table 14.1 (p.362).

The Urgent Issues Task Force issued in December 1992 Abstract 7 dealing with disclosure when a true and fair override is invoked. They considered that in practice there had been a tendency for companies to understate rather than emphasize the significance of an override. The Abstract gives detailed recommendations of how a company should describe, quantify and justify a true and fair override. The fact that this has been thought necessary illustrates the importance of the concept of the true and fair view in UK practice.

Thus, it can be seen that the true and fair view is invoked in practice. If, as pointed out above, there is no clear definition, or even a quasi-definition, in the law or standards,what can this phenomenon mean?

TABLE 14.1

Analysis of the use of the true and fair override

True and fair override invoked in respect of:	%	Selected companies
Investment properties	44	A&J Mucklow, Allied London Properties, Amber Day, Bett Brothers, Bolton, Charter Consolidated, Daily Mail & General Trust, Haynes Publishing, J. Smart, Matthew Clark, McCarthy Stone, Merivale Moore, Ossory Estates, Raglan Property Trust, Scottish Metropolitan Property, Speyhawk, Stanhope Properties, Waverley Cameron, Y.J. Lovell.
Capital instruments	19	Automated Security, BICC, British Airways, Huntingdon International, J. Sainsbury, Ladbroke, Reckitt & Colman, Thorn EMI.
Government grants	16	A&J Mucklow, Anglian Water, Northumbrian Water, North West Water, Severn Trent Water, South West Water, Welsh Water
Consolidation	5	British Assets Trust, Marston, Thompson & Evershed
Post-balance sheet events	5	Cantors, Marston, Thompson & Evershed
Other policies	19	Berisford International, Bett Brothers, Chloride, East Midlands Electricity, Electra Investment Trust, Photo-Me International, Tate & Lyle, Wm Gleadell& Sons

Source: Company Reporting 1993

The Meaning of the True and Fair View in the UK

Walton examined the historical development of the true and fair view in British accounting and came to the conclusion that it is a phrase which is used to represent the application of generally accepted accounting principles (GAAP).[3] This view was given some legal backing in *Lloyd Cheyham & Co.* v *Littlejohn & Co.* (1986) where the courts suggested that third parties are entitled to assume that accounts are drawn up in accordance with approved practice. In an opinion given to the Accounting Standards Board in June 1993 Mary Arden QC (now the Hon. Mrs Justice Arden) states:

> ...while the true and fair view which the law requires to be given is not qualified in any way, the task of interpreting the true and fair requirement cannot be performed by the court without evidence as to the practices and views of accountants. The more authorative these practices and views, the more ready the court will be to follow them. Those practices of course do not stand still. They respond to such matters as advances in accounting and changes in the economic climate and business practice.

The implication of this is that the true and fair view is a code used by accountants and auditors to represent a changing set of practices. The consensus as to what is the currently acceptable set of practices (today's GAAP) is therefore determined by the accounting profession. Thus, as the perspective or interests of the profession change then consensus as to the meaning of GAAP may change. The meaning of the phrase 'true and fair' as a representation of GAAP is continually reconstructed by those who apply the phrase to the outcome of their activities, that is the accounting profession.

It may be argued that the British true and fair view has little operational significance. Its operational sense is limited to being only that of the elaboration of a series of working practices. It means only that the financial statements are accepted practice of the accounting profession. This notion of the profession determining in some exclusive way the meaning of this key phrase may be used to argue that the importance of the phrase is in its symbolic meaning. If the determination and interpretation are based upon, and understood only with, 'specialized knowledge' of accountants and auditors then it plays a key role in securing the status of the profession. The symbolic significance of true and fair, therefore, is in the context of the professional status of accountants and auditors who may operate it as a defence against encroachment of their position from outside. Its operational sense is limited to being only that of the elaboration of a series of working practices.

The European True and Fair View

If we turn to harmonization then these ideas may help us to understand the debates which are taking place. The development of the Fourth Directive brought into sharp focus the fundamentally different perspectives of the British approach and the continental European approach to accounting. The debate on the overriding place of true and fair was much more than an argument about accounting theory or principles (that is the operational nature of true and fair) but became a highly political battle about who regulates accounting. Hopwood puts it thus:

> Operating as a proxy the phraseology of true and fair view had to be imbued with the full significance of the underlying dispute over the territorial claims as to who should regulate and influence accounting and how that influence should be exercised.[4]

In the battle over the status of the true and fair view in the Fourth Directive the British lobby fought fiercely to protect its predominant position. Other member states were either lukewarm, welcomed the challenge of its introduction or at that stage were uncertain as to how it would be implemented. The conventional wisdom of lobbying behaviour suggests that those who have the most to lose lobby hardest and those who are willing to incur the highest costs will often be the winners.

However, even with this apparent victory of the British view, the meaning of true and fair is only as harmonized within the EC as the accounting it represents. The meaning of true and fair, as argued above, is that of the GAAP which has developed in the past and is currently developing. If, as we know to be the case, accounting practice has been developed in different economic and cultural environments to meet different needs by different interest groups (accountants, lawyers, politicians, bankers) then at any moment any accounting jurisdiction will have its own meaning of true and fair. So what real effect will the terms of Article 2 have? It could be predicted that imposing the expression true and fair view through the Fourth Directive would be a waste of time unless it was accompanied by an initiative to construct a common meaning. Instead each jurisdiction has adopted a form of words and set about constructing their own separate meaning in operational terms, based upon the Fourth Directive rules but also on pre-existing national GAAP, which embody different views and expectations of accounting.If these predictions are correct then we would expect to find that there might be differences in the implementation and, in particular, in the interpretation of Article 2. As examples, we will examine the experiences of implementation and interpretation in member states other than the UK.

The implementation of Article 2 in German company law is in s.264(2) of the1986 Commercial Code (HGB) thus:

> Der Jahresabschluß der Kapitalgesellschaft hat unter Beachtung der Grundsätze ordnungsmäßiger Buchführung ein den tatsächlichen Verhältnissen entsprechendes Bild der Vermögens-, Finanz- und Ertragslage der Kapitalgesellschaft zu vermitteln. Führen besondere Umstände dazu, daß der Jahresabschluß eiu den tatsächlichen Verhältnissen entsprechendes Bild in Sinne des Satzes 1 nicht vermittelt,so sind im Anhang zuzätzliche Angaben zu machen.

This is translated by Ordelheide as:

The financial statements of the company must, in compliance with required accounting principles, present a true and fair view of the net worth, financial position and results of the company. If special circumstances result in the financial statements not showing a true and fair view within the meaning of sentence 1, then additional disclosures are required in the notes.[5]

As Alexander points out there are a number of significant differences between this (even in translation) and the Fourth Directive.[6]

1. The phrase 'in compliance with the required accounting principles' is not in the Directive and further the translation does not give full effect to the words used in the German version (note there is no subordinate clause). This additional phrase may be seen as a significant proviso to the true and fair doctrine.

2. The last sentence of the clause seems to indicate that it is only the notes to the accounts which have to be altered to give a true and fair view, the balance sheet and profit and loss account being left in compliance with the accounting rules which may not give a true and fair view. This 'de-coupling' or 'separation' thesis has found acceptance amongst companies, auditors and the German courts. A British view would be that this goes against the philosophy as expressed in the Directive. However, the German view as expressed by Ordelheide is that the British view exceeds the Directive in that the balance sheet and profit and loss account as a whole need to show a true and fair view but not necessarily each individual component.[7]

3. The German law contains no equivalent to Article 2(5) of the Fourth Directive. From a British perspective this would appear to give little possibility of a true and fair override of the accounting legislation. In explanation of the German view Ordelheide puts forward three arguments:

   a In German law the specific rule takes precedence over the general rule. Thus the existence of specific accounting rules overrides the true and fair rule. The exception would be where the specific rule does not cover the specific case in question.

   b Deviation from the accounting rules would have been a tax risk for all German corporations, because of the close link between financial and tax accounts in Germany.

   c The idea of a standard giving a global override of the law has not been accepted in Germany where overrides are envisaged only in relation to a given company and then only in circumstances not specifically dealt with by the law (the exceptional case discussed above).[8]

In French company law the principles of Article 2 are incorporated in Article 9 of the Code de Commerce (1953) thus:

L'annexe complète et comment l'information donnée par le bilan et le compte de résultat.

Les comptes annuels doivent être réguliers, sincères et donner une image fidèle du patrimoine, de la situation financière et du résultat de l'entreprise.

Lorsque l'application d'une prescription comptable ne suffit pas pour donner l'image fidèle mentionnée au présent article, des informations complémentaires doivent être fournies dans l'annexe.

This is translated by Alexander as:

The notes complete and comment on the information in the balance sheet and profit and loss account.

The annual accounts must be regular, sincere and give a true and fair view of the wealth of the enterprise, of its financial position and of its results.

Should the application of an accounting requirement not suffice to give a true and fair view, additional information is to be shown in the notes.[9]

We might again suggest some apparent differences between this implementation, the Fourth Directive itself, and the UK and German versions:

• the introduction of two necessary conditions, that is 'réguliers' and 'sincères' in addition to the expected 'une image fidèle';
• a possible reading of the requirements is that the notes might be used to provide supplementary information to enable a true and fair view to be given.

The interpretation of these differences in approach are problematic and is the subject of some debate in European accounting circles. A similar debate can be observed on the implementation of the Italian 'quadro fedele' and the Spanish 'la imagen fiel'

In the light of the above discussion, it seems likely therefore that the number of true and fair overrides will be negligible in Germany. The same will probably be found in France. As Burlaud states:

*In effect very few companies would take the risk of departing from accounting rules and justifying them by the **extremely vague notion** of true and fair (emphasis added).*[10]

In fact Van Hulle states that he expects 'the override to be unlikely in most continental European countries, **at least for the moment'** (emphasis added).[11]

Comparing this with the UK position examined earlier in this chapter, we can see that the meaning of true and fair and its actual impact on practice differs considerably between member states. The differences are more than operational, that is they go beyond differences in individual practices, they are the result of the different environments in which accounting has in the past and is now operating. The different interpretations of the meaning of true and fair reflect the different political, cultural and legal influences on accounting practice. An appreciation of the symbolic meaning of the true and fair view is important to those wishing to understand accounting in an European context.

These arguments may appear rather 'philosophical' to the analyst but they provide an important perspective to the differences in the development and application of accounting requirements. Further, we believe that the analyst must undertake detailed analysis with these fundamental differences as a constant background consideration.

References

1. Walton, P.J. (1993) 'The true and fair view in British accounting', *European Accounting Review*, **2** (1), 49.
2. Alexander, D.A. (1993) 'European true and fair view?', *European Accounting Review, **2** (1), 59–80.
3. Walton, P.J. (1991) *The True and Fair View: A Shifting Concept*, Occasional Research Paper No.7, ACCA, London.
4. Hopwood, A.G. (1990) 'Ambiguity, knowledge and territorial claims: some observations on the doctrine of substance over form', *British Accounting Review*, March, 92.
5. Ordelheide, D. (1990) 'Soft transformations of accounting rules of the 4th Directive in Germany', *Les cahiers internationaux de la Comptabilité, **3**, 1–15.
6. Alexander, op. cit.
7. Ordelheide, D. (1993) 'True and fair view: a European and a German perspective', *European Accounting Review, **1**, 81–90.
8. Ibid.
9. Alexander, op. cit.
10. Burlaud, A.(1993) 'Commentaires sur l'article de David Alexander', *European Accounting Review, **2** (1), 98.
11. Van Hulle, K. (1993) 'Truth and untruth about true and fair', *European Accounting Review, **2** (1), 99–104.

Problems

1. Using the extracts given in the earlier chapters of this text, identify some further examples of true and fair overrides and categorize them as 'normal' or 'exceptional'.
2. Do you think the problem of translating the concept of true and fair is the cause of different perspectives within the EU? Do you consider that the problem is more than semantic? If so, why?

PART THREE

Financial Statement Analysis: European Case Studies

Overview

In this final part we attempt to answer two questions. The first is whether or not enough information is available within the published report and accounts of a company from one country to enable the user of the accounts to be able to make the necessary adjustments for a meaningful comparison with a company from a different country. The answer to this question would unfortunately appear to be no. In analysing the accounts of six companies, each from a different country, we found that heroic assumptions need to be made about a number of key issues. The measurement practices vary from country to country, and the supporting information is often inadequate for a user of accounts relying on just published information to be able to make meaningful comparisons.

It has to be remembered that the member states of the European Union have adopted a policy of mutual recognition. From an accounting perspective this means that financial accounts prepared according to the present standards of one member state must be accepted by stock exchanges in all the other member states. It is accepted that the standards and laws differ from one country to another, but it is believed by the Commission that there is a sufficient degree of equivalence to enable users in one country to understand accounts prepared according to the standards and laws of another country.

The second question we consider is whether or not it is worthwhile for an outsider to attempt a reconciliation. We demonstrate that a reconciliation is possible and produces interesting results. It must be appreciated, however, that in making adjustments to allow for the differences in reporting practices between countries, some adjustments are more reliable than others. We develop a model that enables users of accounts to assess the reliability that can be attached to each adjustment.

In this part of the book, in order to demonstrate how to make comparisons between companies in different countries we adopt a case study approach and examine the accounts of just two companies (one from Italy, one from France) from different country perspectives. The adjustments to the accounts, to conform with each country's accounting practices were carried out by accounting academics from the appropriate country. We illustrate the adjustments that need to take place for the comparison to be meaningful, explaining the assumptions that need to be made if an external user of accounts is to carry out this exercise and to demonstrate the sensitivity of the reported profit figures to these assumptions and the accounting practices of the different countries.

We believe that because of the dynamic nature of financial reporting rules, and because of assumptions that are necessary to produce accounts, that any attempts to generalize or model relative country reporting procedures are likely to lead to inappropriate conclusions. The case study approach we have adopted for cross-country comparisons deals with the detail of financial reporting in current practice. In our view analysts would be unwise to compromise in their examination of this detail.

It is emphasized that we are not using the standards of any one country as a benchmark. This gets away from the view that any particular country has superior reporting standards and that all other countries should aspire to this standard. All one can really say is that this is the way accounting is done in a particular country and by and large it seems to work for that country.

The earnings and stockholders' equity for each of our two case study companies are adjusted according to the principles and practices of each of the other countries with which this book is concerned. It is the objective of this exercise to demonstrate how it is possible to compare the performance of companies operating and reporting in different countries in a manner which is meaningful to analysts in different countries. To illustrate how to make such a reconciliation and to demonstrate its limitations, the accounts of two companies are used, Pirelli SpA and Rhône-Poulenc SA. It is not suggested that these two companies are in any way representative of particular categories of companies. They are just two large international companies that we chose as case studies. Their accounts were analysed by researchers from Germany, France, Spain, Italy, the Netherlands and the UK. English was the working language of the group, so the English language version of these two companies' accounts were chosen for study. The financial reports for the accounting year ending in 1990 were analysed from the perspective of each country, with the exception of the Netherlands. The 1991 accounts were analysed from the Dutch and British point of view.

15

Pirelli SpA

Pirelli is a major Italian company. In terms of market capitalization it ranks about eighth largest in size in Italy. It is seen as a major international firm with its shares traded in the capital markets of a number of countries. It therefore supplies much more information than is actually required by Italian company law. It should be remembered that Italian companies are tightly controlled. At the beginning of the 1990s, only seven companies had offered more than 50% of their shares to the public, but five of these still had majority control exercised by a small group. In only two companies, therefore, were a majority of shares widely held. Pirelli is not one of these two.

The adjustments necessary for an understanding of the Pirelli financial accounts by non-Italians will be shown for the years ending 31 December 1990 and 31 December 1991. For the first of these years the adjustments will be made to conform to practice in Germany, France, Spain and the UK. For 1991 the adjustments will be to conform to practices in the Netherlands and the UK.

First, however, attention is drawn to an interesting change in the accounting policy of the company that took place between 1990 and 1991.

Current cost versus historical cost

A striking feature of the Pirelli financial statements for 1990 is the preparation of the main accounts according to current cost accounting principles. The historical cost accounts in 1990 were the supplementary statements, presented in order to adhere to a commitment made with Consob.

In the notes to the 1990 accounts this particular treatment is justified thus:

> *The adoption of current cost accounting principles is motivated by the fact that a significant part of the industrial and marketing operations of the Group is carried out in countries with high endemic rates of inflation (Brazil, Argentina, Peru, Turkey).*
>
> *This particular situation – which is not found in any other group based in Italy – is such that financial statements based on current cost accounting principles permit comparison and are better able to*

present the financial position and results of operations of the Pirelli Group.

However, in adherence to commitments made with Consob, our Company has presented an audited consolidated balance sheet on a historical cost basis at December 31, 1990 for the first time, to be followed by the consolidated income statement at historical costs for the year ended December 31, 1991.

Nevertheless, as already communicated to Consob and in the firm belief of rendering a valid sense of informative completeness to the shareholders and public, our Company will continue to furnish financial statement information in the future based on current cost accounting principles which will continue to be the management principles of the Group.

The auditors, Reconta Ernst and Young, express the opinion in the 1990 accounts that the current cost principles adopted by Pirelli allow for a consistent and fair view of the financial position and results of operations.

If these principles are fair for Pirelli why not for companies with similar international operations? Only 14.6% of Pirelli sales are in fact in Central and South America, areas of high inflation. The notes to the accounts also mention Turkey, although it is not possible to say what percentage of the sales are to that country, but from a reading of the very detailed review of operations there is no reason to believe it is particularly high. There are many multinational companies with a higher percentage of their operations in high inflation countries that do not adopt inflation accounting principles.

In 1991 the policy changed. The company reverted to the historical cost convention for the main accounts, with current cost information being given at various places in the accounts in note form. In the notes to the 1991 consolidated financial statements dealing with accounting principles Pirelli explain.

The consolidated financial statements have been prepared using the financial statements of the Group companies and Pirelli S.p.A. at December 31, 1991 and 1990, in accordance with accounting policies based on historical costs. For those countries [sic] operating in high inflation countries (Brazil, Argentina, Peru, Turkey), the financial statements used are those adjusted for inflation, based on Group principles, described later.

In the contribution operation (sic) of June 1988, Pirelli S.p.A. acquired the equity interests in group companies held by Société Internationale Pirelli S.A. at appraisal values that were generally higher than the net equities resulting from the financial statements of these companies. The value in excess of net equity was allocated to fixed assets in the financial statements of the individual companies and depreciated at the same rates used for the fixed asset categories.

These principles reflect those contained in the IV Directive of the European Community, those issued by the National Boards of Dottori Commercialisti e Ragionieri and, in their absence, those of the International Accounting Standards Committee (I.A.S.C.).

A further note explains the figures for 'current cost amounts have been determined in accordance with International Accounting Standard (IAS) No. 15 and No. 29 and the Financial Accounting Standard (FAS), No. 89'.
The 1991 Report of the Independent Auditor 'Reconta Ernst & Young' expresses the opinion that the statements present fairly the position of the Group.

In our opinion, the consolidated financial statements referred to above present fairly the consolidated financial position of the Pirelli Group as at 31, December 1991 and the consolidated results of its operations and changes in financial position for the year then ended in conformity with accounting principles issued by the 'Dottori Commercialisti' and 'Ragionieri' or, in the absence thereof, those issued by the International Accounting Standards Committee (I.A.S.C.).

In order to maintain the continuity and completeness of information provided, the Group has also furnished consolidated financial statement data at December 31, 1991 and 1990 prepared using current values. The elements of the financial statements that are subject to variation on application of current values have been examined by us through verification of the correct and consistent application of inflation accounting principles, the most important of which are described in the paragraph 'Inflation accounting principles' in the 'Notes to consolidated financial statements'.

One wonders why in 1991 a true and fair view could be based on historical cost accounting principles, whereas in 1990 a truer and fairer view was revealed by current cost accounts. To give some idea of the significance of the differences, in 1990:

	[billion lire]
Shareholders' equity with current cost accounting	3853
Shareholders' equity with historical cost accounting	3039
	814

The difference can be explained by the revaluation of three items:

	[billion lire]
Fixed assets	663
Financial assets	101
Inventory	50
	814

The fixed assets have been revalued for current cost purposes by independent appraisers. The financial assets are stated in the historical cost accounts at their cost inclusive of revaluations permitted by law–as opposed to their market value. The inventory is valued for historical cost purposes on the FIFO basis, with the exception of high inflation countries, where replacement cost is used.

Reconciliation – 1990 Adjustments

We now move to the exercise of adjusting the accounts as prepared according to Italian accounting principles so as to conform to the principles in the four other countries, France, Spain, Germany and the UK.

Revaluation of fixed assets

The basic source for principles content, and manner of preparation for financial statements is the Italian Civil Code. Fiscal legislation, however, requires that tax returns be based on accounting records and, consequently, financial statements can be somewhat affected by tax considerations. The Civil Code adopts the historical cost basis. Some fixed assets of Pirelli were, however, revalued under laws passed in 1975 and 1982, applying specified coefficients (calculated from inflation statistics) to fixed asset cost values. The revaluations were only allowed if the asset's current economic value was shown separately in the balance sheet. If this practice was followed the revaluation surplus could be used to increase the shareholders' equity or to cover losses. This surplus was not subject to taxes. In 1990 companies were again given the opportunity to revalue, but if they did, they were to be taxed this time on the revaluation surplus. Very few companies chose to do so.

Therefore, the historical cost accounts show a figure which is the result of adding together assets valued at different dates. Revaluations would clearly only relate to assets purchased prior to 1983, assets purchased subsequent to that year being carried at cost. Some of Pirelli's assets are revalued, but not all to a common date. This is the usual problem with historical cost accounts. The 1990 balance sheet (HC) shows a revaluation reserve figure of only L121 billion. The HC fixed assets are shown as L4208 billion, whereas the CC fixed assets are L4871 billion.

First we attempt to reconcile these figures with UK practice. It is assumed, for our adjustments purposes, that one half of this difference between the current cost and the historical cost figure is the result of the type of partial and occasional revaluation process which takes place in the UK. The other half of the increase (L330 billion) is due to the complete and continuous revaluation required for current cost purposes.

According to this reasoning, the historical cost fixed asset figures prepared to UK standards compared to the current cost Pirelli accounts would show a lower asset figure (L330 billion). However, the accounts, prepared to UK standards, compared with the historical cost Pirelli accounts, would show a L330 billion increase in fixed assets which leads to an increase in depreciation charge and so a reduced profit. In the HC accounts there is a revaluation reserve amounting to L121 billion while in the CC accounts the revaluation reserve is L719 billion. The difference in the reserves is in line with the difference in the fixed asset values in the two balance sheets.

In France, as in Italy, legal revaluations have taken place from time to time. Revaluations at such times do not result in tax charges. The last revaluation that took place which offered tax advantages was in 1977. Between 1978 and 1983 revaluations were permitted but little use was made of the possibilities because a capital gains charge would have resulted from any increase.

From 1984 a new system of regulated revaluations was introduced in France, but again, profitable companies made little use of such opportunities to adjust asset values. We can assume that in 1977 the fixed assets of Pirelli would have had similar values, adopting French practice. Since 1983, no revaluations would have taken place (in the historical cost accounts) in either country.

We have to decide how much lower the fixed assets value would be according to French conventions than it would be according to the Italian as a result of Italian revaluations between 1977 and 1983. The revaluation reserve is shown as L121 billion. We assume that the assets have a 12 to 15 year life and that the revaluation in 1977 would have occurred half way through the life of an asset. At that time this would have resulted in the same reserve according to both French and Italian principles. The revaluation between 1977 and 1983 will have occurred only in the Italian version of the accounts, and we assume this is one half of the total reserve. Therefore, in the French version of the Pirelli accounts, the value of the fixed assets and the revaluation reserve is reduced by L61 billion.

In Spain the general rule for property, plant and equipment is to value them at historical cost. Occasionally, however, revaluation is allowed. One such occasion was in 1983. At that time all assets acquired prior to that date could be legally revalued. We have assumed, therefore, that the assets would have been revalued in Spain as in Italy in 1983, and not since that date. Thus, between the two countries, any differences in the 1990 values would be small and we have not made any adjustment.

In Germany the revaluation of fixed assets is not permitted. An adjustment, therefore, has been made to the accounts as they would appear in Germany in order to eliminate the revaluation reserve.

Depreciation adjustment

The adjustments to the fixed assets figures appearing in the balance sheets required to conform to differing accounting policies necessitate adjustments to be made to the annual depreciation charges. In company accounts we are not always told the depreciation policy. In Germany depreciation would be less because of the lower asset valuations. Assuming the fixed assets have a 12 year life, this would reduce the depreciation charge by L10 billion. In the United Kingdom the depreciation charge would be higher, estimated as L27 billion. There would be no difference in the charge in Spain from that in Italy.

In France, for such a company as Pirelli, straight line depreciation would be the exception. Accelerated depreciation would have been used for tangible assets, except for transport and construction equipment and in some cases (such as equipment to be used for R&D

expenditures) exceptional depreciation would have been used. As a result, the annual depreciation charges would have been higher. On the other hand, the lower asset value figures in France would lead to a lower annual depreciation charge in the income statement. On balance we estimate an amount of L4 billion less annual depreciation in France.

Intangibles

In the Pirelli accounts, both current cost and historical cost, a relatively small amount of intangible assets, L125 billion (only 3% of fixed assets) appears on the balance sheet An inadequate note gives the following breakdown:

	1990 December 31	1989 December 31
	(lire millions)	
Formation expenses	28 737	13 059
Industrial and design patent rights	2 573	1 865
Concessions, licences, trademarks and similar rights	5 387	6 605
Other deferred charges	88 910	89 429
	125 607	110 958

Among the main items included in other deferred charges (L88 910 million) are charges relating to company reorganization, the securing of loans, leased property and software and hardware installations.

The Pirelli accounts tell us that as a rule research and development expenses are charged to income in the year incurred. Nevertheless, they may be capitalized and amortized over a period of five years if certain rigorously specified criteria are met. Goodwill, patents and trademarks are amortized over their expected economic lives not exceeding a period of 10 years. Other costs of various types from which future benefits derive are generally amortized over a maximum period of five years. The costs relating to taking on loans are amortized over a period not exceeding the duration of the loan. The policy statement refers to the write-off of goodwill, but surprisingly, no figure appears in the accounts – perhaps it has all been amortized.

The UK adjustment is based on a faster write-off of the intangibles and can be explained as follows:

	Italy (lire billion)
Opening intangibles (as per accounts)	111
Less Depreciation (as per accounts)	37
	74
Closing intangibles (as per accounts)	125
Therefore additions during year	51

It is assumed that L23 billion of this additional expenditure would in the UK be charged against profit. In the UK the figure for intangibles in the balance sheet is reduced by a similar amount.

The German approach to the intangibles in the Pirelli accounts will be taken as being similar to that of the UK. In France, goodwill, patents and trademarks would have been amortized over a longer period (say from 20 to 40 years) than the ten years which is the Pirelli practice. Thus the asset figure in France might have been higher. However, we did not change the equity and assets figures, given the small amount involved.

The Spanish definition of intangible assets allows only the following items to be included:

- goodwill;
- industrial and design patent rights;
- concessions, licences, trademarks;
- leased property;
- software.

Financial charges due to the securing of loans and leased property may not be included in the balance sheet as deferred expenses to be allocated over future periods. Formation expenses must be charged to the profit and loss account, unless they have been caused by new operations of the firm, and then only before the beginning of the new activity, in which case they are considered to be a particular kind of set-up cost. If these charges relate to company reorganizations they must be charged immediately to the profit and loss account, and they cannot be capitalized.

As Pirelli does not explain the nature of these expenses we have adopted a prudent approach with an adjustment made for Spain that reduces assets and shareholders' equity by L28 737 million. We will assume one half of this is written off against the 1990 profits.

In Spain, Germany and the UK charges resulting from company reorganizations cannot be capitalized. The other items included by Pirelli as deferred charges would in many countries be excluded from intangible assets. The meaning and content of charges referring to software and hardware installations are unclear.

For Spain it was decided to adjust assets and equity by one half of the other deferred charges (L44 495 million), this being the cost of company reorganizations and the charges referred to software and hardware installations. Only one half is capitalized, the other half having been written off in earlier years. The amortization charge for the year will need to be reduced therefore by L13 240 million.

Inventory

In Italy, LIFO is allowed, with the lower of cost or market value rule, market value can be either replacement cost (purchase price) or net realizable value (selling price). The UK does not allow LIFO or replacement cost.

In the historical cost accounts, a note explains that inventory is stated at cost using the FIFO method, with the exception of high inflation countries where replacement cost is used. This valuation of part of the inventory at replacement cost would not be allowed in the UK, therefore some adjustment is necessary. Unfortunately, there is no way of knowing to what percentage of the inventory this revaluation applies.

The effect of such revaluation to replacement cost is to increase the value of the closing inventory above what it would be with a FIFO cost valuation. This will have the effect of increasing profits, but not to the full extent of the increase in the closing inventory valuation. The opening inventory will also be higher. The inventory actually fell by L866 billion over the period. It will be assumed, therefore, that the different methods of valuing inventory (in the HC statement) between Italy and the UK will not result in a change in profits, the higher valuation on some items of inventory being compensated for by the lower inventory level.

The different valuation methods will affect the closing inventory valuations, and the UK asset figure is lowered by L10 billion. A similar adjustment is made for Germany. It was not thought necessary to make an adjustment for Spain or France. In fact the difference, in the Pirelli accounts, between the inventory valuation prepared according to current cost principles and those prepared on an historical cost basis is very small.

In figures the value of stocks and work in progress at 31 December 1990 is:

[million lire]

at current cost	=	1 844 386
at historical cost	=	1 794 211
a difference of only		50 175

On an historical cost total asset figure of L10 997 773 million this is less than half of one per cent.

Pensions

As explained in Part Two of the book the treatment of pension costs varies between countries. In the case of Pirelli there is a self-funded scheme, the balance sheet showing a provision for employees' leaving indemnity of L578 billion and a pension provision of L228 billion. This, however, is a minor part of pension funding in Italy. The state provides the major element of an individual's pension. There is a national social security fund to which all employers and employees contribute. In addition, companies should create a termination reserve for employees by making an annual provision of approximately one-twelfth of the total salaries paid. Thus the treatment of pension costs is based on a self-funded scheme. Upon termination, employees are entitled to a deferred compensation payment out of the reserve of one month's salary times the number of years employed. In the UK the company would provide a major part of an employee's pension which would be externally funded.

In France, there would only have been provisions for retirement indemnities. An adjustment should be made for this difference, but no confidence can be attached to the estimates.

Deferred tax

In Italy the deferred tax provision in the accounts of an individual company arises mainly as a result of accelerated depreciation in fixed assets. In consolidated accounts, accelerated depreciation is not usually applied; in fact the provision is quite small (L44 000 million), with the deferred tax charge for the year being L8000 million. It has been assumed that in the UK the partial liability method would be used, so the L8000 million is added back to increase UK profits.

A similar treatment is adopted for France.

Inflation adjustments

These, of course, only arise in the current cost approach. The notes to the current cost accounts show two adjustments to profits relating to inflation: 'a gain on financial monetary items (low inflation countries)' and an 'Adjustment to cost of goods sold, to commercial monetary items (low inflation countries)' which reduces the costs of raw material and supplies.

At first these two adjustments seem strange. Why is no adjustment made with respect to high inflation countries? In the notes to the historical cost accounts an explanation appears: in detailing the differences in moving from the current cost statement of income to the historical cost statement, mention is made of the fact that 'inflation adjustments relating to high inflation countries are not eliminated'. We do not know what these adjustments are, they are incorporated in both sets of accounts.

Non-recurring items

Pirelli credits the profit and loss account with L44 billion for non-recurring items. These include miscellaneous income from the gains on the disposal of fixed assets, other non-operating income, less non-recurring, non-operating and reorganization expenses. It has been assumed that these items would be treated as extraordinary items in the UK. The Spanish would consider non-recurring income, reorganization expenses and gains on the disposal of fixed assets as extraordinary (L20 155 million). The historical cost accounts give a higher amount of non-recurring expenses in the income statement than the current cost accounts, although this is not clearly explained in the accounts. We will assume that this difference is because of valuation adjustments to investments (L34 613 million).

Foreign currency translation

In the Pirelli accounts balance sheets are translated at exchange rates ruling at year end, whereas in Germany it is assumed that fixed assets, intangibles, investments in affiliated companies and other investments would be translated at average rates in the year of acquisition with all other balance sheet items at year-end rate.

Another difference between German principles and those used by Pirelli is that Germany uses the temporal method whereas Pirelli uses the closing rate method. Therefore an adjustment has been made.

Spanish rules on consolidated accounts also differ from those for Italy. Under Spanish rules, when the foreign company to be consolidated is in a country with hyperinflation its financial statements must be adjusted for inflation before they are translated, although it is also possible to follow the temporal method.

Summary of adjustments

TABLE 15.1
Pirelli SpA earnings adjustments (billion lire) – 1990

	Italy	UK	Germany	Spain	France
Net income	100	100	100	100	100
Depreciation on revalued assets		(27)	10		4
Depreciation on intangibles			10	9	
Deferred tax		8			8
Intangibles		(23)	(23)	(14)	
Pensions					6
Foreign currency translation			(37)		
Adjusted income for distribution	100	58	60	95	118

Table 15.1 summarizes the adjustments that appear to be necessary to move from the profit as shown in Italy to that which would be shown in four of the other countries. In France it is estimated a higher profit would be shown, whilst in the UK and Germany a very much lower profit would be reported. It should be emphasized that these adjustments are those that would appear to be necessary based on the disclosure of policies in the Pirelli accounts. It is very much the reconciliation based on information available to an outsider. Table 15.2 shows the adjustment to shareholder's equity.

TABLE 15.2
Pirelli SpA: adjustments to stockholders' equity (billion lire) – 1990

	Italy	UK	Germany	Spain	France
Total stockholder's equity	3039	3039	3039	3039	3039
Revaluation of fixed assets		330	(121)		(61)
Formation expenses		(23)	(23)	(29)	
Deferred charges			(20)	(44)	
Inventory		(10)	(10)		
Deferred tax		(8)			
Foreign currency translation			193		
Profit &Loss					
Account adjustment		(42)	(40)	(5)	18
Adjusted stockholders' equity	3039	3286	3018	2961	2996

Reconciliation – 1991 Adjustments

For 1991 adjustments have been made to reconcile with accounting standards and practices in the UK and in the Netherlands. The issues involved in a comparison with Dutch principles were not discussed for 1990.

The 1991 balance sheet (historical cost) of Pirelli shows a revaluation reserve figure of L118 864 million. The fixed assets are shown as L4575 billion whereas the current cost fixed assets are L5025 billion.

UK

For the purposes of the UK adjustment we have valued the net fixed
assets as the mid point between the current cost and the historical cost
net asset figures. This assumed that in the UK one half of the
revaluations above the statutory adjustments would have taken place.
This increases the shareholders' equity in the UK by L225 billion above
that in the Italian company's historical cost accounts.

Before moving to the adjustments for the Netherlands we will
complete the UK adjustments.

Depreciation

The higher value of fixed assets according to UK conventions will result
in a higher depreciation charge. We have increased this in 1991 by 20
billion lire.

Intangibles

Note I to the Pirelli accounts is shown below. It will be seen that
goodwill is now being carried in the accounts (at year end 50 billion
lire) as a result of the acquisition of STC. It is possible that a company in
the UK would also choose to carry the goodwill on the balance sheet
but we will adopt the more common policy in 1991 of writing the
amounts off against reserves. If the full goodwill is written off against
reserves there would be no need to amortize this item. We will assume
the amount amortized in 1991 is 10 billion. This means that in the UK
the 10 billion would be added back to profits, and the two amounts
totalling 60 million deducted from reserves.

As explained in the 1990 adjustments we have also adopted a policy of a faster write-off of the other intangible items. For the UK in 1991
we have added a further 25 billion lire to the amortization charge.

Note 1: Intangible assets

	(in millions of lire)	
	December 31 1991	December 31, 1990
Formation expenses	28 111	28 737
Industrial and design patent rights	6 792	2 573
Concessions, licences, trademarks and similar rights	4 143	5 387
Goodwill	49 585	—
Other deferred charges	94 597	88 910
	183 225	**125 607**

Goodwill relates to the acquisition of the STC company which operates
in the sector of land cables for telecommunications. Among the main
items included in other deferred charges are charges relating to

company reorganizations, the securing of loans, leased property, and software and hardware installations, etc.

The reconciliation of the Pirelli profit and shareholders' equity figure from Italian principles to UK principles is shown in Table 15.3

TABLE 15.3
Pirelli SpA earnings and equity (billion lire) – adjusted to UK practice

Adjustment to net income:	
Net income (Italy)	622
Adjustment	
Increased depreciation	(20)
Eliminate depreciation on goodwill	10
Increase amortization of intangibles	(25)
Net income (UK)	587
Adjustments to stockholders' equity:	
Total stockholders' equity (Italy)	2,314
Revalued fixed assets	225
Goodwill written off	(60)
P&L account	35
Stockholders' equity (UK)	2,444

Netherlands

Fixed assets

Contrary to widespread belief, HCA is in fact more common than CCA in Dutch external financial reporting. A number of surveys have shown that current cost accounting has been applied neither universally nor in a uniform manner. Periodic surveys of the annual reports of listed companies demonstrate that replacement value has not been the normal valuation method used in external reporting. For land and buildings replacement value is used by 35% of companies and for plant and equipment replacement value is used by 22% of companies

For example, in the annual report of Akzo 1991 the point is made that 'the principles of valuation and determination of income used in the consolidated financial statements ... are based on historical cost. Current-value data are furnished by way of supplementary information.'

The Dutch Companies Act permits but does not require the use of current cost accounting (CCA). If a company chooses to use CCA, the substance, scope and method of application of CCA are regulated by an asset valuation decree of 22 December 1983.

Tangible fixed assets, financial fixed assets and stocks may be valued at replacement value; recoverable amount or realizable value may be used if necessary. Increases in current cost have to be credited to a revaluation reserve and decreases debited thereto. Irrespective of whether HCA or CCA is chosen, intangible assets and current assets other than inventories are not permitted to be valued at current cost. Corporate taxation is of course based on historical costs, not on replacement costs.

The Act states that the balance sheet and the profit and loss account together with the notes thereto, must reflect 'fairly, clearly and systematically' the financial position and its breakdown into assets and liabilities as at the end of the financial year, and the amount of the profit and loss for the financial year and its deviation from the items of income and expense. The Dutch guidelines use the word 'systematically' which implies that a chosen principle of valuation needs to be maintained as much as possible in the succeeding periods.

The Italian system of incidental revaluation by law is not usual in the Netherlands. Dutch companies choose between HCA or CCA and use the chosen principle systematically. For reconciliation purposes, therefore, an adjustment has been made to the Pirelli accounts in order to eliminate the revaluation reserve, resulting in a decrease of shareholders' equity by L118 864 million.

Depreciation

The Italian Civil Code provides that depreciation should be charged on all categories of assets on the basis of their estimated remaining useful life. The Italian Tax Law gives advice on how to calculate depreciation. We assume the assets have a 12 to 15 year life. Because the revaluation of fixed assets is not permitted in the Netherlands, in historical cost accounts an adjustment has to be made to the annual depreciation charge appearing in the profit and loss account, namely a decrease of L9905 million (118 864m/12 years).

Research and development

The Italian Civil Code does not deal specifically with research and development. The fiscal legislation provides that not more than 50% of the research and development expenses incurred in the financial year are deductible from taxable income. The Pirelli accounts tell us that 'as a rule research and development expenses are charged to income in the year incurred. Nevertheless, they may by capitalized and amortized over a period of five years if certain rigorously specified criteria are met.'

This capitalization and amortization is most usual in the Netherlands. But when capitalization takes place a legal reserve of the size of the capitalized amount has to be formed as a part of the shareholders' equity. Assuming that the 'rigorously specified criteria' agree with the Dutch policy, no adjustment is necessary.

Goodwill, patents and trademarks

The Italian Civil Code requires that patents and trademarks be stated at cost and amortized over their remaining life. According to the Dutch Act goodwill may be charged against income or shareholders' equity. It is also possible to capitalize and amortize it over a period of five years. The capitalized costs of goodwill may be amortized over a period corresponding to the expected useful life. The amortization period may exceed five years only if a substantially longer period can be ascribed to the goodwill; in this case, the amortization period and the reason must be stated. In conclusion therefore no adjustment is made to the Pirelli accounts

Deferred charges

Italian law does not allow individual companies to capitalize lease agreements; thus, for statutory purposes, all leases are treated as operational leases. However, for group accounting purposes lease capitalization is permitted but not mandatory. Pirelli inform us: 'All existing lease contracts in the Group are in the nature of financial leases. Consequently, these assets are recorded in fixed assets, in accordance with international accounting practices. Leased assets are therefore capitalized and depreciated over their estimated useful lives; the major part of the lease payment is considered as a financial expense and residual lease payments are recorded as a financial liability.' This policy corresponds with the guideline in the Netherlands so no adjustment is made.

Some adjustment is necessary, however, with respect to this item because the Dutch Civil Code does not permit capitalization of company reorganization charges. A Dutch company is, however, allowed to form a provision. However, from the information supplied in the notes to the Pirelli financial statements it is not possible to determine the amount of expenditure on company reorganization. From a Dutch perspective the securing of loans, leased property and software and hardware would be better excluded from intangible assets and shown as deferred expenses.

The Pirelli report states that 'work in progress on long-term contracts is valued in proportion to the stage of completion of the work, on the basis of agreed prices and taking into account estimated losses'.

In the Netherlands work in progress may not be valued above production cost. However, two variations from this rule are permitted. One possibility is to take a proportion of the profit to the stage of completion of the work, when this leads to a better understanding of the result. This is done by Pirelli. The other possibility is to bill the client as much as possible of the finished park of the work. This will lead to a decrease of the amount of work in progress. It is concluded that no adjustment is necessary.

Deferred taxes

Pirelli state:

The provision for income taxes relating to current income taxes is determined on the accrual basis, according to fiscal legislation and regulations in the individual countries. Deferred taxation is provided for timing differences arising between income in the financial statements for statutory purposes and the income in the financial statements prepared on the basis of the principles described herein.

When in Italy an item of expense in the financial statements is disallowed by the fiscal authorities because it should be capitalized or deferred and subsequently amortized over a number of years, it is generally reinstated in the financial statements as a fixed asset or deferred charge by crediting the 'tax reserve'. This adjustment is made in the year when the agreement is reached with the fiscal authorities and is amortized in subsequent years.

This policy leads to a deferred tax provision in the accounts of an individual company mainly as a result of accelerated depreciation in fixed assets. In consolidated accounts, however, accelerated depreciation is not usually retained.

In the Netherlands both the deferred credit approach and estimated liability approach are permitted. The application of the comprehensive liability method is the most usual practice. This means that no adjustment is necessary.

Pensions

According to the Pirelli report:

> The accruals for employees' leaving indemnity, pensions and other employee benefits are made on the basis of the legislation in each individual country, local labour agreements and specific benefit programs in effect at certain Group companies. The principle applied is that of allocating the entire cost at maturity over the service lives of the employees based on entitlement earned; this has required the use of actuarial methods, except in the case of employees' leaving indemnity.

In the Netherlands a company, when giving employees the right to a pension, has to recognize the liabilities. Usually in the Netherlands funds are invested in a life insurance company, a company pension fund or an industrial pension fund. In the notes to the financial statements the accounting principles operated in relation to the pension liabilities and provisions has to be explained. The pension costs are externally funded. To reconcile the Italian accounts to Dutch practices, these amounts are deducted from the liabilities and assets sides of the balance sheet, leaving the shareholders' equity unchanged.

Foreign currency translation

The foreign currency issue is not discussed specifically by the Italian Civil Code; however, consistent with its inherent logic, the rate of exchange at the balance sheet date should be used to calculate any unrealized losses. On the other hand, fiscal legislation requires that transactions in foreign currencies be translated into lire at the rates existing at the transaction date and that losses on exchange are to be accounted for only when they are realized. Thus any unrealized losses provided for in the financial statements are not recognized for tax purposes.

Pirelli report that the balance sheets expressed in foreign currency have been translated into Italian lire at exchange rates ruling at year end. The income statements expressed in foreign currency have been translated into Italian lire at the average exchange rate during the year. From this follows, with respect to the balance sheet, that Pirelli uses the closing rate method.

> *Translation differences are charged or credited to reserves... The translation difference represents the difference arising from translating the financial statements at December 31 1991 at exchange rates ruling at December 31 1991 and reflects the slight strengthening of the Italian lire against the currencies in which the individual financial statements are expressed.*

The Dutch Act requires explanation of the bases for the translation of amounts expressed in foreign currencies, with disclosure of how translation and exchange differences have been dealt with. The Act contains no specific directions for the treatment of foreign currencies in the accounts. The guidelines give a specification with respect of the various applicable bases for translation. Practice in this area is not uniform but closing rates are the most common with translation differences in general included in income. It is again concluded that no adjustment is necessary.

Extraordinary items

Pirelli debits the profit and loss account with L567 538 billion for extraordinary items. In the Netherlands the distinction between 'non-recurring item' and 'extraordinary item' is very important. By 'non-recurring item' it is meant that the item occurs only once, while 'extraordinary' means that the item does not belong to the usual operations. We assume that all the items in the Pirelli accounts can be treated as extraordinary items. The reconciliation of the Pirelli profit and shareholders' equity figures from Italian principles to Dutch principles is shown in Table 15.4.

TABLE 15.4
Pirelli SpA income and equity 1991 (billion lire) adjusted to the practices of the Netherlands

Adjustment to net income:	
Net income (Italy)	622
Depreciation revalued fixed assets	10
Adjusted net income (Netherlands)	632
Adjustment to shareholders' equity	
Total shareholders' equity (Italy)	2,314
Revaluation fixed assets	(119)
Profit and loss account adjustment	10
Adjusted shareholders' equity (Netherlands)	2205

Problems

1. What are the reasons that might explain why Pirelli changed from inflation adjusted accounts in 1990 to historical cost accounts in 1991? What is the position taken by the auditor with regard to signing the Pirelli accounts following the change in the principles being applied?

2. The earnings and shareholders' funds of Pirelli show significant variations when adjusted to allow for different country accounting conventions. Briefly summarize the major adjustments.

3. Explain the methods that Pirelli has employed over the years to revalue its assets. Compare and contrast these methods with those that have been adopted in the other five countries.

4. Italy is a leading industrial nation and yet its stock exchanges are not amongst the leading stock markets in the world. Write a brief report on the stock exchanges in Italy explaining why they do not seem to play a major role in the financial environment in that country.

16

Rhône-Poulenc SA

The accounts of Rhône-Poulenc SA will be adjusted to conform to the practices in the other five countries. Rhône-Poulenc (RP) is the largest chemical group in France. To attempt to make meaningful comparisons the adjustments will be based on the actual policies and practices being followed by chemical companies in the other countries, in particular with ICI from the UK, Bayer from Germany, Repsol from Spain and Akzo from the Netherlands

The Rhône-Poulenc group raises finance on a number of international markets and to finance its active acquisition policy has issued a number of different types of security including some sophisticated hybrids. The company was at the time of the 1991 accounts the seventh largest chemical group in the world. Although the company has been controlled by the French government the existence of various outside investors with participation rights in the profits of the company and holders of preferred securities and bonds ensures that reporting standards are of a high quality. Because of the company's policy of preparing consolidated accounts in line with US GAAP the level of disclosure may be higher than in the case for a French company reporting purely for the domestic market.

In 1990 consolidated net income declined by 52.5% from the 1989 level. This decline was attributed to the difficult global chemical market, the economic crisis in Brazil which cut substantially the earnings in that country's subsidiary and the decline in value of the franc, particularly against the US dollar and Japanese yen.

Although the French law on consolidation was enacted in 1985 and came into force in 1986 thereby making preparation of consolidated accounts compulsory, the group has been drawing up such accounts for eighteen years. In 1990 the number of subsidiaries fully consolidated (320) increased by 60% (198 in 1989) and 80 affiliated companies were accounted for by the equity method (83 in 1989).

Policies

In its note on accounting policies Rhône-Poulenc states that:

The Group applies, for its consolidated financial statements, accounting principles which comply with French law and which are

generally accepted in the United States of America. Certain options provided for in the French law on consolidation have been exercised as indicated in notes 1b and g

The accounts satisfy French law and US GAAP while taking options, in this case relating to fixed asset valuation and translation of foreign currencies.

TABLE 16.1
Rhône-Poulenc SA: earning adjustments (FF million) – 1990

	F	G	I	S	UK
Income for distribution to common stockholders	1 097	1 097	1 097	1 097	1 097
Goodwill		484	(1 452)	(1 523)	484
Capitalized interest		(112)	(112)		(112)
Depreciation:					
Capitalized interest		41	41		41
Revalued assets		—	(394)	(394)	
Tangibles			118		
Intangibles other than goodwill			(235)		
Leases		555		555	555
Foreign currency translation			174		174
Taxation		(457)		334	
Restructuration			—		954
		1 608	(763)	69	3 193
Less: Minority interest		4	61	74	242
Adjusted income for distribution	**1 097**	**1 604**	**(702)**	**(5)**	**2 951**

TABLE 16.2
Rhône-Poulenc SA: adjustments to stockholders' equity (FF million) – 1990

	F	G	I	S	UK
Total stockholders' equity	21 047	21 047	21 047	21 047	21 047
Revaluation of fixed assets		—	2 384	2 384	
Depreciation of fixed assets		—	118		
Depreciation of other intangibles		—	(235)		
Depreciation adjustments re:					
capitalized interest		101	41		101
Goodwill adjustment		(20 751)	(1 452)	(3 501)	(20 751)
Leases		555		555	555
Taxation		(457)		334	
Deferred taxation			693		693
Capitalized interest		(412)	(412)		(412)
Minority interest		(348	(388)	(491)	(141)
Foreign currency translation		2533			
Adjusted stockholders' equity	**21 047**	**2 268**	**21 796**	**20 328**	**1 092**

Reconciliation –1990 Adjustments

Tables 16.1 and 16.2 show respectively the adjusted earnings and assets figures prepared by each country analyst. The adjustments in this chapter are made in a slightly different way to those in the previous chapter. The stockholders' equity figures have been adjusted to reflect the position at the end of the year. In some cases (e.g. goodwill) an adjustment has been made to earnings for the depreciation effect. However, because the earnings adjustment in many cases is already incorporated in the adjustment made to stockholders' equity, instead of adjusting for the total change in earnings those items requiring specific adjustment are shown on the stockholders' equity statement (e.g. leases). The adjusted figures show large inter-country differences with the UK earnings figure being nearly three times that of the French, and the Italian figure showing a deficit. The following sections discuss the differences in accounting policies requiring these adjustments.

Property, plant and equipment

RP carries assets at cost (including capitalized interest). Although statutory revaluations were undertaken for individual company purposes the consolidated accounts do not incorporate these. Other French companies adopt different policies. In the UK land and buildings tend to be revalued and this policy appears to have been adopted by ICI in respect of some assets. However, the company does not capitalize interest. The increase in net book value of land and buildings amounts to under 4% of total land and buildings, while the figure for plant and equipment is under 1% of total. These are hardly significant figures and it seems likely that most investment will be in specialized buildings and equipment and that any appreciation will be in respect of office buildings owned. In the circumstances no adjustments have been made to RP values. The current year's interest of FF 112 million has been deducted from earnings and stockholders' equity. In addition interest capitalized in earlier years has been estimated at FF 300 million; the 1988 and 1989 figures amounting to FF 172 million were included in note 19 to the accounts with the balance being estimated. These adjustments also required a reduction in the current year's depreciation of FF 41million and for previous years of FF 60 million.

Revaluation is not permitted in Germany and therefore no adjustment is needed; however, Bayer does not capitalize interest and adjustment has been made for this item. In both Spain and Italy legal revaluations of fixed assets took place in 1983. These revaluations would clearly only relate to assets purchased prior to that year. Assets purchased subsequent to 1983 will be carried at cost. Analysing the depreciation charge from the information contained in the accounts and notes thereto indicates average annual straight line depreciation charges of 4% on buildings and 9% on plant and machinery. Estimates of assets purchased prior to 1984 were made based on available information and the effects of revaluation on asset values and depreciation charges made. Although the new Italian accounting law will provide for the possibility of interest capitalization in the production costs it is not usual for companies to adopt the option allowed by accounting principles followed by Certified Public Accountants and therefore interest charges are assumed to be charged as incurred.

Adjustment to depreciation figures were triggered by revaluations made and these are reflected in the statements of earnings and stockholders' equity. In addition an adjustment was made by the Italian analyst to reflect different rates of write-off between RP and representative Italian companies. All companies computed depreciation on a straight line basis with the exception of the German company. It is often the practice for German companies to provide for special tax depreciation which will only be allowed for taxation purposes if it is accounted for in the financial statements. This results in the depreciation charge being an amalgam of accelerated depreciation on newer equipment to take advantage of tax opportunities and straight line depreciation on older equipment.

Goodwill and other intangibles

RP includes purchased goodwill as an intangible asset and amortizes on a straight line over not more than 40 years. ICI eliminates goodwill against reserves in line with current UK practice. Bayer also writes goodwill off to reserves at the date of first consolidation. Goodwill arising at the time of the first consolidation in German companies can either be offset against equity reserves or can be amortized systematically over the years which are likely to benefit. Although a four-year period is mentioned by law as the regular amortization period, a range of 0–40 years is widely regarded as acceptable. However, in other countries although goodwill is capitalized the writing-off period varies considerably leading to large adjustments in the reporting earnings figures. The figures make the point that a common policy of capitalization and amortization would not lead automatically to comparability. With writing-off periods varying from four to not more than 40 years direct comparability would not be possible without greater standardization. RP depreciates other intangibles, principally patents and trademarks, over 10 years; this is twice the period applied in Italy and the depreciation charge in respect of Italy has been increased accordingly. In Germany intangible fixed assets are to be capitalized, if purchased; they may not be capitalized if created by use of internal resources, (e.g. internally developed brands). The valuation principles to be applied are the same as for property, plant and equipment, although depreciation is usually at a faster rate than for tangible assets.

Inventories

RP values purchased items at lower of average cost or replacement value; manufactured items at manufacturing cost or NRV; and raw materials at lower of cost or replacement value. Although it is not clear what overheads RP would include in manufacturing cost the policies adopted were similar to other companies reporting and no adjustments were thought necessary. In Germany from 1990 LIFO will be accepted as a basis for tax purposes and may therefore change the accounting policy adopted by some companies including Bayer.

Research and development

RP writes off R&D as incurred. Other companies examined also adopt this policy. A new Italian law allows capitalization with amortization over a period not exceeding five years. However, groups are expected to continue immediate write-off. Spain also allows capitalization under certain conditions as do the UK and Germany although current practice favours immediate write-off

Translation of foreign currencies

RP translates income statements at average rates and balance sheet items at closing rates in line with UK and Italian policies. Although Bayer of Germany translates its income statement at average rates it uses the temporal method for balance sheet items. This gives rise to a significant increase in shareholders' equity as the translation reserve which represents the exchange losses on translation of subsidiaries has been eliminated. There may be a compensating increase in depreciation on assets which would be translated at temporal not closing rates but it is impossible to quantity this effect. Neither the German Commercial Code nor the Seventh Directive define a method of translating foreign currency financial statements. Besides, common practice has not yet been established; as a result a broad variety of methods including current/non-current, monetary/non-monetary, temporal, closing and current rate, together with variants thereof are used. This can cause difficulties even when making comparisons between German companies using different methods, since translation of foreign currency statements often materially affects the financial position and results of the group. The Spanish company's note is not clear. It refers to translation of transactions at the rate prevailing at the transaction date with year-end balances being translated at year-end exchange rates. RP distinguishes between countries with highly inflationary economies and others. The Spanish draft on consolidated accounts also makes this distinction requiring adjustment for inflation before translation. The translation loss included in other income (expenses) net of FF 174 million has been excluded from the calculation of income and taken direct to translation reserve for both the Italian and UK presentation.

Deferred taxation

RP has adopted SFAS 96 (US) which requires full provision under the liability method. A similar approach is adopted in Spain and Germany; however, in both the UK and Italy partial provision methods are adopted. This can lead to significant differences in reporting earnings figures. For example ICI when adjusting for US GAAP increase their balance sheet provision by £734 million (excluding ACT recoverable this is an increase of 900%). Note 22(d) in the RP accounts states that: 'The deferred tax balances on the consolidated balance sheets... relate mainly to foreign subsidiaries and originate principally from differences between financial statement and tax depreciation and the translation of Brazilian subsidiaries.' On the other hand part of ICI's note 21 on reserves states: 'No provision has been made in respect of potential taxation liabilities on realization of assets at restated or revalued amounts or on realization of associated undertakings at equity accounted value.' In view of the large loss carry forwards and tax credits, RP note 22(f) and note 22(d) (referred to above) in the accounts, it is considered that both the deferred tax charge and deferred tax provision would be significantly different when adjusted for UK and Italian GAAP. An accurate estimate clearly requires more detailed information but an approximate correction (one third) is proposed to reflect the difference between the full and partial provision methods.

Pensions

RP provides very full information in accordance with SFAS 87. ICI in the UK report in accordance with SSAP 24. These standards differ in both the permitted valuation methods and the date at which pension fund assets are valued. ICI's adjusted statement for US GAAP shows an increased pension charge of 16.5% of the annual charge while share-holders' equity was increased by 69% of the annual charge. Reporting information on pensions varies considerably from country to country in its form and clarity. RP provides superior information showing a full reconciliation. In contrast Bayer provides little detail on this issue. The note on accounting and valuation principles in the accounts simply states that provisions for pensions are made on the basis of actuarial valuations. Because of the way in which German companies can calculate their pension liabilities under the tax law accruals may be understated. This makes adjustment for different assumptions, policies, etc., very difficult to accomplish. This area seems ripe for additional research towards greater standardization given the significant amounts involved.

Leasing

Both RP and ICI capitalize finance leases and depreciate the fair value of the assets. Bayer gives little information about leases, and as with many other issues, accounting for leases is in practice dominated by tax regulations. In Germany standard lease contracts are mostly structured so that leased assets are to be capitalized by lessors rather than lessees. Lessees do not need to disclose details about the amounts of their financial or operating leases. Although companies have to disclose future financial commitments in their notes, they do not need to distinguish between leases and other commitments, and they also do not have to give an analysis of the obligations by year. The impact on the net equity may be small as we might assume that the capitalized assets will be more or less countered by the inclusion of the future lease obligations. However, gearing levels may be affected. Further, the income effect may be small in net terms as depreciation plus interest may equate to lease payments written off. The Spanish General

Accounting Plan (GAP 1990) capitalizes finance leases as intangible assets when there is no doubt that the purchase option will be exercised. In Italy individual companies are not permitted to capitalize leases while for groups it is optional. Although more Italian groups are adopting capitalization currently they are probably still in the minority.

Extraordinary items

Included in RP profits are gains on sales of assets which might be treated as extraordinary in other countries. In the UK profit on the sale of subsidiaries might have been treated as extraordinary as might be the provision for 'restructuration' included in operating expenses. However, as this provision is made for the restructuring of activities often following acquisitions, it seems likely that in the UK provisions would have been made on acquisition and that charges would not be taken through the profit and loss account, thus increasing the reported profit figure and associated figures. The treatment of these items has now changed significantly in the UK following issue of FRS 3. The treatment of extraordinary items would be similar in Italy and Spain. The treatment of extraordinary items in Germany is to disclose by notes to the accounts which means that particular attention needs to be given to these notes. Therefore, as for RP, they would be included in profits. German disclosure levels are, however, low and fall well short of French disclosure levels.

In addition, a major item relates to profit arising on the sale of assets leased back. In accordance with SFAS 98 the gains of FF 1097 million have been reduced by FF 555 million related to future rent payable. The leases appeal to be operating leases (note 23 in the RP accounts) and in the UK all profit would be included. In Spain leaseback is considered to be a financial operation and would not be accounted for as a sale followed by leasing. In Germany the lease would be treated as operating and no adjustment made to profit on sale.

Minority interests

Any changes in levels of profits and/or asset values could be expected to alter the value of minority interest. The extent of this change is a matter of estimation. The changes will affect the minority equity interest in the subsidiary companies and for adjustment purposes their proportionate share of net assets has been estimated as minority equity interest divided by the sum of minority equity interest plus consolidated net assets excluding goodwill. For 1990 this gives a minority interest of 16% and for 1991 of 19%.

Reconciliation – 1991 Adjustments

The 1991 analysis of the Rhône-Poulenc accounts relates to detailed analysis undertaken by a Dutch analyst, together with the adjustments made by the UK analyst. As the UK analysis follows a similar pattern to that adopted for the 1990 accounts reference is only made to differences between the 1990 and 1991 treatments. The adjustments are shown in Tables 16.3, 16.4 and 16.5.

TABLE 16.3
Rhône-Poulenc SA:
reconciliation to Dutch
principles (FF million) –
1991

Income for distribution to common stockholders (France)	1 227
Goodwill	641
Sale and lease back	33
Adjusted income for distribution as per Netherlands	1 901
Difference:	
FF	674
%	54.93%
Adjustments to stockholders' equity:	
Total stockholders' equity (France)	25 238
Goodwill	(21 011)
Leases	33
Adjusted stockholders' equity (Netherlands)	4 260
Difference:	
FF	(20 978)
%	(83.12%)

TABLE 16.4
Rhône-Poulenc SA:
earning adjustments (FF
million) – UK 1991

Income for distribution to common stockholders (France)	1 227
Goodwill	641
Capitalized interest:	(278)
Depreciation: Capitalized interest	88
Leases	33
Foreign currency translation	40
Provision for restructuration	495
Adjustments to stockholders' equity:	2246
Less minority interest	72
Adjusted income for distribution (UK)	2174

TABLE 16.5
Rhône-Poulenc SA:
adjustments to
stockholders' equity (FF
million) – UK 1991

Total stockholders' equity (France)	25 238
Depreciation adjustments re: capitalized interest	188
Goodwill adjustment	21 011
Leases	33
Deferred taxation	584
Capitalized interest:	(878)
Minority interest	14
Adjusted stockholders' equity	4 168

In 1991 consolidated net income of Rhône-Poulenc increased by 12% from 1990. This increase was attributed to the first benefits of the integration of recent acquisitions and the reshaping of the Group's business portfolio which it is claimed is now less vulnerable to economic downturns. The number of fully consolidated subsidiaries declined slightly from 320 to 313 due to the absorption of the former RTZ subsidiaries by Rhône-Poulenc Chemicals Ltd (United Kingdom) and Rhône-Poulenc Inc. (United States).

Netherlands analysis

Fixed assets

In the Netherlands companies are permitted to choose between current cost accounting (CCA) and historical cost accounting (HCA), taking into account that the chosen principle of valuation needs to be maintained as much as possible in the succeeding periods. Irrespective of whether CCA or HCA is chosen, intangible assets and current assets other than inventories are not permitted to be valued at current cost.

In France, as in the Netherlands, accounting law permits consolidated accounts to be based on HCA. However, French fiscal law permits the use of HCA plus legal revaluation, while Dutch fiscal law only permits HCA. This will lead to a permanent difference in France, which does not result in a tax deferral.

We conclude that, assuming the capitalized interest expense consists of only paid interest and not also interest on shareholders' equity, the historical cost principle chosen by RP does not require an adjustment

RP includes capitalized interest when valuing land, plant and equipment. In the Netherlands article 388 of the Dutch Act on financial reporting is applied when using cost price or production price for valuing an asset. The article states that (1) the cost price at which an asset is valued shall comprise the price paid and the related expenses, and (2) the production cost at which an asset is valued shall comprise the cost of the raw and ancillary materials used and the other expenses directly attributable to its production. The production cost may also include a reasonable proportion of the indirect costs and the interest on debts over the period attributable to the production of the asset; in this case, the notes shall state that such interest has been capitalized.

The law requires a fixed policy to be followed when interest is capitalized. Besides, if interest is capitalized, the valuation at the balance sheet may not exceed the appropriate current price. No adjustment has therefore been applied.

RP calculates depreciation on a straight line basis over the estimated useful lives of the respective assets (RP accounts, note 1(c), p. 22). The comparative Dutch company Akzo also uses the straight line method based on estimated life (Akzo accounts, p. 45). Consequently no adjustment is applied.

Goodwill, patents and trademarks

Goodwill represents the excess of the purchase price over the fair market value of net identifiable assets of businesses purchased. Goodwill is amortized on a straight-line basis over a period of not more than forty years. (RP accounts, note 2, p 21.)

Other intangible assets, consisting principally of patents and trademarks, are amortized on a straight-line basis over their estimated useful lives not exceeding forty years. (RP accounts, note 2, p. 21.)

According to the Act: 'The capitalized costs of goodwill may be amortized over a period corresponding to the expected useful life. The amortization period may exceed five years only if a substantially longer period can be ascribed to the goodwill; in this case, the amortization period and the reason must be stated.'

The periodic survey of the Dutch Institute of Chartered Accountants (NIVRA) shows that only 3% of the surveyed companies capitalize goodwill. When the capitalization takes place over a period longer than five years NIVRA found that a very brief reason was given in the notes.

Looking at the Dutch chemical companies Akzo and DSM, we find that these companies charge goodwill directly to shareholders' equity. So, although capitalization is permitted in the Netherlands, based on practice we make the following adjustment: shareholders' equity decreases by FF 21 011 million and net income increased by FF 641 million.

Research and development

'Research and development expenditures are charged to expenses as incurred (RP accounts, p. 22). According to the Dutch guidelines research and development may only be capitalized (thus does not have to be) if the expectation is that the future yield connected with the assets leave enough room for depreciation, otherwise the costs have to be linked to income. Therefore no adjustment is applied.

Inventory

In France, LIFO is not permitted as a basis for cost of goods sold and stock valuation. As an exception to the basis of measurement and valuation permitted by the Plan Comptable Général, groups may use LIFO for determination of cost of sales and value of inventory whether for the group as a whole or for particular segments or regions of activity. Note 1(d) to the consolidated financial statements states:

RP values inventories at the lower of average cost or replacement value (for goods purchased from third parties), or present manufacturing cost (for goods manufactured), without exceeding their net realizable value. Due to the rate of inventory turnover, average cost approximates FIFO. (RP accounts, p. 22.)

In the Netherlands, the principle of valuing inventory is purchase price, production cost or current value. Weighted average cost, FIFO and LIFO rules are all permitted. The RP valuation method equates with the Dutch policy, so no adjustment is applied.

Deferred taxes

'Effective January 1, 1991, RP adopted Statement of Financial Accounting Standard (SFAS) 109 concerning accounting for income taxes' (RP accounts, note 22). SFAS 96 was applied in 1990 and 1989. 'Deferred income taxes are recorded based on the differences between the tax bases on assets and liabilities and their carrying values for financial reporting purposes. Tax rates applicable to future periods are used to calculate year-end deferred income taxes' (RP accounts, p. 23). Thus RP uses the liability method for determining deferred taxes.

Note 22(d) states that:

> The deferred tax balances on the consolidated balance sheet ... relate mainly to foreign subsidiaries and originate principally from differences between financial statement and tax depreciation and the translation of the financial statements of Brazilian subsidiaries.

In the Netherlands both the deferred credit and estimated liability approach are permitted. The liability method is used more in practice. In addition to this it is permitted to charge a change in tariffs to shareholders' equity; the deferred method is no longer to be permitted when a new draft guideline is accepted. It is concluded that no adjustment is required.

Pensions

'The Group accounts for its commitments with respect to pension benefits and other retirement indemnities in accordance with SFAS 87 (note 14)' (RP accounts, note 1(i) p. 23). Based on SFAS 87 RP uses the actuarial principle for calculating the amount of provision for supplementary pension and retirement indemnities on the balance sheet.

Note 14 states:

> Consolidated companies provide pension benefits and retirement indemnities, including a substantial number of defined benefit pension plans which cover the majority of the Group employees. The specific features (benefit formulas, funding policies and types of assets held) of the plans vary depending on regulations and laws in the particular country in which the employees are located... In 1988, the Group irrevocably transferred to an insurance company the vested benefits of retired and early retired employees of French companies.

This agrees with the Dutch policy of effecting the pension liabilities with a life insurance company and entering a provision for pension liabilities on the balance sheet. The conclusion is that no adjustment is necessary.

Foreign currency translation

In France, foreign currency translation rules allow both the temporal and the current rate methods. Foreign exchange translation difference accounts are common on French balance sheets. RP distinguishes between countries with highly inflationary economies and others. For these other countries RP translates income statements at average rates and balance sheet items at closing rates, while exchange differences arising from foreign currency transactions are included in results of operations (RP accounts, p. 22).

For countries with highly inflationary economies (Brazil, Argentina, Mexico), assets recorded at original cost are translated at historical dates, as are related income statement amounts. Gains and losses arising from the translation into French francs of financial statements of subsidiaries located in these countries are included in current year income under the heading 'Other income (expenses) net' (RP accounts, note 21 p.22).

The Dutch Act contains no specific directions for the treatment of foreign currencies in the accounts. It is only required to explain the bases for the translation of amounts expressed in foreign currencies. Guidelines explain the different methods.

For highly inflationary economies, the accounts need to be adjusted for the influence of price changes before translation takes place. The alternative in this situation is to translate non-monetary assets against historical rates while exchange differences are charged to income.

For other countries, the following is applied. The translation differences on direct foreign activities has to be charged directly to income as a result of normal operations. When there is talk of an independent foreign entity, translation differences have to be charged to shareholders' equity. It is concluded that for highly inflationary economies no adjustment is applied.

Leasing

According to the French commercial law, a lessee, being by definition not the owner of a leased asset, may not capitalize future lease rentals, either as an obligation or a receivable. As an exception to the bases of measurement and valuation permitted by the Plan Comptable Général, groups may use lease capitalization.

Note 1(c) to the consolidated financial statements of RP states:

When the group leases assets under the terms of long-term con-
tracts or other arrangement that substantially transfer all of the
benefits and risks of ownership to the Group (financial lease), the fair
market value of the leased property is capitalized and depreciated
and the corresponding obligation is recorded as a liability.

According to Dutch guidelines, the leased asset needs to be capitalized if financial leasing appears to arise from the entire contract conditions. Consequently no adjustment is applied.

Sale and lease back

During 1990 the Group sold a number of fixed assets and leased
back certain of these assets upon their sale, at sale and leaseback

prices related to market conditions. These sale and leaseback transactions resulted in gross gains totalling FF 345 million in 1991 and FF 1097 million in 1990. These gains were reduced, in accordance with SFAS 98, by the present value of future rent payable during the leaseback period totalling FF 33 million and FF 555 million, respectively. (RP accounts, note 20 p. 39).

The leases appear to be operational leases (RP accounts, note 23, p.41).

Because the sale price is independent from the lease terms, profit would be included. RP does not include profit, so an adjustment is required of the size of FF 33 million (see UK adjustments).

Provision for 'restructuration'

Note 15 to the RP accounts explains that: 'Each year the Group, based on its strategies and levels of productivity which it desires to achieve, reviews its activities and production sites. These reviews permit it to decide upon, if necessary, restructuration measures for which a provision is recorded.' In the Netherlands a distinction is made between results from ordinary activities and extraordinary income and expenditure. The Act states: '"Extraordinary income and expenditure" refers to income and expenditure not arising in the ordinary course of the legal entity's business. Unless such income and expenditure are of minor importance for the assessment of the results, the nature and extent thereof shall be explained in the notes.' An example of extraordinary income and expenditure is profits and losses resulting from reorganizations or connected with discontinuity. Consequently the item 'provision for restructuration' needs to be transferred within the statement of income from operating expenses (ordinary expenses) to extraordinary expenses.

Problems

1. The earnings and stockholders' funds of Rhône-Poulenc show significant variations when adjusted to allow for the accounting conventions of different countries. Briefly summarize the main adjustments for 1990 and their significance. Discuss the extent to which international accounting developments in recent years have led to any narrowing of these variations in accounting reporting.

2. An adjustment was made to earnings and stockholders' funds to reflect different policies on leases. Explain the economic difference between operating and finance leases and the effect on financial statements of adopting either a legal or economic approach to reporting for leases. Contrast the policies used by Rhône-Poulenc with another French company Groupe Euro Disney (see Chapter 10) to report their leasing transactions.

3. To what extent may the increasing use of international financial markets by large companies expect to lead to greater standardization in financial reporting?

17

The Use of Adjusted Financial Information

Introduction

This chapter is in two parts. To begin with we show the effect of adjustment on selected financial ratios. In the second part we discuss the reliability of the data obtained from the adjusted accounts.

Effect of Adjustments on Selected Financial Ratios

Having produced the adjusted financial information for Pirelli and Rhône-Poulenc we can now compute some basic ratios from this information. Our analysis produced adjusted statements of earnings and of shareholders' funds. There are many other headings on the financial statements which are used in ratio analysis, such as current assets and liabilities, borrowings, gross profit, etc. Although these items have not been specifically examined the process of adjusting net earnings and shareholders' funds will necessitate the computation of the adjustments needed for these other headings and thus the relevant calculations can be made. For example, in computing the current ratio any adjustments for inventory valuation or taxation provisions can be extracted from the earnings and shareholders' funds adjustment statements. It is possible that in some circumstances an adjustment to one balance sheet or income statement figure will be compensated by another adjustment with no net effect on earnings or shareholders' funds. These items will be relatively uncommon but the process of analysis should identify them even if they have no effect on the principal adjustment statements.

We will now use the adjusted accounts of the two companies to produce the preliminary set of ratios shown in Tables 17.1 and 17.2. These ratios illustrate a number of the factors that have to be considered by the analyst in using adjusted financial information:

1. Adjustment is a complex and detailed operation. There are no systematic ways of adjusting for country differences.
2. The size and nature of certain adjustments can result in very volatile results in the financial ratios. For example, it can be seen that the return on shareholders' funds (ROSF) ratios for Pirelli give a significant but not surprising range of results from 1.76% to 3.94%. The range for Rhône-Poulenc, however, is more

extreme from −3.45% to 270%. Obviously an analyst would need to consider the reasons for this wide range and readers should refer back to the tables of adjustments in the earlier text.

3. Within each company the range of results will be influenced by the components of the ratio being examined. For example the range of sales : shareholders' funds ratios for Pirelli is narrower (323% to 358%) than the range of ROSF results. This is not surprising as the sales figure is not subject to adjustment between the countries in the cases used.

4. Where analysis involves specific items of the accounts which are less subject to diversity of treatment the range of ratios will be narrower. For example, the current ratios for both Pirelli and Rhône-Poulenc have insignificant ranges.

TABLE 17.1
Pirelli accounts 1990: ratios based on adjusted financial statements

	Notes*	Italy	UK	Germany	Spain	France
Return on shareholders' funds (%)		3.29	1.76	1.99	3.21	3.94
Net profit : Sales (%)	1	0.94	0.54	0.57	0.90	1.11
Sales: Shareholders' Funds (%)		3.49	3.23	3.51	3.58	3.58
Gearing (%)	2	45	43	49	46	46
Current ratio	3	1.51:1	1.50:1	1.50:1	1.51:1	1.51:1

Notes*

The unadjusted figures taken from the accounts of Pirelli S.p.A. were as follows (all in lire billion)

1. Sales = 10 603
2. Debt : Debt + Equity (Medium + Long term debt = 2558)
3. Current assets = 5863
4. Current liabilities = 3879

The current asset figure has been adjusted for inventory valuation differences in UK and Germany.

TABLE 17.2
Rhône-Poulenc accounts 1990: ratios based on adjusted financial statements

	Notes*	France	Germany	Italy	Spain	UK
Return on shareholders' funds %		5.21	70.72	-3.45	-0.02	270
Net profit : Sales (%)	1	1.39	2.04	-0.39	0	3.76
Sales: Shareholders' Funds (%)		372	3457	359	385	7180
Gearing (%)	2	50.1	90.0	49.2	50.3	94.9
Current ratio	3	0.98:1	0.97:1	0.99:1	0.99:1	0.98:1

Notes*
The unadjusted figures taken from the accounts of Rhône-Poulenc SA were as follows (all in FF million)

The Use of Adjusted Financial Information

1. Sales = 78 411
2. Debt : Debt + Equity (Medium + Long term debt = 21 166)
3. Current assets = 41 110
4. Current liabilities = 41 861

Borrowing has been adjusted for leasing adjustments for Germany, Spain and the UK. Current liabilities have been adjusted for taxation provision adjustments for Germany and Spain.

The Reliability of Adjusted Information

The detailed adjustments and the underlying discussion and explanation given above will have provided users with an informed insight into the different accounting methods and their impact on reported numbers. It is apparent from this discussion that some of the adjustments are subject to more uncertainty than others and thus analysts and other users may place more reliance on the results of some adjustments for financial statement analysis than on others. It might, therefore, be useful to develop a model to help analysts to assess the relative reliability of both the final result of the adjustment process and each component part of this process. In arriving at our adjustments we adopt the process illustrated in Figure 17.1.

FIGURE 17.1
Model of the adjustment process

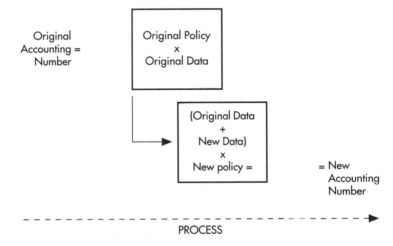

Within this framework we assume that the analyst knows the relevant new policy, that is, the measurement basis that he or she needs for comparative analysis purposes. The information needed therefore is (a) the original policy, (b) the measurement basis, (c) the original data used in producing the original accounting number and (d) any new or additional data needed in applying the new policy. The level of certainty of the resultant figure is therefore subject to:

- the clarity of the explanation of the original policy adopted; and
- the level of disclosure of both the original and the necessary additional data.

We suggest that these certainties may be represented in a matrix as shown in Figure 17.2.

FIGURE 17.2

Matrix of the level of certainty of the adjusted figures

		Accounting Policy/Measurement Base		
		Clear	Unclear	Not Stated
Data disclosure	All available	A	B	C
	Some available	D	E	F
(Original and New)	None available	G	H	I

The level of certainty and thus the quality of each component part of the adjustment process is determined by which cell in Figure 17.2 best describes the nature of the adjustment process which has been carried out. What needs to be attempted next is a ranking of the cells of the matrix in order to arrive at an assessment of the reliability of the adjustment. This ranking process is by its nature subjective and the analysis which follows may not be considered the appropriate one by different analysts or in different cases. However, the assessment process is still relevant as the rankings can reflect this subjectivity. The objective of the process is **relative** reliability and it suffers from the drawbacks and limitations of any similar subjective probability process. It is clear that cell A would result in a high-quality adjustment on which the user could place a high level of reliability. An adjustment described by cell I has almost no reliability as the adjustment would have involved a high level of guesswork. In between these two extremes things are less clear. We would suggest that of the remaining cells the most reliable is cell B, where we have sufficient data and some idea of current policy. The assessment of the next most reliable is problematic in that it could be argued that wherever we have all available data we are able to arrive at our new number (cell C); however, it is difficult to know if the original data was sufficient if the policy is unstated. On the other hand, it could be argued that with a clear opening measurement position some data could be assumed or derived from other sources and thus cell D might be more reliable. We suggest that these rankings would be identical or close depending on circumstances. The same type of argument might be used in distinguishing between cells E and G; however, the low level of data seems to us to be a greater limitation than the combined uncertainty of measurement and data and thus we would favour cell E. Both cells F and H are subject to relatively high levels of uncertainty.

The degrees of uncertainty represented by the different cells in the matrix in Figure 17.2 indicate the levels of reliability which an analyst might attach to the adjusted accounting information. It is possible that this assessment might result in analysts placing more reliance on adjusted accounts of certain countries or identifying those components of financial statements which are less subject to uncertainty. It might be possible to develop a quantified model of relative reliability which analysts can adopt as a yardstick for assessing the usefulness of the adjusted accounting numbers. Research into the practical application of a model of this sort is currently being undertaken.

The Use of Adjusted Financial Information

To conclude, an analyst should always use financial reports and the ratios derived from them with care. In particular when using adjusted financial information the following additional points should be born in mind:

- the reliability of the adjustment;
- the size and nature of the adjustment;
- the components of the ratio.

Financial accounting is not a science and the analysis of financial statements is a complex, uncertain and interpretive activity. The use of adjusted financial information may make the process more uncertain but the process of adjustment itself can be an informative one and give insights into the underlying accounting information. As a means of understanding European accounting practice and diversity we consider it to be an interesting pedagogic approach which complements the more traditional method of country comparisons and system classifications.

Problems

1. Extract 17.1 presents the balance sheet, income statement and notes to the accounts of Bayer AG for the year ended 31 December 1993.

You are required to:

a   prepare a ratio analysis from Bayer's original (German) accounts;

b   prepare statements of adjusted earnings and shareholders' equity based on the generally accepted accounting principles of the United Kingdom and/or another country of your choice;

c   prepare a ratio analysis from your statements of adjusted financial information;

d   comment on the results of the different analyses In **a** and **c**, and discuss any significant differences in accounting policy which have affected these results;

e   assess the relative reliability of your adjusted information.

Extract 17.1 – Bayer AG 1993 accounts, Balance Sheet, Income Statement and Notes.

BAYER GROUP BALANCE SHEET (DM million)

Assets	Note	Dec. 31, 1993	Dec. 31, 1992
Intangibles, fixed assets and investments	[1]		
Intangibles		321	314
Fixed assets		14,412	14,203
Investments	[2]	1,145	1,104
		15,878	**15,621**
Current assets			
Inventories	[3]	8,436	8,517
Receivables and other assets			
Trade accounts receivable	[4]	8,448	7,874
Receivables from subsidiaries		110	128
Other receivables and other assets	[5]	1,364	1,630
		9,922	9,632
Liquid assets	[6]	5,242	3,754
		23,600	**21,903**
Deferred charges	[7]	**693**	**804**
		40,171	**38,328**

Stockholders' Equity and Liabilities	Note	Dec. 31, 1993	Dec. 31, 1992
Stockholders' equity			
Capital stock of Bayer AG	[8]	3,354	3,287
Capital reserves	[9]	3,960	4,065
Retained earnings	[10]	9,040	8,210
Net income		1,327	1,516
Minority interests		479	414
		18,160	**17,492**
Special item with an equity component		**68**	**77**
Provisions			
Provisions for pensions and similar commitments	[11]	7,650	7,239
Other provisions	[12]	4,069	3,802
		11,719	**11,041**
Other liabilities			
Debentures	[13]	2,130	2,080
Liabilities to banks		2,606	2,167
Trade accounts payable	[14]	2,085	2,048
Bills payable		132	147
Payables to subsidiaries		180	169
Miscellaneous liabilities	[15]	2,983	3,005
		10,116	**9,616**
Deferred income		**108**	**102**
		40,171	**38,328**

BAYER GROUP STATEMENT OF INCOME (DM million)

	Note	1993	1992
Net sales	[16]	**41,007**	**41,195**
Cost of goods sold		23,766	23,864
Gross profit		**17,241**	**17,331**
Selling expenses		9,550	9,476
Research and development expenses		3,157	3,096
General administration expenses		1,797	1,858
Other operating income	[17]	1,189	1,383
Other operating expenses	[18]	1,579	1,508
Operating result		**2,347**	**2,776**
Income from investments in affiliated companies – net	[19]	47	53
Interest income (expense) – net	[20]	(51)	(180)
Other non-operating income (expense) – net	[21]	11	44
Non-operating result		**7**	**(83)**
Income before income taxes		**2,354**	**2,693**
Income taxes		982	1,130
Income after taxes		**1,372**	**1,563**
Minority interests	[22]	45	47
Net income		**1,327**	**1,516**

BAYER GROUP STATEMENT OF CASH FLOWS (DM million)

	1993		1992	
Income after taxes		1,372		1,563
Depreciation of fixed assets		2,684		2,547
Increase in long-term provisions		789		586
Cash flow according to German GAAP	4,845		4,696	
Write-downs of current assets		(49)		151
Other changes in working capital		256		(258)
Net cash provided by operating activities		**5,052**		**4,589**
Additions to fixed assets		(3,156)		(2,859)
Retirements of fixed assets		256		229
Additions to investments		(285)		(238)
Retirements of investments		206		83
Net cash used in investing activities		**(2,979)**		**(2,785)**
Dividend paid by Bayer AG		(723)		(838)
Capital contributions		201		184
Utilization of long-term provisions		(238)		(552)
Change in financial obligations		319		(187)
Other changes in stockholders' equity		(144)		(122)
Net cash used in financing activities		**(585)**		**(1,515)**
Increase in liquid assets		**1,488**		**289**
Liquid assets as of December 31		5,242		3,754

Extract 17.1

NOTES TO THE FINANCIAL STATEMENTS OF THE BAYER GROUP

COMPANIES CONSOLIDATED

The Financial Statements of the Bayer Group include Bayer AG and 28 German and 135 foreign subsidiaries in which Bayer AG, directly or indirectly, has a majority of the voting rights or which are under its uniform control. Two joint ventures in which Bayer AG holds a 50 percent interest are consolidated on a pro rata basis. Twelve non-consolidated subsidiaries and one associated company are included according to the equity method.

The total number of companies consolidated has dropped by 13 from the previous year. This does not affect comparability with the previous year's Financial Statements.

Excluded are 135 subsidiaries and 34 associated companies that in aggregate are of minor importance to the net worth, financial position and earnings of the Bayer Group, as well as four companies that exist for social purposes.

ACCOUNTING AND VALUATION PRINCIPLES

The financial statements of most consolidated companies are prepared as of December 31, the balance sheet date for the Bayer Group. Interim statements are prepared for companies having different balance sheet dates. The consolidated assets and liabilities reflected in the Financial Statements of the Bayer Group have been consistently valued in accordance with the following accounting and valuation principles applied by Bayer AG.

Intangibles that have been acquired are shown at cost of acquisition less amortization.

Fixed assets are shown at cost of acquisition or construction less depreciation calculated over their estimated useful lives. Write-downs are made when assets suffer a loss of value that is expected to be permanent. Substantial additions to tax depreciation shown in individual companies' financial statements for the year under report, especially those made under special laws to promote investment in eastern Germany, are not reflected in the Financial Statements of the Bayer Group.

The cost of construction of company-manufactured assets includes the direct cost of materials and direct manufacturing expenses as well as allocations of material and manufacturing overheads including depreciation.

Investments in subsidiaries and in other affiliated companies, and other securities included in investments, are shown at cost of acquisition or, where a lower value was assigned to them, at the lower value. In the case of companies valued at equity, no adjustments are made for variances between their accounting or valuation principles and those used for the Financial Statements of the Bayer Group, since these variances are immaterial.

Loans receivable that are interest-free or bear low rates of interest are carried at present value, other loans receivable are carried at nominal value.

Inventories are valued as follows: raw materials, supplies and goods purchased for resale are normally valued at their weighted average cost of acquisition, while work in process and finished goods are valued at the cost of production. The cost of production includes the direct cost of materials and direct manufacturing expenses as well as allocations of material and manufacturing overheads, including depreciation of fixed assets used for the production. Write-downs are made where inventories have a lower market value and also where permitted for tax purposes.

Receivables and other assets are shown at nominal value less any write-downs.

Marketable securities are shown at the lower of cost of acquisition or market value as of the current or an earlier balance sheet date.

Deferred charges include unamortized debt discounts, stated at nominal value. These discounts are amortized over the life of the liabilities to which they relate.

Allocations to the special item with an equity component were made by German consolidated companies under Art. 6b, Income Tax Act and by foreign companies under comparable tax regulations. German consolidated companies' allocations in the year under report representing gains from the sale of fixed assets and investments are not reflected in the Financial Statements of the Bayer Group.

Provisions for pensions and similar commitments for German consolidated companies are made on the basis of actuarial valuations; for foreign consolidated companies they are made on a similar basis.

Other provisions are established to provide for foreseeable risks and uncertain liabilities. Provisions for maintenance are set up only for maintenance work that is deferred until the first three months of the following year. Provisions for expenses are not established.

Deferred taxes are calculated on timing differences between book income and taxable income of the consolidated companies. Deferred tax assets are offset against deferred tax liabilities. Deferred taxes resulting from the consolidation are combined with the deferred taxes of the individual companies.

Other liabilities are shown at nominal value or redemption value, whichever is higher.

Contingent liabilities arising from guarantees and warranties are shown at an amount equivalent to the loans or commitments actually outstanding as of the balance sheet date.

FOREIGN CURRENCY TRANSLATION

Receivables in foreign currencies that are not hedged and payables in foreign currencies are translated at the rate of exchange as of the recording date or the current or an earlier balance sheet date, whichever yields an amount that is lower for receivables and higher for payables.

Where current assets are hedged, they are translated at the hedged rate.

Foreign consolidated companies' financial statements are translated into DM according to a temporal method which does not affect net income. Subsidiaries in high-inflation countries prepare hard-currency statements.

Foreign currency translation is made as follows:

fixed assets, intangibles, investments in affiliated companies and other securities included in investments
- at the average DM exchange rate in the year of addition (historical average rate)

all other balance sheet items and net income
- at the year-end rate

all income and expenses
- at the weighted average rate for the year.

Bayer's portion of the adjustments resulting from the translation of foreign currency items in the balance sheet is included in capital reserves, while the minority stockholders' portions are included in minority interests.

The adjustments resulting from the translation of foreign currency items in the income statement have no effect on net income as they are included in the operating result.

CONSOLIDATION METHODS

Capital consolidation is made by offsetting investments in subsidiaries and joint ventures against the underlying equities at the date of acquisition or first consolidation. Write-downs and write-ups of investments in consolidated companies are reversed. Differences between purchase price and underlying equity at the date of acquisition or first consolidation are allocated to assets or liabilities and depreciated or amortized over the life of the assets or liabilities. Where goodwill has been acquired, it is offset against retained earnings.

Intercompany sales, profits, losses, income and expenses, and receivables and payables between the consolidated companies are eliminated.

Deferred taxes are recognized for timing differences related to consolidation entries.

Joint ventures that are consolidated are included on a pro-rata basis in accordance with the above principles.

Intercompany profits and losses resulting from transactions in goods and services with companies valued at equity are immaterial and therefore have not been eliminated.

Financial Statements 1993

NOTES TO THE BALANCE SHEET

[1] INTANGIBLES, FIXED ASSETS AND INVESTMENTS

The structure of intangibles, fixed assets and investments and the changes therein are shown in the schedule below.

[2] INVESTMENTS

Lists of Bayer AG's direct and indirect holdings of at least 20 percent have been included in the Commercial Register of the Local Court of Leverkusen. Copies will be furnished, free of charge, upon written request to Bayer AG.

[3] INVENTORIES

	Dec. 31, 1993 DM million	Dec. 31, 1992 DM million
Raw materials and supplies	1,414	1,311
Work in process, finished goods and goods purchased for resale	7,003	7,186
Advance payments	19	20
	8,436	**8,517**

Finished goods include leased products of DM 191 million.

[4] TRADE ACCOUNTS RECEIVABLE

	Dec. 31, 1993 DM million	Dec. 31, 1992 DM million
From		
Subsidiaries	237	207
Other affiliated companies	123	175
Other customers	8,088	7,492
	8,448	**7,874**

[5] OTHER RECEIVABLES AND OTHER ASSETS

	Dec. 31, 1993 DM million	Dec. 31, 1992 DM million
Receivables from other affiliated companies	24	14
Other assets	1,340	1,616
	1,364	**1,630**

Other assets as of December 31, 1993 include DM 168 million that represents income earned in 1993 but not due to be received until after the balance sheet date. This income consists mainly of accrued interest.

CHANGES IN INTANGIBLES, FIXED ASSETS AND INVESTMENTS OF THE BAYER GROUP (DM million)

	Gross Carrying Values					
	Balance Dec. 31, 1992	Changes in companies consolidated	Additions	Retirements	Transfers, Reclassifications	Balance Dec. 31, 1993
Concessions, patents, licenses, trademarks, etc.	578	5	98	70	3	614
Advance payments	9	–	8	–	(3)	14
Intangibles	**587**	**5**	**106**	**70**	**–**	**628**
Land and buildings	12,357	5	111	142	312	12,643
Machinery and technical equipment	29,140	(105)	604	757	1,155	30,037
Furniture, fixtures and other equipment	3,383	(12)	251	263	110	3,469
Construction in progress and advance payments to vendors and contractors	1,918	22	2,084	60	(1,577)	2,387
Fixed assets	**46,798**	**(90)**	**3,050**	**1,222**	**–**	**48,536**
Investments in subsidiaries	419	(42)	20	20	51	428
Loans to subsidiaries	34	3	9	27	–	19
Investments in associated companies	226	(2)	40	9	(51)	204
Investments in other companies	25	47	2	33	–	41
Loans to other affiliated companies	3	–	50	–	–	53
Other securities	148	–	38	26	–	160
Other loans	459	11	82	60	–	492
Investments	**1,314**	**17**	**241**	**175**	**–**	**1,397**
Total	**48,699**	**(68)**	**3,397**	**1,467**	**–**	**50,561**

The Use of Adjusted Financial Information

RECEIVABLES AND OTHER ASSETS MATURING IN MORE THAN ONE YEAR

Receivables and other assets as of December 31, 1993, totaling DM 9,922 million, include the following amounts that mature after 1994:

	Dec. 31, 1993 DM million	Dec. 31, 1992 DM million
Trade accounts receivable	181	157
Receivables from subsidiaries	3	1
Other assets	220	189
	404	**347**

[6] LIQUID ASSETS

	Dec. 31, 1993 DM million	Dec. 31, 1992 DM million
Marketable securities and other instruments	1,837	1,365
Checks, cash on hand, Bundesbank and post office checking accounts, other bank accounts	3,405	2,389
	5,242	**3,754**

[7] DEFERRED CHARGES

Deferred charges as of December 31, 1993 include unamortized debt discounts of DM 95 million and net deferred taxes of DM 270 million.

[8] CAPITAL STOCK

In 1993, the capital stock of Bayer AG increased by DM 67 million to DM 3,354 million through the issue of new shares from the Conditional Capital as a result of warrants being exercised. It is divided into 35,255,635 bearer shares with differing par values.

Authorized Capital of DM 500 million was approved by the Annual Stockholders' Meeting on April 29, 1992. It expires on April 28, 1997. The Authorized Capital can be used to increase the capital stock through the issuance of new shares against cash contributions.

[9] CAPITAL RESERVES

	1993 DM million	1992 DM million
Balance Bayer AG as of January 1	**4,538**	**4,416**
Allocation of paid-in surplus from the exercise of warrants	134	122
Balance Bayer AG as of December 31	**4,672**	**4,538**
Accumulated translation adjustments	(712)	(473)
Balance Bayer Group as of December 31	**3,960**	**4,065**

[10] RETAINED EARNINGS

Included here are retained earnings from prior years and consolidation adjustments recognized in prior years' income. Goodwill of DM 38 million resulting from acquisitions made during the year has been deducted.

[11] PROVISIONS FOR PENSIONS AND SIMILAR COMMITMENTS

This item includes provisions for current and future pension entitlements. It also covers provisions for commitments similar to pensions such as early-retirement and comparable benefits.

Accumulated Depreciation, Amortization and Write-Downs	Net Carrying Values		Depreciation, Amortization and Write-Downs in 1993
	Balance Dec. 31, 1993	Balance Dec. 31, 1992	
307	307	305	102
–	14	9	–
307	**321**	**314**	**102**
7,400	5,243	5,316	403
24,046	5,991	6,194	1,791
2,599	870	915	392
79	2,308	1,778	–
34,124	**14,412**	**14,203**	**2,586**
95	333	369	1
5	14	29	–
79	125	147	–
15	26	13	11
–	53	3	–
5	155	143	–
53	439	400	1
252	**1,145**	**1,104**	**13**
34,683	**15,878**	**15,621**	**2,701**

[12] OTHER PROVISIONS

	Dec. 31, 1993 DM million	Dec. 31, 1992 DM million
Provisions for taxes	646	417
Miscellaneous provisions	3,423	3,385
	4,069	**3,802**

Miscellaneous provisions include amounts for profit-related bonuses, vacations, employee service awards, environmental protection measures, discounts, agents' expenses and other uncertain liabilities.

[13] DEBENTURES

Debentures include the following bonds with warrants attached:

	DM million
Bayer AG	
DM 500 million, 3 $^{1}/_{4}$ % Bonds with Warrants Attached 1984/1994	500
Bayer Capital Corporation N. V.	
DM 600 million, 2 $^{3}/_{4}$ % Bonds with Warrants Attached 1985/1995	600
DM 400 million, 6 $^{1}/_{4}$ % Bonds with Warrants Attached 1987/1997	400
sfrs 250 million, 2 $^{1}/_{2}$ % Bonds with Warrants Attached 1987/2002	294

FURTHER DETAILS OF BONDS WITH WARRANTS ATTACHED

	Subscription rights expire	Subscription price DM	No. of subscription rights not yet exercised
Bayer AG			
Bonds with Warrants Attached 1984/1994	Feb. 28, 1994	140.00	722,164
Bayer Capital Corporation N. V.			
Bonds with Warrants Attached 1985/1995	March 1, 1995	168.00	2,747,929
Bonds with Warrants Attached 1987/1997	Aug. 28, 1997	330.00	1,600,000
Bonds with Warrants Attached 1987/2002	Aug. 28, 1997	330.00	900,000

[14] TRADE ACCOUNTS PAYABLE

	Dec. 31, 1993 DM million	Dec. 31, 1992 DM million
To		
Subsidiaries	22	24
Other affiliated companies	10	24
Other suppliers	2,053	2,000
	2,085	**2,048**

[15] MISCELLANEOUS LIABILITIES

	Dec. 31, 1993 DM million	Dec. 31, 1992 DM million
Advance payments received	47	47
Payables to other affiliated companies	41	29
Other miscellaneous liabilities	2,895	2,929
	2,983	**3,005**

Tax liabilities of DM 228 million and liabilities for social expenses of DM 285 million, included in other miscellaneous liabilities as of December 31, 1993, do not contain amounts that were withheld from employees' salaries in 1993 but not paid over to the respective authorities until after the balance sheet date.

The total amount of other liabilities includes DM 304 million that represents expenses attributable to 1993 but not due to be paid until after the balance sheet date. These expenses consist mainly of accrued interest.

MATURITY OF OTHER LIABILITIES

	Maturing in 1994 DM million	Maturing in 1995-1998 DM million	Maturing after 1998 DM million
Debentures	506	1,275	349
Liabilities to banks	1,854	338	414
Trade accounts payable	2,085	.	–
Bills payable	132	–	–
Payables to subsidiaries	179	1	.
Advance payments received	38	9	.
Payables to other affiliated companies	14	–	27
Other miscellaneous liabilities	2,603	188	104
	7,411	**1,811**	**894**

DM 278 million of other liabilities are secured, mainly by mortgages.

CONTINGENT LIABILITIES

	Dec. 31, 1993 DM million	Dec. 31, 1992 DM million
Issuance and endorsement of bills	256	335
Guarantees	146	165
including guarantees to subsidiaries	[24]	[27]
Warranties	79	74
	481	**574**

OTHER FINANCIAL COMMITMENTS

In addition to provisions, other liabilities and contingent liabilities, certain other financial commitments exist. Those arising from long term leasing and rental agreements, stated at the present value of future payments, amount to DM 1,160 million, including DM 242 million due in 1994, DM 515 million due in 1995-1998, and DM 403 million due after 1998. Those existing under purchase agreements related to capital expenditure projects amount to DM 580 million. Total other financial commitments include DM 28 million to subsidiaries.

NOTES TO THE STATEMENT OF INCOME

[16] NET SALES

A breakdown of net sales and the operating result is included in the Management Report on pages 8-11.

[17] OTHER OPERATING INCOME

The main items of other operating income for 1993 are exchange gains, revenues from sideline operations, and income from other business transactions. Also included are DM 20 million partial reversals of the special item with an equity component.

[18] OTHER OPERATING EXPENSES

Other operating expenses for 1993 include allocations of DM 15 million to the special item with an equity component, exchange losses, cost of goods sold incurred for sideline operations, and other taxes based on items such as property and capital. These other taxes amount to DM 221 million.

[19] INCOME FROM INVESTMENTS IN AFFILIATED COMPANIES — NET

	1993 DM million	1992 DM million
Dividends and similar income	20	40
including amounts from subsidiaries	[8]	[29]
Income from profit and loss transfer agreements	3	1
Expenses resulting from loss transfer	(1)	(3)
Equity income from subsidiaries and associated companies	25	15
	47	**53**

[20] INTEREST INCOME (EXPENSE) — NET

	1993 DM million	1992 DM million
Income from other securities and loans included in investments	55	49
including amounts from subsidiaries	[.]	[1]
Other interest and similar income	452	373
including amounts from subsidiaries	[11]	[14]
Interest and similar expenses	(558)	(602)
including amounts to subsidiaries	[(2)]	[(16)]
	(51)	**(180)**

[21] OTHER NON-OPERATING INCOME (EXPENSE) – NET

	1993 DM million	1992 DM million
Write-downs of investments and marketable securities	(17)	(29)
Miscellaneous non-operating expenses	(48)	(78)
Miscellaneous non-operating income	76	151
	11	**44**

[22] MINORITY INTERESTS

Minority interests in income amount to DM 45 million (1992: DM 49 million), and minority interests in losses, to less than DM 1 million (1992: DM 2 million), yielding net minority interests of DM 45 million (1992: DM 47 million) in Group income after taxes.

Financial Statements 1993

SUPPLEMENTARY DATA

COST OF MATERIALS

	1993 DM million	1992 DM million
Expenses for raw materials, supplies and goods purchased for resale	11,908	11,580
Expenses for purchased services	1,045	778
	12,953	**12,358**

PERSONNEL EXPENSES

	1993 DM million	1992 DM million
Wages and salaries	11,013	11,139
Expenses for compulsory social security contributions, pensions and special financial assistance	3,293	3,295
including pension expenses	[1,337]	[1,325]
	14,306	**14,434**

NUMBER OF EMPLOYEES

The average number of employees was as follows:

Manufacturing	76,807
Sales	36,841
Research and development	12,291
General administration	27,927
	153,866

The joint ventures consolidated on a pro-rata basis account for 3,153 of the above employees.

AMORTIZATION, DEPRECIATION AND WRITE-DOWNS

Valuation write-downs and tax amortization, depreciation and write-downs of intangibles, fixed assets and investments for 1993 total DM 69 million, comprising DM 39 million write-downs due to a permanent loss of value and DM 30 million amortization, depreciation and write-downs for tax purposes. Write-downs of current assets made for tax purposes amount to DM 34 million.

Amortization, depreciation and write-downs for tax purposes and allocations to and partial reversals of the special item with an equity component, made in 1993, as well as similar measures taken in prior years, did not materially affect income after taxes. Higher income taxes resulting from these measures will be spread over several years and therefore will not significantly reduce income after taxes in those years.

Write-ups omitted for tax reasons in 1993 amount to DM 53 million.

TOTAL REMUNERATION OF THE BOARD OF MANAGEMENT AND THE SUPERVISORY BOARD, ADVANCES AND LOANS

The remuneration of the Board of Management for 1993 amounted to DM 10,396,876.00.

Emoluments to retired members of the Board of Management and their surviving dependents amounted to DM 10,661,415.00.

Bayer AG provisions for pensions for these individuals amount to DM 85,676,846.00.

Provisions for remuneration of the Supervisory Board amount to DM 1,710,750.00.

Loans to members of the Board of Management and the Supervisory Board as of December 31, 1993 amounted to DM 11,250.00 and DM 111,851.00, repayments during the year to DM 62,163.00 and DM 3,216.00, respectively. Some of these loans are interest-free, and others are at interest rates of 6.0 % p. a.

The members of the Supervisory Board and the Board of Management are listed on pages 4 and 5.

Leverkusen, March 1, 1994
Bayer Aktiengesellschaft
The Board of Management

AUDITORS' OPINION

The Financial Statements of the Bayer Group, which we have audited in accordance with professional standards, comply with the German statutory provisions. Prepared in accordance with generally accepted accounting principles, they give a true and fair view of the net worth, financial position and earnings of the Group. The Management Report of the Bayer Group, which is combined with the Management Report of Bayer Aktiengesellschaft, is consistent with the Financial Statements of the Bayer Group.

Essen, March 3, 1994
C&L Treuhand-Vereinigung
Deutsche Revision
Aktiengesellschaft
Wirtschaftsprüfungsgesellschaft
Steuerberatungsgesellschaft

C. F. Leuschner	J. Schilling
Wirtschaftsprüfer	Wirtschaftsprüfer
(Certified Public Accountant)	(Certified Public Accountant)

Appendix 1
Extracts from the 1991 Annual Report of ICI plc

GROUP PROFIT AND LOSS ACCOUNT

For the year ended 31 December	Notes	1991 £m	1990* £m
Turnover		**.12,488**	12,906
Operating costs	3	**(11,591)**	(12,057)
Other operating income	3	**136**	180
Trading profit	3	**1,033**	1,029
Share of profits less losses of associated undertakings	4		
As published in the 1990 accounts			154
Extraordinary item restated as exceptional	2		(41)
		30	113
Net interest payable	5	**(220)**	(206)
Profit on ordinary activities before taxation		**843**	936
Tax on profit on ordinary activities	6	**(279)**	(336)
Profit on ordinary activities after taxation		**564**	600
Attributable to minorities		**(22)**	(??)
Net profit attributable to parent company		**542**	578
Extraordinary items	8	**–**	92
Net profit for the financial year		**542**	670
Dividends	9	**(391)**	(389)
Profit retained for year		**151**	281
Earnings before extraordinary items per £1 Ordinary Share	10	**76.4p**	82.3p

* Restated, see note 2.

GROUP RESERVES ATTRIBUTABLE TO PARENT COMPANY

	Note	1991 £m	1990 £m
At beginning of year		**3,963**	4,320
Profit retained for year			
Company		**13**	381
Subsidiary undertakings		**178**	(53)
Associated undertakings		**(40)**	(47)
		151	281
Amounts taken direct to reserves		**(33)**	(638)
At end of year	22	**4,081**	3,963

£m means millions of pounds sterling.

BALANCE SHEETS

At 31 December	Notes	Group 1991 £m	Group 1990 £m	Company 1991 £m	Company 1990 £m
ASSETS EMPLOYED					
Fixed assets					
Tangible assets	11	**5,128**	4,947	**1,079**	1,074
Investments					
Subsidiary undertakings	12			**4,347**	4,189
Participating interests	13	**421**	483	**222**	220
		5,549	5,430	**5,648**	5,483
Current assets					
Stocks	14	**2,025**	2,214	**379**	395
Debtors	15	**2,636**	2,590	**815**	1,301
Investments and short-term deposits	16	**608**	388	**–**	–
Cash	16	**197**	177	**8**	7
		5,466	5,369	**1,202**	1,703
Total assets		**11,015**	10,799	**6,850**	7,186
Creditors due within one year					
Short-term borrowings	17	**(296)**	(447)	**(10)**	(5)
Current instalments of loans	21	**(220)**	(78)	**(156)**	–
Other creditors	18	**(2,894)**	(2,881)	**(1,281)**	(814)
		(3,410)	(3,406)	**(1,447)**	(819)
Net current assets (liabilities)		**2,056**	1,963	**(245)**	884
Total assets less current liabilities		**7,605**	7,393	**5,403**	6,367
FINANCED BY					
Creditors due after more than one year					
Loans	21	**1,788**	1,670	**400**	555
Other creditors	18	**159**	154	**1,053**	1,698
		1,947	1,824	**1,453**	2,253
Provisions for liabilities and charges	19	**526**	549	**14**	119
Deferred income: Grants not yet credited to profit		**52**	63	**5**	6
Minority interests		**288**	286		
Capital and reserves attributable to parent company					
Called-up share capital	20	**711**	708	**711**	708
Reserves					
Share premium account		**469**	446	**469**	446
Revaluation reserve		**56**	50	**–**	–
Other reserves		**399**	381	**436**	533
Profit and loss account		**3,131**	3,014	**2,315**	2,302
Associated undertakings' reserves		**26**	72		
Total reserves	22	**4,081**	3,963	**3,220**	3,281
Total capital and reserves attributable to parent company		**4,792**	4,671	**3,931**	3,989
		7,605	7,393	**5,403**	6,367

The accounts on pages 34 to 59 were approved by the Board of Directors on 9 March 1992 and were signed on its behalf by:

Sir Denys Henderson   *Director*
C. M. Short   *Director*
A. G. Spall   *General Manager – Finance*

Appendix 1

STATEMENT OF GROUP CASH FLOW

For the year ended 31 December	Notes	1991 £m	1990 £m
Cash inflow from operating activities			
Net cash inflow from trading operations	23	**1,651**	1,735
Outflow related to extraordinary provisions	24	**(193)**	(7)
Net cash inflow from operating activities		**1,458**	1,728
Returns on investments and servicing of finance			
Interest and dividends received	25	**97**	142
Interest paid		**(294)**	(278)
Dividends paid by parent company		**(390)**	(384)
Dividends paid by subsidiary undertakings to minority interests		**(7)**	(44)
Net cash outflow from returns on investments and servicing of finance		**(594)**	(564)
Tax paid		**(286)**	(412)
Investing activities			
Cash expenditure on tangible fixed assets	11	**(896)**	(1,019)
Acquisitions and new fixed asset investments	26	**(57)**	(480)
Disposals accounted for as extraordinary items	27	**372**	918
Other disposals	27	**142**	229
Realisation of short-term investments and deposits		**5**	7
Net cash outflow from investing activities		**(434)**	(345)
Net cash inflow before financing		**144**	407
Financing			
Issues of ICI Ordinary Shares		**19**	56
Net increase in loans		**251**	31
Net decrease in lease finance (1990 increase)		**(10)**	75
Net decrease in short-term borrowings		**(71)**	(5)
Net cash inflow from financing	28	**189**	157
Increase in cash and cash equivalents	29	**333**	564

This Statement of Group Cash Flow (prepared in accordance with the provisions of the Accounting Standards Board's Financial Reporting Standard 1) replaces the Statement of Sources and Applications of Group Funds included in previous ICI Group accounts.

ACCOUNTING POLICIES

The accounts are prepared under the historical cost convention and in accordance with the Companies Act 1985, as amended by the Companies Act 1989, and the Accounting Standards issued by the Accounting Standards Board. The following paragraphs describe the main policies. The accounting policies of some overseas subsidiaries do not conform with UK Accounting Standards and, where appropriate, adjustments are made on consolidation in order to present the Group accounts on a consistent basis.

DEPRECIATION
The Group's policy is to write off the book value of each tangible fixed asset evenly over its estimated remaining life. Reviews are made periodically of the estimated remaining lives of individual productive assets, taking account of commercial and technological obsolescence as well as normal wear and tear. Under this policy it becomes impracticable to calculate average asset lives exactly; however, the total lives approximate to 20 years for buildings and 15 years for plant and equipment. Depreciation of assets qualifying for grants is calculated on their full cost.

FOREIGN CURRENCIES
Profit and loss accounts in foreign currencies are translated into sterling at average rates for the relevant accounting periods. Assets and liabilities are translated at exchange rates ruling at the date of the Group balance sheet.

Exchange differences on short-term currency borrowings and deposits are included with net interest payable. Exchange differences on all other transactions, except foreign currency loans, are taken to trading profit. In the Group accounts exchange differences arising on consolidation of the net investments in overseas subsidiary undertakings and associated undertakings are taken to reserves, as are differences arising on equity investments denominated in foreign currencies in the Company accounts. Differences on relevant foreign currency loans are taken to reserves and offset against the differences on net investments.

GOODWILL
On the acquisition of a business, fair values are attributed to the net assets acquired. Goodwill arises where the fair value of the consideration given for a business exceeds such net assets. UK Accounting Standards require that purchased goodwill be eliminated from the balance sheet either upon acquisition against reserves or by amortisation over a period. Elimination against reserves has been selected as appropriate to the goodwill purchases made during recent years.

LEASES
Assets held under finance leases are capitalized and included in tangible fixed assets at fair value. Each asset is depreciated over the shorter of the lease term or its useful life. The obligations related to finance leases, net of finance charges in respect of future periods, are included as appropriate under creditors due within, or creditors due after, one year. The interest element of the rental obligation is allocated to accounting periods during the lease term to reflect a constant rate of interest on the remaining balance of the obligation for each accounting period. Rentals under operating leases are charged to profit and loss account as incurred.

PENSION COSTS
The pension costs relating to UK retirement plans are assessed in accordance with the advice of independent qualified actuaries. The amounts so determined include the regular cost of providing the benefits under the plans which it is intended should remain a level percentage of current and expected future earnings of the employees covered under the plans. Variations from the regular pension cost are spread on a systematic basis over the estimated average remaining service lives of current employees in the plans.

Retirement plans of non-UK subsidiary undertakings are accounted for in accordance with local conditions and practice. With minor exceptions, these subsidiaries recognize the expected cost of providing pensions on a systematic basis over the average remaining service lives of employees in accordance with the advice of independent qualified actuaries.

ASSOCIATED UNDERTAKINGS
The Group's share of the profits less losses of all significant associated undertakings is included in the Group profit and loss account on the equity accounting basis.

The holding value of significant associated undertakings in the Group balance sheet is calculated by reference to the Group's equity in the net tangible assets of such undertakings, as shown by the most recent accounts available, adjusted where appropriate.

RESEARCH AND DEVELOPMENT
Research and development expenditure is charged to profit in the year in which it is incurred.

STOCK VALUATION
Finished goods are stated at the lower of cost and net realizable value, raw materials and other stocks at the lower of cost and replacement price; the first in, first out or an average method of valuation is used. In determining cost for stock valuation purposes, depreciation is included but selling expenses and certain overhead expenses are excluded.

TAXATION
The charge for taxation is based on the profit for the year and takes into account taxation deferred because of timing differences between the treatment of certain items for taxation and for accounting purposes. However, no provision is made for taxation deferred by reliefs unless there is reasonable evidence that such deferred taxation will be payable in the future.

NOTES RELATING TO THE ACCOUNTS

1 COMPOSITION OF THE GROUP

The Group accounts consolidate the accounts of Imperial Chemical Industries PLC (the Company) and its subsidiary undertakings, of which there were 585 at 31 December 1991. Owing to local conditions and to avoid undue delay in the presentation of the Group accounts, 85 subsidiaries made up their accounts to dates earlier than 31 December, but not earlier than 30 September.

2 1990 RESTATEMENT

The comparative figures for the Group for 1990 have been restated to reclassify, as an exceptional item, the ICI share (£41m, less tax relief of £2m) of a provision, previously accounted for as extraordinary by Tioxide Group Ltd while it was an associated undertaking. This restatement is in accordance with the clarification of the accounting treatment of restructuring costs issued by the Accounting Standards Board and has the effect of reducing 1990 profit before tax from £977m to £936m and earnings per share from 87.9p to 82.3p.

3 TRADING PROFIT

	1991 £m	1990 £m
Turnover	**12,488**	12,906
Operating costs		
Cost of sales	**(7,429)**	(7,885)
Distribution costs	**(859)**	(883)
Research and development (£596m (1990 £591m))		
and technical service (£96m (1990 £88m))	**(692)**	(679)
Administrative and other expenses	**(2,580)**	(2,571)
Employees' profit-sharing bonus	**(31)**	(39)
	(11,591)	(12,057)
Other operating income		
Government grants	**17**	30
Royalties	**41**	32
Other income	**78**	118
	136	180
Trading profit	**1,033**	1,029
Total charge for depreciation included above	**549**	525
Gross profit, as defined by the Companies Act 1985	**5,059**	5,021

4 SHARE OF PROFITS LESS LOSSES OF ASSOCIATED UNDERTAKINGS

	1991 £m	1990* £m
Share of profits less losses		
Share of undistributed profits less losses		
As published in the 1990 accounts		66
Tioxide Group Ltd extraordinary item restated as exceptional		(41)*
	(25)	25
Dividend income	**21**	69
Share of profits less losses before tax	**(4)**	94
Gains less losses on disposals of investments	**35**	22
Amounts written off investments (including provisions		
raised £9m (1990 £3m) and released £8m (£nil))	**(1)**	(3)
	30	113*

* Restated, see note 2.

Total dividend income from shares in associated undertakings comprised £11m (1990 £24m) from listed companies and £10m (£45m) from unlisted companies.

In 1990 the Group's 50 per cent share of the results of European Vinyls Corporation (Holdings) BV (EVC) was included in trading profit as the Group retained ownership of certain fixed assets of the business. These assets were transferred to EVC on 31 December 1990.

5 NET INTEREST PAYABLE

	1991 £m	1990 £m
Interest payable and similar charges		
Loan interest	195	155
Interest on short-term borrowings and other financing costs	108	125
	303	280
Interest receivable and similar income from current asset investments		
Listed redeemable securities	(18)	(15)
Short-term deposits	(65)	(58)
	(83)	(73)
Exchange gains on short-term currency borrowings and deposits	–	(1)
	220	206

Loan interest includes £101m (1990 £96m) on loans not wholly repayable within 5 years.

6 TAX ON PROFIT ON ORDINARY ACTIVITIES

	1991 £m	1990* £m
ICI and subsidiary undertakings		
United Kingdom taxation		
Corporation tax	136	109
Double taxation relief	(87)	(43)
Deferred taxation	(20)	2
	29	68
Overseas taxation		
Overseas taxes	205	186
Deferred taxation	31	39
	236	225
	265	293
Associated undertakings	14	43*
Tax on profit on ordinary activities	279	336*

* Restated, see note 2.

UK and overseas taxation has been provided on the profits earned for the periods covered by the Group accounts. UK corporation tax has been provided at the rate of 33.25 per cent (1990 35 per cent).

Deferred taxation
The amounts of deferred taxation accounted for at the balance sheet date and the potential amounts of deferred taxation are disclosed below.

	Group 1991 £m	Group 1990 £m	Company 1991 £m	Company 1990 £m
Accounted for at balance sheet date (see note 19)				
Timing differences on UK capital allowances and depreciation	52	63	–	–
Miscellaneous timing differences	51	10	8	10
	103	73	8	10
Not accounted for at balance sheet date				
UK capital allowances utilized in excess of depreciation charged	329	330	173	151
Miscellaneous timing differences	(44)	(65)	20	11
	285	265	193	162
Full potential deferred taxation	388	338	201	172

NOTES RELATING TO THE ACCOUNTS

7 SEGMENT INFORMATION

Classes of Business

In 1991 the directors decided that the analysis of the Group's activities should be changed to follow more closely the way in which the Group is directed and managed. Results are now presented in four classes of business which group together related product areas or technologies.

	Total assets less current liabilities 1991 £m	1990 £m	Turnover 1991 £m	1990 £m	Profit 1991 £m	1990* £m
Bioscience Products	1,625	1,513	2,953	2,777	682	599
Specialty Chemicals and Materials	2,894	2,704	5,384	5,573	187	202
Industrial Chemicals	1,479	1,694	3,612	3,789	135	205
Regional Businesses	533	617	1,246	1,451	29	23
			13,195	13,590	1,033	1,029
Net operating assets	6,531	6,528				
Inter-class eliminations			(707)	(684)	–	–
Net non-operating assets	1,074	865				
	7,605	7,393	12,488	12,906		
Trading profit					1,033	1,029
Share of profits less losses of associated undertakings					30	113*
Net interest payable					(220)	(206)
Profit on ordinary activities before taxation					843	936*

* Restated, see note 2.

The Group's policy is to transfer products internally at external market prices. £472m (1990 £389m) of the inter-class turnover shown above represents sales from Industrial Chemicals to Specialty Chemicals and Materials.

Net non-operating assets include assets in course of construction, investments in associated undertakings and other participating interests, current asset investments, short-term deposits and cash, less short-term borrowings, and debtors and creditors relating to taxes and dividends. The move to the new Classes of Business referred to above resulted in some net assets previously classified as non-operating being included in operating assets.

	Capital expenditure 1991 £m	1990 £m	Depreciation 1991 £m	1990 £m
Bioscience Products	147	185	112	116
Specialty Chemicals and Materials	317	462	212	202
Industrial Chemicals	339	239	149	128
Regional Businesses	84	127	76	79
	887	1,013	549	525

7 SEGMENT INFORMATION (continued)

Geographic areas

The information opposite is re-analysed in the table below by geographic area. The figures for each geographic area show the net operating assets owned by and the turnover and profit made by companies located in that area; export sales and related profits are included in the areas from which those sales were made.

	Net operating assets		Turnover		Profit	
	1991 £m	1990 £m	**1991** £m	1990 £m	**1991** £m	1990 £m
United Kingdom						
Sales in the UK			**2,571**	2,966		
Sales overseas			**3,079**	3,160		
	2,925	2,964	**5,650**	6,126	**300**	295
Continental Europe	**997**	1,024	**3,194**	3,152	**191**	157
The Americas	**1,569**	1,549	**3,843**	3,651	**391**	382
Asia Pacific	**987**	917	**1,951**	2,047	**119**	136
Other countries	**53**	74	**455**	403	**45**	29
	6,531	6,528	**15,093**	15,379	**1,046**	999
Inter-area eliminations			**(2,605)**	(2,473)	**(13)**	30
			12,488	12,906		
Trading profit					**1,033**	1,029

Inter-area turnover shown above includes sales of £2,075m (1990 £1,982m) from the United Kingdom to overseas subsidiaries.

Geographic markets

	1991 £m	1990 £m
Turnover in each geographic market in which customers are located		
United Kingdom	**2,592**	2,996
Continental Europe	**3,196**	3,352
The Americas	**3,828**	3,656
Asia Pacific	**2,153**	2,251
Other countries	**719**	651
Total turnover	**12,488**	12,906

Employees

	1991	1990
Average number of people employed by the Group in		
United Kingdom	**51,600**	53,700
Continental Europe	**18,000**	17,400
The Americas	**31,000**	32,600
Asia Pacific	**16,400**	16,800
Other countries	**11,600**	11,600
Total employees	**128,600**	132,100

The number of people employed by the Group at the end of 1991 was 123,600 (1990 135,300).

NOTES RELATING TO THE ACCOUNTS

8 EXTRAORDINARY ITEMS

	Group	
	1991 **£m**	1990* £m
Gain on disposal of the investment in Enterprise Oil plc (net of charge for taxation of £9m)		520
Charge for reshaping the ICI Group business portfolio, comprising withdrawals through business divestments, closures and other restructuring measures. The charge is net of estimated disposal proceeds and includes the expense of obtaining substantial cost reductions which are a significant part of the objective (net of tax relief of £50m of which £46m is deferred).		(300)
Charge for the withdrawal from UK compound fertilizer manufacture and restructuring, with a view to ultimate divestment, of the ammonium nitrate business (net of tax relief of £12m of which £9m is deferred)		(128)
	–	92*

* Restated, see note 2.

9 DIVIDENDS

	1991	1990	**1991**	1990
	pence per			
	£1 Share		**£m**	£m
Interim, paid 7 October 1991	**21p**	21p	**149**	148
Second interim, to be confirmed as final, payable 27 April 1992	**34p**	34p	**242**	241
	55p	55p	**391**	389

10 EARNINGS BEFORE EXTRAORDINARY ITEMS PER £1 ORDINARY SHARE

	1991	1990*
Earnings for Ordinary Shareholders, before extraordinary items (£m)	**542**	578*
Average Ordinary Shares in issue during year, weighted on a time basis (millions)	**709**	702
Earnings per £1 Ordinary Share	**76.4p**	82.3p*

* Restated, see note 2.

The effect on earnings per £1 Ordinary Share of the issue of shares under option (note 20) would not be material.

11 TANGIBLE FIXED ASSETS

	Land and buildings £m	Plant and equipment £m	Payments on account and assets in course of construction £m	Total £m
GROUP				
Cost or as revalued				
At beginning of year	1,747	6,921	919	9,587
Exchange adjustments	29	14	16	59
Revaluations and adjustments	(20)	(18)		(38)
New subsidiary undertakings	2	8	1	11
Capital expenditure			887	887
Transfers	158	786	(944)	
Disposals and other movements	(148)	(415)	(5)	(568)
At end of year	1,768	7,296	874	9,938
Depreciation				
At beginning of year	614	4,026		4,640
Exchange adjustments	13	(4)		9
Revaluations and adjustments	2	1		3
Disposals and other movements	(103)	(288)		(391)
Charge for year	70	479		549
At end of year	596	4,214		4,810
Net book value at end 1991	1,172	3,082	874	5,128
Net book value at end 1990	1;133	2,895	919	4,947

Capital expenditure in the year of £887m includes capitalized finance leases of £5m; creditors for capital work done but not paid for decreased by £14m; the resulting cash expenditure on tangible fixed assets was £896m.

The net book value of the tangible fixed assets of the Group includes capitalized finance leases of £48m comprising cost of £119m less depreciation of £71m. The depreciation charge for the year in respect of capitalized leases was £6m and finance charges £14m.

	Land and buildings £m	Plant and equipment £m	Payments on account and assets in course of construction £m	Total £m
COMPANY				
Cost or as revalued				
At beginning of year	382	1,362	205	1,949
Capital expenditure	–	–	153	153
Transfers	49	166	(215)	
Disposals and other movements	(5)	(57)	1	(61)
At end of year	426	1,471	144	2,041
Depreciation				
At beginning of year	114	761		875
Disposals and other movements	(5)	(35)		(40)
Charge for year	15	112		127
At end of year	124	838		962
Net book value at end 1991	302	633	144	1,079
Net book value at end 1990	268	601	205	1,074

The net book value of the tangible fixed assets of the Company includes capitalized finance leases of £5m comprising cost of £8m less depreciation of £3m. The depreciation charge for the year in respect of capitalized leases was £1m and finance charges £1m.

NOTES RELATING TO THE ACCOUNTS

11 TANGIBLE FIXED ASSETS (continued)

	Group		Company	
	1991 **£m**	1990 £m	**1991** **£m**	1990 £m
The net book value of land and buildings comprised				
Freeholds	**1,126**	1,077	**297**	263
Long leases (over 50 years unexpired)	**34**	40	**5**	5
Short leases	**12**	16	**–**	–
	1,172	1,133	**302**	268

	Group			
	Land and buildings		Plant and equipment	
Revalued assets included in tangible fixed assets	**1991** **£m**	1990 £m	**1991** **£m**	1990 £m
At revalued amount	**111**	128	**145**	175
Depreciation	**45**	51	**121**	140
Net book value	**66**	77	**24**	35
At historical cost	**64**	67	**142**	149
Depreciation	**34**	33	**126**	127
Net book value	**30**	34	**16**	22

12 INVESTMENTS IN SUBSIDIARY UNDERTAKINGS

	Shares £m	Loans £m	Total £m
Cost			
At beginning of year	**2,311**	**2,047**	**4,358**
Exchange adjustments	**(106)**	**1**	**(105)**
Transfers to subsidiary undertakings	**(2,839)**	**–**	**(2,839)**
Shares received as consideration for transfers	**2,818**	**–**	**2,818**
New loans	**–**	**912**	**912**
Loans repaid	**–**	**(641)**	**(641)**
At end of year	**2,184**	**2,319**	**4,503**
Provisions			
At beginning of year	**(160)**	**(9)**	**(169)**
Exchange adjustments	**(2)**	**–**	**(2)**
Additions	**(4)**	**(3)**	**(7)**
Releases	**22**	**–**	**22**
At end of year	**(144)**	**(12)**	**(156)**
Balance sheet value at end 1991	**2,040**	**2,307**	**4,347**
Balance sheet value at end 1990	2,151	2,038	4,189

Cost includes scrip issues capitalized £13m (1990 £38m).

	1991 **£m**	1990 £m
Shares in subsidiary undertakings which are listed investments		
Balance sheet value	**9**	63
Market value	**74**	341

The Company's investment in its subsidiary undertakings consists of either equity or long term loans, or both. Normal trading balances are included in either debtors or creditors. Information on principal subsidiary undertakings is given on pages 58 and 59.

18 INVESTMENTS IN PARTICIPATING INTERESTS

	Associated undertakings Shares £m	Loans £m	Other participating interests £m	Total £m
GROUP				
Cost				
At beginning of year	399	10	17	426
Exchange adjustments	4	–	–	4
Additions	15	7	2	24
Disposals and repayments	(25)	–	(5)	(30)
Other movements	(10)	–	(5)	(15)
At end of year	383	17	9	409
Share of post-acquisition reserves less losses				
At beginning of year	74			74
Exchange adjustments	(6)			(6)
Retained profits less losses	(40)			(40)
Other movements	(1)			(1)
At end of year	27			27
Provisions				
At beginning of year	(12)	(4)	(1)	(17)
Other movements	4	(1)	(1)	2
At end of year	(8)	(5)	(2)	(15)
Balance sheet value at end 1991	402	12	7	421
Balance sheet value at end 1990	461	6	16	483

Cost includes scrip issues capitalized £4m (1990 £5m).

The above investments included

1991				
Investments listed on The London Stock Exchange	–	–	–	–
Other listed investments	126	–	–	126
Balance sheet value	126	–	–	126
Market value	118	–	–	118
1990				
Investments listed on The London Stock Exchange	21	–	2	23
Other listed investments	111	–	–	111
Balance sheet value	132	–	2	134
Market value	192	–	10	202

Information on principal associated undertakings is given on page 59.

NOTES RELATING TO THE ACCOUNTS

13 INVESTMENTS IN PARTICIPATING INTERESTS (continued)

	Shares £m	Associated undertakings Loans £m	Total £m
COMPANY			
Cost			
At beginning of year	220	3	223
Exchange adjustments	4	–	4
Additions	–	4	4
Disposals	–	(1)	(1)
At end of year	224	6	230
Provisions			
At beginning of year	(1)	(2)	(3)
Additions	(2)	(5)	(7)
Other movements	–	2	2
At end of year	(3)	(5)	(8)
Balance sheet value at end 1991	221	1	222
Balance sheet value at end 1990	219	1	220

14 STOCKS

	Group 1991 £m	Group 1990 £m	Company 1991 £m	Company 1990 £m
Raw materials and consumables	603	652	110	106
Stocks in process	254	237	82	78
Finished goods and goods for resale	1,168	1,325	187	211
	2,025	2,214	379	395

15 DEBTORS

	Group 1991	Group 1990	Company 1991	Company 1990
Amounts due within one year				
Trade debtors	1,877	1,922	–	–
Amounts owed by subsidiary undertakings			614	1,102
Amounts owed by associated undertakings	34	33	1	1
Other debtors	414	373	56	79
Prepayments and accrued income*	131	151	42	36
	2,456	2,479	713	1,218
Amounts due after more than one year				
Advance corporation tax recoverable†			80	80
Other debtors*	180	111	22	3
	180	111	102	83
	2,636	2,590	815	1,301

* Includes prepaid pension costs (note 35).
† Advance corporation tax recoverable was previously deducted from the balance of deferred tax within provisions for liabilities and charges (note 19) in both the Group and Company accounts. This remains the treatment in the Group accounts.

16 CURRENT ASSET INVESTMENTS AND SHORT-TERM DEPOSITS

	Group 1991 £m	1990 £m
Redeemable securities listed on		
The London Stock Exchange	35	54
Other listed investments	57	47
Total listed investments	92	101
Unlisted investments	4	11
	96	112
Short-term deposits	512	276
	608	388
Included in cash and cash equivalents (see note 29)	506	280
Market value of listed investments	92	101

Included in current asset investments, short-term deposits and cash are amounts totalling £267m (1990 £243m) held by the Group's insurance subsidiaries.

17 SHORT-TERM BORROWINGS

	Group 1991 £m	1990 £m	Company 1991 £m	1990 £m
Bank borrowings				
Secured by fixed charge	9	3	7	–
Secured by floating charge	13	14	–	–
Unsecured	251	353	3	4
	273	370	10	4
Other borrowings (unsecured)	23	77	–	1
	296	447	10	5
Included in cash and cash equivalents (see note 29)	264	346		

18 OTHER CREDITORS

	Group 1991	1990	Company 1991	1990
Amounts due within one year				
Trade creditors	1,004	1,083	162	143
Amounts owed to subsidiary undertakings			519	145
Amounts owed to associated undertakings	8	9	–	–
Corporate taxation	286	284	159	118
Value added and payroll taxes and social security	80	101	–	–
Other creditors*	796	797	140	107
Accruals	478	366	59	60
Dividends to Ordinary Shareholders	242	241	242	241
	2,894	2,881	1,281	814
Amounts due after more than one year				
Amounts owed to subsidiary undertakings			1,045	1,686
Other creditors*	159	154	8	12
	159	154	1,053	1,698

* Includes costs charged as extraordinary in 1990, obligations under finance leases (note 30) and accrued pension costs (note 35).

NOTES RELATING TO THE ACCOUNTS

19 PROVISIONS FOR LIABILITIES AND CHARGES

	At beginning of year £m	Profit and loss account £m	Net amounts paid or becoming current £m	Acquisition and other movements £m	At end of year £m
GROUP					
Deferred taxation (see note 6)	73	11	35	(16)	103
Advance corporation tax recoverable	(80)				(80)
	(7)	11	35	(16)	23
Employee benefits*	212	58	(27)	(1)	242
Reshaping, environmental and other provisions	344	35	(167)	49	201
	549	104	(159)	32	526
COMPANY					
Deferred taxation	10	(18)	16	–	8
Other provisions	109	(8)	(95)	–	6
	119	(26)	(79)	–	14

* Includes provisions for unfunded pension costs (note 35).

In the Company accounts the balance of advance corporation tax recoverable is shown within debtors (note 15).

No provision has been released or applied for any purpose other than that for which it was established.

20 CALLED-UP SHARE CAPITAL OF PARENT COMPANY

	Authorized £m	Allotted, called-up and fully paid 1991 £m	1990 £m
Ordinary Shares (£1 each)	711	711	708
Unclassified shares (£1 each)	139		
	850	711	708

The number of Ordinary Shares issued during the year totalled 2.9m comprising issues in respect of the acquisition in 1990 of Tyler Corporation 0.6m, the Employees' Profit-Sharing Scheme 0.6m, and the exercise of options 1.7m.

At 31 December 1991 there were options outstanding in respect of 16,373,647 Ordinary Shares of £1 under the Company's share option schemes for staff (1990 14,886,235) normally exercisable in the period 1992 to 2001 (1991 to 2000) at subscription prices of £5.95 to £15.12 (£5.95 to £15.12). The weighted average subscription price of options outstanding at 31 December 1991 was £10.66.

Options granted to directors are shown in note 33.

During 1991 movements in the number of shares under option comprised new options issued 3,744,594, options exercised 1,544,834 and options lapsed or waived 712,348. At the end of 1991 there were 16,051,661 shares available for the granting of options (1990 18,996,192).

2 LOANS

	Repayment dates	Group 1991 £m	Group 1990 £m	Company 1991 £m	Company 1990 £m
Secured loans					
US dollars (5½ to 10⅞%)	1992/2012	**39**	38		
Australian dollars (11.1 to 17.1%)	1992/97	**29**	39		
Other currencies	1992/2000	**113**	71		
Total secured		**181**	148		
Secured by fixed charge		**177**	142		
Secured by floating charge		**4**	6		
Unsecured loans					
Sterling					
9¾ to 11¼ % bonds	1992/2005	**400**	400	**400**	400
9¾ % Notes	1993	**75**	75	**75**	75
Others	1992/2002	**129**	128		
		604	603	**475**	475
US dollars					
7½ to 8% Eurodollar bonds	1992/96	**54**	54		
8⅛ to 9.05% bonds	1992/2006	**262**	268		
7.83 to 8.9% medium-term notes	1994/2002	**54**	26		
8¾% Notes	2001	**133**	–		
9½ % Notes	2000	**160**	156		
Others	1992/2013	**102**	73		
		765	577		
Australian dollars (9.5 to 15½%)	1992/94	**137**	86	**81**	80
Canadian dollars (10⅝ to 14½ %)	1992/2000	**67**	68		
Swiss francs (3½ to 4½ %)	1992/99	**162**	175		
Other currencies	1992/2005	**92**	91		
Total unsecured		**1,827**	1,600	**556**	555
Total loans		**2,008**	1,748	**556**	555

Loans from banks included in the table above amounted to £392m (1990 £311m) in the Group of which £126m (£88m) was secured.

New borrowings during the year by subsidiary undertakings included US$250m 8¾% Guaranteed Notes, US$50m 7.83% Medium-Term Notes and two issues of Australian dollar Guaranteed Notes (A$60m repayable in 1993 and A$75m repayable in 1994): the proceeds of these were used for the general purposes of the Group. In addition several project loans were raised through subsidiaries from the European Investment Bank totalling £195m equivalent, repayable at dates between 1992 and 2003.

		Group 1991 £m	Group 1990 £m	Company 1991 £m	Company 1990 £m
Loans or instalments thereof are repayable					
After 5 years from balance sheet date					
Lump sums		**759**	617	**200**	200
Instalments		**292**	222	**–**	–
		1,051	839	**200**	200
From 2 to 5 years		**516**	603	**125**	200
From 1 to 2 years		**221**	228	**75**	155
Total due after more than one year		**1,788**	1,670	**400**	555
Total due within one year		**220**	78	**156**	–
		2,008	1,748	**556**	555
Aggregate amount of loans repayable by instalments any of which fall due after 5 years		**588**	489	**–**	–

NOTES RELATING TO THE ACCOUNTS

22 **RESERVES**

	Share premium account £m	Revaluation £m	Other £m	Profit and loss account £m	Associated under-takings £m	**1991 Total £m**	1990 Total £m
GROUP							
Reserves attributable to parent company							
At beginning of year	**446**	**50**	**381**	**3,014**	**72**	**3,963**	4,320
Profit retained for year				**191**	**(40)**	**151**	281
Amounts taken direct to reserves							
Share premiums	**23**					**23**	127
Goodwill				**(89)**		**(89)**	(355)
Exchange adjustments		**(5)**	**16**	**65**	**(6)**	**70**	(410)
Other movements		**(10)**	**(18)**	**1**	**(10)**	**(37)**	–
	23	**(15)**	**(2)**	**(23)**	**(16)**	**(33)**	(638)
Other movements between reserves		**21**	**20**	**(51)**	**10**		
At end of year	**469**	**56**	**399**	**3,131**	**26**	**4,081**	3,963

In the Group accounts, there was no net exchange movement on foreign currency loans in 1991. (In 1990, gains of £116m were offset in reserves against exchange losses on the net investment in overseas subsidiary and associated undertakings).

The major element of the goodwill taken to reserves in 1991 relates to adjustments to the provisional values attributed to Tioxide Group Ltd net assets following the completion of the fair value assessment initiated at the time of its acquisition at the end of 1990.

The cumulative amount of goodwill resulting from acquisitions during 1991 and prior years, net of goodwill attributable to subsidiary undertakings or businesses disposed of prior to 31 December 1991, amounted to £1,752m (1990 £1,708m).

There are no significant statutory or contractual restrictions on the distribution of current profits of subsidiary or associated undertakings; undistributed profits of prior years are, in the main, permanently employed in the businesses of these companies. The undistributed profits of Group companies overseas may be liable to overseas taxes and/or UK taxation (after allowing for double taxation relief) if they were to be distributed as dividends. No provision has been made in respect of potential taxation liabilities on realization of assets at restated or revalued amounts or on realization of associated undertakings at equity accounted value.

For the purpose of calculating the basis of the borrowing limits in accordance with the Articles of Association, the total of the sums standing to the credit of capital and revenue reserves of the Company and its subsidiary undertakings, to be added to the nominal amount of the share capital of the Company, was £5,259m at 31 December 1991.

	Share premium account £m	Other £m	Profit and loss account £m	**1991 Total £m**	1990 Total £m
COMPANY					
Reserves					
At beginning of year	**446**	**533**	**2,302**	**3,281**	3,077
Profit retained for year			**13**	**13**	381
Amounts taken direct to reserves					
Share premiums	**23**			**23**	62
Purchased goodwill					(4)
Exchange adjustments		**(97)**		**(97)**	(300)
Other movements					65
	23	**(97)**		**(74)**	(177)
At end of year	**469**	**436**	**2,315**	**3,220**	3,281

By virtue of S230 of the Companies Act 1985, the Company is exempt from presenting a profit and loss account.

Appendix 1

23 NET CASH INFLOW FROM TRADING OPERATIONS

	1991 £m	1990 £m
Trading profit	1,033	1,029
Depreciation	549	525
Stocks decrease	171	74
Debtors decrease (1990 increase)	65	(46)
Creditors decrease (1990 increase)	(102)	116
Non-cash items included in trading profit, other operating cash flows	(65)	37
	1,651	1,735

24 OUTFLOW RELATED TO EXTRAORDINARY PROVISIONS

Expenditure relating to the extraordinary items, set up to provide for reshaping the ICI Group business portfolio, and for withdrawal from the UK fertilizer business, including severance and other employee costs, plant demolition and site clearance.

25 INTEREST AND DIVIDENDS RECEIVED

	1991 £m	1990 £m
Dividends received from equity accounted associated undertakings	14	65
Other dividends received	3	4
Interest received	80	73
	97	142

26 ACQUISITIONS AND NEW FIXED ASSET INVESTMENTS

The largest acquisition during 1991 was the purchase of Continental Polymers Inc which has been accounted for by the acquisition method of accounting. The effect of this acquisition on the Group results was not material.

	1991 £m	1990 £m
Acquisitions and new fixed asset investments		
Acquisitions of subsidiary undertakings involving		
Fixed assets	11	402
Current assets	21	339
Total liabilities	(29)	(549)
Minorities	–	(5)
Net assets	3	187
Attributable to interests already owned	–	(101)
Net assets of subsidiary undertakings acquired	3	86
Goodwill	33	210
Fair value of consideration for subsidiary undertakings	36	296
Investment in equity accounted undertakings	9	175
Other investments	15	26
	60	497
Consideration for acquisitions and new investments		
Shares allotted and to be allotted, including share premium	–	79
Cash and cash equivalents acquired	(1)	(61)
Deferred consideration and non-cash consideration	4	(1)
Net cash investment	57	480
	60	497

Fixed and current assets are adjusted to fair value based on external valuations and internal reviews; provisions for closure are made where appropriate.

NOTES RELATING TO THE ACCOUNTS

27 DISPOSALS

	1991 £m	1990 £m
Disposals in the year resulted in the following net asset movements		
Tangible fixed assets	**160**	184
Investments in participating interests	**30**	150
Cash and cash equivalents	**–**	–
Other net current assets	**53**	21
Creditors due after more than one year	**(1)**	11
Provisions for liabilities and charges	**232**	(106)
	474	260
Profit and loss account		
Ordinary activities	**52**	21
Extraordinary items	**–**	626
	526	907
Satisfied by		
Cash consideration	**514**	1,147
Deferred consideration	**9**	(240)
Non-cash consideration	**3**	–
	526	907

The cash consideration for disposals in 1991 includes £372m with respect to items accounted for in previous years as extraordinary (1990 £918m with respect to items accounted for as extraordinary including £239m consideration deferred from 1989 for the US over-the-counter pharmaceuticals business).

The cash consideration for disposals includes £40m (1990 £677m) relating to equity accounted participating interests.

Apart from the disposal proceeds, the contribution of the businesses and subsidiary undertakings divested in 1991 to the cash flows for the year was not material.

CHANGES IN FINANCING DURING THE YEAR

	Share capital £m	Share premium account £m	Loans £m	Finance leases £m	Short-term borrowings* £m	Total £m
At beginning of 1990	694	384	1,736	32	50	2,896
Exchange adjustments	–	–	(174)	(15)	(4)	(193)
New finance	6	50	866	94	68	1,084
Finance repaid	–	–	(835)	(19)	(73)	(927)
Shares issued other than for cash	8	77	(14)	–	–	71
Other movements	–	(65)	169	6	60	170
At beginning of 1991	**708**	**446**	**1,748**	**98**	**101**	**3,101**
Exchange adjustments	**–**	**–**	**3**	**3**	**2**	**8**
New finance	**2**	**17**	**585**	**–**	**32**	**636**
Finance repaid	**–**	**–**	**(334)**	**(10)**	**(103)**	**(447)**
Shares issued other than for cash	**1**	**6**	**–**	**–**	**–**	**7**
Other movements	**–**	**–**	**6**	**2**	**–**	**8**
At end of 1991	**711**	**469**	**2,008**	**93**	**32**	**3,313**

* Amount of short-term borrowings repayable more than 3 months from date of advance.

29 CASH AND CASH EQUIVALENTS

	1991 £m	1990 £m
Balance of cash and cash equivalents		
Cash	**197**	177
Investments and short-term deposits which were within 3 months of maturity when acquired (see note 16)	**506**	280
Short-term borrowings repayable within 3 months from date of advance (see note 17)	**(264)**	(346)
	439	111
Change in the balance of cash and cash equivalents		
At beginning of year	**111**	(454)
Exchange adjustments	**(5)**	1
Cash inflow for year	**333**	564
At end of year	**439**	111

30 LEASES

The total rentals under operating leases, charged as an expense in the profit and loss account, are disclosed below.

	1991 £m	1990 £m
Hire of plant and machinery	**116**	87
Other	**46**	52
	162	139

Commitments under operating leases to pay rentals during the year following the year of these accounts are given in the table below, analysed according to the period in which each lease expires.

	Group 1991 £m	Group 1990 £m	Company 1991 £m	Company 1990 £m
Land and buildings				
Expiring within 1 year	**7**	9	**–**	–
Expiring in years 2 to 5	**18**	10	**1**	–
Expiring thereafter	**15**	14	**3**	4
	40	33	**4**	4
Other assets				
Expiring within 1 year	**18**	24	**4**	3
Expiring in years 2 to 5	**53**	46	**15**	12
Expiring thereafter	**4**	5	**1**	1
	75	75	**20**	16
Obligations under finance leases comprise				
Rentals due within 1 year	**23**	24	**1**	1
Rentals due in years 2 to 5	**80**	100	**5**	4
Rentals due thereafter	**41**	38	**4**	2
Less interest element	**(51)**	(64)	**(5)**	(2)
	93	98	**5**	5

Obligations under finance leases are included in other creditors (note 18).

The Group had no commitments under finance leases at the balance sheet date which were due to commence thereafter.

NOTES RELATING TO THE ACCOUNTS

31 EMPLOYEE COSTS

The average number of people employed by the Group in 1991 was 128,600 (1990 132,100) and the staff costs incurred during the year in respect of those employees were:

	1991 £m	1990 £m
Salaries	2,306	2,270
Social security costs	235	216
Pension costs	175	151
Other employment costs	76	73
Employees' profit-sharing bonus	31	39
	2,823	2,749
Less amounts allocated to capital and extraordinary items	(111)	(50)
Severance costs charged in arriving at trading profit	45	69
Employee costs charged in arriving at trading profit	2,757	2,768
Severance payments and employment costs relating to extraordinary items*	166	6
Total employee costs in respect of people employed by the Group for use in value added calculations	2,923	2,774

* Included in this item is an amount to bring severance costs charged to trading profit from an accrued to a cash paid basis.

32 EMOLUMENTS OF DIRECTORS

The total emoluments of the directors of the Company for the year were £3,023,000 (1990 £2,686,000) including directors' fees of £245,000 (£266,000). Pensions, commutations of pensions and gratuities in respect of executive service of former directors amounted to £5,674,000 (1990 £4,716,000).

The remuneration of executive directors is decided by the Remuneration Committee of non-executive directors. The reward structure includes provision for a performance related bonus. No such bonus was awarded for 1990 or 1991. For 1992 any bonus will reflect the Group's earnings per share and individual performance.

Some directors were also granted options to subscribe for Ordinary Shares under the Company's share option schemes (see note 33).

The table which follows shows the number of directors of the Company whose emoluments during the year were within the bands stated.

Emoluments £	Number 1991	1990	Emoluments £	Number 1991	1990
5,001 – 10,000	1		225,001 – 230,000	1	
15,001 – 20,000	3	3	235,001 – 240,000	1	
20,001 – 25,000	3	1	240,001 – 245,000		1
35,001 – 40,000		1	250,001 – 255,000		2
40,001 – 45,000		1	255,001 – 260,000	1	
45,001 – 50,000	1		260,001 – 265,000	1	
50,001 – 55,000	1	1	265,001 – 270,000	1	1
70,001 – 75,000		1	300,001 – 305,000	1	
75,001 – 80,000	1		305,001 – 310,000		1
125,001 – 130,000		1	325,001 – 330,000	1	
205,001 – 210,000		1	445,001 – 450,000		1
215,001 – 220,000	1		495,001 – 500,000	1	
220,001 – 225,000		1			

Four of the directors whose emoluments are shown above for 1991 were directors for part of the year only (1990 one). The emoluments of the Chairman were £499,000 (1990 £448,000).

33 DIRECTORS' INTERESTS IN SHARES AND DEBENTURES

The interests at 31 December 1991 of the persons who on that date were directors (including the interests of their families) in shares and debentures of the Company and its subsidiaries, are shown below. Their interests at 1 January 1991 (or, if appointed during 1991, at their date of appointment) are shown in parentheses where these differ from the holdings at the year end.

	ICI Ordinary Shares	
J. D. F. Barnes	2,813	
Lord Chilver	1,000	
P. Doyle	2,798	(2,530)
R. C. Hampel	5,492	
C. Hampson	922	
Sir Denys Henderson	20,274	(20,000)
T. O. Hutchison	4,616	
W. G. L. L. Kiep	500	
Sir Patrick Meaney	1,325	
Sir Jeremy Morse	1,819	
Sir Antony Pilkington	500	
A. T. G. Rodgers	600	
Miss Ellen R. Schneider-Lenné	500	
C. M. Short	500	
P. A. Volcker	2,000	
F. Whiteley	14,495	(13,170)
T. H. Wyman	500	

C. Hampson has a beneficial interest in 1,430 ICI Australia Ltd A$1 Ordinary Shares.

During the period 1 January 1992 to 17 February 1992, Sir Denys Henderson acquired an interest in an additional 1,000 shares.

Options to subscribe for Ordinary Shares granted to and exercised by directors during 1991 are included in the table below:

	At 1 January 1991	Options granted	Price £	Options exercised	At 31 December 1991
J. D. F. Barnes	81,800	8,900	10.31	–	90,700
P. Doyle	71,223	7,800	10.31	268	78,755
R. C. Hampel	83,585	15,500	10.31	–	99,531
		446	12.26		
C. Hampson	80,299	13,600	10.31	–	93,899
Sir Denys Henderson	154,700	19,400	10.31	–	174,100
T. O. Hutchison	83,800	–	–	–	83,800
A. T. G. Rodgers	47,192	21,800	10.31	–	68,992
C. M. Short	87,000	3,438	10.31	–	90,438

The options outstanding are exercisable at prices between £6.06 and £15.12.

NOTES RELATING TO THE ACCOUNTS

34 COMMITMENTS AND CONTINGENT LIABILITIES

	Group		Company	
	1991 **£m**	1990 £m	**1991** **£m**	1990 £m
Commitments for capital expenditure not provided for in these accounts (including acquisitions)				
Contracts placed for future expenditure	**365**	357	**40**	37
Expenditure authorized but not yet contracted	**431**	569	**157**	126
	796	926	**197**	163

Contingent liabilities existed at 31 December 1991 in connection with guarantees and uncalled capital relating to subsidiary and other undertakings and guarantees relating to pension funds, including the solvency of pension funds. The maximum contingent liability in respect of guarantees of borrowings and uncalled capital at 31 December 1991 was £24m (1990 £72m) for the Group; the maximum contingent liability for the Company, mainly on guarantees of borrowings by subsidiaries, was £1,182m (1990 £902m).

Other guarantees and contingencies arising in the ordinary course of business, for which no security has been given, are not expected to result in any material financial loss. Litigation and other proceedings against companies in the Group for which provision has not been made are not considered material in the context of these accounts.

A subsidiary company has entered into a take-or-pay contract to purchase electric power commencing 1 April 1993 for fifteen years. The subsidiary is obligated to make monthly payments including a fixed capacity charge and a variable energy charge. The present value of the commitment to purchase electric power over the period of the agreement is estimated at £560m.

In North America the Group's employment practices include the provision of healthcare and life assurance benefits for retired employees. These are currently accounted for on a cash paid basis. The US Financial Accounting Standards Board has issued an accounting standard (FAS 106) which must be implemented in accounts filed in the US for 1993 onwards. This requires the present value of such retiree benefit obligations to be accrued over the working life of the employee. The unprovided obligation at the end of 1991 for the ICI Group, arising from these commitments and calculated in accordance with the US standard, is some £170m. It is also estimated that, leaving aside the accounting for this unprovided initial liability, the application of FAS 106 will reduce profit before taxation reported under US Generally Accepted Accounting Principles by some £20m per annum. UK accounting practice does not currently require the provision of these amounts.

At 31 December 1991, the Group had outstanding forward foreign exchange contracts to purchase £236m (1990 £430m) equivalent and to sell £950m (1990 £1,144m) equivalent. These contracts are taken out with commercial banks for the purpose of hedging currency exposures. The majority of the contracts had a maturity of six months or less from the balance sheet date.

The Group has entered into currency swap, interest rate swap, interest rate option and forward rate agreements to manage the interest rate and currency exposure of its borrowings. At 31 December 1991, the Group had agreements outstanding with commercial banks which had principal amounts of £601m (1990 £608m) equivalent at the exchange rate on that date. The principal amounts under the cross–currency agreements are revalued from contract rate to balance sheet rates with any exchange gains or losses arising treated in accordance with the Group's accounting policy on foreign currencies.

35 PENSION COSTS

The Company and most of its subsidiaries operate retirement plans which cover the majority of employees (including directors) in the Group. These plans are generally of the defined benefit type under which benefits are based on employees' years of service and average final remuneration and are funded through separate trustee-administered funds.

The total pension cost for the Group for 1991 was £175m (1990 £151m). Formal actuarial valuations of the Group's main plans are undertaken triennially. Actuarial valuations of these funds have been undertaken on varying dates. The actuarial assumptions used to calculate the projected benefit obligation of the Group's pension plans vary according to the economic conditions of the country in which they are situated. The weighted average discount rate used in determining the actuarial present values of the benefit obligations was 9.2 per cent. The weighted average expected long-term rate of return on investments was 9.3 per cent. The weighted average rate of increase of future earnings was 6.8 per cent. The actuarial value of the fund assets of these plans was sufficient to cover 106 per cent of the benefits that had accrued to members after allowing for expected future increases in earnings.

The market value of the assets of the major plans in the Group at the date of the latest valuations was £6,281m (1990 £5,902m). Accrued pension costs amounted to £34m (1990 £28m) and are included in other creditors (note 18); provisions for the benefit obligation of a small number of unfunded plans amounted to £162m (1990 £128m) and are included in provisions for employee benefits (note 19). Prepaid pension costs amounting to £85m (1990 £49m) are included in debtors (note 15).

36 STATUTORY AND OTHER INFORMATION

Included in debtors are interest-free loans of £60,000 (1990 £205,000) to two (1990 six) officers of the Company. These loans were provided in accordance with the Company's policy of providing housing assistance to staff who have been transferred.

Remuneration of auditors charged in the Group accounts for 1991 was £4.7m (1990 £4.4m).

PRINCIPAL SUBSIDIARY UNDERTAKINGS

At 31 December 1991	Class of capital	Held by ICI %	Principal activities
EUROPE			
Deutsche ICI GmbH Germany	Ordinary	100†	Manufacture of nylon fibre, paints, pharmaceuticals, chlorine, caustic soda, advanced materials, polyurethanes and specialty chemicals; merchanting of other ICI products
ICI Chemicals & Polymers Ltd England	Ordinary	100†	Manufacture of chemicals, plastics, nylon and polyester fibres and fertilizers; merchanting of ICI and other products
ICI Finance PLC England	Ordinary	100†	Financial services
I.C.I. France SA France	Ordinary	100	Manufacture of bulk and specialty plasticisers, ethylene/propylene oxide derivatives, pharmaceuticals, acrylics and polyurethanes; merchanting of other ICI products
ICI Holland BV Holland	Ordinary	100†	Manufacture of bulk and specialty plastics, films, nylon and polyester polymers and polyurethane chemicals; merchanting of other ICI products
Imperial Chemicals Insurance Ltd England	Ordinary	100†	Insurance
Tioxide Group Ltd England	Ordinary	100†	Manufacture of titanium pigments
THE AMERICAS			
Duperial SAIC Argentina	Ordinary	100	Manufacture of chemicals, plastics and sporting ammunition
ICI American Holdings Inc USA	Common	100†	Manufacture of pharmaceuticals, agrochemicals, seeds, colours, films, paints, advanced materials, polyurethanes, specialty and other chemicals; merchanting of other ICI products
ICI Brasil SA Brazil	Ordinary	89 11†	Manufacture of agrochemicals, colours, seeds, specialty and other chemicals; merchanting of ICI and other products
ICI Canada Inc Canada	Common Preference	100† 100†	Manufacture of fertilizers, industrial explosives, paints and chemicals; merchanting of other ICI products
IPR Pharmaceuticals Inc Puerto Rico	Ordinary	100†	Manufacture of pharmaceutical products
OTHER COUNTRIES			
Chemical Company of Malaysia Berhad Malaysia	Ordinary*	50†	Manufacture of fertilizers, chlor-alkali chemicals, agrochemicals and paints; merchanting of ICI and other products
ICI Australia Ltd Australia (Accounting and reporting date 30 September)	Ordinary*	63†	Manufacture of chemicals, fertilizers, industrial explosives, paints, plastics and pharmaceuticals; merchanting of ICI and other products
ICI (China) Ltd Hong Kong and China	Ordinary	100†	Merchanting of ICI and other products
ICI India Ltd India (Accounting date 31 March; reporting date 31 December)	Ordinary*	51	Manufacture of fertilizers, industrial explosives, polyester fibre, paints, agrochemicals, pharmaceuticals, rubber chemicals and specialty chemicals
ICI Japan Ltd Japan	Ordinary	6 94†	Merchanting of ICI and other products; manufacture of polyester films and other materials; research and development into materials and chemicals

At 31 December 1991	Class of capital	Held by ICI %	Principal activities
OTHER COUNTRIES *(continued)*			
ICI Pakistan Ltd Pakistan	Ordinary*	61†	Manufacture of polyester fibre, soda ash, paints and specialty chemicals; formulation of agrochemicals, merchanting of general chemicals and pharmaceutical products
ICI-Pharma Ltd Japan	Ordinary	60	Marketing of ICI pharmaceutical products
ICI (South Africa) Ltd Republic of South Africa	Ordinary	100	Merchanting of ICI and other products; manufacture of pharmaceuticals

*Listed
†Held by subsidiaries
The country of principal operations and registration or incorporation is stated below each company. The accounting dates of principal subsidiary undertakings are 31 December unless otherwise stated.

PRINCIPAL ASSOCIATED UNDERTAKINGS

At 31 December 1991	Issued share and loan capital at date of latest available audited accounts			Principal activities
	Class of capital	£m	Held by ICI %	
AECI Ltd Republic of South Africa (Accounting date 31 December; reporting date 30 September)	Ordinary* Preference Loan	30 1 94	38† – –	Manufacture of chemicals, fertilizers, fibres, industrial explosives, paints and plastics
European Vinyls Corporation (Holdings) BV Holland (Accounting and reporting date 31 December)	Ordinary	185	50†	Manufacture of vinyl chloride monomer, polyvinyl chloride and fabricated PVC products

*Listed
†Held wholly or partly by subsidiaries (the Group's 38 per cent shareholding in AECI Ltd includes 28 per cent held through Afex Holdings (Pty) Ltd in which the Group's interest is 50 per cent).

The country of registration or incorporation is stated below each company. The principal operations of AECI Ltd are carried out in the Republic of South Africa and those of European Vinyls Corporation (Holdings) BV in the UK, Italy, Germany and Switzerland.

Where audited accounts are not available, the results are taken from unaudited management accounts.

AUDITORS' REPORT

To the Members of Imperial Chemical Industries PLC.

We have audited the financial statements on pages 34 to 59 in accordance with Auditing Standards.

In our opinion these financial statements give a true and fair view of the state of affairs of the Company and the Group at 31 December 1991 and of the profit and cash flow of the Group for the year then ended and have been properly prepared in accordance with the Companies Act 1985.

London
9 March 1992

KPMG Peat Marwick
Chartered Accountants
Registered Auditor

GROUP FINANCIAL RECORD

For the years ended 31 December	1987 £m	1988 £m	1989 £m	1990* £m	1991 £m
Balance sheet					
Tangible fixed assets	3,750	4,092	4,856	4,947	5,128
Investments	417	524	767	483	421
Current assets					
Stocks	1,812	2,004	2,380	2,214	2,025
Debtors	2,162	2,324	2,885	2,590	2,636
Cash and short-term investments	646	456	383	565	805
	4,620	4,784	5,648	5,369	5,466
Total assets	8,787	9,400	11,271	10,799	11,015
Creditors due within one year					
Short-term borrowings	(559)	(289)	(771)	(447)	(296)
Current instalments of loans	(46)	(50)	(109)	(78)	(220)
Other creditors	(2,365)	(2,671)	(2,738)	(2,881)	(2,894)
Total assets less current liabilities	5,817	6,390	7,653	7,393	7,605
Creditors due after more than one year					
Loans	1,511	1,627	1,627	1,670	1,788
Other creditors	70	137	86	154	159
Provisions and deferred income	434	397	591	612	578
Minority interests	357	304	335	286	288
Capital and reserves attributable to parent company	3,445	3,925	5,014	4,671	4,792
	5,817	6,390	7,653	7,393	7,605
Capital gearing					
Total borrowings as a percentage of total borrowings, shareholders' funds and minority interests	36.8	32.1	32.2	31.6	32.1
Turnover and profits					
Turnover	11,123	11,699	13,171	12,906	12,488
Trading profit (after depreciation)	1,297	1,470	1,467	1,029	1,033
Depreciation	464	484	536	525	549
Share of profits less losses of associated undertakings	157	162	279	113	30
Interest other than loan interest (net)	8	(2)	(44)	(51)	(25)
Profit before loan interest	1,462	1,630	1,702	1,091	1,038
Loan interest	(150)	(160)	(175)	(155)	(195)
Profit before taxation	1,312	1,470	1,527	936	843
Taxation	(504)	(540)	(531)	(336)	(279)
Attributable to minorities	(48)	(49)	(66)	(22)	(22)
Net profit attributable to parent company, before extraordinary items	760	881	930	578	542
Extraordinary items	–	(44)	127	92	–
Dividends	(277)	(341)	(381)	(389)	(391)
Profit retained, transferred to reserves	483	496	676	281	151
Return on assets					
Profit before loan interest as a percentage of assets employed (average total assets less current liabilities)	24.4	26.7	24.2	14.5	13.8

* Restated, see note 2 on page 38.

For the years ended 31 December	1987 £m	1988 £m	1989 £m	1990 £m	1991 £m
Cash flow					
Net cash inflow from operating activities	1,517	1,700	1,518	1,728	**1,458**
Net cash outflow from returns on investments and servicing of finance	(359)	(406)	(492)	(564)	**(594)**
Tax paid	(349)	(459)	(593)	(412)	**(286)**
Net cash outflow from investing activities	(1,094)	(882)	(1,002)	(345)	**(434)**
Net cash inflow (outflow) before financing	(285)	(47)	(569)	407	**144**
Net cash inflow from financing	113	135	69	157	**189**
Increase (decrease) in cash and cash equivalents	(172)	88	(500)	564	**333**

ICI ORDINARY SHARE COMPARISONS

	1987	1988	1989	1990*	1991
Millions					
Shares in issue					
At year end	676	683	694	708	**711**
Weighted average for year	669	679	689	702	**709**
£ per £1 Ordinary Share					
Stock Market price					
Highest	16.45	11.84	13.35	12.51	**13.76**
Lowest	9.65	9.50	10.13	8.08	**8.52**
At year end	10.82	10.13	11.34	8.66	**12.10**
Earnings per £1 Ordinary Share	114p	130p	135p	82p	**76p**
Dividends					
Dividends (net)	41p	50p	55p	55p	**55p**
Dividends grossed up for imputed tax credit	56p	67p	73p	73p	**73p†**
Dividends (net) in 1991 money (adjusted by RPI)	54p	62p	64p	58p	**55p**
Balance sheet value of Ordinary Shareholders' equity at end of year – £ per £1 Ordinary Share	5.10	5.75	7.22	6.60	**6.74**
Indexed value of the £, expressed in average 1991 £s, based on RPI	1.31	1.25	1.16	1.06	**1.00**

* Restated, see note 2 on page 38.
† Assumes a basic rate of income tax of 25 per cent.

SOURCES AND DISPOSAL
OF VALUE ADDED

For the year ended 31 December	Notes	1991 £m	1990* £m	Change %
SOURCES OF INCOME				
Sales turnover		12,488	12,906	−3%
Royalties and other trading income		119	150	−21%
Less materials and services used		(8,285)	(8,764)	
Value added by manufacturing and trading activities		4,322	4,292	+1%
Share of profits less losses of associated undertakings		30	113	−73%
Total value added		4,352	4,405	−1%
DISPOSAL OF TOTAL VALUE ADDED				
Employees	1			
Pay, plus national insurance contributions, pension costs and severance payments		2,892	2,735	
Profit-sharing bonus	2	31	39	
Total employee costs		2,923	2,774	+5%
Severance payments and other employment costs relating to extraordinary items	3	(166)	(6)	
	4	2,757	2,768	−
Governments				
Corporate taxes	5	279	336	
Less grants		(17)	(30)	
		262	306	−14%
Providers of capital				
Interest cost of net borrowings		220	206	
Dividends to shareholders		391	389	
Minority shareholders in subsidiary undertakings		22	22	
		633	617	+3%
Re-investment in the business				
Depreciation		549	525	
Extraordinary items		−	(92)	
Profit retained		151	281	
		700	714	−2%
Total disposal		4,352	4,405	−1%

* Restated, see note 2 on page 38.

Notes
1   The average number of employees in the Group worldwide decreased by 3 per cent.
    The average number employed in the UK decreased by 4 per cent.
2   The 1991 UK bonus rate was 3.5p per £1 of remuneration (1990 4.7p).
3   See note 31 on page 54.
4   Employee costs charged in arriving at trading profit (see note 31).
5   Does not include tax deducted from the pay of employees. Income tax deducted from
    the pay of UK employees under PAYE amounted to £201m in 1991 (1990 £185m).

This table, which is used for calculating the bonus under the Employees' Profit-Sharing Scheme, is based on the audited accounts; it shows the total value added to the cost of materials and services purchased from outside the Group and indicates the ways this increase in value has been disposed.

SHAREHOLDER INFORMATION

DIVIDEND PAYMENTS

A second interim dividend for the year 1991, which the Annual General Meeting will be asked to confirm as the final dividend for that year, is payable on 27 April 1992 to Ordinary shareholders registered in the books of the Company on 19 March 1992. Dividends are normally paid as follows:

First Interim: Announced on the last Thursday in July and paid early in October.

Second Interim: Announced on the last Thursday in February and paid late in April.

Quarterly Results

Unaudited trading results of the ICI Group for 1992 are expected to be announced as follows:

First quarter	30 April 1992
Half year	30 July 1992
Nine months	29 October 1992
Full year	25 February 1993

TAXATION

In certain circumstances, when a shareholder in the UK sells shares, his liability to tax in respect of capital gains is computed by reference to the market value of the shares on 31 March 1982 adjusted for inflation between that date and the date of disposal. The market value of ICI Ordinary Shares at 31 March 1982, for the purposes of the capital gains tax, was 309p.

The Company is not, and has not been, a close company within the meaning of the Income and Corporation Taxes Act 1988.

SHAREHOLDERS

The following table analyses the holdings of £1 Ordinary Shares at the end of 1991:

Size of holding	Number of Ordinary shareholders' accounts	Millions of shares	%
1-250	146,176	18,140,042	2.6
251-500	86,541	32,220,406	4.5
501-1,000	61,845	44,903,807	6.3
1,001-5,000	32,030	55,625,187	7.8
5,001-10,000	1,080	7,803,352	1.1
10,001-50,000	1,124	26,699,551	3.8
50,001-1,000,000	821	174,939,745	24.6
Over 1,000,000	102	350,610,229	49.3
All holdings	329,719	710,942,319	100

In addition to the number of registered shareholders shown, there are approximately 14,000 holders of American Depositary Receipts. The ADRs, each of which is equivalent to four £1 Ordinary Shares, are issued by Morgan Guaranty Trust Company of New York.

As at 17 February 1992 (one month prior to the date of Notice of Meeting) Morgan Guaranty Trust Company of New York had a non-beneficial interest in 26,691,584 Ordinary Shares of the Company (being 3.75 per cent of the issued Ordinary Share Capital), all of which were registered in the name of their nominee company, Guaranty Nominees Limited. At that date the Prudential Corporation group of companies had an interest in 26,002,591 Ordinary Shares of the Company (being 3.65 per cent of the issued Ordinary Share Capital) of which 17,572,237 shares were

registered in the name of Prudential Assurance Company Limited.

No other person held an interest in shares comprising three per cent or more of the issued Ordinary Share Capital of the Company.

ICI Ordinary Shares are listed on all the major European Stock Exchanges and on the Tokyo Stock Exchange. In the form of ADRs, they are also listed on the New York Stock Exchange.

Index of Company Accounts Extracted

Subject Index